SUSTAINABILITY DEVELOPMENT THROUGH GREEN ECONOMICS

CONTEMPORARY STUDIES IN ECONOMIC AND FINANCIAL ANALYSIS

Series Editor: Simon Grima

Volume 106:	Contemporary Issues in Social Science *Edited by Simon Grima, Ercan Ozen and Hakan Boz*
Volume 107:	A New Social Street Economy: An Effect of the COVID-19 Pandemic *Edited by Simon Grima, Osman Sirkeci, and Kamuran Elbeyoğlu*
Volume 108A:	Managing Risk and Decision Making in Times of Economic Distress *Edited by Simon Grima, Ercan Özen and Inna Romānova*
Volume 108B:	Managing Risk and Decision Making in Times of Economic Distress *Edited by Simon Grima, Ercan Özen and Inna Romānova*
Volume 109A:	The New Digital Era: Digitalisation and Emerging Risks and Opportunities *Edited by Simon Grima, Ercan Ozen and Hakan Boz*
Volume 109B:	The New Digital Era: Digitalisation and Emerging Risks and Opportunities *Edited by Simon Grima, Ercan Ozen and Hakan Boz*
Volume 110A:	Smart Analytics, Artificial Intelligence and Sustainable Performance Management in a Global Digitalised Economy *Edited by Pallavi Tyagi, Simon Grima, Kiran Sood, B. Balamurugan, Ercan Ozen and Thalassinos Eleftherios*
Volume 110B:	Smart Analytics, Artificial Intelligence and Sustainable Performance Management in a Global Digitalised Economy *Edited by Pallavi Tyagi, Simon Grima, Kiran Sood, B. Balamurugan, Ercan Ozen and Thalassinos Eleftherios*
Volume 111A:	Smart Analytics, Artificial Intelligence and Sustainable Performance Management in a Global Digitalised Economy *Edited by Pallavi Tyagi, Simon Grima, Kiran Sood, B. Balamurugan, Ercan Ozen and Thalassinos Eleftherios*
Volume 111B:	Digital Transformation, Strategic Resilience, Cyber Security and Risk Management *Edited by Simon Grima, Eleftherios Thalassinos, Gratiela Georgiana Noja, Theodore V. Stamataopoulos, Tatjana Vasiljeva and Tatjana Volkova*
Volume 111C:	Digital Transformation, Strategic Resilience, Cyber Security and Risk Management *Edited by Kiran Sood, B. Balamurugan and Simon Grima*
Volume 112A:	Contemporary Challenges in Social Science Management: Skills Gaps and Shortages in the Labour Market, Part A *Edited by Anne Marie Thake, Kiran Sood, Ercan Özen and Simon Grima*
Volume 112B:	Contemporary Challenges in Social Science Management: Skills Gaps and Shortages in the Labour Market, Part B *Edited by Anne Marie Thake, Simon Grima, Ercan Özen and Kiran Sood*
Volume 113A:	Sustainable Development Goals: The Impact of Sustainability Measures on Wellbeing, Part A *Edited by Ridhima Sharma, Indira Bhardwaj, Simon Grima, Timcy Sachdeva, Kiran Sood and Ercan Özen*
Volume 113B:	Sustainable Development Goals: The Impact of Sustainability Measures on Wellbeing, Part B *Edited by Ridhima Sharma, Indira Bhardwaj, Simon Grima, Timcy Sachdeva, Kiran Sood and Ercan Özen*

CONTEMPORARY STUDIES IN ECONOMIC AND FINANCIAL ANALYSIS VOLUME 114

SUSTAINABILITY DEVELOPMENT THROUGH GREEN ECONOMICS

EDITED BY

SANJAY TANEJA
Graphic Era Deemed to be University, India

PAWAN KUMAR
Chandigarh University, India

REEPU
Chandigarh University, India

BALAMURUGAN BALUSAMY
Shiv Nadar University, India

KIRAN SOOD
Chitkara Business School, Chitkara University, Punjab, India; Research Fellow, Women Researchers Council, Azerbaijan State University of Economics (UNEC)

AND

SIMON GRIMA
University of Malta, Malta

emerald PUBLISHING

United Kingdom – North America – Japan
India – Malaysia – China

Emerald Publishing Limited
Emerald Publishing, Floor 5, Northspring, 21-23 Wellington Street, Leeds LS1 4DL.

First edition 2024

British Library Cataloguing in Publication Data
A catalogue record for this book is available from the British Library

ISBN: 978-1-83797-425-2 (Print)
ISBN: 978-1-83797-424-5 (Online)
ISBN: 978-1-83797-426-9 (Epub)

ISSN: 1569-3759 (Series)

Printed and bound by CPI Group (UK) Ltd, Croydon, CR0 4YY

CONTENTS

LIST OF FIGURES AND TABLES

FIGURES

TABLES

ABOUT THE EDITORS

Sanjay Taneja is an Associate Professor in Research at Graphic Era deemed to be University in Dehradun, India and an Affiliate Professor at Usak University in Turkey. With a focus on areas such as Banking Regulations, Fin Tech, Sustainable Finance, and Environmental Finance, he holds a double Master's degree in management with a specialisation in green finance and marketing. He completed his PhD in Banking and Finance and his Post-doctoral degree on the impact of the European Green Deal on Carbon Emission in Turkey. He has published extensively in SCOPUS/Web of Science/SCI/ABDC/UGC Care Journals, with over 50 publications, including research papers, e-books, text books, and edited books. He has also published cases in Case Centre, ABDC-B, and Scopus journals and holds several patents. He has a strong academic record, with citations on Google Scholar and Scopus, and a history of participation in conferences and FDPs. He is frequently invited as a speaker and has served as a session chair, resource person, and judge at various conferences. He is known for his dynamic and positive approach, with a commitment to personal and professional growth.

Pawan Kumar has 16 years of experience in teaching. He obtained his highest degree from Kurukshetra University in India and worked in educational institutions. At present, he is working as an Associate Professor in Finance at the University School of Business Chandigarh University Mohali, India. He presented more than 30 papers at various national and international conferences and published more than 25 research papers in various reputed journals. He has published three books on the Indian financial system, economics, and insurance fundamentals and principles. Two published patents have also been in his credit. Moreover, five PhD scholars are under his supervision.

Reepu is an accomplished Associate Professor at Chandigarh University, India, with a PhD in Finance and a decade of academic expertise. Her extensive research contributions are showcased through numerous presentations at both international and national conferences. Driven by innovation, she holds patents reflecting her commitment to advancing knowledge. Additionally, her publications in reputable journals indexed by Scopus, ABDC, and UGC Care underscore her scholarly impact. With a rich blend of academic and research accomplishments, she stands as a dedicated professional contributing significantly to the academic community and the field of finance.

Balamurugan Balusamy is currently working as an Associate Dean Student at Shiv Nadar University, Delhi-NCR. Prior to this assignment, he was Professor at the School of Computing Sciences & Engineering and Director of International

Relations at Galgotias University, Greater Noida, India. His contributions focus on engineering education, blockchain, and data sciences. His academic degrees and 12 years of experience working as a Faculty in a global university like VIT University, Vellore have made him more receptive and prominent in his domain. He does have 200 plus high-impact factor papers in Springer, Elsevier, and IEEE. He has written more than 80 edited and authored books and collaborated with eminent professors across the world from top QS ranked universities. He has served up to the position of Associate Professor in his stint of 12 years of experience with VIT University, Vellore. He had completed his Bachelor's, Master's and PhD degrees from top premier institutions in India. His passion is teaching and adapting different design thinking principles while delivering his lectures. He has published 80+ books on various technologies and visited 15+ countries for his technical course. He has several top-notch conferences in his resume and has published over 200 quality journal, conference and book chapters combined. He serves on the advisory committee for several start-ups and forums and does consultancy work for the industry on industrial IoT. He has given over 195 talks at various events and symposiums.

Kiran Sood is a Professor at Chitkara Business School, Chitkara University, Punjab, India. She received her undergraduate and postgraduate degrees in Commerce from Panjab University, respectively, in 2002 and 2004. She earned her Master of Philosophy degree in 2008 and Doctor of Philosophy in Commerce with a concentration on Product Portfolio Performance of General Insurance Companies in 2017 from Panjabi University, Patiala, India. Before joining Chitkara University in July 2019, she had served four organisations with a total experience of 18 years. She has published various articles in various journals and presented papers at various international conferences. She serves as an Editor of the refereed journals, particularly the *IJBST International Journal of BioSciences and Technology*, *International Journal of Research Culture Society*, and *The Journal of Corporate Governance, Insurance, and Risk Management*. Her research mainly focusses on regulations, marketing and finance in insurance, insurance management, and economics and management of innovation in insurance. She has edited more than 10 books with various international publishers such as Emerald, CRC, Taylors & Francis, AAP, WILEY Scrivener, IET, Rivers Publishers, and IEEE.

Simon Grima is the Deputy Dean of the Faculty of Economics, Management, and Accountancy, Associate Professor and the Head of the Department of Insurance and Risk Management which he set up in 2015 and started and coordinates the MA and MSc Insurance and Risk Management degrees together with the Undergrad degree in Insurance. He is also a Professor at the University of Latvia, Faculty of Business, Management, and Economics and a Visiting Professor at UNICATT Milan and Hahxi Zeka University, Peja, Kosovo. He served as the President of the Malta Association of Risk Management and President of the Malta Association of Compliance Officers between 2013 and 2015, and between 2016 and 2018 respectively. Moreover, he is the Chairman of the Scientific Education Committee of the Public Risk Management Organization. His research focus is on Governance, Regulations, and Internal Controls and has over 30 years of experience varied between financial services, academia and public entities. He has acted as co-chair and is a member of the scientific programme committee at some international conferences and is a chief editor, editor, and review editor of some journals and book series. He has been awarded Outstanding Reviewer for the *Journal of Financial Regulation and Compliance in the 2017 and 2022 Emerald Literati Awards*. Moreover, he acts as an Independent Director for Financial Services Firms, sits on Risk, Compliance, Procurement, Investment and Audit Committees and carries out duties as a Compliance Officer, Internal Auditor, and Risk Manager.

ABOUT THE CONTRIBUTORS

Shikha Agnihotri, PhD, is presently working as an Assistant Professor in the Institute of Management Studies, Ghaziabad. She is a keen researcher and academician having an experience of 11 years in the corporate and academic industry. She has a Doctorate in HR from Amity University, Noida. She is a UGC-NET-qualified professional having forte in teaching HR and marketing subjects. Her research area includes HR analytics, employability readiness, competency mapping, and skill gap analysis of management students. She has several publications in Scopus, Web of Science, ABDC, and UGC-indexed journals. Her research works have been applauded at several international conferences which include the conferences at IIT-Roorkee, IMT-Ghaziabad and Amity University to name a few. She has hands-on experience of using SMARTPLS, Jamovi, and SPSS for data analysis.

Paiman Ahmad is an Assistant Professor at the University of Raparin, Rania-Kurdistan Region-Iraq. She is a researcher with research interest in energy economics, sustainable development in developing economies, climate change, migration, and public sector in the developing world. She holds a PhD degree in Public Administration from the National University of Public Service-Budapest-Hungary-2018. Her research works have been published in reputable journals such as *International Environmental Agreements: Politics, Law and Economics, Journal of Public Affairs, Sustainable Development Wiley, Journal of Cleaner Production, Renewable Energy, Environmental Science, Pollution Research, Environmental Impact Assessment Review, Public Policy and Administration, and Economic Research-Ekonomska Istraživanja* and top-tier academic publishers: Elsevier, Palgrave Macmillan, Springer, Taylor & Francis, Routledge, and Wiley.

Aamer Al Aflak is a Research Scholar at Chandigarh University, Mohali, Punjab. Holding a Master of Business Administration (MBA) degree in Marketing and International Business, from Lovely Professional University, Jalandhar, he brings a multidisciplinary perspective to his current pursuits. His research endeavours are primarily focussed on the dynamic intersection of consumer behaviour and sustainability, probing the intricate connections between market dynamics and environmental consciousness.

Alhamzah Alnoor holds a PhD in Management and Administration, currently working as a Senior Lecturer of Strategic Management at the Management Technical College, Southern Technical University, Basrah, Iraq. He received a BSc degree with first-class honours from Southern Technical University in 2013. After completing his BSc in Operation Management, he was awarded a Master's degree in Business Administration from the University of Basrah, Iraq 2016. He obtained his PhD from the School of Management, Universiti Sains Malaysia, Malaysia 2022. His research interests lie in the areas of strategic management, business ethics, leadership, human resources management, organisational psychology, organisational sociology, innovation, entrepreneurship, SMEs, technology adoption, and social commerce. He has published numerous scientific journal articles and conference papers. He is a regular reviewer of numerous prestigious journals. He has many handbooks that were published under Springer publisher. During his career, he was engaged in more than 50 projects.

Shivangi Shukla Bhavsar a born mentor, coach, and education reformer. She holds a PhD in Management and an MBA, offering expert assistance. She specialises in innovative teaching tools, student motivation, time management, and creative approaches. She is proficient in E-learning, SharePoint, content management systems, and gamified learning. As an Associate Professor of Marketing at Narayana Business School, Ahmedabad, she delivered insightful webinars on various marketing aspects. She presented and published papers at national and international conferences, focussing on rural healthcare management, service quality, and women in STEM. She maintains high standards of quality, discipline, and time management, helping employers achieve their goals.

Ioana Birlan is a Master's student at the Bucharest University of Economic Studies, specialising in applied statistics and data science. With a Bachelor of Science in Statistics and Economic Forecasting from the Faculty of Cybernetics, Statistics, and Economic Informatics, she has a solid foundation in quantitative analysis. Her academic journey is enriched by a deep interest in machine learning and its applications. She has actively participated in several datathons and attended numerous conferences focussed on artificial intelligence, data science, algorithmic governance, and sustainability.

Arnab Chakraborty has more than 17 years of corporate and academic experience. He is currently working as an Associate Professor in the School of Leadership and Management, MRIIRS, Faridabad. He has also worked as a Programme Manager in Amity University, Noida; and HOD, Department of Management, College of Applied Education and Health Sciences, Meerut. He has conducted several MDPs, FDPs, and training programmes. He has published many research papers in Scopus indexed, UGC Care list, and peer-reviewed national and international journals. He has also written two books and has one patent publication. His area of interest is developmental economics, digital marketing, and marketing management. He has a PhD in Economics. He is UGC-NET qualified and has MBA, PGDBM, and MA (Economics) degrees.

Tanya Chouhan is an Assistant Professor at the Galgotias College of Engineering and Technology, Greater Noida, India. She has a specialisation in human resources and Indian ethos. She holds a PhD in HR and Indian Ethos from Banasthali Vidyapith, Rajasthan. She has published several book chapters in Scopus-indexed journals and has presented papers at various national and international conferences on *Emotional-Social Intelligence, Human Resources, and Indian Ethos*.

Adriana AnaMaria Davidescu is a Full Professor in the Department of Statistics and Econometrics of the Bucharest Academy of Economic Studies and Senior Researcher at the National Institute for Scientific Research in Labour and Social Protection, with over 14 years of experience in socio-economic research and labour market analysis. She has a PhD from the Bucharest University of Economic Studies and has been a Visiting Scholar at the University of Salerno, Italy. She has over 14 years of experience in the analysis of informal economy issues, coordinating or being a member of the research team of over 50 national and international projects.

Shuchi Dawra is Professor at Chitkara Business School, Chitkara University, Punjab, India. Her area of expertise includes Global HRM practices, AI in HR, digital transformation, sustainable practices, high-potential workplaces and employees. She has a Doctorate in the domain of HRM and OB from Panjab University, Chandigarh, India. She has MCom and MBA (HR) degrees; she is UGC-NET Commerce qualified; and is HR Analytics certified from the IIM, Rohtak. She has administrative leadership, teaching, consultancy, and research experience of over 18 years in industry and academia. She has her publications in reputed international and national journals, holds four copyrights and two patents granted, and has successfully supervised three doctoral research. She is also a reviewer and has chaired sessions in the conferences.

Narayanage Jayantha Dewasiri is a Professor attached to the Department of Accountancy and Finance, Sabaragamuwa University of Sri Lanka. Further, he currently serves as the Brand Ambassador at Emerald Publishing, UK and the Vice President of the Sri Lanka Institute of Marketing. He is a pioneer in applying triangulation research approaches in the management discipline. He is currently serving as the Co-editors-in-Chief of the *South Asian Journal of Marketing* published by Emerald Publishing, Managing Editor of the *Asian Journal of Finance* and the *South Asian Journal of Tourism and Hospitality* published by the Faculty of Management Studies, Sabaragamuwa University of Sri Lanka.

Gökçe Sinem Erbuğa received BSc and MSc degrees from Ankara University, Turkey; PhD degree from Dokuz Eylul University, Turkey. Her research interests span both forensic accounting and the economics of criminology. She won first place in the new venture competition Massachusetts Institute of Technology in 2018. She took short-term courses at the London School of Economics and the University of Groningen. Her researches are both qualitative and quantitative and focusses mostly on the motivations for committing fraud. She is currently working as an Assistant Professor at the Faculty of Economics and Administrative Sciences at Dokuz Eylul University.

Deepali Gala is an Assistant Professor at Bharati Vidyapeeth, I.M., Kolhapur, with 15 years of teaching experience. Holding an MBA, MPhil, and PhD in Management from Shivaji University, Kolhapur, she specialises in marketing and finance. Her research focusses on entrepreneurship development and marketing management. With 10 published papers, including one in a Scopus listed journal, she explores topics such as women's entrepreneurship, government schemes and technical indicators in option trading. She has also contributed chapters to books and participated in national and international conferences. She has extensive teaching experience and has conducted workshops on communication skills and interview techniques. Passionate about education, she continuously enhances her skills through workshops and faculty development programmes.

Kritika Gupta is presently a Research Scholar and is working as an Assistant Professor at the University School of Business at Chandigarh University, Mohali, India. She is having a vast experience of more than 12 years in the field of academics and research. She has expertise in subjects like marketing research, services marketing, consumer behaviour, and research methodology. She has published her research work in international and national journals.

Prachi Gupta, Associate Professor, Director – Centre for Digital Marketing, Strategy and Analytics at Chitkara Business School, Chitkara University, Punjab, carries more than 20 years of work experience in corporate and academics. Her skills lie in extensive analysis of customer and branding stories and drawing insights from them leading to learning. Her insights and analysis on different aspects of marketing have been published as case studies in a book on Indian cases by Pearson publications for their title *Marketing Management* by Philip Kotler. She is Content Contributor at the World Advertising Research Center. She has been Subject Matter Expert and Faculty in Brand Management with upGrad. Her research interest and her PhD is in the area of branding, with different research papers in the area published in international and national journals.

Ayşegül Gürsoy is an Associate Professor at the Faculty of Economics and Administrative Sciences, Dokuz Eylul University, Turkey, since 2020. She was awarded with Jean Monnet Scholarship Programme funded by the European Union and received her MSc degree in Investment Management from Cranfield University, UK, in 2014. She has published various articles in national and international journals in the fields of sustainable finance and emerging financial markets.

Mawarala Vitharanage Probodika Hanshani is a dedicated student pursuing a BSc Honours in Financial Management at Sabaragamuwa University of Sri Lanka. Known for her academic excellence, she actively participates in campus organisations related to finance and business. With a passion for numbers and problem-solving, she has excelled in internships, gaining practical experience in financial management.

Md. Motahar Hossain is a Research Scholar and Instructor in the Department of Business Management, University School of Business, Chandigarh University, Punjab, India. He has more than 12 years of teaching and research experience at different universities in Bangladesh. He has published 12 journal articles and 4 conference papers on different issues concerning business management, finance, economics, etc. Currently, he has been pursuing a PhD focussing on Small Business Management.

Md. Shajedul Islam has been serving as an Associate Professor (Management) at the Department of Business Studies, North Bengal International University, Rajshahi, Bangladesh. He has more than 12 years of teaching and research experience at different universities in Bangladesh. He has published more than 10 research articles concerning business management, human resource development, banking, etc. Currently, he has been pursuing a PhD focussing on Human Resource Management.

Bhavesh P. Joshi is an IIM Ahmedabad alumnus. He has a Doctorate in Commerce, Master's degree in Business Administration, and MPhil in Management. He has experience of more than two decades in industry and academics at various positions and profiles. He has published 40 research papers and case studies in various journals of repute and five doctorate scholars were awarded under his guidance in the area of finance and management. He is certified in consulting from Consultancy Development Center, New Delhi. He had trained students as SAP trainer in SAP (FICO) at Manav Rachna SAP Academy (the First private university in North India to have an SAP Student Academy). His areas of interest include behavioural finance, security analysis and portfolio management, corporate finance, business law and business environment, and strategic management.

Sezer Bozkus Kahyaoglu is currently an Associate Professor at Izmir Bakircay University from 2018 to the present. She has certifications in CIA, CFSA, CRMA, CICP, CFE, and CPA. Her research interests mainly include applied econometrics, data analytics, financial markets and instruments, sustainability, corporate governance, risk management, fraud accounting, auditing, coaching, mentoring, and NLP. She has various refereed articles, books, and book chapters published via international publishing companies. She has previously worked in a variety of management positions in the banking, audit, and risk sectors.

Reet Kaur, an accomplished professional, holds a Bachelor's and Master's degrees in Commerce, complemented by an MBA, and is UGC-NET Commerce qualified. She also holds a PhD degree in Commerce. With over 12 years of teaching expertise in finance and marketing, she is dedicated to academic excellence. She has contributed significantly to her field, presenting and publishing research papers in national seminars, international conferences, and journals. Her commitment to education and the dissemination of knowledge is evident in her impactful contributions, driven by a commitment to excellence, she continues to inspire and impart valuable insights in the realms of commerce, making a lasting impact in the academic arena.

Twana N. Mohamad Khan holds a PhD from the University of Sulaymania, Faculty of Economics and Management, Economic Department, MSc in Economics from the University Putra Malaysia, and BSc in Economics from the University of Sulaymania. He worked at the University of Sulaymania and Cihan University of Sulaymania as a Faculty Member and has several years of work experience in the areas of teaching, research, administration, programming, student affairs, seminars, workshops, and events. He has several research publications in well-known international journals and local journals. He has become a Director General of Administration and Finance in the Ministry of Higher Education and Scientific Research since 2019 until now. His research interests include topics directly related to economic sciences, including but not limited to unemployment, poverty, inflation, interest rate fluctuation and finance, economic development, and financial crises.

Kirti Khanna is an Assistant Professor in the Department of UG Management Studies, FMS, MRIIRS. She is postgraduate in Commerce (International Business) and has MPhil in Accountancy and Law (Commerce). She is an academician engaged in research and teaching for the last 10 years. She has the honour of receiving the Best Paper Award in the International Conference Organised by the Research Development Association & RDRF, Jaipur in collaboration with the Rajasthan Chamber of Commerce and Industry, Jaipur. She has experience in organising conferences, FDPs/MDPs, and has also taken sessions as resource person in workshops. She has published several research papers in journals of international repute.

Sanjeev Kumar is a Professor cum HOD in School of Hotel Management and Tourism, Lovely Professional University, Punjab, India. He holds a Bachelor's degree in Hotel Management from Osmania University. He earned his Master's degree in Tourism Management from Madurai Kamaraj University and his Doctorate from Amity University, Rajasthan. He has worked as a teacher for the past 18 years. While in Kuwait, he worked as an Assistant Dining Manager for Gulf Catering Company and other hotels. He has published 20 research articles and has presented more than 12 papers at national and international conferences. He supervises six PhD research scholars and has directed many MBA and MSc research projects in hospitality and tourism. He has taken part in several FDPs and workshops. He also travelled throughout the country to attend international and national conferences.

Shivani Malhan is working as an Assistant Professor at Chitkara University. She has done her MBA from University Business School, Panjab University and PhD in Marketing Management in the area of Brand Loyalty. She has a corporate experience of two years in Tata Motors and an experience of nine years in teaching. Moreover, she has published many research papers in UGC Care listed journals and Scopus-indexed journals and has attended many national and international conferences and seminars. She has been awarded the 'Best research paper presentation award' by IIT Roorkee. Furthermore, she was a member of the team which organised Carpe Diem in collaboration with IIM Ahmedabad and was given the award of honour for being an active member of NSS while she was working in DAV University.

Eduard Mihai Manta is a PhD student at the Doctoral School of Cybernetics and Statistics and has over seven years of experience in model risk management, holding various positions in data teams. In the last few years, he focussed on machine learning and data science. The subject studied in the PhD is the COVID-19 pandemic – an accelerator of the implementation of sustainable development concepts, resilience, green, and inclusive of the global economy. He has experience working with one of the principal NGOs in the field of education, working on reports that underlie decision-making within the organisation.

Rekha Mewafarosh is working as an Assistant Professor at the Indian Institute of Forest Management, Bhopal. She obtained her PhD degree in Management from the Institute of Commerce and Management, Jiwaji University, Gwalior in 2014. She has more than nine years of teaching and research experience and has published papers in several reputed journals. She has also attended many FDPs, national and international conferences, and workshops. Her area of expertise is human resource management and organisational behaviour. She has authored a book on team building and leadership. She is a member of the editorial board of the *International Journal of Research in Business Studies*. She has also published several papers at national and international conferences. Her research interests include subjective well-being, diversity management, and training and development.

Eva Militaru is a Senior Researcher with 20 years of experience in academic research. She holds a PhD in Economics and she has completed a Postdoctoral Research Programme in Economics at the Bucharest University of Economic Studies. Her research interests include the topics of labour market participation, forecasting and anticipation of labour demand, and labour market transitions, and she has an extensive expertise in quantitative analysis and econometric modelling, survey design, and qualitative analysis techniques. She has participated in over 40 projects and widely published on topics regarding labour market developments, forecasting and anticipation of labour demand, wages, social, and fiscal policy evaluation.

Farah Naeem is currently working as an Assistant Professor at Shriram Institute of Management & Technology, Kashipur, Uttarakhand, India. She holds an MBA (HR) and PhD in the area of Work Stress from Kumaun University, Nainital. She has completed BSc from Aligarh Muslim University, India and has teaching experience of around eight years in various management colleges. Her research interests are in field work-related stress, workplace well-being, and HRM. She has also qualified for UGC-NET and has published papers in national and international journals, conference proceedings, and book chapters as well.

Lethiwe Nzama-Sithole, PhD, is a Senior Lecturer and Deputy Head in the Department of Commercial Accounting at the University of Johannesburg, South Africa since 2015. She is a Certified Internal Auditor. Her research interests mainly include corporate governance, auditing, computer auditing, accounting education, and mentoring. She has published various refereed articles, book chapters, and conference papers. She has over 19 years of work experience and has previously held positions such as accountant and internal auditor.

Nitin Pathak is a Professor and HOD-Commerce at the University School of Business at Chandigarh University. His forte is accounting and finance and he has mentored research work on many topics in this domain for papers, case studies, chapters in books, and several publications in referred journals. His research work has been presented and published in conference proceedings at multiple national and international conferences. He has also made many contributions to edited books. He has devoted 21 years as a profound academician, holding decision-making positions in various committees and teams focussed on making the institution a centre of excellence.

Bhaskar Vijayrao Patil, an Assistant Professor with 18+ years of teaching experience in Computer Applications, holds a PhD from Shivaji University, Kolhapur. As a recognised PhD guide, he contributes actively to research and academia. With over 30 published research papers, including a Scopus-indexed article, his expertise spans areas such as web technology, Android, Dot.Net, Linux, and database management. His significant involvement in academia is reflected in roles such as university exam in-charge, web site coordinator, and AICTE coordinator. As a prolific researcher, he explores topics like machine learning, financial markets, and IoT. His dedication is evident through his guidance to PhD students and authorship of book chapters.

Bhakti Pawar specialises in economics, marketing, and ecotourism with over 13 years in academia and industry. She holds a 'Leadership and Management in New-Age Business' certificate from Wharton School. She actively contributed to skill development in the National University Students Skill Development project and received an RBI scholarship for her Project on Fintech. As a prolific researcher, she has presented papers globally, authored a book on economic analysis for business decision, and is a Life Member of INSEE – Indian Society for Ecological Economics, New Delhi. She is a sought-after guest speaker at events organised by FIDD-RBI, K L University, and Bharati Vidya Bhavan.

Mădălina Ecaterina Popescu is a Professor at the Department of Informatics and Economic Cybernetics at the Bucharest University of Economic Studies and Senior Researcher at the National Scientific Research Institute for Labour and Social Protection in Romania. She has a PhD in Economics and over 16 years of experience in socio-economic research and advanced knowledge in the labour market, budgetary policy, counterfactual impact evaluation, econometric modelling, forecasting, and numerical simulations. She participated in international training courses and conferences on the labour market, coordinated 7 research projects, and participated in over 40 research projects.

Mananage Shanika Hansini Rathnasiri is a Lecturer in the Department of Marketing Management, Faculty of Management Studies (FMS), Sabaragamuwa University of Sri Lanka (SUSL). She serves as an Associate Editor cum Editorial Assistant of the *South Asian Journal of Marketing*, published by Emerald Publishing. She is also an Editor of the book *Shaping Entrepreneurial Marketing: A South Asian Perspective* by Emerald Publishing. Furthermore, she contributes as the Associate Editor of the *Sri Lankan Marketer Magazine*, published by the Sri Lanka Institute of Marketing, and Editor-in-Chief of the *FMS Today* published by the FMS, SUSL.

Rajiv Saini is a Research Scholar at Chitkara Business School, Chitkara University, Punjab, India. He is a working professional and has 25 years of working experience as Head – learning and development in the corporate sector and pursuing his research in human resource management function. He has presented papers at various national and international conferences on E-learning, HR, and organisation development.

Selim Şanlisoy completed his undergraduate education at Dokuz Eylül University, Department of Economics in 1997. In 2000, he completed his Master's degree in Economics at Dokuz Eylül University with a thesis on *The Effects of Export-Oriented Industrialisation Strategy on Income Distribution: The Case of Turkey*. In 2008, he completed his PhD in Economics with his thesis titled *Analysis of Economy-policy Interaction in Terms of Process Policy: The Case of Turkey*. He received the title of Associate Professor in 2017 and Prof. Dr. in 2023. He is currently working as a Faculty Member at Dokuz Eylül University in the Department of Economics.

Arjita Singh, an Assistant Professor at Ram Kumar Goel Institute of Technology in Ghaziabad, India, specialises in human resources and Indian ethos, holding a PhD from Banasthali Vidyapith, Rajasthan. With multiple book chapters in Scopus-indexed journals and presentations at national and international conferences, she actively contributes to academia. She also aids in teaching courses like Indigenous Management Systems and Indian Ethos in Management, bringing her expertise to the classroom. Attending conferences and research seminars on ethos and Indian management keeps her knowledge current and enriches her teaching approach.

Navjit Singh is presently working as a Professor in the University School of Business at Chandigarh University, Mohali, India. He is having a vast experience of more than 18 years in the field of Academics and Research. He has expertise in subjects like marketing research, services marketing, consumer behaviour, research methodology, quality management, decision science, etc. He has published his research work in many international and national journals of repute like *The TQM Journal, BE, VINE Journal of Information Systems, IJQRM*, etc. to name a few and many others.

Larisa Stănilă is a Senior Researcher with 15 years of experience in socio-economic research. She holds a PhD degree in Economic Cybernetics and Statistics since 2013. She participated in numerous research projects, acquiring significant knowledge in labour market, econometric analysis and forecasting, qualitative analysis, and counterfactual impact evaluation. She has published more than 35 scientific articles in nationally and internationally renowned journals and she has participated in numerous national and international conferences.

Mohammad Badruddoza Talukder is an Associate Professor at the College of Tourism and Hospitality Management, International University of Business Agriculture and Technology, Dhaka, Bangladesh. He completed his PhD in Hotel Management at the School of Hotel Management and Tourism, Lovely Professional University, India. He holds a Bachelor's degree and a Master's degree in Hotel Management from India. He has been teaching various courses in the Department of Tourism and Hospitality at various universities in Bangladesh since 2009. His research areas include tourism management, hotel management, hospitality management, food and beverage management, and accommodation management, where he has published research papers in well-known journals in Bangladesh and abroad. He is one of the executive members of the Tourism Educators Association of Bangladesh. He has led training and counselling for various hospitality organisations in Bangladesh. As an administrator, he served as a Debate Advisor at the University and Coordinator for Courses and Exams in the Department of Tourism and Hotel Management. He has experience as a manager in various business-class hotels in Bangladesh. He is one of the Certified Trainers for the Food and Beverage Service Department of the SIEP Project from Bangladesh. He became an Honorary Facilitator at Bangladesh Tourism Board's Bangabandhu International Tourism and Hospitality Training Institute.

Anita Tanwar is working as an Assistant Professor at Chitkara University. She has done her MBA from Maharishi Dayanand University and MPhil and PhD in the area of banking. She has a corporate experience two years in the Ambala Central Cooperative Bank and an experience of nine years in teaching. Moreover, she has published many research papers in UGC Care listed journals and Scopus-indexed journals and has attended many national and international conferences and seminars. She has been awarded the NCC 'C' certificate and best cadet award. Furthermore, she reviewed six papers for the Academy of Management and she is a reviewer in *Global Business and Finance Review*–Scopus indexed journal.

Sinem Atici Ustalar graduated from Dokuz Eylül University, Faculty of Economics and Administrative Sciences, Department of Economics. She completed her

Master's degree in the Financial Economics and Banking Programme at the same University in 2017 and completed his Doctorate in Economics in 2023. Her doctoral study was conducted on the effect of investors' knowledge level on financial market risk. She started working at Atatürk University as a Research Assistant in 2019 and continues to work as an Assistant Professor in the Department of Economic Theory at the same university.

Maria Denisa Vasilescu is an Associate Professor in the Department of Statistics and Econometrics at the Bucharest University of Economic Studies and Senior Researcher at the National Scientific Research Institute for Labour and Social Protection. She holds a PhD degree in Cybernetics and Statistics. She participated in over 30 research projects and has experience in project management and coordination of multidisciplinary teams. She published widely, having extensive expertise in advanced statistical analysis, econometric modelling, impact analysis and policy recommendations. Her areas of interests are employment, inequalities and discrimination, earnings, labour market imbalances, migration, health policies, green economy, and renewable energy.

Priya Vij has a Master's in Business Economics from Panjab University, Chandigarh, and a PhD in Management from Punjab Technical University, Jalandhar. With a work experience of more than 14 years in academics, she is currently associated with Chandigarh University, Punjab as Professor and Programme Leader–Economics.

FOREWORD

In an era defined by pressing global challenges, the pursuit of sustainable and equitable economic development stands as a shared commitment for nations worldwide. The book *Sustainability Development Through Green Economics*, by Emerald Publishing, serves as a comprehensive exploration of critical topics ranging from the diverse landscape of the European Union's green transition to the details of green HRM, sustainable organisations, and the impact of green banking practices.

In the contemporary landscape, the importance of a green economy cannot be overstated, represents a transformative approach that integrates environmental considerations into economic decision-making, fostering a harmonious coexistence between human activities and the planet. However, the lack of accessible information and resources regarding green economy practices remains a significant impediment to its widespread adoption. The book emerges as a beacon, illuminating the path towards green growth and sustainability, addressing the information gap and catalysing a collective understanding of the imperatives of environmental responsibility. It not only serves as a repository of knowledge but also as a clarion call to raise awareness and disseminate scientific information about green growth and green economy practices. Through the collective expertise and insights shared by esteemed authors, this compilation strives to bridge the informational divide, empowering readers with the tools to navigate the complexities of integrating sustainability into economic frameworks.

The transition to a green economy requires not just commitment but unified responsibility, a collective effort that unfolds gradually. It is a journey that necessitates consistent awareness and understanding and this book is a significant step towards that collective awakening. The authors, through their insightful contributions, have introduced the importance of these sensitive issues, shedding light on the complexities and challenges that lie ahead. Their efforts are commendable and their works guide us towards a more sustainable future. In extending our gratitude to the authors, I acknowledge the significance of their contributions to the *Sustainability Development through Green Economics* book. I do hope that this book becomes a basis for individuals across various spheres, providing them with the knowledge and stimulus needed to contribute to the ongoing dialogue on sustainable development through green economics.

Nargiz Hajiyeva
Ph.D., Political Scientist
Director of 'Organization of Scientific Activities' Unit
Chair of Women Researchers Council
Academic Lecturer on Political Science
Azerbaijan State University of Economics
Co-Director of 'Empirical Methods' Working Group
Swiss Political Science Association

PREFACE

The book titled *Sustainability Development Through Green Economics* provides findings of research in the field of *sustainability development in economics*, finance, and computer science. This book commits to providing approaches, theories, risks, tools, and techniques in finance using technology along with SDE goals.

Sustainable development satisfies existing demands without jeopardising the capacity of subsequent descendants to fulfil their respective needs. Economies at their core, are made up of a set of laws and standards that encourage certain conduct and penalise others. Our economies currently encourage excessive consumerism, weaken social ties, and deplete natural resources. But this is just the way our economies have developed to work; it is neither inevitable nor necessary. It takes a fresh economic vision to address these issues which is green economy. The concept of a 'green economy' does not supplant sustainable development but instead places a fresh emphasis on the region's economy, investments in infrastructure, job and skill needs, and favourable social and environmental consequences.

The book describes first about green economy and how it contributes towards sustainable development. This book would elucidate sustainable development. The book traverses the power of economic as well as financial policy, green investment, green insurance as well as green infrastructural development to ensure sustainable development.

This book provides a link between technology, finance, economics, and sustainability and thus, is relevant for undergraduate, graduate, and executive students, and researchers in the field of business, finance, economics, and computer science. The book is also relevant for practitioners, industry people, policymakers, investors, corporate executives, etc. This can be offered as an elective course for undergraduate and postgraduate students to impart knowledge on the newest technology for sustainable living with harnessed usage.

Unique sales points:

1. Offers a thorough exploration of sustainability through the lens of green economics.
2. Provides actionable strategies and real-life examples for practical implementation.
3. Incorporates insights from various disciplines to appeal to diverse audiences.

4. Presents up-to-date research and trends in the field.
5. Inspires readers to make meaningful contributions towards sustainable development.

Kiran Sood
Chitkara Business School, Chitkara University, Punjab, India;
Research Fellow, Women Researchers Council,
Azerbaijan State University of Economics (UNEC)

Simon Grima
University of Malta, Malta
University of Latvia, Latvia

CHAPTER 1

SOCIAL AND ECONOMIC DIVERSITY IN THE EUROPEAN UNION ON THE ROAD TO GREEN ECONOMY*

Maria Denisa Vasilescu[a, b],
Mădălina Ecaterina Popescu[a, b],
Larisa Stănilă[b] and Eva Militaru[b]

[a]*Bucharest University of Economic Studies, Bucharest, Romania*
[b]*National Scientific Research Institute for Labour and Social Protection, Bucharest, Romania*

ABSTRACT

Purpose: *The chapter analyses the diversity of the European Union (EU) member states in terms of the transition to a sustainable, green, and just economy.*

Need for the study: *Sustainable development is an important concern that the EU approaches by aiming to transition to a greener economy, fairly and inclusively. Moreover, the actual context, post-pandemic period and ongoing war at the EU border, makes the social and economic development of the EU countries matter even more in the light of this just transition.*

*Part of this work was supported by the NUCLEU Programme funded by the Romanian Ministry of Research, Innovation and Digitalization (Project PN 22100201).

Sustainability Development through Green Economics
Contemporary Studies in Economic and Financial Analysis, Volume 114, 1–19

Published under exclusive licence by Emerald Publishing Limited
ISSN: 1569-3759/doi:10.1108/S1569-375920240000114001

Methodology: The authors relied on a multidimensional approach, using principal component analysis (PCA) to reduce the dimensionality of the dataset. The cluster analysis allowed us to group the countries in such a way that made it possible to identify the best and worst performers, as well as certain patterns that can be the basis for the formulation of good practices and transferable to the states that need more support in the transition to a green economy.

Findings: The results indicated that EU member states can be grouped into five clusters, each needing specific policies to ensure sustainable and inclusive development. Denmark, Finland, and Sweden turned out the best performers, while Estonia, Lithuania, Bulgaria, and Romania proved to have the most unfavourable situation.

Practical implications: The findings provide relevant policy implication insights for policy decision-makers in the field of green economy, economic development, and social policies, with directions for future research.

Keywords: Sustainable development; green economy; inequalities; just transition; cluster analysis; principal component analysis; European Union;

JEL Codes: C38; O44; O52; Q01; Q56; Q58

1. INTRODUCTION

Economic sustainability is a permanent concern in Europe and around the world. The financial crisis from 2008 had put the economic development on hold for several years; there was a relatively calm period after 2012–2014 until the COVID-19 pandemic started. The war in Ukraine came in a period of a slight recovery from the pandemic, the two recent events putting a lot of pressure on all EU Member States' economies and individuals' welfare: the pandemic had put pressure on health systems all over the world, the labour markets, public budgets; the war at the edge of EU affected the energy prices, the food chains (Lee, 2022).

On top of all these events, the climate crisis comes with its specificities: it differs pretty much from other crises, in that the cause and effect are distant from one another: the cause is now and here and the effect might be distant in the future and another place on the planet. This type of causal relationship makes it difficult for some individuals to realise that cause A produces the effect B and therefore they are not interested in changing their behaviour. In other words, the fact that future generations will suffer from our actions, and maybe the vulnerable individuals will suffer the most, does not make some of us today act more wisely and consciously. When talking about air, water, and soil pollution, only the local accidents make individuals aware of the danger. Thus, it is widely considered that only coordinated efforts and actions could make a difference in the future.

Buch-Hansen and Nesterova (2022) argue that we need a deep societal transformation, a change in 'our inner being' to become more empathetic, less egocentric and possessive, more capable of seeing ourselves as a part of a community and aware of our actions' consequences.

Under such context, it becomes essential to properly investigate the post-pandemic social and economic diversity of the EU countries in the context of green economies and sustainable development. To serve this scope, we relied on a multidimensional approach to cluster and find patterns between the EU countries in terms of income inequalities, unemployment, green economy, and economic development. The novelty of the chapter consists of the holistic methodological approach designed for such investigation, in which a generous dataset was initially considered with indicators reflecting the social, demographic, education and employment, green economy, and economic development dimensions. It was followed by a PCA to reduce the dimensionality of the dataset with a minimum information loss and then a cluster analysis based on the extracted factors. In this manner, we ensure a rather holistic approach when clustering the EU countries and investigating the patterns between them. On the one hand, our findings provide relevant policy implication insights for policy decision-makers in the fields of green economy, economic development, and social policies. On the other hand, our methodological approach could be useful for researchers and academicians by providing directions for future studies.

The chapter is structured in the following manner. Section 2 covers the literature review in the field, followed by the data and methodology in Section 3, in which the steps of our investigation are thoroughly explained. The chapter's main findings are discussed and analysed in Section 4, while the conclusions and limitations of our investigation are tackled in the last section.

2. LITERATURE REVIEW

One definition of the 'green economy' concept is that of the United Nations, which states that for a green economy, we should aim for a low level of carbon, efficient use of resources, and an inclusive society (Lee, 2022). Therefore, the political discourse around the just transition to a net-zero carbon economy should always consider not only the practical aspects of the transition, but also the social dimension of it: inevitable, despite all the adaptation measures, at least in the first phase some will lose and a straightforward result will be the exacerbation of the social inequalities. Because of that, a crucial debate should be on what measures should be adopted to minimise the negative effects, protect the most vulnerable individuals and/or communities, and take the action needed to move forward sustainably.

It is expected that millions of jobs to be created during this transition, but a significant number of other jobs will disappear. Rather more often than less often, the sectors/regions/areas where jobs are created and lost are not the same, meaning that workers must be relocated. Many of them will need training, reskilling, and upskilling (Akgüç et al., 2022). Not only between regions and economic activities will appear unequal effects, but also among men and women, among young and elders, among natives and migrants, among highly educated and less educated. In other words, all those who already are in some form of vulnerability, who already must face a form or another of discrimination, inequality, or poverty, will most likely suffer significant challenges (Galgóczi & Akgüç, 2021).

In Europe, the European Green Deal is meant to manage the transition to a greener economy. It aims to 'leave no one behind' and to ensure a 'just, fair and inclusive' transition, as Frans Timmermans pointed out at the launch of the programme in December 2019 (European Commission, 2019a). This ambitious political initiative aims to transform Europe into the first climate-neutral continent by 2050, in an attempt to tackle environmental changes (European Commission, 2019b). Despite the official declaration, it is to be expected that the entire process will not be just, fair, and inclusive for all. Some will benefit from this transition, while some will lose. Unfortunately, great chances are that the 'losers' will be the vulnerable and disadvantaged members of today's society.

Who are the vulnerable? To whom should the policies be addressed? One definition that might be useful is that vulnerable individuals are those who suffer from any kind of discrimination, lack of jobs, education, development opportunities, and unequal access to health and other public services. Unfortunately, all too often the vulnerabilities are multiple and cumulative. As a result of the exposure to this kind of systematic barriers, these individuals face poverty, health problems, and a higher risk of social exclusion, they do not take part in any way in the political decision-making and they feel that they do not matter for the rest of the society. In consequence, the political decision-makers need to correctly identify the vulnerable communities at all levels; they also need to understand what makes them so vulnerable, what needs they have, and how those needs can be optimally addressed so that the phrase 'no one is left behind' to turn true at the end of the day.

In a recent study, Eurofound and EEA (2023) investigated the convergence of the quality of life of the Member States, by analysing a set of important variables (at the macro-, meso- and micro-levels). They reached important conclusions, one of them being that the macro-indicators pointed towards progress on reaching the targets, but the convergence was not that straightforward. The evidence showed that there is a reduction in disparities between Member States regarding greenhouse gas emissions, but not regarding the share of renewable energy in energy consumption, for example. They also examined the correlation between socioeconomic and environmental indicators, concluding that high performance on socioeconomic indicators is positively correlated with progress in environmental factors (the higher the income, the better the performance of environmental factors; the better performance of social indicators, the greater improvement observed of environmental performance). The interdependences between social, economic, and environmental development are not a surprise anymore (Daniek, 2020), one country cannot have steady and healthy economic growth without taking care of the social aspects and the well-being of the citizens.

Another hindrance that can prevent sustainable development is corruption. Maybe the connection between corruption and a greener economy is not as straightforward sometimes, but studies are showing that where corruption dominates a country's government, that country is less likely to be able to improve its environmental development (Biswas et al., 2012; Tawiah et al., 2023).

Tawiah et al. (2023) obtained a negative and significant relationship between corruption and green growth, using a panel of 123 countries for the period 2000–2017. They argue that corrupt countries inefficiently exploit their natural resources. Corruption also prevents the increase of renewable energy use and may contribute to the continued use of fossil fuels, as pointed out by Sinha et al. (2019).

Several studies used cluster analysis to obtain homogenous groups of countries when analysing aspects of sustainable development, economic growth, social indicators, and climate change. Some of them looked at worldwide evolutions (Çağlar & Gürler, 2022) and classified 110 countries in terms of sustainable development goals (SDGs); Li et al. (2019) investigated 67 countries to highlight the relationship between economic growth and CO_2 emissions.

Others, such as Petrov et al. (2018), Drastichová and Filzmoser (2019), Onuferová et al. (2020), Drastichová (2020), Rybak et al. (2022) and Jančovič (2022), investigated the dynamics and evolutions inside the EU. Drastichová (2020) used several SDG indicators to classify the EU-28 plus Norway, looking at the performance in sustainability in these countries. She employed data from 2007 to 2016, made use of Ward's method for clustering, and obtained a total of four clusters. She concluded that the Northern countries represent the most sustainable group, while the cluster composed of the countries in the Baltic, Southeast, and South areas is the worst-performing group of countries.

Onuferová et al. (2020) analysed the EU28 countries from the perspective of social and economic development, using a set of indices for 2011 and 2018. Their result indicated that several countries improved their performances and moved from one cluster in 2011 to another in 2018 (UK, Germany, Latvia, Estonia, Lithuania, and the Czech Republic), but most of them remained in the same clusters.

Jančovič (2022) investigated the progress made by EU countries regarding the SDG indicators, performing a cluster analysis for data from 2015 and 2020. He obtained for each of the two years a set of five clusters, with the best performers being Belgium, France, Luxembourg, Denmark, Germany, and the Netherlands. Similar results, with good results towards achieving the SDGs, were identified in Austria, Sweden, Slovenia, and Finland. At the opposite pole, Jančovič (2022) obtained that Bulgaria and Romania were the worst performers.

Petrov et al. (2018) investigated the sustainability of the southern European countries. They investigated 15 indicators for a group of 10 countries, performing a cluster analysis. They obtained three clusters: Serbia Albania, Macedonia, Bosnia and Herzegovina, Montenegro (being the group of the candidate or potential candidate countries for accession in the EU), Bulgaria, Romania, Croatia (the group of countries with moderate performance), and Slovenia and Greece (the best performers in the area).

Rybak et al. (2022) performed a cluster analysis for the EU27 countries, aiming at identifying the groups of countries that are performing like each other when considering a set of indicators regarding Climate Change, Environment, and Energy (as provided by Eurostat database, 2024). They obtained 10 clusters, leading to the conclusion that each country has different energy systems in place. It emerged that each member state was following, in 2019, its specific path to achieve climate and energy policy objectives.

3. DATA AND METHODOLOGY

The chapter intends to study the post-pandemic social and economic diversity of the EU countries in the context of green economies. To serve this scope, we proposed a multidimensional approach to cluster and find relevant patterns between the EU countries in terms of income inequalities, unemployment, green economy, and economic development.

The methodological approach of our investigation consisted of the following main steps.

Step 1. Data Collection: First, we gathered an initial set of potential indicators at the EU level for the year 2022 which were considered relevant for our investigation. The following main five categories of indicators were considered:

(1) *Social indicators*: Gini coefficient, gender employment gap, at-risk-of-poverty rate (AROP), and the impact of social transfers on poverty reduction.
(2) *Demographic indicators*: old-age dependency ratio and life expectancy.
(3) *Education and employment indicators*: unemployment rate, the share of women in top management positions, high-tech employment, adult participation in learning, and the share of the population with low or high education level.
(4) *Green economy indicators*: carbon dioxide emissions, renewable energy, material footprint, and resource productivity.
(5) *Economic development indicators*: GDP per capita, trade openness and the corruption perception index (CPI).

The set of indicators is summarised and described in Table 1.1. The main source of our data was the Eurostat online database, only for the variable *trade openness* we used as a source the UNCTAD database (2024).

Table 1.1. Main Indicators.

Data Dimensions	Indicator	Definition
Social indicators	Gini	The Gini coefficient is used to represent the distribution of the population's income and is considered a measure of inequality. The indicator is used to assess the income distribution of equivalised disposable income
	AROP	The at-risk-of-poverty rate indicates the percentage of people who have an adult-equivalent disposable income with values below the poverty risk threshold (60% of the median income)
	Employment_gap	The gender employment gap measures the difference between the employment rates of men and women of working age (20–64 years)
	Social_transfers	The effect of social transfers, without taking pensions into account, on poverty reduction

Table 1.1. (*Continued*)

Data Dimensions	Indicator	Definition
Demographic indicators	Life_expectancy	Life expectancy indicates the average number of years a new born can expect to live under current mortality conditions
	Old_age_dependency	Old-age dependency ratio represents the ratio between the elderly (people aged 65 and over) and people of working age (15–64 years)
Education and employment indicators	Unemployment	Unemployment rate is the number of unemployed persons as a percentage of the labour force
	Hightech_employment	Share of people employed in knowledge-intensive activities: science, engineering, and ICT (% of total employment)
	Women_manag	Share of women occupying senior managerial positions (%)
	Adult_learning	Quantifies the lifelong learning of adults, based on the share of people who participated in learning activities in the last month (%)
	ISCED02	The share of people with a low level of education, less than primary, primary, or lower secondary education: International Standard Classification of Education (ISCED) levels 0–2 (%)
	ISCED58	The share of people with a high level of education, (tertiary education, ISCED levels 5–8) (%)
Green economy indicators	Carbon_dioxide_ emissions	Total air emissions (greenhouse gases in CO_2 equivalent), originating both from productive activities and from domestic consumers (tons per capita)
	Renewable_energy	Share of energy obtained from renewable sources (%)
	Material_footprint	Represents the total amount of raw materials extracted to satisfy the need for final consumption and to support economic growth (tons per capita)
	Resource_productivity	Resource productivity represents the ratio between the total amount of materials used and the gross domestic product (GDP) and measures whether economic growth is correlated with the use of natural resources in a country (PPS/kilogram)
Economic development	GDP_per_capita_pps	The ratio between GDP and population, expressed in purchasing power standards (PPS)
	Trade_openness	Represents the sum of exports and imports, divided by GDP
	CPI	CPI, calculated by Transparency International, with values between 0 (very high corruption) and 100 (very low corruption)

Source: Authors' selection of data.

Step 2. Data Preparation and Standardisation: Before performing a PCA or a cluster analysis on the EU countries based on the selected data, we checked and prepared the data for the investigation. Thus, the dataset was initially checked for missing values to make sure that the investigation was not compromised.

Next, a correlation matrix was computed to check the strength of the relationship between the considered indicators and the results were below the 0.8 cut-point. Finally, since the indicators were expressed in different measurement units, we decided to standardise the dataset using the min–max method (Davidescu et al., 2015; Popescu et al., 2018).

Step 3. Performing a PCA: Since a generous dataset consisting of 19 relevant indicators was gathered for this study, we first had to reduce the dimensionality of the initial dataset with a minimum information loss to be able to perform a cluster analysis on the EU countries. Therefore, a PCA was applied. PCA is a statistical procedure that allows a dimensionality reduction of the initial dataset to fewer uncorrelated factors (called principal components) that keep a maximum of the variance of the initial dataset. These principal components are computed as a weighted linear combination of the initial dataset and are ranked decreasingly according to the variation of the initial indicators. Thus, the first principal component keeps the largest variation, followed by the second factor with the highest variation uncontained in the previous factor, and so on. The choice of the total number of selected principal components was based in this chapter on the number of principal components with eigenvalues higher than one.

Before conducting a cluster analysis based on the resulting principal components, we checked the robustness of the PCA by conducting a sensitivity analysis. Several statistical tests were therefore used to check the quality of the PCA results using the SPSS 21 software. On the one hand, we conducted the Kaiser–Meyer–Olkin (KMO) test to evaluate the adequacy of the sampling by comparing the magnitudes of the observed correlation coefficients to those of the partial correlation coefficients. On the other hand, we applied Bartlett's test of sphericity to check for redundancies between indicators to make sure that all indicators from the correlation matrix are uncorrelated.

The results are summarised in Table 1.2.

Since the KMO test registered a value higher than 0.5, we can conclude that the PCA is indeed appropriate to be applied and that the sampling is adequate (Davidescu et al., 2015; Popescu et al., 2018), although values higher than 0.8 are optimal to indicate the most reliable results possible for a PCA. Moreover, since the *p*-value of Bartlett's test of sphericity is lower than 0.05 for an approximate Chi-square of 198.46, we confirm that the test is statistically significant and that the indicators considered in the PCA are related and suitable for structure detection.

Step 4. Performing the Cluster Analysis: The cluster analysis was next performed using the previously computed principal components and a hierarchical cluster algorithm to find patterns between the EU countries in terms of income inequalities, unemployment, green economy, and economic development.

Table 1.2. Sensitivity Analysis to Test the Robustness of the PCA.

KMO measure of sampling adequacy	0.57
Bartlett's test of sphericity (approx. Chi-square)	198.46 (0.00)

Source: Authors' calculations in SPSS.

Among the existing hierarchical cluster methods available in the literature (Everitt et al., 2001), we opted for Ward's minimum variance method for the following reasons. This method is among the most reliable cluster algorithms as it minimises the total within-cluster variance. Its objective function consists of the error sum of the squared deviations from the mean, which assures a minimum information loss. When implemented, the method finds at each step the optimal pair of clusters to merge that could lead to the minimum increase in total within-cluster variance, using a weighted metric, such as the squared Euclidian distance or the Euclidian distance between cluster centres. In our approach, we opted for computing the Euclidian distance between clusters instead of the squared Euclidian distance. This allowed us to cluster the EU countries based on the main principal components extracted from the PCA that was previously conducted and to better represent the five main categories of indicators targeted in this chapter (social, demographic, education and employment, green economy, and economic development respectively), with a minimum information loss.

4. RESULTS AND DISCUSSIONS

In Table 1.3, we first present the main results of the PCA conducted to reduce the dimensionality of the initial dataset, with minimum information loss. The main results of the PCA are summarised in Table 1.3 and indicate that only the first four components have values above one ($\lambda_1 = 3.99$; $\lambda_2 = 2.86$; $\lambda_3 = 1.63$ and $\lambda_4 = 1.23$), having altogether a minimum information loss of approximately 25.35%. Therefore, based on the Kaiser criterion, we keep only the first four principal components for further investigation. Some of the initial variables had to be, however, excluded from the PCA analysis to assume a minimum information loss when reducing the dimensionality of the initial dataset. Those particular variables were: Employment_gap, Life_expectancy, Old_age_dependency, ISCED02, ISCED58 and Trade_openness.

Table 1.3. The Total Variance Explained.

Components	Initial Eigenvalues		
	Total	% of Variance	Cumulative %
1	3.986	30.660	30.660
2	2.862	22.015	52.676
3	1.627	12.512	65.188
4	1.230	9.459	74.647
5	0.920	7.079	81.726
6	0.810	6.229	87.955
7	0.553	4.251	92.205
8	0.293	2.252	94.457
9	0.255	1.958	96.415
10	0.206	1.587	98.003
11	0.124	0.954	98.957
12	0.091	0.699	99.655
13	0.045	0.345	100.000

Source: Authors' calculations in SPSS.

The rest of the indicators are summarised in Table 1.4, through the rotated matrix of the four principal components using the Varimax normalised variation method. For each principal component, we can check which are the strongest correlated indicators according to Table 1.4.

The first principal component (PC1 – The economic development factors) is strongly correlated with the following macroeconomic indicators: GDP per capita, CPI, as well as the adult's participation in learning and the percentage of employment in knowledge-intensive activities of the total employment. It explains 30.7% of the total variance of the initial dataset and can practically be considered to gather some of the most relevant economic development factors.

The second principal component (PC2 – The social factors) explains 22% of the total variance of the initial dataset and can practically be considered an element describing some of the most relevant social factors in an economy, as it is strongly correlated with the social indicators of income inequality, at risk of poverty rate, unemployment rate, and the impact of social transfers on poverty reduction.

The third principal component (PC3 – The green and productive economy) is strongly correlated with indicators of renewable energy, material footprint, resource productivity, and the share of women in top management positions. It explains 12.5% of the total variance of the initial dataset and can practically be considered an element describing the green and productive economy.

Finally, the *fourth principal component (PC4 – The degree of pollution)* explains 9.5% of the total variance of the initial dataset, being highly correlated only with the carbon dioxide emissions factor. It can be considered, therefore, to explain the degree of pollution in an economy.

Table 1.4. Rotated Component Matrix.[a]

PC	The Standardised Indicators	Component			
		1	2	3	4
PC1 – The economic development factors	Zscore(GDP_capita_pps)	0.460	0.180	0.094	−0.184
	Zscore(CPI)	0.784	−0.226	0.101	0.442
	Zscore(Adult_learning)	0.821	−0.367	0.183	0.034
	Zscore(Hightech_employment)	0.674	−0.232	−0.391	0.325
PC2 – The social factors	Zscore(Gini)	−0.081	0.906	0.153	0.019
	Zscore(Unemployment)	0.276	0.549	−0.079	−0.369
	Zscore(Social_transfers)	0.338	−0.629	0.057	0.480
	Zscore(AROP)	−0.199	0.897	0.158	−0.049
PC3 – The green and productive economy	Zscore(Renewable_energy)	0.607	0.060	0.691	−0.219
	Zscore(Material_footprint)	0.214	0.008	0.775	0.362
	Zscore(Resource_productivity)	0.334	−0.061	−0.888	0.021
	Zscore(Women_manag)	0.237	0.140	0.593	−0.257
PC4 – The degree of pollution	Zscore(Carbon_dioxide_emissions)	0.052	−0.097	−0.079	0.927

Source: Authors' calculations in SPSS.
[a]Rotation converged in 14 iterations.

The cluster analysis was next performed based on these four principal components to find patterns between the EU countries in terms of income inequalities, unemployment, green economy, and economic development. The dendrogram presented in Fig. 1.1 can help us visualise how the EU countries have grouped themselves after applying Ward's minimum variance method, while Fig. 1.2 represents a geographic representation of the resulting EU cluster countries.

The results of the cluster analysis indicated the following grouping for the EU member states:

- Cluster 1: Cyprus, Germany, Austria, Belgium, Ireland, Netherlands and Luxembourg.
- Cluster 2: Czechia, Poland, Slovakia, Slovenia and Hungary.
- Cluster 3: Denmark, Finland and Sweden.
- Cluster 4: Estonia, Lithuania, Bulgaria and Romania.
- Cluster 5: Croatia, Portugal, France, Malta, Greece, Italy, Spain and Latvia.

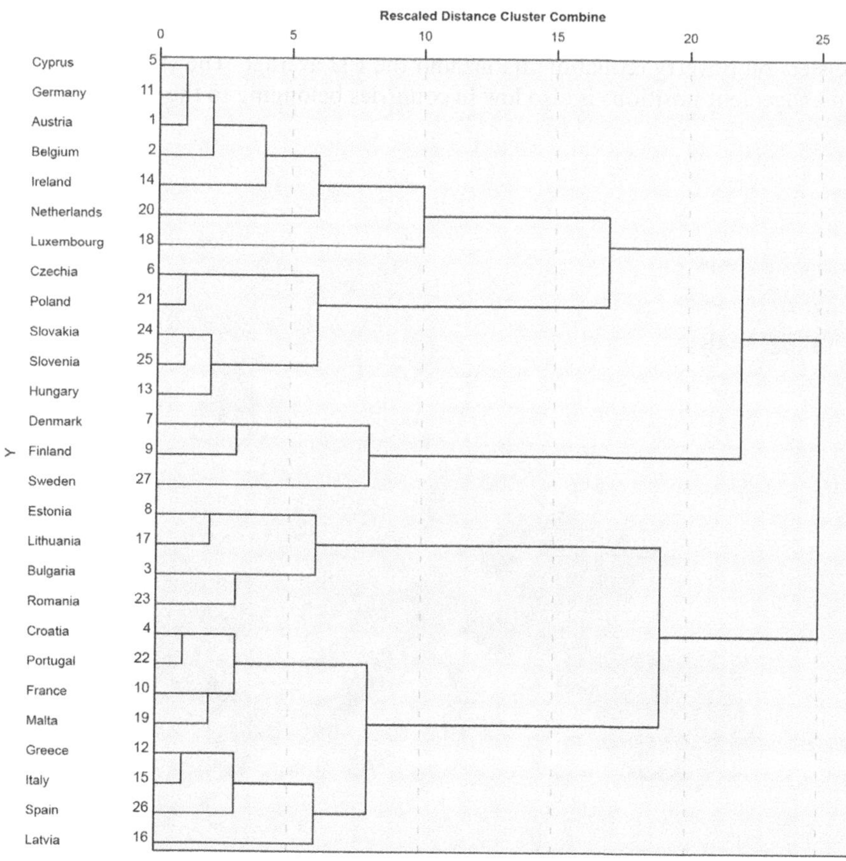

Fig. 1.1. The Dendrogram. *Source:* Authors' calculations in SPSS.

Countries in *Cluster 1* are characterised by a perceived level of corruption below the EU average in Fig. 1.1, by a relatively high share of workers in high-tech sectors, and by average values for the adult participation rate in lifelong learning. At the same time, the results indicated a relatively low or medium level of inequalities, low unemployment rates, as well as small shares of people at risk of poverty and social exclusion. In the countries belonging to this cluster, the impact of social transfers on poverty is high, which indicates the effectiveness of social policies. These countries are characterised by high emissions of carbon dioxide (tons/capita), Ireland and Luxembourg being the top two in the EU in terms of pollution. At the same time, the share of energy obtained from renewable sources is relatively low for this cluster. But the resource productivity is high, even very high for some countries, such as the Netherlands and Luxembourg.

Cluster 2 is composed of countries with relatively low GDP per capita, low share of workers in high-tech sectors, as well as low shares of lifelong learning adults. Also, perceived corruption is relatively low. The results indicated that in these countries inequalities are reduced, with Slovakia, Slovenia, and the Czech Republic recording the lowest values for the Gini coefficient. Unemployment rates are generally low, as is the share of people at risk of poverty, while the effects of social transfers on poverty reduction are around the EU average. The share of women in management positions is also low in countries belonging to the second cluster.

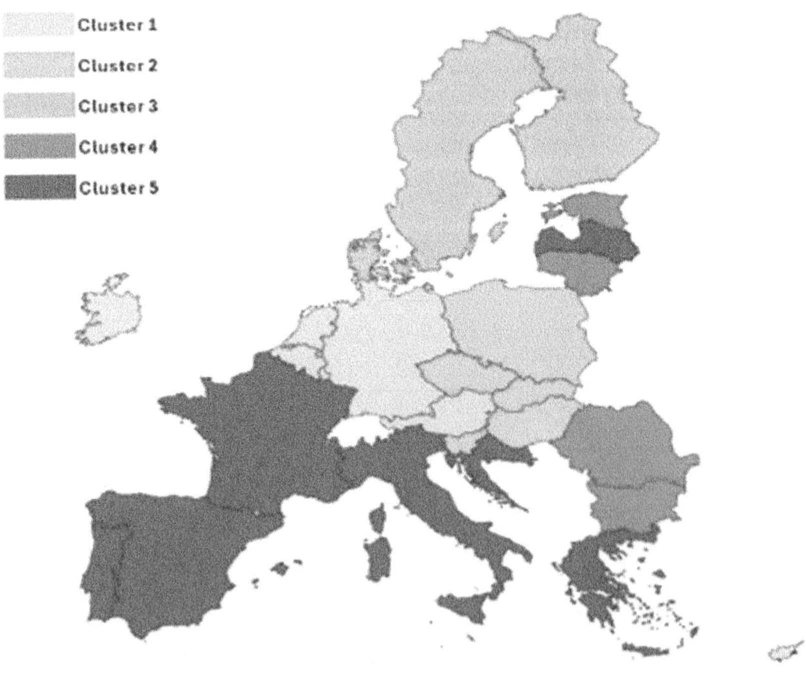

Fig. 1.2. The Countries Belonging to the Five Clusters. *Source:* Authors' design in Excel based on the results obtained in SPSS.

Regarding the indicators for the green economy, the states in this group are characterised by reduced productivity of resources used, low or around average material footprint, small shares of renewable energy, and average values for carbon dioxide emissions.

The countries in *Cluster 3*, Denmark, Finland, and Sweden, stand out especially due to the economic development component: high values of GDP per capita expressed in PPS, the lowest level of corruption (they are top three in the EU), very high proportions of lifelong learning adults, as well as large shares of high-tech employees. Also, income inequalities are reduced, the share of women in top management positions is high, the risk of poverty is low, social transfers are effective in reducing poverty, only unemployment rates are relatively high. In terms of sustainable economic development, these countries are characterised by a very high share of renewable energy (first, second, and fourth places in the EU member states' hierarchy), material footprint is also high, but they register low resource productivity.

Cluster 4 is composed of countries with low performances, especially from an economic and social perspective: the lowest values of GDP per capita, the share of lifelong learning adults is low, as is the share of employees in the high-tech sectors, the states in this cluster being dominated by corruption. At the same time, these countries recorded high values of income inequalities (Lithuania and Bulgaria, the highest values among EU countries), very high shares of people at risk of poverty (especially in Romania and Bulgaria), unemployment rates around the average, and a reduced impact of social transfers on poverty. However, the share of women in top management positions is relatively high, with the highest value in the EU being registered in Lithuania. Values around the average were recorded for the share of renewable energy and carbon dioxide emissions, material footprints are above average, while resource productivity is particularly low, with Bulgaria registering the lowest value in the EU.

Finally, *Cluster 5* contains countries generally characterised by relatively high or around the average values for indicators such as GDP per capita, corruption, inequalities, unemployment, or risk of poverty. On the other hand, relatively low or close to average values were recorded for adult lifelong learning, high-tech employment, the impact of social transfers on poverty reduction, material footprint, and resource productivity. It is worth mentioning that carbon dioxide emissions are the lowest in this cluster.

The positioning of each cluster according to the four principal components can be seen in Fig. 1.3.

Cluster 3 stands out as the best performer on all levels: it contains countries with very good economic and social development, as well as a sustainable green economy. The results obtained are in line with those of Jančovič (2022), Drastichová (2020) and Drastichová and Filzmoser (2019). It is worth noting that the three countries in this cluster, Denmark, Finland, and Sweden, have a good quality of governance, attested by the lowest perceived corruption in the EU and supported by the efficiency of the implemented policies. Among the aspects analysed in this study, we noticed that social policies are well tailored to the needs of the vulnerable population, and social transfers have a great impact on reducing poverty.

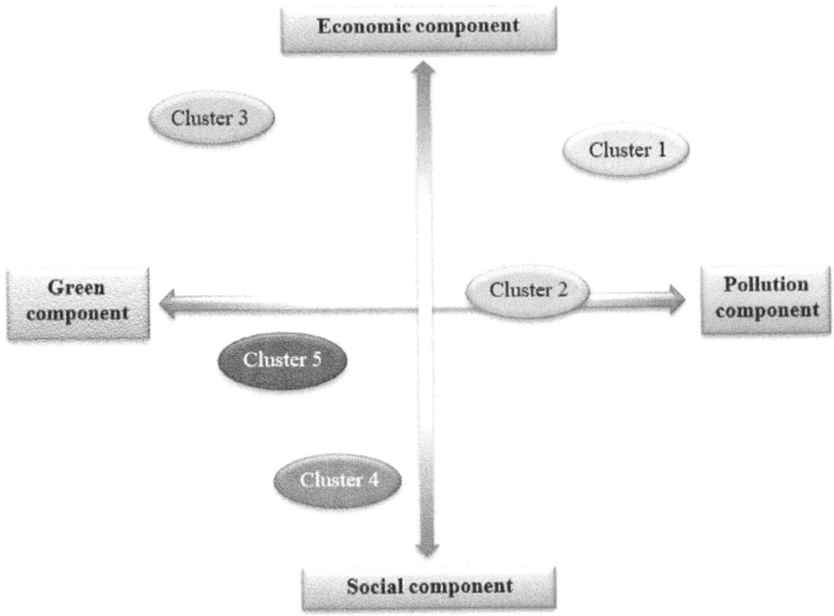

Fig. 1.3. The Distribution of Clusters According to the Principal Components.
Source: Authors' design based on the results obtained in SPSS.

Income inequalities are also reduced, indicating well-designed equality policies. All this is possible thanks to the high level of economic development, indicated in our analysis mainly by the level of GDP per capita. The high proportion of lifelong learning adults should also be highlighted, which proves that these countries place a great emphasis on education. Innovation and knowledge-intensive activities are well valued, a fact demonstrated by the high proportion of employees from high-tech sectors, such as science, engineering, and ICT. At the same time, the results indicated that the countries in this cluster also focus on green and sustainable development, a fact mainly supported by the use of a large share of energy from renewable sources, although they could improve the material footprint.

Cluster 1 (composed of Cyprus, Germany, Austria, Belgium, Ireland, Netherlands, and Luxembourg) contains relatively well-developed states from an economic and social point of view, but on the green economy side, the indicators do not indicate a very favourable situation. A more in-depth analysis shows that, although the level of education is high, activities in the high-tech sectors are well represented, income inequalities and the risk of poverty are reduced, and social and labour market policies are effective, and all of this is accompanied by reduced corruption, we see that the sustainability of the development is not ensured by the implementation of a greener economy and the reduction of the effects on the environment: carbon dioxide emissions are high and the use of renewable energy is scarce. The countries in this cluster have a high potential for transition to a green economy because they already benefit from economic and social stability. Sustainable development can coexist with maintaining competitiveness and protecting vulnerable groups, with the help of well-designed and implemented government policies, higher corporate social responsibility, and increased awareness among citizens. In this case, it may be of help to involve the citizens in the decision-making process, to co-opt them on the green side of the development.

About Cluster 2 we can say that it has the advantage of the social component. With low at-risk-of-poverty rates, low unemployment, low level of income inequalities, and a relatively good impact of social transfers on poverty reduction, we can conclude that policies targeting the labour market and people's well-being are effective. On the other hand, the countries in this group (Czechia, Poland, Slovakia, Slovenia, and Hungary) do not have very good economic performances, considering their low values of GDP per capita and, at least in the short term, they have a reduced potential to improve their status because of the low performance of the education system (estimated based on adult lifelong learning rate) and the low investments in knowledge-intensive activities (quantified by the share of employees in high-tech sectors). Regarding the green economy, the results indicated that these countries have low resource productivity, a low share of renewable energy, and CO_2 emissions around the EU average, which seems normal for their level of economic development. The optimal approach for these countries for a transition to a sustainable economy is to prioritise the policies that target the educational system to ensure a high-quality human resource, as well as investments in innovation and value creation, to increase productivity and sustainable competitiveness, with an emphasis on the development of green sectors. Good quality green jobs have the potential to increase the share of workers in hi-tech sectors, but also to maintain a low level of inequalities, poverty, and unemployment. Also, because the results indicated low shares of women in top management positions for the countries in this cluster, we recommend more effective policies aimed at reducing the gap between men and women, as gender equality in management can contribute to sustainable development (Apostu et al., 2023).

The countries in Cluster 5 recorded values around the average for the economic component, but the specific indicators for the social component indicate an unfavourable situation: high unemployment rates, pronounced income inequalities, and high proportions of people at risk of poverty. On the axis of pollution and green development components, this cluster stands out for its low values of carbon dioxide emissions and material footprint. Our results are confirmed by other similar studies, such as Rybak et al. (2022), Petrov et al. (2018), and Jančovič (2022). It seems that the countries in this cluster have already embarked on a greener economic path but at the cost of social indicators. The steps to follow would be to develop the green economy more, a suitable way for this group of countries being to expand the production capacities and use of renewable energy, but with great attention to the social component. Policies and strategies for sustainable development must be very carefully designed, so as not to affect vulnerable groups, especially in terms of energy poverty or energy inequality, both of which are highly likely to be accentuated during the transition to the green economy (Kashour, 2023). Therefore, the policies should aim at reducing poverty and inequalities and promoting social cohesion.

Cluster 4 contains the countries (Estonia, Lithuania, Bulgaria and Romania) with the worst performances: low levels of economic and social development, marked by the most pronounced income inequalities and very high at-risk-of-poverty rates, as well as very strong corruption. They are also characterised by high material footprints and very low resource productivity. These shortcomings have of course been identified in several other studies, such as those conducted by Rybak et al. (2022), Jančovič (2022) or Drastichová and Filzmoser (2019). Policy recommendations for countries in this cluster are difficult to formulate because many issues need to be addressed. In a broader way and subject to the purpose of the current study, we will recommend balanced approaches, which do not only aim at pure economic development but also consider social and environmental aspects, so that the road to convergence is a just and sustainable one.

5. CONCLUSIONS

The European Green Deal includes so far several initiatives: the Fit for 55 package is meant to translate the Green Deal's goals into law (July 2021); the European Climate Law (May 2021); the EU strategy on adaptation to climate change (June 2021); EU biodiversity strategy for 2030 (turned into a law in June 2023); Farm to fork strategy (October 2020); European industrial strategy (November 2020); Circular economy action plan (December 2020); Batteries and waste batteries (July 2023); Just Transition Mechanism for financial and technical support (the Just Transition Fund was adopted in June 2021). Europe is determined to grow into the first climate-neutral continent by 2050 and it seems some of the Member States took this ambitious plan very seriously. Of course, much work still needs to be done, not only on the carbon emissions or the material footprint reduction but also on the social component of this transition.

Our chapter analysed the diversity of the EU member states in terms of the transition to a sustainable, green, and just economy. We focussed on putting together variables that indicate the performance of countries in the green economy area with those that indicate inclusive development. We added variables that quantify the level of economic development, the emphasis on lifelong education, and the extent of knowledge-intensive sectors, considering them among the most important catalysts of the green economy. At the same time, we included several variables that characterise the social side of economies, such as the level of income inequality, the risk of poverty, unemployment, and the impact of social transfers on poverty, to identify the effectiveness of social policies and the extent of vulnerabilities. We also included corruption in the analysis as it is one of the barriers to the adoption and implementation of strategic decisions for sustainable development.

We chose to use cluster analysis because it allowed us to group the countries in such a way that we could identify the best and worst performers, as well as certain patterns that can be the basis for the formulation of good practices, transferable to the states that need more support in the transition to the green economy.

The results indicated that the EU member states can be grouped into five clusters. Denmark, Finland, and Sweden are the best performers, with a high level of green development, supported by a strong and competitive economy and characterised by an inclusive society, based on reduced inequalities and vulnerabilities. Cyprus, Germany, Austria, Belgium, Ireland, Netherlands, and Luxembourg have high potential, the economic and social structure offering them good support for the development of the green economy. Although Poland, Czechia, Slovakia, Slovenia, and Hungary do not have such good economic performances as the states mentioned before, they have the advantage of the social component, having better chances that the transition to the green economy to not harm the vulnerable. Another pattern was observed for Croatia, Portugal, France, Malta, Greece, Italy, Spain, and Latvia: it seems that the countries in this cluster already embarked on a greener economic road, but at the cost of social indicators, therefore the policies should aim at reducing poverty and inequalities and promoting social cohesion. Estonia, Lithuania, Bulgaria, and Romania proved to have the most unfavourable situation, they need to improve their economic, social, and governance performance, to place themselves on a positive trend towards sustainable development.

The policymakers should always bear in mind that for this transition to be just, inclusive, and sustainable they should address all dimensions of socioeconomic inequalities (in other words, to consider the inequalities regarding gender, age, race, ethnicity, disability, and other factors). Also, the burden should not be put on the most vulnerable in society, which almost certainly are the least responsible for climate change; the richest groups in society are more likely to be responsible, and consequently, they should bear most of the weight of this transition to a greener society (Akgüç et al., 2022). Also, the recent crisis showed everyone that relying on one or only a few producers (or exporting countries) of different goods is not a very good idea (e.g., the batteries crisis for electric vehicles during the COVID-19 pandemic; Ajanović, 2022 or the gas supply interruption due to the Russian aggression against Ukraine; Cui et al., 2023).

A straightforward conclusion is that we need to become more aware of the communities we all live in. If we promote social cohesion, design and create good quality green jobs, and provide access to these opportunities to the ones in the most vulnerable situations, we build a better tomorrow for all of us. It is time for a societal shift, from the top-down approach to a bottom-up one (Arabadjieva et al., 2023).

Regarding the limitations of our investigation, we are aware of the following two-fold caveats. First, both the PCA and the cluster analysis can only allow for a static analysis among the EU member states, corresponding to the year 2022, as being the most recent year with data availability. Second, in terms of methodological approaches, we are also aware that cluster analysis cannot serve as a correlation-causality tool for the diversity of factors considered in the study. Instead, it focusses on the similarities and differences between the EU countries from a rather holistic approach, allowing us to cluster the EU economies in terms of good practices of sustainable development strategies implementation.

We believe that the topic of just transition will not be saturated with research studies anytime soon, and consider the following to be just a few future ideas for research, out of a large number of others: (i) identifying green skills and jobs; (ii) more insight on how many people are really in energy poverty in Europe; (iii) understanding the role and impact of digitalisation; (iv) searching the optimal investment (type and cost) to renovate the worst-performing dwellings and to decarbonise low-income households; and (v) determining if the planned measures are reaching vulnerable groups and also identifying those groups that are not benefiting those measures.

REFERENCES

Ajanović, A. (2022). The impact of COVID-19 on the market prospects of electric passenger cars. *WIREs Energy and Environment*, *11*(5). https://doi.org/10.1002/wene.451

Akgüç, M., Arabadjieva, K., & Galgoczi, B. (2022). *Why the EU's patchy 'just transition' framework is not up to meeting its climate ambitions* [Policy Brief 2022.06]. ETUI Research Paper. https://ssrn.com/abstract=4220500

Apostu, S., Vasilescu, M. D., & Sood, K. (2023). Gender inequality in management and sustainable competitiveness. In P. Tyagi, S. Grima, K. Sood, B. Balamurugan, E. Özen, & T. Eleftherios (Eds.), *Smart analytics, artificial intelligence and sustainable performance management in a global digitalised economy* (Contemporary Studies in Economic and Financial Analysis, Vol. 110, pp. 243–259). Emerald Group Publishing Limited. https://doi.org/10.1108/S1569-37592023000110A013

Arabadjieva, K., Casamenti, A., & Naydenova, V. (2023). *Empowering vulnerable groups in the green economy*. https://alliancejusttransition.eu/wp-content/uploads/2023/11/Empowering-Report-2023-online.pdf

Biswas, A. K., Farzanegan, M. R., & Thum, M. (2012). Pollution, shadow economy and corruption: Theory and evidence. *Ecological Economics*, *75*(C), 114–125. https://doi.org/10.1016/j.ecolecon.2012.01.007

Buch-Hansen, H., & Nesterova, I. (2022). Less and more: Conceptualising degrowth transformations. *Ecological Economics*, *205*(C), 107731. https://doi.org/10.1016/j.ecolecon.2022.107731

Çağlar, M., & Gürler, C. (2022). Sustainable development goals: A cluster analysis of worldwide countries. *Environment, Development and Sustainability*, *24*(6), 8593–8624. https://doi.org/10.1007/s10668-021-01801-6

Cui, L., Yue, S., Nghiem, X.-H., & Duan, M. (2023). Exploring the risk and economic vulnerability of global energy supply chain interruption in the context of Russo-Ukrainian war. *Resources Policy*, *81*, 103373. https://doi.org/10.1016/j.resourpol.2023.103373

Daniek, K. (2020). Green economy indicators as a method of monitoring development in the economic, social and environmental dimensions. *Social Inequalities and Economic Growth*, *62*(2), 150–173. https://doi.org/10.15584/nsawg.2020.2.10

Davidescu, A. A., Vass Paul, A. M., Gogonea, R. M., & Zaharia, M. (2015). Evaluating Romanian eco-innovation performances in European context. *Sustainability*, *7*, 12723–12757.

Drastichová, M. (2020). Cluster analysis of sustainable development goal indicators in the European Union. In M. Bilgin, H. Danis, G. Karabulut, & G. Gözgor (Eds.), *Eurasian economic perspectives* (Vol. 12(1), pp. 99–124). Springer.

Drastichová, M., & Filzmoser, P. (2019). Assessment of sustainable development using cluster analysis and principal component analysis. *Problems of Sustainable Development*, *14*(2), 7–24.

Eurofound & EEA. (2023). *Green, clean and keen to converge? A convergence analysis of environmental quality of life in the EU*. https://www.researchgate.net/publication/372968178_Green_clean_and_keen_to_converge_A_convergence_analysis_of_environmental_quality_of_life_in_the_EU

European Commission. (2019a). *Press release from December 2019*. Retrieved January 19, 2024, from https://ec.europa.eu/commission/presscorner/detail/e%20n/ip_19_6691

European Commission. (2019b). *The European Green Deal. COM (2019) 640 final, Brussels*. Retrieved January 19, 2024, from https://eur-lex.europa.eu/legal-content/EN/TXT/?uri=COM%3A2019%3A640%3AFIN

Eurostat. (2024). *Database*. https://ec.europa.eu/eurostat/data/database
Everitt, B. S., Landau, S., & Leese, M. (2001). *Cluster analysis* (4th ed.). Arnold.
Galgóczi, B., & Akgüç, M. (2021). The inequality pyramid of climate change and mitigation. In N. Countouris, R. Jagodzinski, & S. Theodoropoulou (Eds.), *Benchmarking working Europe 2021: Unequal Europe* (pp. 108–131). ETUI. https://www.etui.org/publications/benchmarking-working-europe-2021
Jančovič, P. (2022, December 1–2). Cluster analysis of European Union member states performance in terms of SDG indicators. In *Proceedings of the 23rd international scientific conference, International relations 2022: Current issues of world economy and politics* (pp. 251–262), Bratislava, Slovakia. https://fmv.euba.sk/www_write/files/veda-vyskum/konferencia-smolenice/2022/zbornik.pdf
Kashour, M. (2023). A step towards a just transition in the EU: Conclusions of a regression-based energy inequality decomposition. *Energy Policy*, *183*(C), 113816. https://doi.org/10.1016/j.enpol.2023.113816
Lee, S. (2022). *Toward a just green economy transition*. Field Actions Science Reports (Special Issue 24). The Social and Economic Challenges of Ecological Transformation (pp. 38–43). http://journals.openedition.org/factsreports/6903
Li, W., Yang, G., Li, X., Sun, T., & Wang, J. (2019). Cluster analysis of the relationship between carbon dioxide emissions and economic growth. *Journal of Cleaner Production*, *225*(2019), 459–471. https://doi.org/10.1016/j.jclepro.2019.03.220
Onuferová, E., Čabinová, V., & Matijová, M. (2020). Categorization of the EU member states in the context of selected multicriteria international indices using cluster analysis. *Review of Economic Perspectives*, *20*(3), 379–401. https://doi.org/10.2478/revecp-2020-0018
Petrov, V., Trivić, N., & Ćelić, Đ. (2018). Assessing sustainability of the Southeast European economies. *Economics of Agriculture*, *65*(2), 519–529. https://doi.org/10.5937/ekoPolj1802519P
Popescu, M. E., Militaru, E., Cristescu, A., Vasilescu, M. D., & Maer Matei, M. M. (2018). Investigating health systems in the European Union: Outcomes and fiscal sustainability. *Sustainability*, *10*(9), 3186. https://doi.org/10.3390/su10093186
Rybak, A., Rybak, A., Joostberens, J., & Kolev, S. D. (2022). Cluster analysis of the EU-27 countries in light of the guiding principles of the European Green Deal, with particular emphasis on Poland. *Energies*, *15*(14), 5082. https://doi.org/10.3390/en15145082
Sinha, A., Gupta, M., Shahbaz, M., & Sengupta, T. (2019). Impact of corruption in public sector on environmental quality: Implications for sustainability in BRICS and next 11 countries. *Journal of Cleaner Production*, *232*, 1379–1393. https://doi.org/10.1016/j.jclepro.2019.06.066
Tawiah, V., Zakari, A., & Alvarado, R. (2023). Effect of corruption on green growth. *Environment, Development and Sustainability*. https://link.springer.com/article/10.1007/s10668-023-03152-w
UNCTAD. (2024). Statistics – Empowering development through data. Data Centre. https://unctadstat.unctad.org/datacentre/

CHAPTER 2

THE DEVELOPMENT OF HUMAN CAPITAL IN THE HOSPITALITY BUSINESS

Mohammad Badruddoza Talukder[a] and Sanjeev Kumar[b]

[a]*College of Tourism and Hospitality Management, International University of Business Agriculture and Technology, Dhaka, Bangladesh*
[b]*School of Hotel Management and Tourism, Lovely Professional University, Phagwara, India*

ABSTRACT

Purpose: *Human capital development strategies and components in hospitality are covered in this chapter. This study examines hospitality human capital development, including training, leadership, technology integration, staff well-being, diversity, equality, and inclusion (DEI).*

Design/methodology/approach: *This chapter uses secondary data from the relevant research article literature. The design shows how human capital development techniques affect hospitality. This study addresses human capital development needs in the hospitality business as technology becomes increasingly essential.*

Findings: *Hospitality worker adaptation and flexibility for human capital development, including wellness efforts for work–life balance, are discussed in the chapter. The results also address recognition and incentive systems to foster a healthy hospitality workplace culture that supports employee human capital development.*

Sustainability Development through Green Economics
Contemporary Studies in Economic and Financial Analysis, Volume 114, 21–38

Published under exclusive licence by Emerald Publishing Limited
ISSN: 1569-3759/doi:10.1108/S1569-375920240000114002

Research limitations: *Human capital research in hospitality is minimal. Future research should examine additional human capital determinants affecting hospitality sector success and their relevance in varied settings for global hospitality and tourism growth.*

Practical implications: *This study can help hospitality and tourism stakeholders, policymakers, and local communities improve the symbiotic relationship for human capital development. Practical implications emphasise the necessity of inclusive development initiatives that empower hospitality communities and maintain global hospitality and tourism.*

Originality/value: *This study examines how human capital development affects hospitality, particularly tourism. The novelty is studying development strategies as drivers for good change, teaching sustainable global human capital development in international tourism.*

Keywords: Human capital; hospitality business; global hospitality and tourism leadership; technology integration; well-being; work–life balance

JEL Codes: 040; 043; 044

1. INTRODUCTION

Within the hospitality sector, human capital is the most essential factor in determining success (Yusaini et al., 2023). This industry is located at the junction of providing excellent service and satisfying customers. Today, marked by rapid technological breakthroughs and increasing consumer expectations, the requirement for a highly competent, adaptive, and engaged staff has never been more vital than it is now (Hanushek, 2013). This introduction provides the groundwork for further investigation into the various techniques and components involved in human capital development within the hospitality industry (Zhang et al., 2021). Because the sector is navigating a landscape formed by globalisation, digital transformation, and a broad consumer base, it is becoming increasingly apparent that investing in the knowledge, skills, and well-being of employees throughout the industry is vital. Rather than focussing on the more traditional aspects of training and development, this chapter delves into the comprehensive approach necessary to cultivate a workforce capable of providing exceptional service and successfully navigating the challenges in the contemporary hospitality landscape (Ogiemwonyi et al., 2023).

Onboarding programmes and efforts for continuing training are examples of the core components of human capital development that are the primary focus of the initial planning phase. These are the fundamental building blocks for cultivating the vital skills and competencies for providing exceptional customer experiences (Ogiemwonyi et al., 2023). There is a strong emphasis on developing soft skills, cultural sensitivity, and a clear grasp of the various requirements of each consumer. As a result of the recognition of the importance that successful management plays in generating employee engagement and organisational success, leadership development emerges as a crucial component. This part examines management training programmes specifically designed for, as well as the significance of, succession planning, which is designed to ensure a smooth transition of leadership and a culture of excellence maintained throughout time (O'Neill & Bagchi-Sen, 2022). This study aims to investigate how digital literacy training and cybersecurity education might be integrated in an environment that is becoming increasingly influenced by technology. The workforce needs to be able to navigate and use technology tools to achieve optimal productivity and customer satisfaction. Additionally, cybersecurity training serves to protect against the hazards that are linked with digital operations.

In this chapter, cross-training activities and change management techniques are discussed. This is done to recognise the significance of a diverse and resilient workforce. Not only can these improve the adaptability of employees, but they also help to prepare the workforce for upheavals and interruptions in the sector. Wellness programmes and the development of a good work–life balance are discussed, and the well-being of employees is the primary focus of these conversations (Slavković et al., 2023). To lower staff turnover rates and create sustained employee engagement, it is widely understood that a work environment that is both pleasant and helpful is an essential component. In addition, the introduction discusses the significance of recognition and incentive systems in developing a constructive workplace culture. Employees' morale, motivation, and general job satisfaction may all be improved when employers recognise and celebrate the accomplishments of their staff members (Olusegun Adedipe & Olusola Adeleke, 2016). The chapter investigates the importance of DEI in developing human capital capacity. Creating a workplace that not only represents the diversity of its client base but also values and supports individuals from various backgrounds is a discussion topic. One way to do this is through the implementation of inclusive training initiatives.

The purpose of this chapter is to give a complete analysis of the many approaches and factors involved in the human capital development process within the hospitality sector. When firms acknowledge the linked nature of training, leadership development, technology integration, employee well-being, diversity and inclusion, and other related topics, they may prosper in a continually growing and competitive marketplace (Wynn & Jones, 2023). The hospitality sector is continuously changing, driven by technological advancements, evolving consumer habits, and worldwide trends. As a result, a growing demand for highly trained and flexible staff is growing. The capacity of personnel working in hospitality firms to not only meet but also exceed customers' expectations is critical to the profitability of these businesses. Given the dynamic nature of the environment, it is necessary to take a strategic and comprehensive approach to the development of human capital that goes beyond the standards of traditional training paradigms. The basis for employee success is laid by effective onboarding programmes, which provide a smooth integration into the firm's culture when new employees are hired. The purpose of these programs is not only to perform procedures but also to introduce the core values, mission, and customer-centric ethos that underframe the hospitality sector (Talukder et al., 2023).

Furthermore, they offer a crucial chance to connect newly hired employees with the expectations of the business, which helps to build a sense of belonging and commitment from the beginning of the employment relationship. Continuous training is becoming increasingly important as a foundational component in creating a trained workforce that can adjust to the ever-evolving needs of the business. Staff must be provided with the most recent information and skills to remain competitive in this fast-changing client expectations and technological landscape. Developing soft skills, such as effective communication, empathy, and problem-solving, is essential to exceptional customer service. Training efforts go beyond developing technical abilities, including these soft skills (Anastasiya, 2023).

Leadership development in the hotel sector questions administrative expertise and needs to be met strategically. Influential leaders play a crucial role in converting corporate goals into achievable tactics, as well as those responsible for driving employee engagement and creating a great work culture. This chapter investigates management training programmes and succession planning as critical components of cultivating a leadership pipeline that guides firms through obstacles and opportunities. In a time when technology is everywhere, it is essential for personnel working in the hospitality industry to have training in digital literacy. It is a technical need and a critical facilitator of operational efficiency and increased guest experiences to understand point-of-sale systems, reservation platforms, and customer relationship management tools. At the same time, as technology becomes more prevalent, there is an increasing demand for cybersecurity training. This training allows businesses to protect sensitive consumer information and preserve their clients' confidence (Talukder, 2021).

Adaptability is a defining characteristic of a workforce that is resilient. This chapter explores the concept of cross-training programmes to enhance the adaptability of employees within the organisation. When employees can fill various positions within the firm, they develop the skills necessary to handle a wide range of responsibilities and contribute to a more adaptable workforce. To ensure that workers continue to be productive in the face of disruptions, change management methods are being investigated as crucial tools for training employees to navigate upheavals in the sector (Akintunde et al., 2023). It is widely acknowledged that the well-being of employees is a factor in a firm's success. A correlation exists between wellness programmes and greater productivity, less absenteeism, and improved employee morale. Wellness programmes not only contribute to the physical and emotional health of employees, but they also promote confidence. In addition, enabling a good work–life balance is essential for ensuring the happiness and retention of employees, preventing burnout, and encouraging long-term commitment (Agba et al., 2023). The recognition and incentive mechanisms significantly influence a company's culture in place. Recognising and honouring the achievements made by employees helps cultivate a pleasant environment in the workplace, which in turn motivates people and reinforces a feeling of purpose (Kumar et al., 2024). This, in turn, adds to better levels of job satisfaction and a workforce that is more engaged within their careers.

Successful hospitality firms must include DEI in their organisational structure. It is not just that inclusive training efforts reflect the diversity of the client base. However, they also create an atmosphere where employees from various backgrounds feel respected and supported. This chapter investigates how DEI programmes contribute to a more inventive, dynamic workforce aligned with a global clientele's varied demands and expectations. This chapter details the many techniques and issues involved in human capital development within the hospitality sector. Organisations can position themselves not only to thrive in the present but also to adapt and excel in the future by adopting a holistic approach encompassing onboarding, continuous training, leadership development, technology integration, employee well-being, recognition systems, and diversity and inclusion. This approach incorporates all these elements (Smagulova et al., 2023).

Objectives of the chapter:

(a) To contemplate the possibility of improving the leadership abilities of supervisors and managers working in the hospitality industry.
(b) To provide workers with continual training in digital literacy to guarantee that they are adept in using technology pertinent to their positions in the hospitality industry.
(c) Ensure the efforts align with the hospitality industry's overarching strategic aims and mission.

2. REVIEW OF THE RELEVANT LITERATURE

The hospitality sector's chapter on human capital development highlights the significant role that well-trained and engaged workers play in achieving organisational success. Studies highlight the significance of effective training programmes, the development of leadership skills, and the use of technology to improve the quality of service and the level of pleasure experienced by guests. The chapter demonstrates that the hotel industry has a persistent positive association between employee training and enhanced performance. Training and development are integral to this relationship. Effective training programmes not only improve employees' technical abilities but also contribute to developing vital soft skills, which in turn helps employees build a mentality focussed on providing service to customers (Talukder et al., 2023).

Leadership and management: The development of leadership skills is recognised as an essential component in the achievement of organisational success. The chapter highlights the influence of good leadership on employees' morale, the level of work satisfaction they experience, and overall productivity. Leadership training programmes and succession planning are necessary to ensure that the sector continues to have a pool of skilled executives (Fokina et al., 2023). The literature emphasises the centrality of technology in the contemporary hospitality business and technological integration contributes to its significance. It has been demonstrated that the successful integration of technology, which includes training in digital literacy and steps to protect against cybersecurity threats, significantly improves operational efficiency, enhances visitor experiences, and protects customer information (Collins Ii et al., 2023).

Ability to adapt and cross-training: It is well acknowledged that the flexibility of the workforce is an essential component in successfully navigating changes in the business. Implementing cross-training programmes has contributed to employee flexibility, resulting in a more adaptable force capable of managing various jobs and responsibilities (Shekhar et al., 2023).

Well-being of employees: Numerous studies have highlighted the connection between employees' well-being and organisations' success. Several studies have demonstrated that wellness programmes and activities promoting work–life balance may lower employee turnover rates, enhance employee happiness, and influence a firm's overall success (Azizah et al., 2023).

Recognition and reward systems: The chapter on the topic strongly emphasises the role that recognition and reward systems play in providing a positive culture in the workplace. There is a correlation between organisations that recognise and celebrate their employees' achievements and organisations with better employee engagement, increased motivation, and work satisfaction (Rajeswari & Balamurugan, 2022).

DEI: It is widely acknowledged that various inclusive training efforts are essential to promote diversity and develop an inclusive workplace culture. According to the chapter, businesses promoting DEI are more likely to attract and retain top personnel, increasing customer creativity and happiness (Azizah et al., 2023).

Continuous learning and development: The literature emphasises the significance of continuous learning, highlighting its role in developing employees and strengthening their skills. Companies that prioritise possibilities for continuing growth are better positioned to modify their strategies in response to changes in the industry and to keep their competitive advantage (International Research & Training Center for Information Technologies & Systems of the NAS & MES of Ukraine & Synytsya, 2023).

Engagement of employees and contentment of employees: Employee engagement and satisfaction are constantly linked to customer satisfaction and overall business performance, according to the chapter conducted. It has been demonstrated that engaged employees are more devoted, productive, and likely to provide outstanding service, ultimately positively influencing customers' experience (Daryono, 2023).

Quantifiable performance metrics: Academics argue for adopting measurable performance metrics to evaluate the efficacy of efforts in human capital development. Key performance indicators are defined to assess the influence on employee performance, customer happiness, and organisational results (Tsai et al., 2023).

Cost-effective training solutions: The chapter investigates the significance of adopting training solutions that are both cost-effective and of high quality without sacrificing the former. According to the chapter, effective training programmes can contribute to a favourable return on investment and long-term success (Kumar et al., 2023).

Compatibility with organisational objectives: The body of the chapter emphasises how important it is to ensure that human capital development activities align with the company's overarching objectives. According to studies, it is essential to take a strategic approach, which involves ensuring that the organisation's overarching goal and vision are supported by its employees' training and development initiatives (Odeibat, 2023).

Approach that is focussed on the customer: The chapter about human capital development in the hotel sector emphasises the importance of a customer-centric approach. The findings of studies highlight the need for training programmes concentrating on technical skills and instilling a profound comprehension of customers' requirements and preferences. It has been demonstrated that there is a considerable influence on guest happiness, loyalty, and positive word-of-mouth when personnel have a mindset centred on the customer (Puška et al., 2024; Yerpude et al., 2022).

Globalisation and cultural competence: The literature acknowledges the significance of cultural competence in human capital development, acknowledging that the hospitality sector is becoming increasingly globalised. It has been determined that training programmes that encourage cultural understanding and sensitivity are essential when it comes to catering to a range of client demographics and establishing an inclusive atmosphere for employees from various cultural backgrounds (Negedu & Ojomah, 2022).

Technology's changing role: Ongoing study investigates the changing role that technology plays in the hospitality industry and the implications that this has for the growth of human capital. Studying how organisations can better prepare their workforce for technological advancements like artificial intelligence and automation is becoming increasingly important as these technologies become more widespread. This ensures that employees maintain their skills and adaptability in the face of technological disruption (Talukder et al., 2023).

Employee empowerment and autonomy: According to the chapter conducted, empowering workers and giving them some degree of autonomy may be a factor in increased job satisfaction and enhanced customer relationships (Talukder et al., 2023). An increase in innovation is frequently observed in organisations that cultivate a feeling of ownership among their workforces. This is because frontline employees feel more engaged in the organisation's decision-making processes (Yang & Ok Choi, 2009).

Sustainability and social responsibility: Human capital development is becoming more intertwined with considerable corporate social responsibility (CSR) and sustainability activities. The chapter has shown that businesses prioritising ethical standards and environmentally responsible operations are more likely to recruit and retain individuals who share similar values successfully. Training programmes that combine environmental and social awareness benefit the organisation's image and contribute to its overall success (Moura, 2023).

Decision-making through the application of data analytics: As big data and analytics continue to increase in popularity, there is an increasing focus on utilising data-driven insights in human capital development. The purpose of this chapter is to investigate how businesses may use data analytics to determine skill gaps, customise training programmes, and make educated decisions on talent management, which will ultimately lead to development plans that are more effective and targeted (Zaimoglu et al., 2023).

Flexible work arrangements: The literature acknowledges the growing significance of flexible work arrangements, particularly in light of shifting expectations on the balance between work and personal life. It has been shown that businesses that provide employees with various work times and locations are more likely to find and keep diverse and skilled staff. Strategies for developing human capital are adapting to satisfy these shifting desires (Kumar et al., 2024).

Trends in the economy and industrial recent pieces of the chapter: Trends in the Economy and Industrial Recent chapter pieces have brought attention to the need to monitor economic and industry trends continuously. Organisations that stay abreast of economic shifts and industry developments are better equipped to proactively address challenges and capitalise on emerging opportunities. This allows them to influence the design and implementation of human capital development initiatives.

The impact of the COVID-19 pandemic: In a recent chapter, the impact of the COVID-19 pandemic has been examined, with particular attention paid to the specific issues that the pandemic has presented to the hotel sector and its workers. The literature investigates how organisations have modified their strategies for developing human capital in response to the pandemic. These modifications include the implementation of remote training, enhanced health and safety protocols, and the role of resilience in overcoming challenges that have never been seen before (Southwest State University & Charochkina, 2021).

Tactics for employee retention: The hospitality industry's chapter on employee retention techniques dives into practical strategies. Studies investigate the influence of competitive salary, career progression possibilities, and a favourable organisational culture in addition to traditional training in keeping talented and motivated employees.

Collaboration with Educational Institutions, it has been determined that collaboration between organisations involved in hospitality and educational institutions is a viable option for increasing human capital development. By forming partnerships with academic institutions, it is possible to facilitate the development of individualised training programmes, internships, and mentorship opportunities that align with the industry's requirements and foster an environment that encourages and supports continuous learning (Sojan, 2023).

3. CONCEPTUAL ANALYSIS AND MANAGERIAL IMPLICATIONS

The process of conceptual analysis is dissecting and analysing the fundamental ideas included inside a particular chapter framework, theoretical framework, or academic subject. When it comes to the development of human capital in the hospitality sector, conceptual analysis is a method that investigates the essential concepts and components that make up the theoretical underpinning of this field. The following is a conceptual examination of the development of human capital in the hospitality industry (Talukder et al., 2023):

A capital of humans: In the workplace context, 'human capital' refers to the aggregate of individuals' skills, knowledge, talents, and experiences. One of the essential assets in the hospitality sector is human capital. This is because the quality of service and the experiences that customers have are strongly dependent on the skills of the workers.

The significance of human capital development lies in the fact that it guarantees that personnel have the essential abilities and attitudes to provide high-quality services, which contributes to hospitality firms' overall success (Odeibat, 2023).

Instruction and professional growth: Employees' knowledge, abilities, and competencies may be improved through training and development, which include systematic attempts to improve these aspects of job performance. Concerning the hospitality sector, these programmes emphasise technical abilities (such as operating reservation systems) and soft skills (e.g., communication and customer service).

The significance of training and development efforts lies in the fact that they are necessary for ensuring that staff are adequately equipped to face the ever-changing problems that the sector presents, hence encouraging continual progress and flexibility via development.

Development of leadership skills: An organisation's leadership development programme comprises many activities and programmes designed to cultivate competent leaders inside the company. Leadership in the hospitality industry encompasses more than just standard management responsibilities; it includes those who motivate and direct teams towards providing outstanding service. It is essential to have strong leadership to keep a pleasant work culture, motivate employees, and effectively match organisational goals with methods for human capital development (Wynn & Jones, 2023).

Synchronisation of technologies: Regarding the hospitality sector, technology integration incorporates technological tools and systems into the business's day-to-day operations. This involves providing staff with training in digital literacy to use technology efficiently.

Technology integration is essential in this digital transformation era to optimise operational efficiency, enrich guest experiences, and ensure personnel are equipped to traverse technological changes (Gao et al., 2022).

Workplace health and safety: Employee well-being is defined as being physically and mentally well, having a healthy work–life balance, and being satisfied with one's employment. In the hotel industry, where work may be high-pressure, well-being programmes are essential to keep a healthy and engaged staff. It is necessary to prioritise the well-being of employees since doing so adds to higher job satisfaction, less attrition, and improved general morale, creating a pleasant atmosphere for work (Dixit & Aggarwal, 2023).

Inclusion, diversity, and equity (abbreviated as DEI): DEI efforts aim to establish a workplace culture that recognises and respects individuals from various backgrounds, including variances in colour, gender, ethnicity, and other categories. Variety, equity, and inclusion (DEI) activities in the hospitality industry encourage a more inclusive atmosphere, increasing the likelihood that staff will represent the diversity of the client base and encouraging creativity and innovation (Azizah et al., 2023).

Acquiring new knowledge and continuing education: Creating a culture in which employees are encouraged to pursue continual education and skill upgrading throughout their careers is an essential component of continuous learning and development when it comes to the definition of the term. Employees must continuously learn to stay current with industry trends, technology, and best practices. This is especially true in industries undergoing fast change (Nieva Boza et al., 2023).

Organisations for acknowledgement and reward: The term 'recognition and reward systems' refers to recognising and honouring the accomplishments made by employees through the delivery of various incentives, prizes, and positive feedback. Implementing efficient recognition and reward systems is important because they enhance employee morale, motivation, and work satisfaction, contributing to a positive culture inside the firm.

Alignment of strategic objectives: The term 'strategic alignment' refers to ensuring that activities about human capital development are closely connected to the overarching aims and objectives of the business. The significance of this is that ensuring that human capital initiatives are aligned with organisational goals guarantees that efforts contribute directly to the success and sustainability of the hospitality industry.

Collaboration and partnerships in educational institutions: In the context of educational institutions, cooperation, and partnership refer to working together to develop individualised educational opportunities, internships, and training programmes. The importance of such collaboration lies in the fact that they establish a culture of continual learning, bridge the gap between academic knowledge and business requirements, and contribute to developing a pipeline of competent individuals. This study aims to provide nuanced knowledge of the fundamental ideas involved in developing human capital in the hospitality business. The strategies and practices that contribute to the success and sustainability of hospitality businesses are shaped mainly by each component, which plays a critical role in the process (Owuondo, 2023).

Concerns about management: Several management implications are associated with the conceptual framework and suggestions for human capital development in the hospitality industry. These implications apply to businesses operating in this sector. By implementing these guidelines, the workforce's effectiveness can be improved, customer happiness can be increased, and the firm may succeed significantly. The following are the consequences for management (Ahun et al., 2023):

Investment in human capital with a strategic focus at: The implication is that managers should consider human capital a strategic asset and commit resources to developing leadership skills, employee well-being, and organisational training. It is recommended that a budget and resources be allocated for comprehensive training programmes, leadership development efforts, and staff well-being activities (Talukder & Hossain, 2021).

Development of leadership for succession planning: The success of an organisation is directly proportional to the quality of its leadership. The results of leaders should be a top priority for managers to guarantee a steady supply of competent leaders. To cultivate future leaders, it is imperative to implement specific leadership development programmes, mentorship efforts, and succession planning techniques (Johnson, 2022).

Literacy in digital technology and the integration of technology: It is essential to embrace technology to improve operations' efficiency and guests' experiences. For employees to efficiently utilise technology tools, they must possess digital literacy. Make investments in technological solutions pertinent to the hotel business, give continual training in digital literacy, and remain current on developing technologies (Ramli & Mohamad Arsad, 2023).

The priority of employee health and well-being: It is essential to acknowledge the influence that employees' well-being has on a firm's success. Managers need to give activities that improve both physical and mental health a high priority. The action that should be taken is to incorporate wellness programmes and flexible work arrangements and cultivate a good work atmosphere that promotes the well-being of employees (Talukder, 2020).

Organisations for acknowledgement and reward: Therefore, it is essential to acknowledge the significance of recognising and acknowledging employee efforts. The establishment and constant implementation of efficient recognition and reward systems should be the responsibility of managers. To take action, we should design and implement recognition programmes, celebrate successes, and establish a culture where good contributions are acknowledged at all levels.

Inclusion, diversity, and equity (abbreviated as DEI): Therefore, it is essential to acknowledge the significance of diversity and inclusion in improving the performance of a business. Managers need to give DEI initiatives priority. Implement inclusive training programmes, encourage diversity in recruiting procedures, and cultivate an inclusive organisational culture.

Learning on an ongoing basis and improvement of professional skills: The implication is to foster an environment that welcomes ongoing education. Managers are responsible for encouraging their staff to explore chances for continued professional development.

Acting will involve providing access to educational materials, workshops, and training events. Encourage and assist staff members in obtaining certifications and furthering their education.

Ability to adapt using cross-training: Observe the significance of having a staff that can adjust to changing circumstances. Managers should implement cross-training projects to increase adaptability (Talukder, 2021). Cross-training programmes should be developed so workers can experience various positions inside the firm. Foster the development of a wide range of talents among personnel.

The importance of strategic alignment and making decisions based on data: Context – Ensure that the strategies for human capital are aligned with the organisation's aims. Managers should utilise data analytics to facilitate informed decision-making. Regularly assess and change processes to align with the company's goals.

Data analytics may identify talent gaps and workforce planning can be optimised.

Institutional collaboration with educational organisations: The implication is that we should acknowledge the significance of working together with educational institutions. Establishing collaborations to develop individualised training programmes and internship opportunities is something that managers should do. Engage in collaborative efforts with educational institutions to provide training programmes pertinent to the business. Students should be allowed to gain hands-on experience in the hospitality industry through establishing internship programmes.

Implementing these managerial measures has the potential to contribute to creating a suitable and adaptable corporate culture, improving employee engagement, and ultimately enhancing the overall performance of hospitality firms. To manage human capital effectively, it is necessary to use a comprehensive approach because these acts are interrelated.

Fig. 2.1 shows the foundation's pillar of human capital development and confirms that strategic components assure human capital development in hospitality. It is also mentioned in the Fig. 2.1 that the scope of human capital in hospitality and its features ensure human capital development in hospitality. Moreover, the foundation's pillars of human capital development impact the scope of human capital in hospitality.

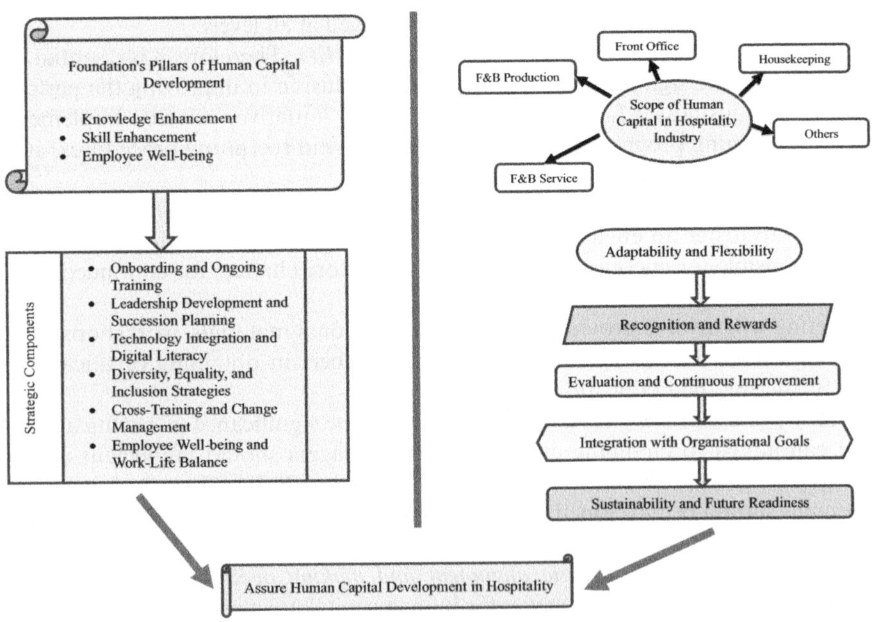

Fig. 2.1. Conceptual Framework.

4. RECOMMENDATIONS

Based on the conceptual framework and study of human capital development in the hospitality sector, the following recommendations are provided for businesses that are looking to improve the efficacy of their personnel and their overall success:

Put money into all-encompassing training programmes: The hotel sector requires that comprehensive training programmes be developed and implemented. These programmes should address both technical and soft skills critical to the industry. It is essential to regularly update training content to connect it with the ever-changing trends in the industry and the expectations of customers.

Make the development of leadership a priority: To cultivate successful leaders inside the business, it is necessary to establish leadership development programmes that are specifically targeted. Succession planning should be considered to ensure a continual pipeline of qualified leaders who can guide teams and create organisational success.

Engage with technology and improve digital literacy: Training in digital literacy should be provided continuously to ensure that employees are proficient in using relevant technological tools. Keeping up with the latest technological breakthroughs and incorporating creative solutions may help improve the efficiency of operations and the quality of customer experiences.

Increase the well-being of the staff: Establish wellness programmes that consider both the physical and emotional well-being of individuals. Create a constructive atmosphere at work that encourages a healthy balance between work and personal life, minimises feelings of burnout, and boosts overall job satisfaction.

Ensure that a culture of acknowledgement and rewards is fostered: Establish recognition and incentive systems that appreciate employees' efforts and apply them effectively and consistently. It is essential to foster a culture that recognises and celebrates achievements at all levels of the business and it is also necessary to encourage peer recognition.

Encourage DEI by offering:

- To foster diversity and cultural understanding, inclusive educational programmes should be implemented.
- To foster an atmosphere in which employees feel appreciated and supported, it is essential to establish and demonstrate a commitment to equity and inclusion.
- Continuous learning should be encouraged.
- Develop an organisational culture that highly emphasises ongoing education and professional growth.
- It is essential to allow workers to participate in seminars and obtain further knowledge about their positions.
- Strategies for human capital should be aligned with the goals of the organisation.
- The efforts to develop human capital must follow the company's broader goals and mission.
- It is essential to regularly examine and alter plans to remain in line with the shifting goals of the company.

Ability to adapt using cross-training: Implementing cross-training programmes to improve employees' versatility and adaptability is essential. The business culture should be one in which employees are encouraged to learn a wide range of talents and contribute to various parts of the organisation.

Keep an eye on the trends in the economy and the industry, and react by: Maintaining awareness of the economic and business developments that may affect the hospitality industry is crucial. Adapt the strategy for human capital proactively to align with the market's shifting dynamics.

Develop the ability to bounce back from adversity: It is necessary to develop crisis response strategies to handle workforce-related difficulties, such as those posed by global events such as the COVID-19 pandemic. Encourage workers to be resilient by emphasising flexibility and offering support systems when facing difficult circumstances.

Participate in partnerships with educational establishments: Developing individualised training programmes and internship opportunities can be accomplished by establishing collaborations with educational institutions.

Participate in academic institutions to close the knowledge gap between educational institutions and the industry's requirements.

5. CONCLUSION

Human capital development in the hospitality sector is a dynamic and varied process. It is an essential component in achieving success and the continued existence of organisations. The purpose of this in-depth chapter was to emphasise the most critical aspects, techniques, and recommendations for efficient human capital development within the framework of the hospitality industry. The conceptual framework provides a holistic understanding of the interconnected nature of human capital in the hospitality industry. This understanding encompasses foundational elements such as training and leadership development and critical aspects such as technology integration, employee well-being, diversity, and inclusion. The implementation of recognition and reward systems, ongoing learning, and strategy alignment are further factors that contribute to developing a constructive work culture and promoting engaging employees.

For firms looking to improve the efficiency of their workforce, the ideas offered provide insights that may be put into action. Organisations can develop a resilient and adaptable workforce that can meet the industry's ever-changing demands by investing in comprehensive training, prioritising leadership development, embracing technology, and promoting employee well-being. An approach centred on the customer, a dedication to diversity and inclusion, and strategic alignment with the organisation's goals are all additional factors contributing to developing a positive and sustainable organisational culture. The professional development of personnel is enhanced via the implementation of recognition and reward systems, continuous learning initiatives, and cross-training programmes. This, in turn, contributes to higher job satisfaction and overall performance.

It can be concluded that developing human capital in the hospitality business is an ongoing journey that involves both refinement and adaptability. Organisations that prioritise the health and development of their workforce, adopt strategies that align with the trends in their industry, and cultivate a culture that encourages innovation and inclusivity are in a better position to thrive in a highly competitive environment.

6. DIRECTIONS FOR THE FUTURE STUDY

As the hospitality sector continues to change, several areas require more study to improve our understanding of effective methods for human capital development and to put those strategies into practice:

- Investigate the influence of emerging technologies, such as artificial intelligence, virtual reality, and automation, on human capital development in the hospitality industry. It is essential to investigate how firms may get their workforce ready to implement these advancements.
- Carry out an in-depth chapter on the globalisation of the hospitality industry's workforce and the significance of having cross-cultural competence. Explore how firms may effectively manage diverse teams while catering to a consumer base spanning different country.
- Investigate the unique techniques and interventions contributing to employee well-being during crises, such as worldwide pandemics. Explore the long-term consequences of crisis-related stresses on the workforce and discover optimal practices for organisational resilience.
- Explore innovative recognition and reward systems methods, including the integration of gamification, tailored incentives, and social recognition platforms. Examine these systems' effects on the workforce's motivation and engagement level.
- It is essential to do a longitudinal chapter to monitor the long-term effects of leadership development programmes on organisations' performance. Determine the extent to which successful leadership contributes to the retention of employees, the contentment of customers, and the organisation's overall performance over a prolonged period.
- Conduct a chapter on applying data analytics for talent management within the hospitality industry. Investigate how firms may use data-driven insights to locate workers with high potential, fill up skill shortages, and improve workforce planning.
- Exploring the ramifications of flexible work arrangements, particularly the possibility of working remotely, on human capital development is an important topic to investigate. Assess the difficulties and advantages of working remotely in the hospitality industry and develop solutions to ensure employees remain engaged.
- In the context of human capital development, it is essential to investigate how sustainable practices and CSR may be included in human capital development initiatives.

Investigate how firms might match their workforce's growth with environmental and social sustainability aims.

- Investigate the possibility of collaborating across different sectors in human capital development. It is essential to investigate the possibility of forming partnerships between companies in the hotel industry, educational institutions, and other businesses to develop new training programmes and initiatives for knowledge exchange.
- Conduct a qualitative chapter to get insights directly from workers on their experiences with human capital development programmes. This will allow for the understanding of employee perspectives on development programmes. Investigate employees' views, preferences, and ideas to maximise training effectiveness, leadership development, and well-being activities.

To ensure that organisations remain adaptable, resilient, and thriving in the face of dynamic challenges and opportunities, scholars and practitioners can contribute to the evolution of human capital development practices in the hospitality industry by delving into these chapter directions.

REFERENCES

Agba, M. S., Agba, G. E. M., Abang, P. O., Enang, A. U., Ozumba, L. N., Duke, O. O., Ata-Agboni, J. U., Eja, T. R., Odinka, G. E., Okpa, J. T., Bassey, A. E., & Nwagboso, C. I. (2023). University governance: TET fund and human capital development in perspective. *Corporate and Business Strategy Review*, *4*(4), 295–309. https://doi.org/10.22495/cbsrv4i4siart11

Ahun, E., Demir, A., Yiğit, Y., Tulgar, Y. K., Doğan, M., Thomas, D. T., & Tulgar, S. (2023). Perceptions and concerns of emergency medicine practitioners about artificial intelligence in emergency triage management during the pandemic: A national survey-based study. *Frontiers in Public Health*, *11*, 1285390. https://doi.org/10.3389/fpubh.2023.1285390

Akintunde, T. S., Isayomi, A. S., & Nigeria. (2023). The effect of the informal economy on human capital development. *Izvestiya Journal of the University of Economics – Varna*, *67*(3), 182–195. https://doi.org/10.56065/IJUEV2023.67.3.182

Anastasiya, I. (2023). State regulation of innovative development of human capital. *Journal of Law and Sustainable Development*, *11*(11), e2289. https://doi.org/10.55908/sdgs.v11i11.2289

Azizah, S. N., Raharjo, A. P., & Kristiana, I. F. (2023). Humility and psychological well-being of hospital employees. *Proceedings of International Conference on Psychological Studies (ICPsyche)*, *4*, 280–286. https://doi.org/10.58959/icpsyche.v4i1.45

Collins Ii, R. T., Algaze, C., & Posner, B. Z. (2023). The leadership/management concept scale: Differentiating between actions constituting leadership and management. *Leadership & Organization Development Journal*, *44*(5), 657–677. https://doi.org/10.1108/LODJ-06-2022-0299

Daryono, D. (2023). An assessment of employee engagement: Understanding organisation with employees to increase high performance. *Journal of Business & Management*, *1*(3), 188–205. https://doi.org/10.47747/jbm.v1i3.1131

Dixit, A., & Aggarwal, P. (2023). Safety and health in the workplace. *International Journal for Research in Applied Science and Engineering Technology*, *11*(3), 592–598. https://doi.org/10.22214/ijraset.2023.48043

Fokina, O., Ivanovskaya, Z., Mottaeva, A., & Khubaev, A. (2023). The conceptual role of leadership in project management. *E3S Web of Conferences*, *458*, 04020. https://doi.org/10.1051/e3sconf/202345804020

Gao, Q., Liu, Y., Ayub, B., & Hussain, M. (2022). Does health crises effect tourism: Role of financial inclusion for green financial development. *Frontiers in Public Health*, *10*, 896894. https://doi.org/10.3389/fpubh.2022.896894

Hanushek, E. A. (2013). Economic growth in developing countries: The role of human capital. *Economics of Education Review*, *37*, 204–212. https://doi.org/10.1016/j.econedurev.2013.04.005

International Research and Training Center for Information Technologies and Systems of the NAS and MES of Ukraine, &Synytsya, K. M. (2023). Model of development of continuous-learning. *Control Systems and Computers*, *2*(302), 45–60. https://doi.org/10.15407/csc.2023.02.045

Johnson, B. L. (2022). Pass the torch: Leadership development and succession planning in nonprofit organizations. *Journal of Philanthropy and Marketing*, *27*(4), e1770. https://doi.org/10.1002/nvsm.1770

Kumar, S., Talukder, M. B., Kabir, F., & Kaiser, F. (2024). Challenges and sustainability of green finance in the tourism industry: Evidence from Bangladesh. In S. Taneja, P. Kumar, S. Grima, E. Ozen, & K. Sood (Eds.), *Advances in finance, accounting, and economics* (pp. 97–111). IGI Global. http://dx.doi.org/10.4018/979-8-3693-1388-6.ch006

Moura, C. (2023). Investing in social responsibility to achieve full sustainability. *Worldwide Hospitality and Tourism Themes*, *15*(6), 681–683. https://doi.org/10.1108/WHATT-09-2023-0117

Negedu, I. A., & Ojomah, S. O. (2022). Remedial approach to cultural globalization and intercultural competence. In J. O. Chimakonam, E. Etieyibo, & I. Odimegwu (Eds.), *Essays on contemporary issues in African philosophy* (pp. 193–207). Springer International Publishing. https://doi.org/10.1007/978-3-030-70436-0_13

Nieva Boza, C., Aguilà González, S., & Mas Parera, M. T. (2023). La importancia de los Proyectos de Aprendizaje Tutorados en la formación permanente de los docen-tes de Educación Física [The importance of project oriented learning in continuing training of physical education teachers]. *Retos*, *51*, 1282–1292. https://doi.org/10.47197/retos.v51.97879

Odeibat, A. (2023). Exploring the impact of managerial capabilities on the innovation potential of artificial intelligence and organizational capabilities: A literature review. *Review of Applied Socio-Economic Research*, *26*(2). https://doi.org/10.54609/reaser.v26i2.420

Ogiemwonyi, O., Alam, M. N., & Alotaibi, H. S. (2023). Connecting green HRM practices to pro-environmental behavior through green human capital in the hospitality sector. *Business Strategy & Development*, *6*(4), 1053–1071. https://doi.org/10.1002/bsd2.297

Olusegun Adedipe, C., & Olusola Adeleke, B. (2016). Human capital development in the Nigerian hospitality industry: The imperative for a stakeholder driven initiative. *Worldwide Hospitality and Tourism Themes*, *8*(2), 195–206. https://doi.org/10.1108/WHATT-11-2015-0051

O'Neill, M., & Bagchi-Sen, S. (2022). Public universities and human capital development in the United States. *Geo Journal*, *88*(1), 733–751. https://doi.org/10.1007/s10708-022-10636-1

Owuondo, J. (2023). Fostering educational development and innovation in the global south: Incentivizing research and development (R&D). *International Journal of Research and Scientific Innovation*, (Special issue), 186–195. https://doi.org/10.51244/IJRSI.2023.101018

Puška, A., Hodžić, I., Štilić, A., & Murtič, S. (2024). Evaluating European Union countries on climate change management: A fuzzy MABAC approach to the climate change performance index. *Journal of Green Economy and Low-Carbon Development*, 3(1), 15–25.

Rajeswari, R., & Balamurugan, A. (2022). An empirical analysis of factors influencing reward and recognition systems followed in selected garments industries in Tirupur. *Management Journal for Advanced Research*, *2*(4), 9–15. https://doi.org/10.54741/mjar.2.4.2

Ramli, F. N. A., & Mohamad Arsad, N. (2023). Stem teacher digital literacy: Relationship between digital literacy and technology integration in teaching and learning post COVID-19. *Journal of Nusantara Studies (JONUS)*, *8*(2), 316–333. https://doi.org/10.24200/jonus.vol8iss2pp316-333

Shekhar, S., Zhou, Z.-H., Chiang, Y.-Y., & Stiglic, G. (Eds.). (2023). *Proceedings of the 2023 SIAM international conference on data mining (SDM)*. Society for Industrial and Applied Mathematics. https://doi.org/10.1137/1.9781611977653

Slavković, M., Ognjanović, J., & Bugarčić, M. (2023). Sustainability of human capital efficiency in the hotel industry: Panel data evidence. *Sustainability*, *15*(3), 2268. https://doi.org/10.3390/su15032268

Smagulova, N. T., Elshibekova, K. Zh., & Assanova, A. Zh. (2023). Efficiency of investments in human capital: Priorities and prospects for their development. *Bulletin of "Turan" University*, *3*, 121–140. https://doi.org/10.46914/1562-2959-2023-1-3-121-140

Sojan, T. (2023). A study on the causes of employee turnover and different retention tactics developed by business. *International Scientific Journal of Engineering and Management*, *2*(3). https://doi.org/10.55041/ISJEM00126

Southwest State University, &Charochkina, E. Yu. (2021). Trends in the technological transformation of the industrial sector of the economy at the present stage. *Proceedings of the Southwest State University. Series: Economics, Sociology and Management*, *11*(5), 85–94. https://doi.org/10.21869/2223-1552-2021-11-5-85-94

Talukder, M. B. (2020). The future of culinary tourism: An emerging dimension for the tourism industry of Bangladesh. *I-Manager's Journal on Management*, *15*(1), 27. https://doi.org/10.26634/jmgt.15.1.17181

Talukder, M. B. (2021). An assessment of the roles of the social network in the development of the tourism industry in Bangladesh. *International Journal of Business, Law, and Education*, *2*(3), 85–93. https://doi.org/10.56442/ijble.v2i3.21

Talukder, M. B., & Hossain, M. M. (2021). Prospects of future tourism in Bangladesh: An evaluative study. *I-Manager's Journal on Management*, *15*(4), 1–8. https://doi.org/10.26634/jmgt.15.4.17495

Talukder, M. B., Kabir, F., Muhsina, K., & Das, I. R. (2023). Emerging concepts of artificial intelligence in the hotel industry: A conceptual paper. *International Journal of Research Publication and Reviews*, *4*(9), 1765–1769. https://doi.org/10.55248/gengpi.4.923.92451

Talukder, M. B., Kumar, S., Sood, K., & Grima, S. (2023). Information technology, food service quality and restaurant revisit intention. *International Journal of Sustainable Development and Planning*, *18*(1), 295–303. https://doi.org/10.18280/ijsdp.180131

Tsai, C., Patel, H., Horbal, P., Dickey, S., Peng, Y., Nwankwo, E., Hicks, H., Chen, G., Hussein, A., Gopinathannair, R., & Mar, P. L. (2023). Comparison of quantifiable electrocardiographic changes associated with severe hyperkalemia. *International Journal of Cardiology*, *391*, 131257. https://doi.org/10.1016/j.ijcard.2023.131257

Wynn, M. G., & Jones, P. (2023). Natural capital and natural asset management in the hospitality industry. *Athens Journal of Tourism*, *10*(1), 9–20. https://doi.org/10.30958/ajt.10-1-1

Yang, S., & Ok Choi, S. (2009). Employee empowerment and team performance: Autonomy, responsibility, information, and creativity. *Team Performance Management: An International Journal*, *15*(5/6), 289–301. https://doi.org/10.1108/13527590910983549

Yerpude, S., Sood, K., & Grima, S. (2022). Blockchain-augmented digital supply chain management: A way to sustainable business. *Journal of Risk and Financial Management*, *16*(1), 7.

Yusaini, M. H., Hassan, M. A., & Hasnisham, Q. M., (2023). Flexible work arrangements: Experience of a Malaysian manufacturing company. *NUST Business Review*, *4*(2), 1–18. https://doi.org/10.37435/NBR23010801

Zaimoglu, A. K., Pratt, L., & Fisher, B. (2023). Epistemological role of human reasoning in data-informed decision-making. *Frontiers in Communication*, *8*, 1250301. https://doi.org/10.3389/fcomm.2023.1250301

Zhang, Y., Xiong, Y., Lee, T. J., Ye, M., & Nunkoo, R. (2021). Sociocultural sustainability and the formation of social capital from community-based tourism. *Journal of Travel Research*, *60*(3), 656–669. https://doi.org/10.1177/0047287520933673

CHAPTER 3

EXPLORING THE LINKAGE BETWEEN SUSTAINABILITY AND WELL-BEING AT THE WORKPLACE: THE PRISMA APPROACH

Rekha Mewafarosh[a], Farah Naeem[b], Shivani Malhan[c] and Shikha Agnihotri[d]

[a]*Indian Institute of Forest Management, Madhya Pradesh, India*
[b]*Shri Ram Institute of Management and Technology, Uttarakhand, India*
[c]*Chitkara Business School, Chitkara University, Punjab, India*
[d]*Institute of Management Studies, Uttar Pradesh, India*

ABSTRACT

Purpose: *This chapter explores the linkage between sustainability and subjective well-being (SWB) in the workplace. This scoping review aims to present rational approaches to the linkage between sustainability and SWB at the workplace.*

Need of the study: *Sustainability aims to achieve social equity and justice through various initiatives so that present and future generations can enjoy resources without exploiting them. By adopting sustainable initiatives in our day-to-day lives, we can create a healthier equation between humans, work and nature.*

Methodology: *This scoping review explores the relationship between sustainability and SWB in the workplace. Employing the PRISMA method for*

Sustainability Development through Green Economics
Contemporary Studies in Economic and Financial Analysis, Volume 114, 39–53

Published under exclusive licence by Emerald Publishing Limited
ISSN: 1569-3759/doi:10.1108/S1569-375920240000114003

synthesis, which is qualitative in nature, the review includes research papers published from 2014 to 2023.

Findings: *Sustainable HRM encourages employees to engage in socially responsible initiatives and activities. Research demonstrated a positive correlation between well-being and desirable outcomes, including improved job performance, increased productivity and reduced employee turnover intention.*

Practical implications: *This review underscores the significance of implementing sustainable practices to enhance well-being across various levels within organisations, encompassing individual employees, teams, organisations as a whole and inter-organisational processes. Organisations can pave the way for a resilient future by prioritising sustainable actions today.*

Keywords: Sustainability; subjective well-being; workplace; PRISMA; systematic literature reviews; sustainable HRM; well-being

JEL Codes: Q56; I31

INTRODUCTION

Sustainability involves meeting present needs while safeguarding the needs of future generations. The concept of sustainability encompasses multiple aspects, including environmental, social, and economic. Sustainability enables better resource management and focusses on minimising waste and pollution. It also aims to achieve social equity and justice by promoting renewable energy sources so that present and future generations can enjoy resources without exploiting them (González-Díaz et al., 2021).

We can create a healthier equation between human development and nature by adopting sustainable practices in our day-to-day lives, businesses, and communities. Since sustainable actions of today will lead to a more resilient future. A study on climate change and mental well-being establishes that an alteration in climatic conditions can lead to helplessness, hopelessness, and pessimism, particularly among younger employees (Clayton et al., 2017; Majedul Islam, 2022). According to a 2021 World Economic Forum study, 59% of workers who leave their jobs do so to work for a company that is more aligned with their ideals. There is reason to suppose that many personnel who are on the move prioritise sustainability. In a recent survey by IBM in 2021, it was found that the majority of employees (71%) perceive organisations practising environmental responsibility as more desirable.

These results demonstrate that integrating sustainability into one's fundamental business offer may benefit the environment and the company's bottom line (Preston, 2022). The United Nations 2030 Sustainable Development Goals (SDGs) stresses protecting people's health and well-being to ensure a sustainable future (Parsons et al., 2020).

In this chapter, researchers establish the linkage between SWB and organisational sustainable practices. The chapter focusses on the relevance of adopting sustainable practices in the context of social practices like wellness programmes by companies to achieve their employees' SWB.

The concept of sustainability and SWB has recently gained popularity for many reasons. Firstly, organisations understand that sustainability is crucial for long-term survival as the world faces numerous challenges like resource depletion, climate change, pandemics, and many more. In order to survive and thrive amidst such a challenging environment, organisations need to adopt a more sustainable approach to stay relevant and profitable in the long run. Moreover, sustainable practices bring many benefits, including cost savings, resource optimisation, better supply chain management, waste reduction, etc. (Barletta et al., 2021).

Employers foster sustainability through regulatory relevance and support the employee by attracting and retaining talent, participation of employees, and motivation (Renwick et al., 2011). Organisations are encouraged to establish policies and strategies that promote job satisfaction while maintaining a harmonious alignment between economic, social, and environmental objectives. The literature emphasises the importance of various policies and practices. These factors create organisational cultures, climates, and capabilities conducive to achieving positive environmental outcomes (Kramar, 2014). Leading organisations recognise the importance of cultivating a world-class talent pool to gain a competitive edge in the global business landscape and align with SDGs. Research suggests that organisations that prioritise effective resource utilisation, enhanced productivity, profitability, and long-term growth are more likely to achieve their strategic objectives (Ambec & Lanoie, 2008; De Prins et al., 2014; Jackson et al., 2011; Khandekar & Sharma, 2005).

In this chapter, researchers establish the linkage between SWB and organisational sustainable practices. The chapter focusses on the relevance of adopting sustainable practices in the context of social practices like wellness programmes by companies to achieve their employees' SWB.

WORKPLACE WELL-BEING

The culture where employees feel respected and get the opportunity to learn, as well as the clarity on job descriptions and the expectations, as well as the assigned responsibilities that people are assigned and all contribute to the organisational environment. All of these elements foster workplace happiness because such elements facilitate a culture that will promote the happiness and well-being of employees (Danna & Griffin, 1999). Employee satisfaction is based on the leader's willingness to listen to the subordinates' questions, which is the cornerstone of effective leader-subordinate dynamics (Bates & Thompson, 2007). When job demands exceed the resources available, it will cause tension and dissatisfaction among employees, negatively impacting workplace well-being (Naeem, 2021). In today's world, work–life balance has a profound impact on the lives of working professionals. Studies indicate that the average workweek for full-time employees in the United States has increased significantly, with individuals working longer hours, including weekends (Saad, 2014 ; USBoL, 2015). This extended workload takes a toll on workers' well-being, leading to stress, burnout, and work overload for a significant proportion of full-time professionals (Kelton, 2014; Naeem, 2018). As a result, researchers in organisational settings increasingly focus on understanding the relationship between work and individual well-being (Briner & Walshe, 2015; Wright et al., 2007).

Workplace well-being is significant for organisational success and has become a subject of organisational study (Danna & Griffin, 1999). Employees' experiences at work are portrayed in their jobs and even in matters outside the workplace. The workplace well-being companies provide their employees is what causes the employees' association with the organisation. It helps foster optimism, hope, and self-efficacy among the personality traits of employees (Aryanti & Widiana, 2020). Employees who reported feeling good at work are happier, behave well, and appear in a good state of physical and mental health compared to those who reported feeling less well (Kurniadewi, 2017; Schwarz & Strack, 1999). The organisational atmosphere and demographic features are just two factors that influence the happiness of workers at work.

SUBJECTIVE WELL-BEING

SWB encompasses individuals experiencing positive emotions, joy, and contentment while acknowledging a few negative emotions and challenges (Diener, 2000). SWB often manifests through simple phrases like 'I feel good' or 'I feel happy'. SWB is a subjective evaluation of one's overall quality of life (Diener, 2000), providing insight into how individuals perceive their circumstances, activities, and psychological resources (New Economics Foundation, 2018). Well-being gained attention when the World Health Organisation acknowledged in 1948 that health extends beyond the absence of disease to encompass well-being (La Placa & Knight, 2014). Well-being is subjective and multidimensional (Organization for Economic Cooperation, 2013). Research indicates a significant association between demographic variables and an individual's SWB (Agarwal & Mewafarosh, 2021). The term 'happiness' is often used interchangeably with SWB to represent overall well-being.

SUSTAINABILITY AND SWB

SWB refers to the perception of one's own happiness and life satisfaction (LS) by an individual. Studies establish happier employees are more committed and engaged, resulting in higher productivity and profits.

Employee well-being has been linked to higher job satisfaction and a positive work climate, promoting creativity and innovation (Naeem, 2022). The concept of sustainability has profoundly impacted various management functions, like organisational behaviour, people management, supply chain, and strategic management. In response to the adverse effects of conventional human resource management approaches on the workforce, environment, and society, sustainable HRM has gained significant attention from practitioners and academics (Mariappanadar, 2003, 2014a, 2014b). Sustainable HRM practices are desired by both employees and organisations due to their significant implications. Thriving employees exhibit positive energy, lower turnover intentions, reduced burnout, emotional attachment to organisations, innovation, and creativity (Abid et al., 2015; Porath et al., 2012).

SYSTEMATIC LITERATURE REVIEWS

A systematic literature review (SLR) is a robust and thorough approach employed in research to systematically identify, assess, and integrate existing scientific literature on a particular subject. Its purpose is to offer an impartial and objective overview of the available evidence, enabling researchers to derive dependable conclusions and make well-informed decisions. By following a structured methodology, an SLR ensures the inclusion of relevant studies, minimises bias, and enhances the reliability and validity of the findings.

The benefits of conducting a SLR are numerous. It provides a comprehensive overview of the existing evidence, identifies research gaps, and helps identify areas for further investigation. SLRs are widely used in healthcare, social sciences, and other disciplines to inform policy-making, clinical practice guidelines, and academic research. However, it is important to acknowledge that SLR have limitations. They rely on the availability and quality of published studies, potentially excluding unpublished or grey literature (Puška et al., 2024; Yerpude et al., 2022).

Additionally, the conclusions drawn from an SLR are only as reliable as the studies included, and biases can still exist despite rigorous methodology. In summary, SLR are valuable for synthesising and analysing existing research systematically and unbiasedly. By following a structured process, researchers can provide a comprehensive summary of the evidence, contributing to evidence-based decision-making and advancing knowledge in their respective fields.

Well-being and sustainable employee performance have become critical considerations for organisational sustainable development (Di Fabio, 2017). Previous studies have demonstrated the association between SWB and various positive outcomes such as knowledge sharing, innovation behaviour, job performance, organisational citizenship behaviours, productivity, and reduced turnover intention. Today, artificial intelligence is used to create knowledge repositories, and the Internet of Things (IoT) has grown immensely and is contributing to the development of recent technological advancements in every sector; this change in work dynamism is affecting the SWB of employees (Verma et al., 2019; Zhang et al., 2021). The importance of SWB in the organisational context is highlighted theoretically and practically (Robertson et al., 2012). While factors at the individual, organisational, and group levels have been identified as influencing SWB, there is still ongoing research on the predictors of well-being. Further investigation is needed, as suggested by Butt et al. (2018) and Nielsen et al. (2017).

PROBLEM DEFINITION AND SCOPE

Sustainable practices combat climate change by reducing emissions, promoting renewables, and adopting efficiency. Businesses can contribute to reducing their carbon footprint, which is crucial for combating global warming and its adverse impacts on ecosystems, communities, and economies. Social Inequities: Sustainable business practices can address social inequities by promoting fair labour practices, providing decent working conditions, and supporting supply chains that uphold human rights. Businesses can implement fair wages, ensure safe working environments, and engage in responsible sourcing practices to avoid exploitation and improve the well-being of workers.

METHODS

Search and Sources

The study's results were obtained using a SLR based on the PRISMA model. Databases, search terms, and strategies were carefully chosen to ensure comprehensive coverage and high-quality analysis (Page et al., 2021). The search was performed on Scopus, Web of Science, and ProQuest in July 2022, with a follow-up search in January 2023. As shown in Table 3.1, keywords included sustainability (sustainable practices, sustainable HRM, SWB, well-being, and climate change) and methods (model, methods and practices). Snowballing was also utilised to examine references from included papers.

Formulation of Search String

Table 3.1. Keywords and Associated Terms.

Keywords	Associated Terms
Sustainable practices	waste reduction, recycling, and responsible disposal; resource efficiency; social responsibility
Well-being	Subjective Well-being; work engagement; Psychological well-being; Resilience; emotional well-being; stress management
Climate change	greenhouse gas; mitigation; renewable energy; extreme weather event
Sustainable HRM	Social Sustainability; Sustainability; Sustainable Development; Work–life Balance; Green HRM; Talent Management

Source: *Secondary sources* (from the database of Scopus, Web of Science, and ProQuest).

Data Collection and Study Selection

As shown in Fig. 3.1, this study included practices and initiatives promoting sustainability in work settings. Peer-reviewed papers presenting clear and tangible approaches to sustainability, focussing on English language publications, were included. Studies involving larger or staged processes and commentaries, posters, protocols, editorials, and perspectives were excluded. As exhibited in Fig. 3.1, papers solely defining sustainability concepts without relating to SWB were also excluded. Authors independently screened the initial 20% of full-text articles, resolving discrepancies through discussion and refining the inclusion/exclusion criteria. One author then screened the remaining papers for inclusion.

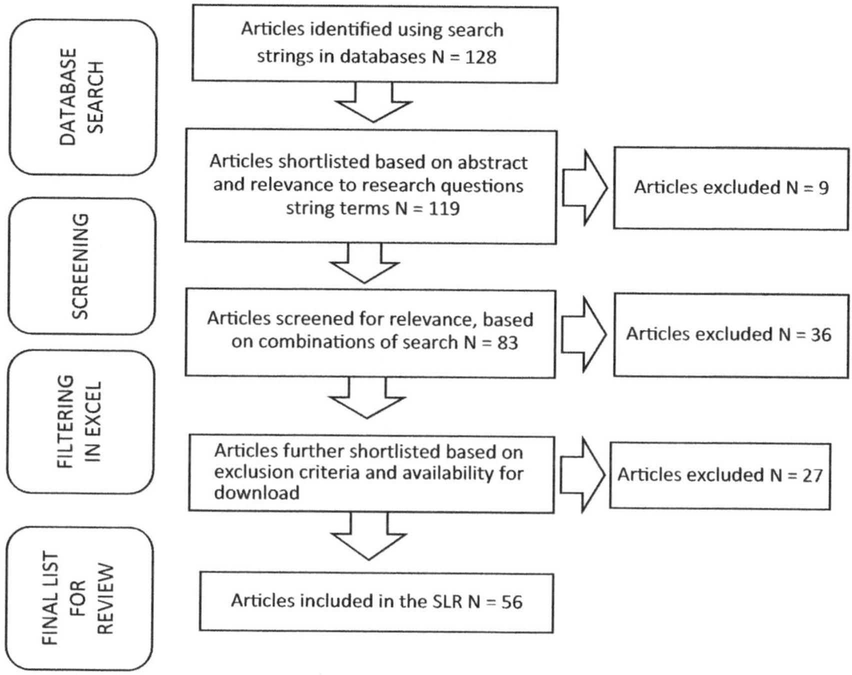

Fig. 3.1. Literature Search Strategy and Review Process: Flow Diagram (PRISMA Model). *Source*: https://www.bmj.com/content/372/bmj.n71; retrieved on February 2023.

Table 3.2 shows the details of the chapters, including the authors' names, the papers' titles, the research aims, the research methodology, and the study's findings.

QUALITY ASSESSMENT AND DATA EXTRACTION STRATEGY

The data extraction and quality assessment form were developed to refine the search for articles. In some cases, quality assessment fails in data extraction in the context of the relevancy of studies. To extract the data, the exclusion of qualitative research is not recommended as the applied to extract the data does not capture the 'significance' studies. The included studies have provided an overview of data extraction's sustainability and SWB. Data extraction aims to report the descriptions and incite the relevant information to ascertain the aim of this study. Each article is assessed in a structured manner to meet the expected baseline quality of the research paper. The strategy behind the data extraction includes the objective of the paper, the purpose of the study, the research gap, initiatives

Table 3.2. Details of Papers/Research Used in SLR.

Authors/Year	Title/Journal	Objective of Research	Research Methodology	Key Findings
Siddiqui and Ijaz (2022)	Conceptualizing the sustainable workplace well-being: a measurement framework/*Pakistan Journal of Social Sciences (PJSS)*	The study aims to do an SLR on well-being at work and link it with sustainable well-being at the job	Around 52 workplace well-being papers were gathered and screened to achieve objectives	General well-being is now replaced with sustainable well-being at workplaces, a new theme supporting the triple-bottom-line approach towards a sustainable business policy
De Neve and Sachs (2020)	Sustainable development and human well-being; World Happiness Report	The research analyses the experiential association between the SDGs and employee wellness.	Information was derived from the SDGs index and Gallup survey	A robust association between acquiring sustainable growth and self-report questionnaire of wellness. Furthermore, the results show a growth in insignificant outcomes to sustainable development on the dimension of well-being
Kubiszewski et al. (2022)	Toward better measurement of development, which is sustainable and better well-being: A few indicators of SDG reliably predict satisfaction related to life; Sustainable Development	To highlight some of the issues with this approach, the authors model LS survey scores by country as a proxy for overall well-being and as the dependent variable against the official 232 SDG indicators	The study utilises the 232 SDG indicators; using a constrained linear regression approach, authors identified a model that includes only 8 out of the 232 pointers and reflects variation in LS	Results show that the maximum of the current pointers are not essential and seem to be on the list only because they could be measured. The present slots of indicators are not able to assess overall responsible development and sustainable well-being. The eight dimensions are representations of financial, societal, and ecological variables. Authors clustered countries based on the pointers, and LS shows a correlation between topographical and social areas

Abid et al. (2020)	Antecedents and mechanism of employee well-being for social sustainability: A sequential mediation; *Sustainable Production and Consumption*	The paper aims to analyse the consequences of fair perception on the wellness of the workforce	Two wave-lagged study approaches were utilised together with information from a sample of 804 participants employed in various roles	Results show empirical support for the direct and indirect association through process macros. It was found that workplace civility and thriving on the job have a crucial role in establishing a relationship between fair perception and subjective wellness
Singh et al. (2019)	Self-efficacy and workplace well-being: moderating role of sustainability practices; *Benchmarking: An International Journal*	It aims to identify how psychological variables concerning self-efficacy play a pertinent role in achieving employee prosperity	A sample of 527 executives working in public and private manufacturing sectors of India was utilised to collect data	The result shows an important association between self-efficacy and employee wellness. Moreover, it was found that the linkage between efficacy related to oneself and work wellness was stronger among employees practising higher sustainable practices and vice versa
Chillakuri and Vanka (2021)	Examining the effects of workplace well-being and high-performance work systems on health harm: a sustainable HRM perspective ***Society and Business Review***	The research seeks to analyse the role of well-being at work and its indirect impact on job intensification. Moreover, understand sustainable goals through the lenses of sustainable HRM	The data were gathered from 324 executives	Analysis results ensure that workplace well-being practices minimise the negative impact arising from work intensification
Mariappanadar and Kramar (2014)	Sustainable HRM: The synthesis effect of high-performance work systems on organizational performance and employee harm. *Asia-Pacific Journal of Business Administration*	The paper aims to study sustainable HRM based on the combination and concurrent impact of high-performance working systems	Information was gathered by employing survey methods with the help of twin canonical correlation analysis	Results show that a flexible and enhanced productivity work schedule like telephonic work and reduced work hours are likely to have an adverse impact on organisational performance

(*Continued*)

Table 3.2. *(Continued)*

Authors/Year	Title/Journal	Objective of Research	Research Methodology	Key Findings
Randev and Jha (2019)	Sustainable human resource management: A literature-based introduction. *NHRD Network Journal*	The paper intends to analyse current studies on sustainable human resource management to build a better understanding of the subject	A detailed literature review was scanned to achieve results	Results show that, nowadays, organisational practices primarily focus on absenteeism, attrition, worker performance, and forecasting financial productivity
Sadick and Kamardeen (2020)	Enhancing employees' performance and well-being with nature exposure embedded office workplace design. *Journal of Building Engineering*	The study aims to show the effect of nature exposure on employees by synthesising empirical research to understand their contribution to holistic sustainability	Forty-two articles that met the inclusion criteria were chosen, followed by SLR and meta-analyses	Results show that internal nature contributes to societal sustainability by affecting employee health and motivation
Madero-Gómez et al. (2023)	Companies could benefit when they focus on employee well-being and the environment: A systematic review of sustainable human resource management. *Sustainability*	The paper examines the work's adverse effect on workers' wellness and its indirect consequences on the SDGs	Data for the literature review were gathered from the Scopus scholarly database, ranging from 2008 to 2022	It was found that adopting sustainable practices in organisational settings is likely to boost wellness and minimise pollution, which is beneficial for the company's viability

Source: Secondary sources (from the database of Scopus, Web of Science, and ProQuest).

taken, sustainable practices, and the theoretical underpinning of the study. One of the authors extracted significant data and others assessed it. If any data seem missing, we discussed it among authors and reached a consensus point. Finally, based on a common consensus, we reached an agreement on the accuracy of the research work.

DATA SYNTHESIS AND PRESENTATION

After applying the inclusion criteria, the search revealed 128 articles published on sustainability, sustainable practices, well-being, and employees. Further, each article was assessed manually in the context of its relevance concerning the research study; 9 articles were excluded. The articles are shortlisted based on abstract and relevance to research questions.

The thematic structure of 119 papers was assessed by performing by discussing and revealing the important themes of the studies. We contribute to the literature by assessing existing theoretical concepts, research gaps, and implications in our study. The study concludes by discussing themes and sub-themes and offers suggestions that will be helpful to organisations. Then the articles are shortlisted to 83, as the excluded 37 articles' themes are relevant in the context of our research work. Finally, 56 articles were included in this study and 27 were again excluded as they were unrelated to our research purpose.

The study analysis provides a framework by assessing the past literature and ascertaining the new directions for future researchers. The findings of the study assert that: (1) Sustainable HRM is the need of the hour; this approach will emphasise integrating sustainable principles and practices within the domain of HRM. It recognises the crucial role of HRM in promoting environmental stewardship, social responsibility, and economic viability within organisations. Sustainable HRM involves aligning HR strategies and practices with the broader sustainability goals of an organisation.

Organisations practising Sustainable HRM understand that their employees are key drivers of sustainable development. They prioritise the well-being and engagement of employees, fostering a culture of sustainability and providing opportunities for learning and growth. Sustainable HRM also promotes diversity, inclusion, and equal opportunities, recognising that diverse perspectives and experiences contribute to sustainable outcomes. Furthermore, Sustainable HRM recognises the importance of responsible leadership and ethical decision-making. HR professionals play a crucial role in promoting ethical behaviour, ensuring transparency, and enforcing sustainability policies and practices throughout the organisation. By adopting Sustainable HRM practices, organisations can achieve several benefits. These include enhanced reputation and brand value, improved employee satisfaction and retention, increased innovation and creativity, better risk management, and long-term organisational resilience. Sustainable HRM integrates sustainability principles into HR strategies, processes, and practices, recognising that employees are key change agents. By facilitating a culture by aligning HR initiatives with broader sustainable goals, organisations can contribute to a sustainable future, which results in benefits like motivated and engaged employees.

(2) Sustainable practices in managing manpower in organisations can be an antecedent for employee well-being. When organisations prioritise sustainability and incorporate sustainable HRM practices, they create an environment that supports and enhances the employees' well-being. Sustainable HRM promotes work–life balance by offering flexible work arrangements, promoting a healthy work culture, and encouraging employees to prioritise their well-being. This can reduce stress, increase job satisfaction, and improve overall well-being. Sustainable HRM focusses on employee development and growth, offering training programmes, mentorship, and opportunities for learning and advancement. Employees feeling valued and supported in their professional development positively impacts their well-being. Sustainable HRM emphasises employee health and safety, ensuring a safe and healthy work environment. By implementing wellness programmes, promoting physical and mental health, and providing resources for employee well-being, organisations contribute to the overall well-being of their employees. Sustainable HRM recognises the importance of fostering an inclusive and diverse workplace. Employees feeling valued, respected, and included contributes to their well-being and overall job satisfaction.

SUSTAINABLE HRM AS THE PREDICTOR OF EMPLOYEE WELL-BEING

Sustainable HRM encourages employees to engage in socially responsible initiatives and activities. When employees feel a sense of purpose and are given opportunities to contribute to meaningful causes, it enhances their well-being and job satisfaction. Sustainable HRM focusses on fostering employee engagement and involvement. Organisations empower employees by providing opportunities for participation, feedback, and involvement in decision-making processes, leading to higher levels of satisfaction and improved well-being. By prioritising sustainable HRM practices, organisations demonstrate their commitment to employee well-being. These practices create a positive work environment and better work–life balance, aid in the development of employees, ensure health and safety, foster inclusivity, encourage social responsibility, and enhance employee engagement. All these factors contribute to overall organisational success.

DISCUSSIONS

CB Bhattacharya, in his study, stressed that sustainable practices forge engaged employees, and engaged employees are more productive, happy, and satisfied. He stressed in his interview that to successfully implement sustainable practices, environmental and societal considerations are to be given for the growth of an enterprise. The experiences that employees get at work are reflected in their work and job, and sometimes, it also reflected outside the workplace. The workplace well-being companies provide their employees is what causes the employees' association with the organisation. It helps in emerging optimism, hope, and self-efficacy among employees' personality traits (Aryanti et al., 2020). Employees who reported feeling good at work are happier, behave well, and appear in a good state of physical and mental health compared to those who reported feeling less well (Kurniadewi, 2017). To build a sustainable workplace, the organisation should focus on integrating individual and organisational goals. Companies like Starbucks, Unilever, Ikea, and IBM have initiated programmes to cultivate sustainable cultures for the happiness and engagement of employees.

CONCLUSIONS

Organisations/corporations have realised the relevance of the psychological wellness of people at work. Researchers' interest in research on mental health challenges, SWB, and happiness in the organisational setting is limited. Due to cutthroat competition, the world of work is changing, creating a lot of pressure and stress among professionals. It is high time that organisations strategise their system through sustainable practices to address the psychological wellness of workers. They need to address the issue by focussing on the organisational challenges, urging employees to seek counselling and help if they feel isolated, lonely, anxious, and stressed. The desired changes in the organisational dynamics can only be handled by a few persons, but they should be implemented with sustainable approaches and in a collaborative manner. Organisations have to develop mechanisms to achieve sustainable goals where the focus is on the well-being of employees for better productivity and growth of an enterprise.

IMPLICATIONS

This study suggests that sustainable practices act as an underlying mechanism that improves well-being and results in the satisfaction of employees. The study focusses on promoting sustainability to enhance overall performance, as well-being directly affects the performance of employees. This study provides evidence that sustainable practices at the workplace improve the well-being of manpower (Madero-Gómez et al., 2023). Improved well-being leads to satisfied, engaged, active, and involved employees, which balances the pressure and promotes employee performance.

REFERENCES

Abid, G., Ahmed, S., Elahi, N. S., & Ilyas, S. (2020). Antecedents and mechanism of employee well-being for social sustainability: A sequential mediation. *Sustainable Production and Consumption*, *24*, 79–89.

Agarwal, S., & Mewafarosh, R. (2021). Linkage of social media engagement with FoMO and subjective well-being. *Journal of Content, Community & Communication*, *13*(7), 46–57.

Ambec, S., & Lanoie, P. (2008). Does it pay to be green? A systematic overview. *The Academy of Management Perspectives*, 45–62.

Aryanti, R. D., Sari, E. Y. D., & Widiana, H. S. (2020). *A literature review of workplace well-being* [Paper presentation]. *International conference on community development (ICCD 2020)*. https://www.atlantis-press.com/proceedings/iccd-20/125945161

Barletta, I., Despeisse, M., Hoffenson, S., & Johansson, B. (2021). Organisational sustainability readiness: A model and assessment tool for manufacturing companies. *Journal of Cleaner Production, 284*, 125404.

Briner, R. B., & Walshe, N. D. (2015). An evidence-based approach to improving the quality of resource-oriented well-being interventions at work. *Journal of Occupational and Organizational Psychology, 88*(3), 563–586.

Butt, T. H., Abid, G., Arya, B., & Farooqi, S. (2020). Employee energy and subjective well-being: a moderated mediation model. *The Service Industries Journal, 40*(1–2), 133–157.

Chillakuri, B., & Vanka, S. (2021). Examining the effects of workplace well-being and high-performance work systems on health harm: A sustainable HRM perspective. *Society and Business Review, 16*(1), 71–93. https://doi.org/10.1108/SBR-03-2020-0033

Clayton, S., Manning, C. M., Krygsman, K., & Speiser, M. (2017). *Mental health and our changing climate: Impacts, Implications, and guidance*. American Psychological Association, and ecoAmerica.

Danna, K., & Griffin, R. W. (1999). Health and well-being in the workplace: A review and synthesis of the literature. *Journal of Management, 25*(3), 357–384.

Di Fabio, Annamaria. "The psychology of sustainability and sustainable development for well-being in organizations." *Frontiers in psychology 8* (2017): 296938

De Prins, P., Van Beirendonck, L., De Vos, A., & Segers, J. (2014). Sustainable HRM: Bridging theory and practice through the'Respect Openness Continuity (ROC)'-model. *Management revue*, 263–284

De Neve, J. E., & Sachs, J. D. (2020). The SDGs and human well-being: A global analysis of synergies, trade-offs, and regional differences. *Scientific Reports, 10*(1), 15113.

Diener, E. (2000). Subjective well-being: The science of happiness and a proposal for a national index. *American Psychologist, 55*(1), 34–43. https://doi.org/10.1037//0003- 066x.55.1.34

González-Díaz, R. R., Acevedo-Duque, Á., Salazar-Sepúlveda, G., & Castillo, D. (2021). Contributions of subjective well-being and good living to the contemporary development of the notion of sustainable human development. *Sustainability, 13*(6), 3298.

Kelton. (2014, September). *The state of workplace productivity report* [Internet]. https://www.cornerstoneondemand.com/sites/default/files/research/csod_rs_state_of_the_workplace_2014.pdf

Khandekar, A., & Sharma, A. (2005). Managing human resource capabilities for sustainable competitive advantage: An empirical analysis from Indian global organisations. *Education+ Training, 47*(8/9), 628–639

Kramar, R. (2014). Beyond strategic human resource management: Is sustainable human resource management the next approach? *The International Journal of Human Resource Management, 25*, 1069–1089.

Kubiszewski, I., Mulder, K., Jarvis, D., & Costanza, R. (2022). Toward better measurement of sustainable development and wellbeing: A small number of SDG indicators reliably predict life satisfaction. *Sustainable Development, 30*(1), 139–148.

Kurniadewi, E. (2017). Psychological capital dan workplace well-being sebagai prediktor bagi employee engagement. *Jurnal Psikologi Integratif, 4*(2), 95–112.

La Placa, V., & Knight, A. (2014). Well-being: Its influence and local impact on public health. *Public Health, 128*(1), 38–42.

Madero-Gómez, S. M., Rubio Leal, Y. L., Olivas-Luján, M., & Yusliza, M. Y. (2023). Companies could benefit when they focus on employee well-being and the environment: A systematic review of sustainable human resource management. *Sustainability, 15*(6), 5435.

Majedul Islam, M. M. (2022). Threats to humanity from climate change. In *Climate change: The social and scientific construct* (pp. 21–36). Springer International Publishing.

Mariappanadar, S., & Kramar, R. (2014). Sustainable HRM: The synthesis effect of high performance work systems on organisational performance and employee harm, *Asia-Pacific Journal of Business Administration, 6*(3), 206–224. https://doi.org/10.1108/APJBA-03-2014-0039

Mariappanadar, S. (2003). Sustainable human resource strategy: The sustainable and unsustainable dilemmas of retrenchment. *International Journal of Social Economics*, *30*(8), 906–923.

Mariappanadar, S., & Kramar, R. (2014). Sustainable HRM: The synthesis effect of high performance work systems on organisational performance and employee harm, *Asia-Pacific Journal of Business Administration*, *6*(3), 206–224. https://doi.org/10.1108/APJBA-03-2014-0039

Naeem, F. (2018). Antecedents of organisational stress among bank executives. *Jaipuria International Journal of Management Research*, *4*(2), 82–91.

Naeem, F. (2021). Achieving work life balance through remote working in troubled times. In *Management functions in Covid-19 era* (p. 113). Bloomsbury Publishing. ISBN 978-93-54355-37-0

Naeem, F. (2022). Understanding stress in role and well-being in manufacturing sector: An analysis of major sources. *Journal of Global Information and Business Strategy (JGIBS)*,*14*(1).

Nielsen, L. (2017). Measuring the subjective well-being of diverse populations in the US. *Applied research in quality of life*, *12*, 237–240

Organization for Economic Cooperation. (2013). *How's life? 2013: Measuring well-being*. OECD Publishing. https://doi.org/10.1787/9789264201392-en

Page, M. J., McKenzie, J. E., Bossuyt, P. M., Boutron, I., Hoffmann, T. C., Mulrow, C. D., Shamseer, L., Tetzlaff, J. M., Akl, E. A., Brennan, S. E., et al. (2021). The PRISMA 2020 statement: An updated guideline for reporting systematic reviews. *BMJ*, *372*, 71.

Parsons, H., Houge Mackenzie, S., Filep, S., & Brymer, E. (2020). Subjective well-being and leisure. In *Good health and well-being* (pp. 678–687). https://doi.org/10.1007/978-3-319-69627-0_8-1

Porath, C., Spreitzer, G., Gibson, C., & Garnett, F. G. (2012). Thriving at work: Toward its measurement, construct validation, and theoretical refinement. *Journal of organizational behavior*, *33*(2), 250–275.

Puška, A., Hodžić, I., Štilić, A., & Murtič, S. (2024). Evaluating European Union countries on climate change management: A fuzzy MABAC approach to the Climate Change Performance Index. *Journal of Green Economy and Low-Carbon Development*, *3*(1), 15–25.

Randev, K. K., & Jha, J. K. (2019). Sustainable human resource management: A literature-based introduction. *NHRD Network Journal*, *12*(3), 241–252.

Renwick, D. W. S., Redman, T., & Maguire, S. (2011). Green human resource management: A review and research agenda. *International Journal of Management Reviews*, *15*, 1.

Saad, L. (2014). *The "40-hour" workweek is actually longer*, Seven Hours.

Sadick, A. M., & Kamardeen, I. (2020). Enhancing employees' performance and well-being with nature exposure embedded office workplace design. *Journal of Building Engineering*, *32*, 101789.

Schwarz, N., & Strack, F. (1999). Reports of subjective well-being: Judgmental processes and their methodological implications. In D. Kahneman, E. Diener, & N. Schwarz (Eds.). *Well-being: The foundations of hedonic psychology* (pp. 61–84). Russell Sage Foundation.

Siddiqui, S. H., & Ijaz, A. (2022). Conceptualizing the sustainable workplace well-being: A measurement framework. *Pakistan Journal of Social Sciences*, *42*(2), 363–380. http://pjss.bzu.edu.pk/index.php/pjss/article/view/1095

Singh, S. K., Pradhan, R. K., Panigrahy, N. P., & Jena, L. K. (2019). Self-efficacy and workplace well-being: Moderating role of sustainability practices. *Benchmarking: An International Journal*, *26*(6), 1692–1708. https://doi.org/10.1108/BIJ-07-2018-0219

Verma, K., Bhardwaj, S., Arya, R., Islam, U. L., Bhushan, M., Kumar, A., & Samant, P. (2019). Latest tools for data mining and machine learning. *International Journal of Innovative Technology and Exploring Engineering (IJITEE)*,*8*(9S), 18–23.

Wright, T. A., Cropanzano, R., & Bonett, D. G. (2007). The moderating role of employee positive well-being on the relation between job satisfaction and job performance. *Journal of Occupational Health Psychology*, *12*(2), 93.

Yerpude, S., Sood, K., & Grima, S. (2022). Blockchain-augmented digital supply chain management: A way to sustainable business. *Journal of Risk and Financial Management*, *16*(1), 7.

Zhang, X., Rane, K., Kakaravada, I., & Shabaz, M. (2021). Research on vibration monitoring and fault diagnosis of rotating machinery based on Internet of things technology. *Nonlinear Engineering*, *10*(1), 245–254. https://doi.org/10.1515/nleng-2021-0019

CHAPTER 4

SUSTAINABLE ORGANIZATIONS, HIGH POTENTIAL EMPLOYEES, AND BLENDED LEARNING EFFECTIVENESS IN THE MANUFACTURING INDUSTRY

Rajiv Saini and Shuchi Dawra

Chitkara Business School, Chitkara University, India

ABSTRACT

Introduction: *The idea of sustainability has become increasingly popular across many industries. To meet the demands of the present without compromising the capacity of future generations to meet their requirements, sustainable organisations prioritise integrating environmental, social, and economic aspects into their operations.*

Purpose: *To analyse the inter-relationship between sustainable organisations, high-potential employees (HPEs), and blended learning (BL) effectiveness. Organisations can gain a competitive edge, spur innovation, and contribute to a more sustainable and inclusive future by incorporating sustainability into their operations and offering sustainable workspaces.*

Design/methodology/approach: *This research approach offers a thorough understanding of the connections between sustainable organisations, HPEs, and workspaces by combining a literature review of 77 research papers, case studies, and surveys.*

Sustainability Development through Green Economics
Contemporary Studies in Economic and Financial Analysis, Volume 114, 55–74

Published under exclusive licence by Emerald Publishing Limited
ISSN: 1569-3759/doi:10.1108/S1569-375920240000114004

Findings: *The dedication to sustainability draws high-potential workers and environmentally aware customers who favour supporting socially conscientious businesses.*

Practical implications: *The study provides valuable implications and suggestions for businesses looking to improve their sustainability and recruit top talent. These proposals should include the techniques for integrating sustainability into organisational culture, employee engagement programmes, talent recruiting and retention tactics, and designing environmentally friendly workspaces.*

Originality/value: *This research approach offers a thorough understanding of the connections between sustainable organisations, HPEs, and workspaces by combining literature reviews, case studies, surveys, interviews, and data analysis.*

Keywords: High-potential employees; sustainable organisation; employee engagement; training and development; sustainable practices; blended learning

JEL Codes: M51; M53; J24

1. INTRODUCTION

Global technology advancements influence our everyday lives; we must stay abreast and educate ourselves on the latest innovations. Remember that 'evolving' means progressing to the next level without erasing the previous one, that is, using the best of both worlds by combining benefits from the past with those from the present (Tang, 2018).

Face-to-face training and eLearning are combined in a BL programme to satisfy the ever-changing demands of today's HPEs. A BL programme allows HPEs to study outside the classroom. HPEs who like conventional learning and those who learn best via semi-autonomous, computer-based instruction can benefit from this approach. On the other hand, online learning allows HPEs of manufacturing industries to study at their own speed and in various ways, including via interactive media such as movies and quizzes that are possible through a learning management system from their home page.

BL programmes have exploded in popularity in the past several years, with learning experts praising their benefits. In BL programmes, conventional classroom teaching methods are combined with newer, more cutting-edge technologies to enhance learning in real time and with more engagement. A BL programme gives HPEs additional learning and engagement opportunities, making them more likely to be considered HPEs. Face-to-face training is available, and if HPEs need additional time to work on a new idea or technique, they may always go to online resources. If HPEs have concerns or issues, they may meet with a trainer to address them face-to-face (Polat et al., 2021).

A BL programme allows HPEs to learn in various ways, depending on their learning styles. Only face-to-face learning has the potential to develop a reliance on instructors. It is empowering and encouraging for HPEs to have the ability to study both individually and in a face-to-face setting. Additionally, it enables trainers to handle training sessions more effectively, which is very useful when working with big groups of people. HPEs of manufacturing industries have more opportunities to study on their own, at their speed, and on their own time than other employees. In addition, training instructors are no longer required to cover everything during face-to-face sessions with participants. They can break the course to maximise efficiency and choose whatever they want to focus on during training sessions. Additionally, if all HPEs are performing at a different level, employing an e-learning platform allows each person to be assessed and get the focus they need to learn and improve. In general, BL programme effectiveness helps close the gap in training sessions; instructors teach various concepts; and participants learn multiple skills and knowledge.

Large-scale changes in organisational contexts need the constant learning of employees in every manufacturing industry to make them more sustainable. Individual and organisational growth is crucial to creativity and learning (Collis et al., 2005), while others say it is a source of competitive advantage. Technological advancement and developing an 'experience and understanding economy' have provided new economic growth opportunities. Because of this development, non-traditional learning options began to be used widely among HPEs in academic and professional contexts, marking the transition from the industrial to the information age. BL, also known as 'hybrid learning', has been used effectively in higher education and business in numerous cases (Bonk et al., 2002). Before the 'blended learning program', the phrase 'hybrid course' was used. Both terms are now interchangeable in higher education (Graham, 2013). 'Integrated learning' and 'multi-learning approaches' are two more Arabic words for BL programmes (Al-Shahwan, 2015).

BL programme effectiveness may be offered at four levels: institutional, activity, course, and programme. Organisations make decisions on how to adopt BL at the institutional level. On the other hand, activity-level blends include instructors and stakeholders, and BL happens as part of the training process. The trainer in the manufacturing industry should prepare ahead for course-level mixes. Combined programmes assume individuals with high potential participate in Internet and face-to-face interpersonal training programmes (Graham, 2013). People who employ a variety of learning and educational methodologies learn in the manufacturing industries. Although BL is widely accepted, several difficulties must be addressed when offering this training in the manufacturing industry (Kim et al., 2008).

For online learning, we have yet to learn how success predictors connect to outcomes like student satisfaction and learners' ability to transfer material, even though BL programmes use a wide range of technology and delivery methods (Prifit, 2022). This is a method of teaching that puts the focus on HPEs and makes use of educational technology to get the material over. The instructor only serves to aid the learning process. People work quickly and can access resources anytime and from any location. In manufacturing industries, HPEs learning may benefit from a wide range of BL applications and models, including synchronous chat and teleconference (Bonk et al., 2002). As a result of the many BL techniques and technologies available, BL practitioners may find it challenging to determine which BL approaches and technologies are optimal and how to evaluate BL software or tools. Some gaps in HRD experts' understanding of the most successful BL ways to educate manufacturing's high-potential personnel need to be filled (Kim et al., 2008).

As a result of this research, BL practitioners will be better prepared to deal with rapid changes in their professions and their organisations will be more successful. As per recent survey data, BL techniques in manufacturing industries boosted employee satisfaction, quality of work, and production levels (Kim et al., 2008). According to most businesses and employees, BL programme efficacy is more efficient and effective, as well as low-cost, adaptive, and flexible for manufacturing industry training.

Businesses and employees alike recommend the BL programme for the following reasons: greater accessibility for a broader spectrum of HPEs while reducing costs and enhancing effectiveness compared to more traditional teaching methods. Mixed learning programmes are more effective than more traditional online training, according to academics from the American Culture for Learning and Development, Stanford University, the University of Tennessee, and Penn State, among others. Training strategies that are more accessible to a broader range of HPEs while both cutting expenses and increasing effectiveness in the opinion of experts from the American Culture for Training and Development, Stanford University, the University of Tennessee, and Penn State BL programmes are more effective than typical online training programmes.

Because the BL programme is the most effective and commonly utilised teaching method in schools, businesses, and organisations, researchers advocate that it be an essential element of manufacturing industries training settings. In training, for example, smartphones may make learning more convenient and adaptable for busy professionals since they can access learning materials wherever they are (Dzakiria et al., 2012). Since 'on-the-job training' has largely been replaced by 'online training', the quality of the online environment continues to be a significant concern when considering BL in the context of the organisational manufacturing industry. As a result, the key advantages of e-learning, such as the ability for business owners to get 'just-in-time' training, are realised (Bielawski & Metcalf, 2003).

The term 'learning organisation' in a BL programme has been coined since learning is the only competitive advantage that can be sustained over time. The learning organisation is seen as a reaction to a corporate environment that is becoming more unpredictable and dynamic. Unlike traditional organisations, learning organisations have implemented systems, structures, and processes to improve their capabilities and continuously accomplish long-term goals (Mubayrik, 2018). The goal of a learning organisation is not to provide 'more training'. While training may assist in developing skills, the development of cognitive levels of knowledge and skill is the goal of a learning organisation. Table 4.1 presents the four-level model as follows:

Table 4.1. Four-level Model of Training Criteria to Evaluate Training Programmes.

Level 1	Learning information, knowledge, methods, and procedures is a lifelong endeavour. This rule applies to well-known situations in which only minimal modifications have occurred
Level 2	Learning new work abilities that can be applied to different scenarios is a priority. This rule applies to new scenarios in which previous answers must be modified. Bringing in outside knowledge may be a beneficial tool in this situation
Level 3	Learning to be flexible. This applies to more dynamic circumstances in which new solutions must be developed. It is through experimentation and taking lessons from both success and failure that learning takes place in this environment
Level 4	It is developing the ability to learn. Instead of just adapting to the future, it is necessary to innovate and be creative to shape the future. This is the stage at which assumptions are called into question and expertise is reframed

Source: Alsalamah and Callinan (2021).

2. THE RATIONALE OF THE STUDY

Considering the unpredictable times, turbulent corporate environment, pandemics, and other factors, a shift in BL programme approaches is urgently required today for businesses to be sustainable. Management expects the human resources and training departments to develop innovative, time-saving, travel-saving, and cost-effective learning and development approaches. The learning-on-the-move solutions learning paradigm is in high demand since it is quick and efficient. Creative learning technologies significantly influence the organisation's long-term sustainability when engaging, developing, and retaining HPEs in manufacturing industries (Sivapalan, 2017).

Initiatives and tactics that lessen technology's environmental impact make up green IT. This results from lower consumption of consumables and energy, including hardware, electricity, gasoline, and paper, among other things. Due to these decreases, Green IT initiatives also result in financial savings, environmental advantages, energy use, procurement, administration, and support, which are all important. Some efforts may satisfy the needs and desires of stakeholders and regulatory bodies in addition to cost savings and environmental advantages. For instance, server virtualisation enables businesses to cut back on operational costs like energy, support, and the board, as well as future server purchases' capital costs. The amount of equipment that needs to be reused in the future is continuously reduced, and the company frequently accepts incentives or rebates from local utilities to preserve energy (Singla & Singh, 2020). The acceptance and deployment of these technologies must be accomplished smoothly and effortlessly by policymakers, who must also make constructive contributions (Shalender et al., 2023).

3. BL PROGRAMME EFFECTIVENESS IN SUSTAINABLE ORGANISATIONS

The model provides a solution to all the needs and is gaining popularity because of its simplicity. During the height of BL programme effectiveness's prominence, a great deal of research was conducted to determine its effectiveness. Learning efficacy is examined in the following reviews: (Akyüz & Samsa, 2009; Hughes, 2007; Melton et al., 2009); examine attainment, contentedness, comportment, critical reasoning, learner support, involvement, interplay, impact, as well as retention. Hughes (2007) conducted a study to examine the efficacy of BL programmes effectiveness is based on support and retention and the results were published. Organisations have invested in HIPOs to develop their skill sets and better prepare HPEs for future manufacturing industries. Organisations focus highly on technological engagement in learning and development to save money, travel time, and other resources. The participation of HIPOS in the blending programme is very significant for the organisation's ability to strengthen its technical skills, effectiveness for future growth, and other aspects of establishing and preparing a leadership pipeline, among other things.

This study explores theoretical and conceptual frameworks and analyses primary research data from earlier studies to identify significant market changes in BL programmes and the development possibilities in industrial industry-learning contexts for the sustainability of business organisations. The studies from various perspectives were analysed for this research study to enable the development of a body of evidence on the topic under consideration. As a result, this chapter aims to explore the effectiveness of the BL programme as a measure for sustainable solutions in manufacturing industry contexts based on the outcomes of previous studies in this area.

Sustainable business and optimisation of learning solutions:

- A similar structure and vocabulary throughout the talent lifecycle – through selection to onboard, succession planning, and leadership development – may help organisations become more productive.
- Research and thoroughly grasp the 'organisation's requirements to adequately describe the employee's ongoing development aim.
- Contextualise your strategy to ensure it is appropriate for the existing work environment, culture, and climate.
- Identify the abilities and quantifiable behaviours crucial to achieving on-the-job success and putting them into action.
- Learners' learning styles should be assessed using good, scientifically established instruments to detect untapped potential and knowledge gaps.
- Incorporate real-world situations, applicable applications, and a call to action into your presentation.
- Create a learning environment that blends the advantages of technology-based approaches with interactive, assisted sessions and tailored reinforcement to provide a comprehensive learning experience.

The benefits of the BL programme are practical in making business sustainable: Incorporating the right balance of learning activities into a lesson plan has apparent advantages; the specifics of that mix will rely on what is being learned, but it may include a combination of observation, analysis, practice, and accessing learning content through reading, listening, or watching. Including technologies and online learning in the activities may also be beneficial. The following are seven advantages of implementing a BL programme to make an organisation sustainable.

Multi-mode and media learning: While process diagrams on paper or in PowerPoint might be confusing, an animated, narrated process is more straightforward to understand and follow since it can be rewound as necessary. Richard Mayer & Ruth Clark 3 and other scientists have researched to support this claim.

The ability to videotape internal experts expressing their well-considered views on a subject is now readily available to learners in ways that would not be conceivable without video and the technology to transmit it properly. Even if you cannot bring in your organisation's finest authority on a given issue to make an introductory speech at the beginning of every classroom training programme, you may film that person and use that video at the beginning of a blend instead.

Practice in a safe environment: Researchers Broad and Newsom have shown that giving practice opportunities, case studies, and simulations are critical in helping employees learn in manufacturing. Workshops in the BL programme environment may better concentrate on practice by shifting active learning to eLearning courses. Using case studies and practice situations online can also enhance the learning experience. In a simulation focussing on soft skills or decision-making, users may practise skills in a manner that's not practicable or economical in a classroom setting. Sara de Freitas did intriguing research in which she found that digital simulations may be much more successful than conventional learning methods in certain situations.

More effective use of time: Ambitious and senior managers increasingly desire to learn quickly and frequently use technology-supported learning outside regular working hours. As a result, educational materials must be considered while being developed. In many minds, not having enough time is a hindrance to learning, a 'process, where participants may practice and enhance their abilities over time'. According to client internal research, learners needed to be more specific about the effectiveness of one-off classroom interventions.

Scaffolding and learner journeys: To help learners participate with new concepts, BL can present information and practice opportunities sequentially. This helps learners understand new concepts, understand their relevance, and identify skills gaps. Then, they can concentrate on learning new ideas and mastering new skills, and finally, they can embed these into working practices in the manufacturing industries.

Increased reach and take-up: Making it more straightforward for individuals to incorporate learning into their work should result in greater reach and take-up. Also significant from a strictly practical standpoint, based on virtual classroom technology allows individuals to meet at the same time for a session without necessarily having to be in the exact location.

Furthermore, digital online forums facilitate conversation between persons who live in various time zones and would otherwise find it challenging to maintain a regular online debate or discourse.

Improved transfer of learning: For many years, the inability of face-to-face workshop learning to transfer to work has been acknowledged as a problem.

Broad and Neustrom's book *Transfer of Training*, published around 25 years ago, summarised several research findings on the efficacy of training transfer and made essential suggestions that are still relevant today. Recently, PhD research on transitioning from school to a face-to-face executive education programme organised by a top business school showed similar problems with participants' inability to bring classroom insights back to their working practice.

4. ROLE OF LEARNING THEORIES IN BL FOR SUSTAINABLE ORGANISATIONS

According to Carman (2005), there are a variety of beliefs about BL that might be used in various professional settings. While in training and educational settings, he focusses on the link between the learning tasks nature and their qualities in actual application.

Behaviourism: The focus of behaviourism, as the name implies, is on how people behave in different settings. Due to a significant positivist view of cause and effect, it came into being and acquired form. In a nutshell, an action brings forth a response. Behavioural psychology looks at how HPEs behave when they are studying. Behaviourism means tracking how kids respond to various stimuli and assessing, analysing, and quantifying those responses to better control individual responses. Rather than the intellect or cognitive functions, behaviourism focusses on what could be observed in a particular situation. You cannot learn about something that you cannot see.

Cognitivism: Conductors anticipated stimulus and response, and a response or reaction to the 'stiff' weights was considered (Harasim, 2012). Researchers who believed that our brains are essential for learning focussed on the discrepancy between the frequency of environmental cues and HPEs responses. In their research, they found and emphasised the importance of mental processes like motivation and creativity in helping HPEs learn online. A key feature of cognitive science is that it draws from various disciplines to better understand the mind's workings and stages of cognitive development, which are critical to learning and information processing. Therefore, the behaviourist approach is one of the most widely accepted learning theories. Cognitivism has exciting and creative possibilities as powerful online software transforms into highly configurable and individualised learning systems that attempt to merge artificial insight and cognitive computing into modules.

Bloom's taxonomy:

- *Creating*: Consolidate and rearrange the components into a new format, design, or structure once they have been integrated into a functional whole.
- *Evaluating*: Using checks and critiques, predefined criteria and standards are employed to make judgments.
- *Analysing*: Using checks and critiques, predefined criteria and standards are employed to make judgments.

- *Applying*: Presently implementing or performing a method to get it started or used.
- *Understanding*: To make sense of spoken, textual, graphical communications, people employ various techniques, including explanation, representation, breaking down, enlightening, inferring, and comparing.
- *Remembering*: Retrieving relevant information and knowledge from good memory by extrapolating.

Social constructivism: Educational theorists like Lev Vygotsky, John Dewey, and Jean Piaget have relied extensively on behaviourism and cognitivism. The teacher and the student played an essential role in teaching and learning. According to Vygotsky, acquisition is a problem-solving process and the social construction of problem-solving solutions is the basis for learning's efficiency. A 'near-growth zone' is a situation where the instructor, the trainee, and the issue to be solved are all near one other. By providing an educational setting where learners may gather, evaluate, and develop the knowledge required to solve an issue, trainers help HPEs learn more effectively (Ruey, 2010). However, John Dewey believed that learning occurs due to a series of new practical interactions in which HPEs learn from one another while also attempting, cooperating, and analysing. Many social constructionist educational ideas may still be identified today despite Dewey's technique being developed in the early 20th century. Table 4.2 presents the elements of the BL process stemming from the learning theories as follows:

Table 4.2. Elements of the BL Process Stem from the Learning Theories as Follows.

Live Events	A 'virtual classroom' is a synchronous, instructor-led learning session in which all HPEs engage simultaneously
Online content	Interactive web or CD-ROM training is a learning opportunity that HPEs complete independently, at their own pace, and on their schedule
Collaboration	E-mail, threaded chats, and online chat are ways students may engage with one another
Assessment	How well students understand a subject. Pre- and post-assessments can be performed before or after live or self-paced activities to establish prior knowledge and measure learning and information transfer
Reference material	On-the-job reference items that help HPEs retain and apply what they have learned, such as PDA downloads and PDF documents

Source: Hassan et al. (2018).

5. OBJECTIVES AND RESEARCH QUESTIONS

BL programme effectiveness is beneficial in terms of HPE happiness, knowledge creation, performance, and intrinsic motivation. Thus, it impacts building awareness among the HPEs and the BL programme's effectiveness, acting as a core for sustainability. This chapter aims to understand how these factors connect to HPEs characteristics and BL programme effectiveness design aspects to make organisations sustainable.

The following questions guide the study:

- What is the need for a BL programme?
- What are the benefits of a BL programme and its effectiveness?
- How is a BL programme and its valuable effectiveness for HPEs of manufacturing industries to make them sustainable?
- How do manufacturing high-potential personnel see BL practice?
- This document aims to do the following things in particular.
- Give a complete picture of how high-potential factory employees see the practice of the BL programme's effectiveness.
- Outline the advantages of the (BL) programme and its effectiveness.
- Acquire a grasp of the BL programme that may be used soon as a tool for training HPEs.
- Analyse previously published studies examining the effectiveness of the BL programme in the manufacturing industry learning environment.

Another goal of this research is to determine how different learning settings impact HIPOs' learning ability by looking at demographics, instructional design, and learner motivation. With this, to look at the ability of HPEs and also to enhance their abilities, the four criteria were looked upon:

- Characteristics of trainer.
- Practice events.
- Aid in education.
- Weight of research.

Prior studies have indicated that the unique character of these features influences HPEs learning and application of knowledge, which is why they were included in this study as well (Ford, 1992; Wlodkowski, 1985). Our research included employees' real learning, educators' assessed learning, and HPEs educational application as dependent variables.

6. SIGNIFICANCE OF THE STUDY

This study is intended for professionals working in online learning in general and business learning. Therefore, it does a more in-depth investigation of the effectiveness of BL programmes in manufacturing industries. While a few research papers have tried to determine the structure of BL programme effectiveness, few have aimed to characterise the current and the future of BL programmes in the manufacturing industries. Finally, the study outcomes will present an overview of the BL programme's effectiveness in the manufacturing industries, which will serve as important information for future research in both HPEs education and manufacturing industries' training fields. Furthermore, the results may serve as a guide for policymakers in the future. Analysis of original research data from past studies and a review of theories and ideas are used to evaluate major current trends in

BL programmes and upcoming innovations in manufacturing industry-learning settings. The studies analysed for this research study enable the development of a specific viewpoint and body of evidence on the topic under consideration (Puška et al., 2024; Yerpude et al., 2022).

7. CHARACTERISTICS OF THE STUDIES

Ten surveys, five subjective studies, and two case studies were among the 18 evaluated papers selected for inclusion. These papers were selected to overview BL in corporate contexts in HPE education and training. The articles reviewed for this study are the primary method of gathering descriptive data. Between 2005 and 2014, these reviews were published in peer-reviewed journals. All the research is scientific publications that have been peer-reviewed. Additional articles analysed include those from countries like China, Korea, and Taiwan as well as the United States (Kim et al., 2008), Australia (Allan, 2007), and Taiwan (Teng et al., 2009). Intervening for a period ranging from four weeks to seven months was considered successful. In the studies under consideration, researchers looked at how BL is already functioning and how it could develop in the learning environments of manufacturing industries. With the specific criteria in place, it was possible to identify papers mainly concerned with BL in manufacturing industries' learning environments. The researchers' own created interviews and questionnaires, together with various approaches, provide the most essential contribution to the research. The number of reviews was 77 (Prifit, 2022). They performed studies in the United States and Canada, respectively (Collis et al., 2005). They conducted two case studies in the Netherlands and the United States.

8. RESEARCH METHODOLOGY

The 'Preferred Reporting Items for Systematic Reviews and Meta-Analyses' (PRISMA) statements have been used as the basis for this SR's methodology. PRISMA is an evidence-based compilation of systematic reviews and meta-analyses. Systematic reviews with aims other than assessing therapies can also be documented using PRISMA, albeit more commonly used for this purpose. Examples: sustainability, learning, BL, or HPEs. In this study, four strategies were employed to find relevant literature and gather data on the problem under investigation:

Conventional subject searching: For this investigation, we did a thorough search of English-language peer-reviewed publications. We also checked the references of relevant primary and review literature. Many databases and academic publications were used to compile the data, such as EBSCOhost, LexisNexis, and Google Scholar, as well as ProQuest and Emerald, Business Source Complete, PsycINFO, and ERIC.

Mixed learning, HPEs education, manufacturing industries learnings, sustainable business, sustainable development goals (SDGs), and emerging developments in BL programme effectiveness were some of the keywords utilised in the study. The literature covered the years 1990 through June of this year. Peer-reviewed publications were sought, but abstracts were examined for relevant references to the issue. An examination of the bibliography of necessary research turned up additional sources of information.

Reference list checking: Identification of relevant and worthwhile research was accomplished via reference list checking.

Contact with experts: Collaboration with specialists was a key research strategy employed in this study to search for relevant material, and it was one of the most important. BL specialists with a solid knowledge base and competence in HPE learning were enlisted to help identify the most important research articles. Among other things, these experts assisted in the identification and evaluation of important and exciting research.

Citation searching: Various databases, particularly Google Scholar and Get Cited, were used to conduct the reference search.

The primary studies selection procedure for 77 studies is divided into four stages: identification, multiple screening, admissibility, and inclusion (Mohr et al., 2009). The first stage involves identifying all potentially relevant studies, totalling 549 articles. One hundred forty-four duplicate studies and research reduced this number. This included studies that were duplicated in different databases as well as research that was duplicated in peer-reviewed articles and conference proceedings. The second stage does a preliminary evaluation by screening titles, keywords, and abstracts. Three hundred records have been eliminated so far because they need to meet the inclusion criteria, twenty-seven publications were non-English, notably in terms of study scope and optimisation subject. Both records marked as included and those marked as unclear were forwarded for further review.

9. BL PROGRAMME EFFECTIVENESS AND HPES

The benefits of BL are well acknowledged, yet previous research suggests its effectiveness is still debateable (Bruff et al., 2013). When compared to face-to-face or purely online training, several studies indicated that BL was more successful than either. Castle and McGuire (2010) revealed that students preferred traditional classroom instruction over online or mixed learning. It was found that students who got an education in an online mixed-learning environment performed 'modestly' better than those who received instruction in a regular classroom setting, according to a meta-analysis of 45 studies. A study by Al-Qahtani and Higgins (2013) indicated that BL outperformed face-to-face and online learning in terms of academic attainment. Students in the BL group scored much higher on exams. They showed higher satisfaction levels with their learning experiences than students in the traditional face-to-face group (Smith & Suzuki, 2015). Wei et al. (2017) conducted a three-month quasi-experiment comparing traditional in-class education versus BL and found that the latter group outperformed the former. Students in BL groups outperformed traditional face-to-face training academically, according to Zhang and Zhu (2018). According to Zou et al. (2020), a BL technique that incorporates Internet resources has been demonstrated to be more successful in promoting student cooperation and engagement in order to promote active learning.

In contrast to the previous research, Griffiths et al. (2014) found that test scores and pass rates for BL and face-to-face learning were not statistically different and students in the BL group reported lower overall satisfaction. Similarly (Bowen et al. (2014) discovered no significant differences in learning outcomes between traditional face-to-face and BL despite the BL group receiving a lower overall rating (Güzer & Caner, 2014). A literature review determined no significant difference in student achievement between BL and traditional face-to-face learning. By analysing numerous BL experiments, Israel (2015) concluded that students' proficiency in BL was slightly higher than in face-to-face learning. However, students reported lower satisfaction levels due to fewer face-to-face interactions with instructors. Likewise, Owston et al. (2019) found that in-class tutorials and online lectures had higher overall satisfaction when compared to mixed learning. The efficacy of BL varied depending on the type of information being taught and the social presence of instructors.

Furthermore, it is essential to understand what 'HPE' means. The words 'high-potential' refer to an employee who has outstanding or uncommon talents and abilities that enable him to grow and contribute to the company's achievement of corporate goals and future success. Thus, a high-potential worker can enhance his talents and gain more experience during his career (Lombardo & Eichinger, 2000). This is a close approximation of what skill is. Employee talent is defined as a person who has a unique blend of talents, skills, expertise, personal attributes, and future potential. As a result, the performance and potential of a person should be the criteria for talent. However, the essential elements determining a company's significant potential might vary. As a result, defining a uniform definition of a HPE is challenging because it depends on various circumstances (sector of business, organisational hierarchy, firm position, and so forth).

People's perceptions of what it means to be a person with great potential vary widely. Managers may be tempted to choose high potentials based on factors they are already familiar with, such as past performance and results because there is no clear concept of high potential. A study of 1,000 worldwide organisations done in 2007 found that 78% of these corporations use past performance to identify high-potential individuals.

Employees with high potential and their managers are aware of this and convey a strong message: 'We believe that you have skills that will allow you to accede to the posts in upper levels in the company in the future'. As a result, the 'high-potential label' is excellent evidence of the company's trust in the employee and raises the individual's expectations. Because of the significance and variety of his expectations, high-potential workers may sometimes feel as though they are not getting what they were promised (Martin & Schmidt, 2010).

Data extraction: To begin, we used the terms 'blended learning programme effectiveness in sustainable organisations', 'learner satisfaction with the blended learning program', and 'manufacturing industries learning strategies' to conduct a literature search. We gathered information on participants based on their characteristics, the sample size, and how they were recruited. We also looked at the year the study was published and the country of origin.

There were 495 abstracts retrieved in the literature search and the citations revealed 54 research (549 papers). The abstract review rejected 301 abstracts, 86 publications being non-English, and 144 papers that did not meet the inclusion requirements for the study's focus. The inclusion criteria selected 77 appropriate peer-reviewed publications, which were then assessed for their acceptability.

Quality assessments: Studies were qualitatively appraised using standardised checklists with acceptable criteria since much research was expected to be included (Ritchie et al., 2003). Essential checklists for qualitative investigations were employed in this study. Gough (2007) used evidence weights for the assessment of the quality of the review.

The document's design is done in a descriptive manner, which implies that all the paper's critical information is presented clearly and concisely. Instruments utilised in the research comprise case study techniques, past research papers, and articles. The assessment of training and development for HPEs, research, and evaluation of employees' perceptions about BL programme success in manufacturing companies. The BL programme for high-potential workers in manufacturing industries was studied utilising all the research tools utilised by researchers in the analysed studies to identify the impact of the BL programme and its effectiveness on HPEs.

10. DISCUSSIONS, RESULTS, AND CONCLUSION

A combination of online and face-to-face learning is utilised in BL to deliver various scheduled and organised learning courses, organised and structured experiential learning, and natural accomplishment disparities among learners and trainers. Also, they were influenced by several criteria to choose BL programme effectiveness over alternative learning choices, including pedagogic richness, social contact, cost efficiency, availability of information, individual agency, and ease of revision (Graham, 2013). The existing body of research supports implementing BL methods in educational institutions and businesses. All the research acknowledged the apparent benefits of a BL programme and its effectiveness as a vehicle for organisational training; nevertheless, most of the studies also identified impediments and problems to effectively adopting a BL programme in working environments (Iyer-Raniga, 2022).

Lack of understanding of the concept of 'blended learning program efficacy' significantly impacts participants' opinions of BL's effectiveness and success (Teng et al., 2009). Yes, even if their company uses this method. According to Rossett et al. (2003), the development of BL systems is set by six primary challenges: 'Stability of content, duration of programme implementation and development, the importance of human connection in the learning process, budget, educational resources, and the individual or group character of active learning are all factors to consider'. Although many BL ideas and concepts are theoretically accessible, HRD practitioners have not adequately investigated and proven their application by HRD professionals (Kim et al., 2008).

It is projected that the BL programme will increase significantly in manufacturing industries-learning contexts despite the problems and limitations observed by researchers and study participants (Kim et al., 2008; Teng et al., 2009). According to research, companies are now adopting BL programmes to teach their staff and this trend is predicted to grow drastically in the future. The BL method is expected to become a popular and prominent delivery mode in the future because it enhances the quality of teaching and learning experience, contributes to improved knowledge transfer, encourages cooperation and communication, reduces costs, and provides new strategic directions for the organisation. Furthermore, the BL programme will be made available via technologies enabling learners to participate in performance assistance or just-in-time training sessions.

Employee professional learning strategies (extra skills, information, learning, and relearning) will be the focus of most learning and training companies in the 21st century (Berge, 2007; Kazerounian & Foley, 2007). A growing number of professions, as well as the public and private sectors, are turning to BL to improve the quality of instruction. Businesses in the public and private sectors and higher education institutions are increasingly embracing BL programmes, their effectiveness, technologies, and methodology in their training programmes, particularly in multi-site and global administrations (Prifiti, 2022). Students, professors, instructors, lecturer/lecturer/administrators, training developers, and high-potential workers, who worked in teaching positions were surveyed (Bonk, 2008), expect significant changes in learning and teaching approaches because of their results, with a particular emphasis on the widespread usage of BL as a primary learning strategy in manufacturing industries-learning contexts. Furthermore, it is projected that BL will increase significantly and become even more important than online learning.

HPEs, training professionals, and employees have shown a favourable attitude towards integrating the BL programme and its effective methods in manufacturing industries-learning environments; according to Bonk et al. (2002), A and B, the results are consistent. According to the poll, more than half of those who participated said their company plans to increase its business intelligence (BL) use in the next decade. They found that businesses commonly use e-learning because of the opportunity for BL to thrive in the future. Organisations routinely employ BL despite the problems they face owing to a need for more awareness about this learning technique (Kim et al., 2008). There is no denying that HR professionals need education and direction on what BL means and how to put it into practice in their manufacturing industries. Since most respondents in the 18 articles under consideration recognised the importance of authentic learning methodologies, HPEs and managers expect technology to give employees just-in-time and authentic learning.

Regarding HPEs success and job performance, a new study shows that the BL programme's effectiveness significantly benefits. However, Chang and Chen (2015) found that BL had the most significant impact on HPEs self-assessment scores rather than their achievement test results.

According to the BL programme, a new method for working environments is a success, which practically any organisation's management would agree on

(Collis et al., 2005). By enhancing collaboration and altering work habits, this learning may be used to discover and address present company challenges, making corporate processes more effective. The BL programme is expected to help manufacturing industries grow by serving as an expertise-building block that enables theory to be used immediately in manufacturing.

Many firms value the effectiveness of BL programmes because employees are encouraged to learn on the job by participating in work-based activities that include HPEs as learning partners and using business resources they have developed. For example, according to Dzakiria et al. (2012), the rise in popularity of the BL programme may be traced back to technological innovation, which has created new opportunities for training and learning and the integration of various technologies with pedagogical (HPEs education) or pedagogical (academic education).

The BL programme was superior to other training and learning approaches in well-regarded research (Graham, 2013). The BL programme's effectiveness is a pedagogical option that may motivate global projects to promote lifetime learning. When considering the future of the BL programme, it is critical to continue identifying successful BL models that may be used in the industrial industries at the programme, course, activity, and institutional levels.

To help HPEs improve their skills, find work, or continue their studies as part of their lifelong learning, the BL programme may assist them in completing programmes or training while they are still working. Participants said they anticipate financial resources to be allocated to adopting the BL programme in their manufacturing industries during the next several years. However, they acknowledge that several challenges must be solved if BL can be provided successfully in manufacturing industries. Even though HPEs are optimistic about the rising use of BL in manufacturing industries, the most severe problem is that they need to comprehend what it means (Kim & Bonk, 2006). Due to the lack of management commitment and support, there are significant roadblocks in the way of BL's practical introduction and implementation.

According to Bonk et al. (2002), the BL programme has been used in specific organisations, but it is expected to become more widespread soon. Manufacturing industries currently use BL programmes as a common form of delivering content. The present chapter shows how the BL programme, its effectiveness, and training methods are applied to the HPEs of the manufacturing industry. Most often these days, virtual learning environments are used to enhance or replace in-person learning experiences, such as fostering learning communities and facilitating the usage of guest experts, as well as giving access to follow-up tools and additional material (Hylén et al., 2012).

11. PRACTICAL IMPLICATIONS

Because of this research, recommendations for HRD experts should be developed on adopting the BL programme in their manufacturing industries. This research should assist practitioners in better understanding how to create, provide, and analyse techniques used in manufacturing industries' learning contexts based on the primary data from the most relevant studies. There are several concerns and obstacles that HRD professionals experience when applying the BL programme in manufacturing industries in the context of HPEs ability to learn and build sustainable networks (Tulowitzki, 2021).

12. RECOMMENDATIONS FOR FUTURE RESEARCH

There are several difficulties in the BL programme's effectiveness in manufacturing industries related to learning criteria for HPEs and building sustainable organisations. These difficulties should be investigated further to see whether any improvements have occurred and what procedures or approaches are being established to address current problems effectively since the research revealed numerous obstacles in the BL programme. The study of career development for HRD, HRT, and training professionals may also concentrate on developing a paradigm for the effective and efficient use of new technologies in the BL programme. Consequently, future research should focus on developing 'best practice' scenarios and sustainable organisational theories to equip practitioners with the necessary methodological competence and knowledge to obtain management support for the BL programme (Bordoloi et al., 2021). The effectiveness of the BL programme has been hampered by management's lack of enthusiasm for and dedication to the strategy.

13. LIMITATIONS OF THE STUDY

As a result, a significant gap remains in our knowledge of how the BL programme is used in HPEs learning processes now and in the future. The study's primary goal was to collect as many evaluations, qualitative investigations, and case studies as possible. The problem is that these kinds of studies are typically restricted or unavailable. It is also conceivable that participants' replies reflect distorted beliefs and perspectives.

The research also has limitations due to the publications' expiration dates. Published studies in the previous 5–10 years would have been appropriate because the present research focusses on future developments in the BL programme. As many evaluations, qualitative studies, and case studies as possible were collected as part of the study's primary goal. In most cases, research of this nature is limited or unavailable.

Another possibility is that the responses of those who took part reflect skewed viewpoints and assumptions:

- New, upgraded, or developed training programmes or systems are expensive.
- Lack of organisational BL training cultures in the manufacturing industries or employee opposition to the latest trends in training or management (resistance to change).
- Problems with technology and a lack of technical support (Guiney, 2015).

This research suggests that future studies should focus on overcoming challenges, barriers, and technologies rather than just effectiveness since all studies have shown that it works regardless of company size and sample differences. Moreover, independent studies on the effect and influence of BL programmes and their effectiveness on businesses from other perspectives, such as knowledge and skills, may be required.

REFERENCES

Akyüz, H. İ., & Samsa, S. (2009). The effects of blended learning environment on the critical thinking skills of students. *Procedia – Social and Behavioural Sciences*, *1*(1), 1744–1748. https://doi.org/10.1016/j.sbspro.2009.01.308

Allan, B. (2007). *Blended learning: Tools for teaching and training*. Facet Publishing.

Al-Qahtani, A. A., & Higgins, S. E. (2013). Effects of traditional, blended and e-Learning on students' achievement in higher education. *Journal of Computer Assisted Learning*, *29*(3), 220–234. https://doi.org/10.1111/j.1365-2729.2012.00490

Alsalamah, A., & Callinan, C. (2021). Adaptation of Kirkpatrick's 4-level model of training criteria to evaluate training programmes for head teachers. *Education Sciences*, *11*, 116.

Berge, Z. L. (2007). Barriers and the organization's capabilities for distance education. *Distance Learning*, *4*(4), 1–15.

Bielawski, L., & Metcalf, D. S. (2003). *Blended elearning: Integrating knowledge, performance, support, and online learning*. HRD Press Inc.

Bonk, C. J., Olson, T. M., Wisher, R. A., & Orvis, K. L. (2002). Learning from focus groups: An examination of blended learning. *Journal of Distance Education*, *17*(3), 97–118.

Bordoloi, R., Das, P., & Das, K. (2021). Perception towards online/blended learning at the time of Covid-19 pandemic: An academic analytics in the Indian context. *Asian Association of Open Universities Journal*, *16*(1), 41–60.

Bowen, W., Chingos, M., Lack, K., & Nygren, T. (2014). Interactive learning online at public universities: Evidence from a six-campus randomized trial. *Journal of Policy Analysis and Management*, *33*(1), 94–111.

Bruff, D. O., Fisher, D. H., McEwen, K. E., & Smith, B. E. (2013). Wrapping a MOOC: Student perceptions of an experiment in blended learning. *Journal of Online Learning and Teaching*, *9*(2), 187–199.

Carman, J. M. (2005). Blended learning design: Five key ingredients. *Agilent Learning*, *1*(11), 1–10.

Castle, S. R., & McGuire, C. J. (2010). An analysis of student self-assessment of online, blended, and face-to-face learning environments: Implications for sustainable education delivery. *International Education Studies*, *3*(3), 36–40.

Chang, N. C., & Chen, H. H. (2015). A motivational analysis of the ARCS model for information literacy courses in a blended learning environment. *Libri*, *65*(2), 129–142.

Collis, B., Bianco, M., Margaryan, A., & Waring, B. (2005). Putting blended learning to work: A case study from a multinational oil company. *Education, Communication & Information*, *5*(3), 233–250.

Dzakiria, H., Don, M. S., & Rahman, H. D. A. (2012). Blended learning (B.L.) as a pedagogical alternative to teaching business communication course: A case study of UUM executive diploma program. *Turkish Online Journal of Distance Education*, *13*(3), 297–315.

Ford, M. (1992). *Motivating humans: Goals, emotions, and personal agency beliefs*. Sage Publications, Inc.

Gough, D. (2007). Weight of evidence: A framework for the appraisal of the quality and relevance of evidence. *Research Papers in Education*, *22*(2), 213–228.

Graham, C. R. (2013). Emerging practice and research in blended learning. In M. G. Moore (Ed.), *Handbook of distance education* (pp. 351–368). Routledge.

Griffiths, R., Mulhern, C., Spies, R., & Chingos, M. (2015, March). Adopting MOOCs on campus: A collaborative effort to test MOOCs on campuses of the university system of Maryland. *Online Learning*, *19*(2).

Guiney. (2015). The present and future state of blended learning at workplace-learning settings in adult education: A systematic review. *Journal of Social Studies Education Research*, *9*(4), 247–273.
Harasim. (2012). An investigation into students' views on blended learning at the English Language Institute at King Abdulaziz University. *Arab World English Journal*, *1*(Special issue 1), 164–178.
Hassan, N. F. B., Puteh, S. B., & Sanusi, A. B. M. (2018). Elements of technology enabled/enhanced active learning (TEAL) to enhance the quality and employability of bachelor's students. *MATEC Web of Conferences*, *150*, Article 05005.
Hughes, G. (2007). Using blended learning to increase learner support and improve retention. *Teaching in Higher Education*, *12*(3), 349–363.
Hylén, J., D'Antoni, S., Mulder, F., & Van Damme, D. (2012). Open educational resources: Analysis of responses to the OECD country questionnaire [OECD Education Working Paper No. 76, OECD Publishing].
Israel, M. J. (2015). Effectiveness of integrating MOOCs in traditional classrooms for undergraduate students. *International Review of Research in Open and Distributed Learning*, *16*(5), 102–118.
Iyer-Raniga, U. (2022). Intercultural and interdisciplinary engagement for embedding sustainability. In W. Leal Filho & C. R. Portela de Vasconcelos (Eds.), *Handbook of best practices in sustainable development at university level: World sustainability series*. Springer Publishing. https://doi.org/10.1007/978-3-031-04764-0
Kazerounian, K., & Foley, S. (2007). Barriers to creativity in engineering education: A study of instructors' and students' perceptions. *Journal of Mechanical Design*, *129*(7), 761–768.
Kim, K. J., & Bonk, C. J. (2006). The future of online teaching and learning in higher education. *Educause Quarterly*, *29*(4), 22–30.
Lombardo, M. M., & Eichinger, R. W. (2000). High potentials as high learners. *Human Resource Management*, *39*(4), 321–329.
Martin, J., & Schmidt, C. (2010). How to keep your top talent. *Harvard Business Review*, *88*, 54–61.
Melton, B., Graf, H., & Chopak-Foss, J. (2009). Achievement and satisfaction in blended learning versus traditional general health course designs. *International Journal for the Scholarship of Teaching and Learning*, *3*(1), article 26.
Mohr, D. C., Spring, B., Freedland, K. E., Beckner, V., Arean, P., Hollon, S. D., Ockene, J., & Kaplan, R. (2009). The selection and design of control conditions for randomized controlled trials of psychological interventions. *Psychotherary and Psychosomatics*, *78*(5), 275–284.
Mubayrik, H. F. H. (2018). The present and future state of blended learning at workplace-learning settings in adult education: A systematic review. *Journal of Social Studies Education Research*, 9(4), 247–273.
Owston, R., York, D. N., & Malhotra, T. (2019). Blended learning in large enrolment courses: Student perceptions across four different instructional models. *Australasian Journal of Educational Technology*, *35*(5), 29–45.
Polat, E., Van Dam, S. S., & Bakker, C. A. (2021). Shifting from blended to online learning: Students' and teachers' perspectives. *Proceedings of the Design Society*, *1*, 2651–2660.
Prifit, R. (2022). Self-efficacy and student satisfaction in the context of blended learning courses. *Open Learning: The Journal of Open, Distance and e-Learning*, *37*(2), 111–125.
Puška, A., Hodžić, I., Štilić, A., & Murtič, S. (2024). Evaluating European Union countries on climate change management: A fuzzy MABAC approach to the climate change performance index. *Journal of Green Economy and Low-Carbon Development*, *3*(1), 15–25.
Ritchie, J., Spencer, L., & O'Connor, W. (2003). Carrying out qualitative analysis. *Qualitative research practice: A guide for social science students and researchers*, *2003*, 219–262.
Rossett, A., Douglis, F., & Frazee, R. V. (2003). Strategies for building blended learning. *Learning Circuits*, *4*(7), 1–8.
Ruey, S. (2010). A case study of constructivist instructional strategies for adult online learning. *British Journal of Educational Technology*, *4*(5), 706–720.
Shalender, K., Singla, B., & Sharma, S. (2023). Emerging technologies and their game-changing potential: Lessons from corporate world. In S. Grima, K. Sood, & E. Özen (Eds.). *Contemporary studies of risks in emerging technology, Part A* (Emerald Studies in Finance, Insurance, and Risk Management, pp. 61–70). Emerald Publishing Limited.

Singh, H. (2003). Building effective blended learning programs. In *Challenges and opportunities for the global implementation of E-learning frameworks* (pp. 15–23). IGI Global (*Issue of Educational Technology*, *43*(6), 51–54).

Singla, B., & Singh, A. (2020). An initiative to green information technology. *International Journal of Advanced Science and Technology*, *29*(4), 363–372.

Sivapalan, S. (2017). Sustainability, blended learning, and the undergraduate communication skills classroom: Negotiating engineering undergraduates' expectations and perceptions. *On the Horizon*, *25*(1), 7–23.

Smith, J. G., & Suzuki, S. (2015). Embedded blended learning within an Algebra classroom: A multimedia capture experiment. *Journal of Computer Assisted Learning*, *31*(2), 133–147.

Tang, K. H. D. (2018). Correlation between sustainability education and engineering students' attitudes towards sustainability. *International Journal of Sustainability in Higher Education*, *19*(3), 459–472.

Teng, Y. T., Bonk, C. J., & Kim, K. J. (2009). The trend of blended learning in Taiwan: Perceptions of HRD practitioners and implications for emerging competencies. *Human Resource Development International*, *12*(1), 69–84.

Tulowitzki, P. (2021). Cultivating a global professional learning network through a blended-learning program – Levers and barriers to success. *Journal of Professional Capital and Community*, *6*(2), 164–178.

Wlodkowski, R. J. (1985). Enhancing adult motivation to learn. *The Canadian Journal for the Study of Adult Education*, *1*(1), 69.

Yerpude, S., Sood, K., & Grima, S. (2022). Blockchain-augmented digital supply chain management: A way to sustainable business. *Journal of Risk and Financial Management*, *16*(1), 7.

Zhang, Q., & Zhu, S (2018). Visual interpretability for deep learning: A survey. *Frontiers Information Technology Electronic Engineering*, *19*, 27–39.

Zou, L.-C. , Zhang, J.-H., Miao, J.-J., Zhang, Y.-X., Hwang, G.-J., & Zhu, Y. (2020). An individualized intervention approach to improving university students' learning performance and interactive behaviours in a blended learning environment. *Interactive Learning Environment*, *28*(2), 231–245.

CHAPTER 5

A SYSTEMATIC REVIEW OF LITERATURE ON GREENWASHING*

Kritika Gupta and Navjit Singh

University School of Business, Chandigarh University, Gharuan, Punjab, India

ABSTRACT

Purpose: *The study focusses on the systematic review of the greenwashing literature to present the research gaps to researchers for future studies.*

Design/methodology/approach: *The systematic review has been used to analyse past studies on 'greenwashing'. The 325 research articles of the previous 10 years (2014–2023) were downloaded from the Scopus-indexed database using the keyword 'greenwashing'.*

The findings: *There is a need for a study on greenwashing in developing countries like India. An attempt should be made to analyse the research with a large sample size.*

Research limitations: *The scope of the data used in this study is limited by the source of retrieval, that is, the Scopus. The current source adequately serves the study's purpose, as the Scopus database is one of the most significant citation databases. This study analyses data from the years 2014 to 2023 to improve credibility and reduce biases.*

*This research did not receive any specific grant from funding agencies in the public, commercial, or not-for-profit sectors.

Sustainability Development through Green Economics
Contemporary Studies in Economic and Financial Analysis, Volume 114, 75–90

ISSN: 1569-3759/doi:10.1108/S1569-375920240000114005

Practical implications: The research findings will significantly help researchers, green marketers, and practitioners be aware of the emerging markets of greenwashing and consumers' rising greenwashing perception of green products.

Originality/value: This study is a novel attempt to explore a better understanding of greenwashing for researchers. The study is original; work has yet to be performed on this topic.

Keywords: Greenwashing; greenwashing perception; systematic review of literature; green marketing; consumers; green products

JEL Codes: M10; M31; Q56

INTRODUCTION

Greenwashing, coined from blending 'whitewash', exemplifies a well-known phenomenon within advertising and marketing. It involves the strategic deployment of green public relations and marketing tactics to convey that corporate products, objectives, and rules are inherently environmentally benign and deceitful (Sandeen, 2009; Simon, 2000). Such deliberate engagement in greenwashing communication strategies is frequently motivated by the desire of companies to dissociate themselves from their environmental transgressions or those perpetuated by their suppliers (Pizzetti et al., 2021). By employing these tactics, these entities aim to create a favourable public image of environmental responsibility while obscuring the true nature of their practices, thus misleading consumers and deflecting attention away from their ecological shortcomings.

Greenwashing is a pervasive issue that transcends geographical boundaries and industry sectors. Its prevalence is not restricted to a particular area or country but extends globally. The global green technology and sustainability market has witnessed substantial growth, with a value of $10.32 billion in 2020 and a projected value of $74.64 billion by 2030 (Maiti, 2022). Correspondingly, the ratio of consumers who have not purchased environmentally friendly products has reduced significantly in the past decade (Dagher & Itani, 2014). In light of this shifting consumer preference, many organisations focus on achieving public and clean environment goals, emphasising the 'triple bottom line' approach encompassing people, the planet, and profits (Cronin et al., 2011).

This chapter analyses the gaps in past studies related to greenwashing. The main objective of this research chapter is to show the existing research gaps from a literature review of 32 articles downloaded from the Scopus-indexed database. This chapter comprehensively reviews and analyses previous studies on greenwashing. The present systematic review was done in order to identify the published literature describing studies related to greenwashing. Then, a thorough review of the articles was done. The major characteristics of the articles and the classification and coding of the major characteristics of the study were done. Finally, the main gaps derived from the detailed study of the research papers were presented. The main conclusions and recommendations for future studies are also given.

THEORETICAL FRAMEWORK

In order to recognise the main themes, a detailed study of all the articles was done. A systematic study of all papers downloaded from the Scopus-indexed database was done. The following themes were explored from published literature:

- Green marketing.
- Consumer scepticism.
- Environmental concern.
- Environmental knowledge.
- Consumers' attitude towards green products.

Green Marketing

Since the late 1980s, the firms have made significant improvements in green marketing efforts as more firms recognise the importance of minimising the environmental impact of their products (Easterling et al., 1996). The concept of green marketing is gaining importance in today's world globally. While many companies have made genuine attempts to adopt environmentally friendly practices, there is also a concerning trend of firms exaggerating or fabricating environmental claims in the advertisements of their products (de Freitas Netto et al., 2020).

Consumer Scepticism

Greenwashing has emerged as a major problem or common issue in the marketplace as companies strive to appeal to environmentally conscious consumers. However, the consequences of greenwashing extend far beyond consumer scepticism. It undermines consumer trust and hampers progress towards achieving sustainable consumption patterns (Cherry & Sneirson, 2012). When consumers are confronted with greenwashed advertisements, they face a dilemma: whether to believe the claims made by companies or approach them sceptically.

Environmental Concern

Environmental concerns have gained significant prominence among global consumers, surpassing other pressing issues such as the economic crisis, terrorism in the counties, war conditions, and security issues (Dagher & Itani, 2014; Grimmer & Woolley, 2014; Mara et al., 2022). Individuals acknowledge day-to-day business activities' detrimental impact on the environment (Saha & Darnton, 2005). In response to this evolving consumer sentiment, governments and companies alike recognise the significance of adopting 'green marketing' strategies (Almossawi, 2014; Durif et al., 2010; García-Salirrosas & Rondon-Eusebio, 2022) to enable consumers to purchase and make environmentally conscious choices.

Environmental Knowledge

It is essential to acknowledge that consumers' responses to greenwashing are not uniform. Consumers with excellent environmental knowledge and expertise may be more discerning in evaluating green advertisements, while others may exhibit high levels of scepticism (Parguel et al., 2015). This displays the benefits of consumer education in changing their perception related to the greenwashing of green products. By increasing environmental literacy and awareness, consumers can develop a critical mindset and better differentiate between genuine environmental claims and greenwashing tactics.

Consumer's Attitude Towards Green Products

Consumers feel the companies do not display complete details about their green activities or products. They feel less confident about green companies and their green products, so the consumers are suspicious regarding the quality level of the green products available in the nearby market (Li et al., 2022). Hence, they are less confident in purchasing green products. The higher the degree of greenwashing, the more negative the attitude of consumers towards green products.

RESEARCH METHODOLOGY

The systematic review has been used in the analysis of past studies on the topic of greenwashing. It helps to analyse the main studies and characterise the research field more comprehensively to identify the gaps for future studies. The following steps are followed for the study:

(a) Research articles from the previous 10 years (2014–2023) were downloaded from the Scopus-indexed database using the keywords 'greenwashing'.
(b) As displayed in Fig. 5.1, after following the inclusion and exclusion criteria, the remaining research articles were deeply analysed.
(c) Further analysis of the research articles was done by creating a data classification sheet based on major categories involved in the study of the research articles.
(d) Then, logical coding was done based on the above classification to structure the existing study related to the topic.
(e) Finally, the interpretation of the results based on the coding sheet was made to ascertain the gaps related to the topic of study for further future studies in the area.

The procedure followed in selecting the research article for the study is displayed in Fig. 5.1. A total of 325 research articles were downloaded from the Scopus-indexed database by using the keywords greenwashing. Of them, 32 papers were related to the greenwashing perception of the consumers related to green products, green purchase intention, and green products. A total of 238 papers were rejected from the study as they were not related to the main subject of the study. Eight doubtful papers were discussed within the panels that constituted

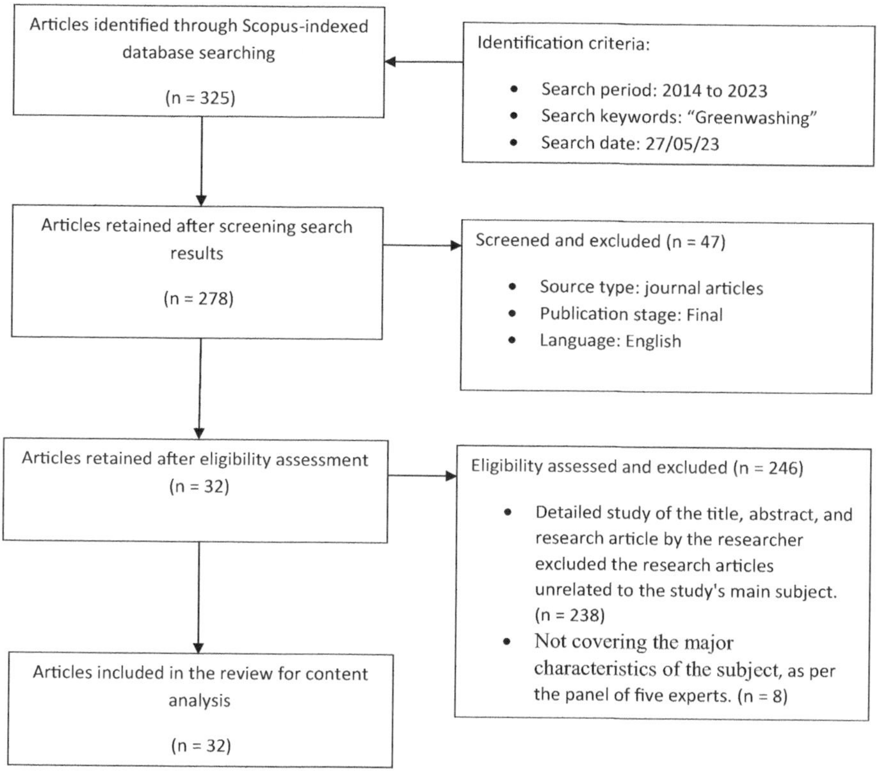

Fig. 5.1. The Procedure Followed in Selecting the Research Article for the Study. *Source*: Authors' compilation.

five subject experts. The subject experts found that the papers did not cover the major characteristics of the subject and were rejected from the study.

After a thorough review of the papers, a classification sheet was formed based on major characteristics of work reported in the literature (Table 5.1). The classification describes eight main categories for which logical coding was done to provide structure to existing knowledge. These categories numbered 1–8 and consisted of coding P, Q, R, S, T, U, and so on. As per the analysis, one article may have more than one code for a particular main category.

The first classification describes the context of the study. The analysis has been carried out in developed and developing countries. These are coded as letters P, Q, and R. Context is important in the study related to greenwashing. While designing a research process, it is important to know the areas where the study has already been carried out. It helps to identify the areas where maximum work on this topic has already been done and also ascertains the area to be explored in future studies. This systematic review can help evaluate the relationship between developed and developing or underdeveloped countries regarding greenwashing. The code 'others' displays the studies that have not been done in developing countries and not in developed countries.

Table 5.1. The Categories Used for the Classification and Coding in This Research Chapter for the Study.

Category	*Meaning*	*Codes for Alternatives*
1.	Context	P– Studies done in the developed countries Q – Studies done in the developing countries R – Non-applicable
2.	Geographic region	P – Europe Q – Asia R – North America S – South America T – Africa U – Others
3.	Time period	P – 2014–2015 Q – 2016–2017 R – 2018–2019 S – 2020–2021 T – 2022–2023 till date
4.	Main subject	P – Greenwashing perception Q – Green purchase intention R – Green products S – Others
5.	Method	P – Qualitative Q – Quantitative R – Literature review S – Case study T – Others
6.	Sample size	P – Less than 250 or 250 Q – 251 to 500 R – 501 to 750 S – More than 751 T – Non-applicable
7.	Topics	P – Green marketing Q – Consumer scepticism R – Environmental concern S – Environmental knowledge T – Consumers attitude towards green products U – Others
8.	Products type	P – Convenience goods Q – Shopping goods R – Specialty goods S – Unsought goods T – Others

Source: Authors' compilation.

The second classification represents the geographical region where the study has been carried out. The P, Q, R, S, T, U, and V codes were assigned to the geographic regions of various continents like Europe, Asia, North America, South America, Africa, and Australia, where greenwashing is noticed. The code 'non-applicable' has been applied to studies not covering the above-stated continents.

The third classification discusses the time period of the study, which is labelled by the letters P, Q, R, S, and T. The time period of study is from 2014 to 2023.

The fourth classification is framed according to the main subjects on which the research is designed, coded by the letters P, Q, R, and S. These main subjects include topics that are directly related to the study of greenwashing. It helps to analyse the key topic discussed in the various research articles.

The fifth classification relates to the method used in the past studies coded as P, Q, R, S, and T. Coding helps to verify which method was most frequently used by researchers and which methods were the predominant methods for studying greenwashing by the researchers.

The sixth classification is related to the sample size used for the research, coded with the letters P, Q, R, S, and T. Obtain a sample size that possesses the appropriate capability to produce valuable results. An under-sized study leads to a waste of resources for not producing valid results. A large sample size broadens the collected data range and forms a better picture for analysis to draw meaningful results.

The seventh classification relates the subtopics of the main subjects studied in the papers and is coded by letters P, Q, R, S, T, and U. These subtopics include those topics that help to study the main topic in depth. Coding helps to describe which subjects were focussed on by the researchers in the past studies and where future studies need to focus. This classification is supplementary to the third classification of the main subject and makes the theme of the study gain insights for better analyses.

The eighth classification analyses the product type found in the research articles, coded by letters P, Q, R, S, and T. It describes whether the product is a convenience product, a shopping product, a speciality product, unsought goods, or others (Puška et al., 2024; Yerpude et al., 2022).

RESULTS AND DISCUSSION

In this section, the classification and categorisation of each selected research article (Akturan, 2018; Braga et al., 2019; Bulut et al., 2021; de Alencar et al., 2021; de Sio et al., 2022; Guerreiro & Pacheco, 2021; Kahraman & Kazançoğlu, 2019; Le et al., 2019; Lemke & Luzio, 2014; Li et al., 2022; Liu et al., 2023; Lu et al., 2022; Naderer & Opree, 2021; Neureiter & Matthes, 2022; Nyilasy et al., 2014; Okbagaber, 2023; Olk, 2021; Rivai, 2020; Singh et al., 2022; Sun & Shi, 2022; Taufik & Dagevos, 2021; Topal et al., 2020; Ulusoy & Barretta, 2016; Urbański & Ul Haque, 2020; van et al., 2022; Volschenk et al., 2022; Wang et al., 2020; Xiao et al., 2022; Zhang et al., 2018, 2022; Zhang & Sun, 2021) for the study is shown in Table 5.2. Then, based on the overall classifications, the results are analysed.

Context

The first classification, presented in Fig. 5.2, comprises the context in which past studies are concentrated. Codes P, Q, and R are assigned to the context of past studies in articles, where P – studies are done in developed countries, Q – studies are done in developing countries, and R – others. The results from the analysis of the 32 research articles are presented in Fig. 5.2. The results depict that most studies (56.25%) belong to developed countries, followed by developing countries (43.75%).

- *Gap 1*: Greenwashing in developing countries needs to be studied.

Table 5.2. The Classification and Categorisation of Each Research Article for the Study.

S. No.	Context	Geographical Region	Time Period	Main Subject	Method	Sample Size	Topic	Products Type
1	P	R	P	P	Q	Q	P	T
2	P	S	P	Q,R	P	P	Q	P,Q,R
3	P	S	Q	Q,R	Q	P	R	R
4	P	P	R	Q,R	Q	Q	U	P,Q,R,S
5	Q	Q	R	P,Q	Q	R	R	R
6	Q	T	T	P,Q	Q	P	S,R,P	P
7	P	P	T	R	Q	P	R	P
8	P	P	R	P,Q,R	P	P	R,T	P
9	P	S	R	P,Q,R	Q	S	T	T
10	Q	Q	R	R	Q	Q	Q,T	T
11	Q	Q	T	R	Q	Q	R	T
12	Q	Q	R	P,Q,R	Q	Q	U	R
13	P	S	S	Q,R	Q	S	R	P
14	P	P	R	R	Q	T	R,S	R
15	Q	Q	S	P	Q	Q	R	R
16	P	P	S	P	Q	S	Q	R
17	P	P	S	Q,R	Q	Q	P,R	P,R
18	Q	Q	T	P	Q	Q	U	T
19	Q	Q	S	P	Q	P	R,S	P,Q,R
20	P	S	S	R	P,Q	P	P,R	R
21	P	P	S	R	Q	Q	R,S	T
22	P	P	S	P,Q,R	Q	P	R	T
23	P	P	S	P	Q	Q	P,Q	T
24	P	P	T	Q,R	Q	Q	Q,S	P
25	P	P	T	P	Q	R	S,R,P	T
26	Q	Q	T	R	Q	P	P,Q	P
27	Q	Q	T	P,Q,R	Q	Q	P	Q
28	Q	Q	T	Q,R	Q	Q	Q	T
29	Q	Q	T	P,Q	Q	P	R	Q
30	Q	Q	T	R	R	T	R	R
31	Q	Q	T	P	Q	P	R	T
32	P	P	T	R	P	T	R,S	T

Source: Authors' compilation.

Geographic Region

The second classification, displayed in Fig. 5.3, involves the analysis of the geographic region in which past studies are focussed. Codes P, Q, R, S, T, U, and V codes were assigned to the geographic region, where P – Europe, Q – Asia, R – North America, S – South America, T – Africa, U – Australia, and V – others. This classification considers the diversity of the analysis of the research articles studied in the past years. The geographic region analysis of the 32 research articles is displayed in Fig. 5.3. Results depict that most of the studies (40.63%) belonged to Asia, followed by Europe (37.50%). This topic is less studied in North America (3.13%), South America (15.63%), and Australia (3.13%). These results show that consumers in these countries are gaining awareness of greenwashing

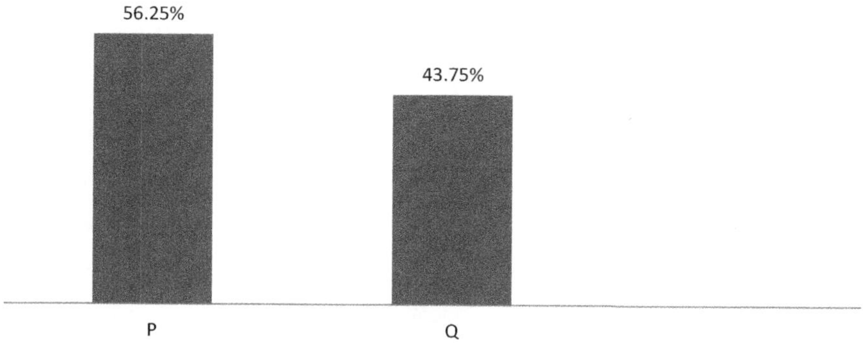

Fig. 5.2. The Context of Studies Analysed. *Source*: Authors' compilation. *Categories*: P – studies done in developed countries and Q – studies done in developing countries.

in developing countries of Asia and developed countries of Europe. Therefore, the developed world of America and Africa must pay attention to greenwashing.

Time Period

The third classification, presented in Fig. 5.4, shows the time period of the research articles studied. They were labelled as P – 2014–2015, Q – 2016–2017, R – 2018–2019, S – 2020–2021, and T – 2022–2023.

Fig. 5.4 displays the time period of the study. Results depict that most researchers have done studies on greenwashing in the years 2022–2023 (40.63%). Followed by 28.13% in 2020–2021, 21.88% in the years 2018–2019, 3.13% in the years 2016–2017, and 6.25% in the years 2014–2015.

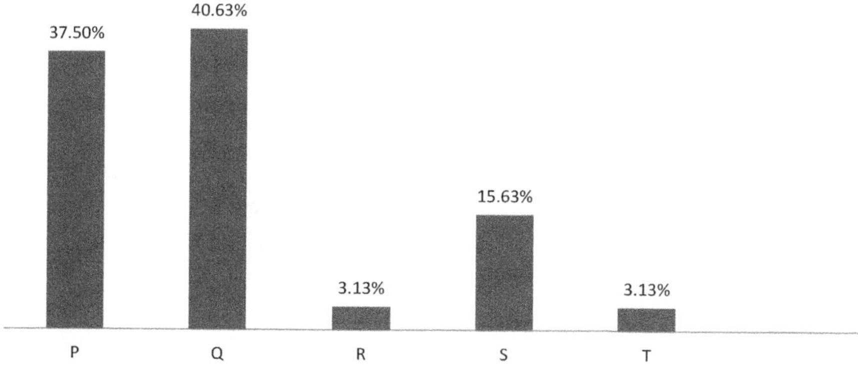

Fig. 5.3. The Geographic Region in the Studies Analysed. *Source*: Authors' compilation. *Categories*: P – Europe, Q – Asia, R – North America, S – South America, and T – Africa.

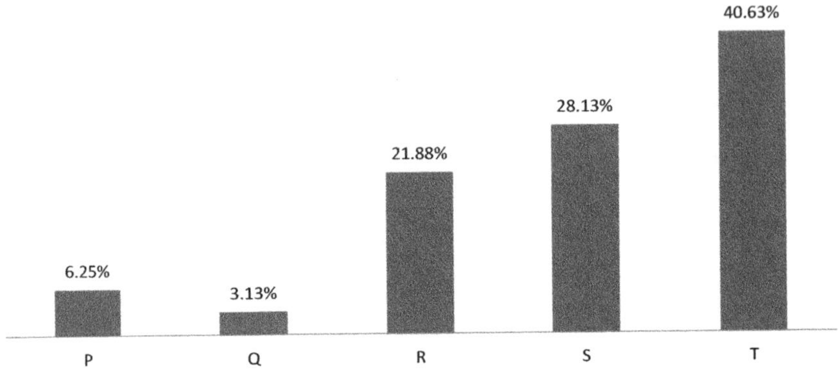

Fig. 5.4. The Time Period of the Study. *Source*: Authors' compilation. *Categories*: P – 2014–2015, Q – 2016–2017, R – 2018–2019, S – 2020–2021, and T – 2022–2023.

Main Subject

The fourth classification, displayed in Fig. 5.5, presents the main subject of the study. The research articles were analysed as they were related to greenwashing perception, green purchase intention, and green products coded as P – greenwashing perception, Q – green purchase intention, R – green products, and S – others, as shown in Fig. 5.5. This analysis would help to create an overview of various subtopics discussed in the literature like greenwashing perception, green purchase intention, and the green products used by the consumers. Results indicate that the maximum number of papers were related to green products (28.13%). In comparison, 25% of the studies were on greenwashing perception and 18.75% of the studies were on green purchase intention about green products, and 12.50% of the studies were based on the greenwashing perception of the consumers concerning

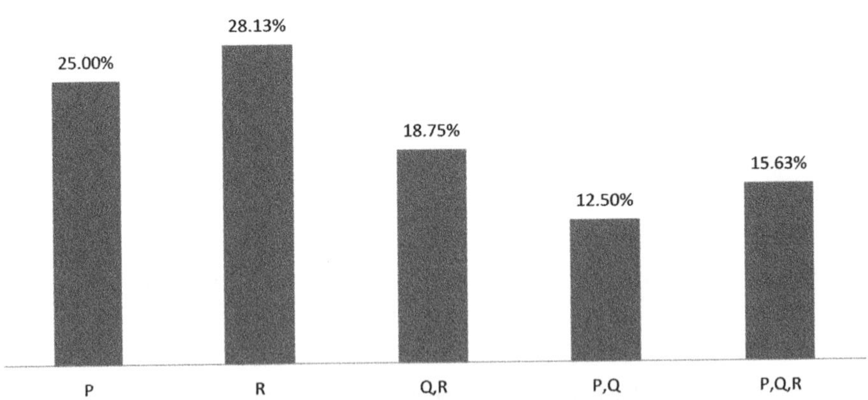

Fig. 5.5. The Main Subject of the Study Analysed. *Source*: Authors' compilation. *Categories*: P – greenwashing perception, Q – green purchase intention, R – green products, and S – others.

green products. It is noticed from a study that only 15.63% of the studies focus on the greenwashing perception of the consumers, green purchase intention, and green products. Based on these data, we have noticed fewer studies done by research scholars on the greenwashing perception of consumers, green purchase intention, and the green products available in the market. This research area has a broad scope of study when categories are P, Q, and R studied jointly.

Methods

The fifth classification, displayed in Fig. 5.6, shows the method used in the analyses of the articles. The codes are P, Q, R, S, and T represented as follows: P – qualitative, Q – quantitative, R – literature review, S – case study, and T – others. The results are shown in Fig. 5.6. The method used in the research articles has displayed different results. Most of the studies focus on quantitative methods (84.38%). Few research articles used qualitative methods (9.38%) and literature review (3.13%) as the study method. The study used combinations of different methods in research articles, such as qualitative and quantitative methods (3.13%).

From the above results, it can be concluded that there is a need for new studies. Thus, we can notice the Gap 2:

- *Gap 2*: New studies on greenwashing require using a qualitative method, literature review, and case study.

Sample Size

The sixth classification, presented in Fig. 5.7, relates to the sample size of the studies in articles, coded in the following way: P – less than 250 or 250, Q – 251–500, R – 501–750, S – more than 750, and T – non-applicable.

As shown in Fig. 5.7, in the bulk of research papers analysed, the sample size was less than 250 (34.38%). Around 40.63% research articles analysed a sample size of 251–500, 6.25% analysed a sample size of 501–750, and 9.38% analysed a

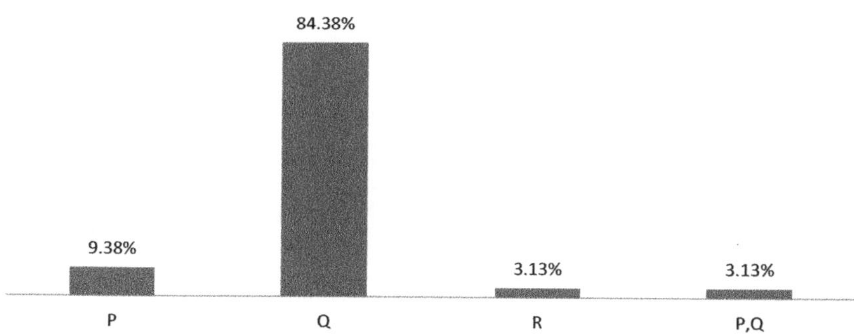

Fig. 5.6. Methods. *Source*: Authors' compilation. *Categories*: P – qualitative, Q – quantitative, R – literature review, S – case study, and T – others.

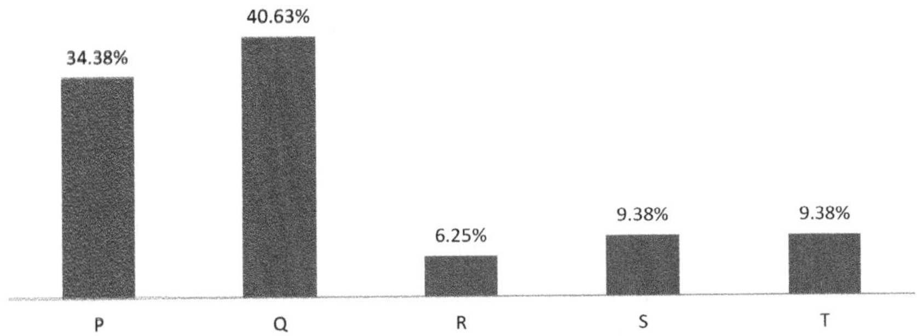

Fig. 5.7. Sample Size. *Source*: Authors' compilation. *Categories*: P – less than 250 or 250, Q – 251–500, R – 501–750, S – more than 750, and S – non-applicable.

sample size of more than 750. In some of the research studies, the sample size was not considered. Hence, for more reliable studies in the future, an attempt should be made to do the research analysis with a sample size of more than 500.

- *Gap 3*: For more reliable studies in the future, an attempt should be made to do the research analysis with a large sample size.

Topics

The seventh classification, presented in Fig. 5.8, describes the various topics on which the work has been undertaken in past studies. The codes for the topics are as follows: P – green marketing, Q – consumer scepticism, R – environmental concern, S – environmental knowledge, T – consumer attitude towards green products, and U – others. As shown in Fig. 5.8, most of the previous research

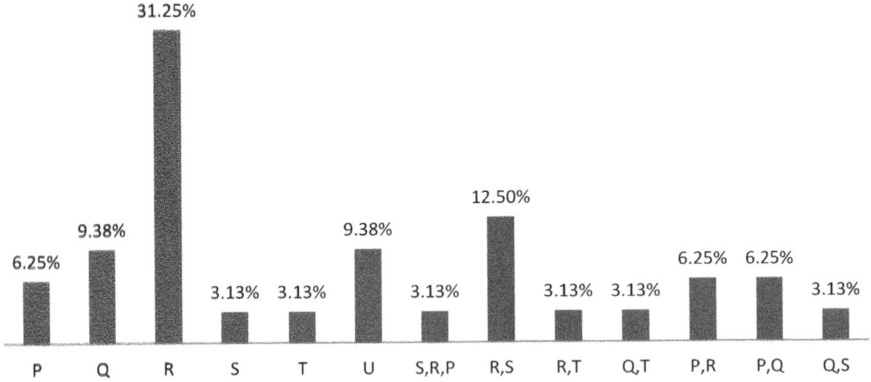

Fig. 5.8. Topics. *Source*: Authors' compilation. *Categories*: P – green marketing, Q – consumer skepticism, R – environmental concern, S – environmental knowledge, T – consumer attitude towards green products, and U – others.

(31.25%) is focussed on environmental concerns. Around 9.38% studies are about consumer scepticism.

Only 6.25% of studies were related to green marketing and 3.13% were related to environmental knowledge. A very small percentage of studies (3.13%) were combined studies related to greenwashing perception, green purchase intention, and focussing on green products.

- *Gap 4*: Very few combined studies have been done on the greenwashing perception of the consumer related to green products and green purchase intention. Researchers can use this for future studies and explore new perspectives on this issue.

Products Types

Lastly, the eighth category, displayed in Fig. 5.9, displays the product type of the research articles and was coded as P – convenience goods, Q – shopping goods, R – specialty goods, S – unsought goods, and T – others. The result is shown in Fig. 5.9. The studies focussing on convenience goods are 18.75%. The majority of the researchers have contributed to the study related to speciality goods (25%). Only 6.25% studies are performed on shopping goods.

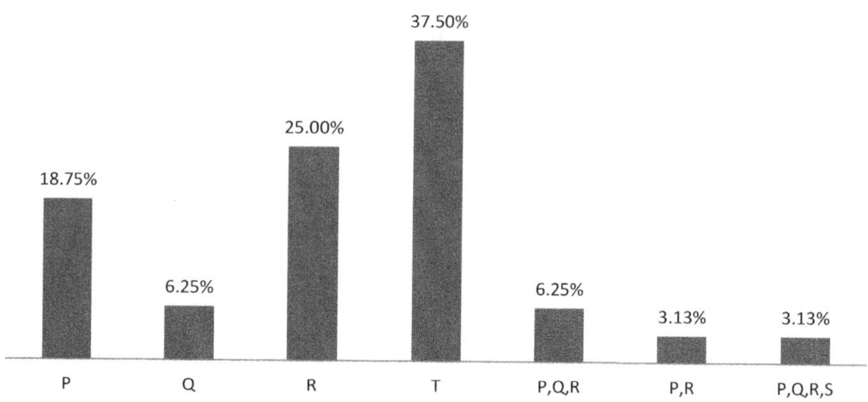

Fig. 5.9. Product Type. *Source*: Authors' compilation. *Categories*: P – convenience goods, Q – shopping goods, R – specialty goods, S – unsought goods, and T – others.

CONCLUSION

This chapter focusses on the topic of 'greenwashing'. There is no dearth of sources, but there is an acute shortage of consumer awareness of greenwashing globally. This study downloaded research articles from the previous seven years (2014–2023) from the Scopus-indexed database using the keywords 'greenwashing'. The selected 32 papers revealed that developed countries are more concerned and aware of the greenwashing problem. The coding sheet was designed with the main subject of study in mind to give structure to eight classifications. Further, the gaps in each classification were consequently identified, which provides the basis for future studies. After the comprehensive analysis of all the categories in the coding sheet, four gaps have been identified in the literature that show a need for research to be carried out to remove the gap in existing studies.

The results of this systematic review indicate that researchers need to focus on the following four existing gaps:

- Need to study in developing countries on greenwashing.
- New studies on greenwashing require the use of a qualitative method, literature review, and case study.
- For more reliable studies in the future, an attempt should be made to do the research analysis with a large sample size.
- Only some combined studies are done on greenwashing perception of the consumer related to green products and green purchase intention. Researchers can use this for future studies and explore new perspectives.

The identified gaps in the available literature will strengthen future research and consequently help avoid fraudulent practices promoting greenwashing perception.

REFERENCES

Akturan, U. (2018). How does greenwashing affect green branding equity and purchase intention? Empirical research. *Marketing Intelligence and Planning*, *36*(7), 809–824. https://doi.org/10.1108/MIP-12-2017-0339

Almossawi, M. (2014). Promoting green purchase behavior to the youth (case of Bahrain). *British Journal of Marketing Studies*, *2*(5), 1–16.

Braga, S., Jr, Martínez, M. P., Correa, C. M., Moura-Leite, R. C., & Da Silva, D. (2019). Greenwashing effect, attitudes, and beliefs in green consumption. *RAUSP Management Journal*, *54*(2), 226–241. https://doi.org/10.1108/RAUSP-08-2018-0070

Bulut, C., Nazli, M., Aydin, E., & Haque, A. U. (2021). The effect of environmental concern on conscious green consumption of post-millennials: The moderating role of greenwashing perceptions. *Young Consumers*, *22*(2), 306–319. https://doi.org/10.1108/YC-10-2020-1241

Cherry, M. A., & Sneirson, J. F. (2012). Chevron, greenwashing, and the myth of green oil companies. *Journal of Energy, Climate, and the Environment*, *3*, 133.

Cronin, J. J., Smith, J. S., Gleim, M. R., Ramirez, E., & Martinez, J. D. (2011). Green marketing strategies: An examination of stakeholders and the opportunities they present. *Journal of the Academy of Marketing Science*, *39*, 158–174.

Dagher, G. K., & Itani, O. (2014). Factors influencing green purchasing behavior: Empirical evidence from the Lebanese consumers. *Journal of Consumer Behaviour*, *13*(3), 188–195.

de Alencar Caldas, M. V., Veiga-Neto, A. R., de Almeida Guimarães, L. G., de Castro, A. B. C., & Pereira, G. R. B. (2021). Greenwashing in environmental marketing strategy in the Brazilian furniture market. *Revista de Economia e Sociologia Rural*, *59*(3), 1–19. https://doi.org/10.1590/1806-9479.2021.225336

de Freitas Netto, S. V., Sobral, M. F. F., Ribeiro, A. R. B., & Soares, G. R. D. L. (2020). Concepts and forms of greenwashing: A systematic review. *Environmental Sciences Europe*, *32*(1), 1–12.

de Sio, S., Zamagni, A., Casu, G., & Gremigni, P. (2022). Green trust as a mediator in the relationship between green advertising skepticism, environmental knowledge, and intention to buy green food. *International Journal of Environmental Research and Public Health*, *19*(24). https://doi.org/10.3390/ijerph192416757

Durif, F., Boivin, C., & Julien, C. (2010). In search of a green product definition. *Innovative Marketing, 6*(1), 25–33.

Easterling, D., Kenworthy, A., & Nemzoff, R. (1996). The greening of advertising: A twenty-five year look at environmental advertising. *Journal of Marketing Theory and Practice, 4*(1), 20–34.

García-Salirrosas, E. E., & Rondon-Eusebio, R. F. (2022). Green marketing practices related to key variables of consumer purchasing behavior. *Sustainability, 14*(14), 8499.

Grimmer, M., & Woolley, M. (2014). Green marketing messages and consumers' purchase intentions: Promoting personal versus environmental benefits. *Journal of Marketing Communications, 20*(4), 231–250.

Guerreiro, J., & Pacheco, M. (2021). How green trust, consumer brand engagement and green word-of-mouth mediate purchasing intentions. *Sustainability (Switzerland), 13*(14), 1–13. https://doi.org/10.3390/su13147877

Kahraman, A., & Kazançoğlu, İ. (2019). Understanding consumers' purchase intentions toward natural-claimed products: A qualitative research in personal care products. *Business Strategy and the Environment, 28*(6), 1218–1233. https://doi.org/10.1002/bse.2312

Le, A. N. H., Jain, M., Tam, T. D., & Tam, L. T. (2019). Attitudinal ambivalence towards green products: An empirical study in an emerging market. *International Journal of Economics and Business Research, 18*(3), 292–303. https://doi.org/10.1504/IJEBR.2019.102726

Lemke, F., & Luzio, J. P. P. (2014). Exploring green consumers' mindset toward green product design and life cycle assessment: The case of skeptical Brazilian and Portuguese green consumers Lemke and Luzio exploring green consumers' mindset toward design and LCA. *Journal of Industrial Ecology, 18*(5), 619–630. https://doi.org/10.1111/jiec.12123

Li, W., Li, W., Seppänen, V., & Koivumäki, T. (2022). How and when does perceived greenwashing affect employees' job performance? Evidence from China. *Corporate Social Responsibility and Environmental Management, 29*(5), 1722–1735. https://doi.org/10.1002/csr.2321

Lu, X., Sheng, T., Zhou, X., Shen, C., & Fang, B. (2022). How does young consumers' greenwashing perception impact their green purchase intention in the fast fashion industry? An analysis from the perspective of perceived risk theory. *Sustainability (Switzerland), 14*(20). https://doi.org/10.3390/su142013473

Maiti, M. (2022). Does development in venture capital investments influence green growth? *Technological Forecasting and Social Change, 182*, 121878.

Mara, D., Nate, S., Stavytskyy, A., & Kharlamova, G. (2022). The place of energy security in the national security framework: an assessment approach. *Energies, 15*(2), 658.

Naderer, B., & Opree, S. J. (2021). Increasing advertising literacy to unveil disinformation in green advertising. *Environmental Communication, 15*(7), 923–936. https://doi.org/10.1080/17524032.2021.1919171

Neureiter, A., & Matthes, J. (2022). Comparing the effects of greenwashing claims in environmental airline advertising: Perceived greenwashing, brand evaluation, and flight shame. *International Journal of Advertising, 42*(3), 461–487. https://doi.org/10.1080/02650487.2022.2076510

Nyilasy, G., Gangadharbatla, H., & Paladino, A. (2014). Perceived greenwashing: The interactive effects of green advertising and corporate environmental performance on consumer reactions. *Journal of Business Ethics, 125*(4), 693–707. https://doi.org/10.1007/s10551-013-1944-3

Olk, S. (2021). The effect of self-congruence on perceived green claims' Authenticity and perceived greenwashing: The case of EasyJet's CO2 promise. *Journal of Nonprofit and Public Sector Marketing, 33*(2), 114–131. https://doi.org/10.1080/10495142.2020.1798859

Parguel, B., Benoit-Moreau, F., & Russell, C. A. (2015). Can evoking nature in advertising mislead consumers? The power of 'executional greenwashing'. *International Journal of Advertising, 34*(1), 107–134.

Pizzetti, M., Gatti, L., & Seele, P. (2021). Firms talk, suppliers walk: Analyzing the locus of greenwashing in the blame game and introducing 'vicarious greenwashing'. *Journal of Business Ethics, 170*, 21–38.

Puška, A., Hodžić, I., Štilić, A., & Murtič, S. (2024). Evaluating European Union countries on climate change management: A fuzzy MABAC approach to the climate change performance index. *Journal of Green Economy and Low-Carbon Development, 3*(1), 15–25.

Rivai, A. (2020). Seeking for sustainable electronic brands' performance: Role of perceived greenwashing and perception dimensions. *Journal of Security and Sustainability Issues, 10*, 218–230. https://doi.org/10.9770/jssi.2020.10.Oct(16)

Saha, M., & Darnton, G. (2005). Green companies or green con-panies: Are companies really green, or are they pretending to be? *Business and Society Review*, *110*(2), 117–157.

Sandeen, C. (2009). It is not easy being green: Green marketing and environmental consumerism in continuing higher education. *Continuing Higher Education Review*, 73, 93–113.

Simon, D. R. (2000). Corporate environmental crimes and social inequality: New directions for environmental justice research. *American Behavioral Scientist*, *43*(4), 633–645.

Sun, Y., & Shi, B. (2022). Impact of greenwashing perception on consumers' green purchasing intentions: A moderated mediation model. *Sustainability (Switzerland)*, *14*(19). https://doi.org/10.3390/su141912119

Taufik, D., & Dagevos, H. (2021). Driving public acceptance (instead of skepticism) of technologies enabling bioenergy production: A corporate social responsibility perspective. *Journal of Cleaner Production*, *324*. https://doi.org/10.1016/j.jclepro.2021.129273

Topal, İ., Nart, S., Akar, C., & Erkollar, A. (2020). The effect of greenwashing on online consumer engagement: A comparative study in France, Germany, Turkey, and the United Kingdom. *Business Strategy and the Environment*, *29*(2), 465–480. https://doi.org/10.1002/bse.2380

Ulusoy, E., & Barretta, P. G. (2016). How green are you, really? Consumers' skepticism toward brands with green claims. *Journal of Global Responsibility*, *7*(1), 72–83. https://doi.org/10.1108/JGR-11-2015-0021

Urbański, M., & Ul Haque, A. (2020). Are you environmentally conscious enough to differentiate between greenwashed and sustainable items? A global consumer's perspective. *Sustainability (Switzerland)*, *12*(5), 1–25. https://doi.org/10.3390/su12051786

van der Schyff, V., Suchánková, L., Kademoglou, K., Melymuk, L., & Klánová, J. (2022). Parabens and antimicrobial compounds in conventional and "green" personal care products. *Chemosphere*, *297*, 1–8. https://doi.org/10.1016/j.chemosphere.2022.134019

Volschenk, J., Gerber, C., & Santos, B. A. (2022). The (in)ability of consumers to perceive greenwashing and its influence on purchase intent and willingness to pay. *South African Journal of Economic and Management Sciences*, *25*(1), 1–9. https://doi.org/10.4102/sajems.v25i1.4553

Wang, H., Ma, B., & Bai, R. (2020). The spillover effect of greenwashing behaviours: An experimental approach. *Marketing Intelligence and Planning*, *38*(3), 283–295. https://doi.org/10.1108/MIP-01-2019-0006

Yerpude, S., Sood, K., & Grima, S. (2022). Blockchain-augmented digital supply chain management: A way to sustainable business. *Journal of Risk and Financial Management*, *16*(1), 7.

Xiao, Z., Wang, Y., & Guo, D. (2022). Will greenwashing result in brand avoidance? A moderated mediation model. *Sustainability (Switzerland)*, *14*(12), 1–15. https://doi.org/10.3390/su14127204

Zhang, H., Ul Ainn, Q., Bashir, I., Ul Haq, J., & Bonn, M. A. (2022). Does greenwashing influence the green product experience in emerging hospitality markets post-COVID-19? *Sustainability (Switzerland)*, *14*(19), 1–16. https://doi.org/10.3390/su141912313

Zhang, J., & Sun, J. (2021). Green talk or green walk: Chinese consumer positive word-of-mouth to corporate environmental actions in polluting industries. *Sustainability (Switzerland)*, *13*(9), 1–22. https://doi.org/10.3390/su13095259

Zhang, L., Li, D., Cao, C., & Huang, S. (2018). The influence of greenwashing perception on green purchasing intentions: The mediating role of green word-of-mouth and moderating role of green concern. *Journal of Cleaner Production*, 187, 740–750. https://doi.org/10.1016/j.jclepro.2018.03.201

CHAPTER 6

ROLE OF GREEN INVESTMENT ON ECONOMIC ASPECTS OF SUSTAINABLE DEVELOPMENT

Reet Kaur and Anita Tanwar

Chitkara Business School, Chitkara University, India

ABSTRACT

Introduction: *Investments in environmentally friendly initiatives can bolster infrastructure projects, agricultural methods, and water management systems that improve the ability to withstand climate-related difficulties. Green investments encompass endorsing carbon markets and financial instruments that incentivise reducing emissions. This research helps attain the climate objectives described in sustainable development goal 13 (SDG 13).*

Purpose: *This chapter aims to investigate the relationship between greenhouse gases (GHG) and gross domestic product (GDP), with the underlying objective of understanding the relevance of green investment for sustainable development.*

Methodology: *For the analysis, the top five countries: the USA, China, Germany, Japan, and India, were chosen based on the world's largest economies in 2023, as per their GDP data. For testing the hypothesis, data from the World Bank database during the period 2002-2022 was retrieved and GDP is used as a dependent variable and GHG as an independent variable. For the study, panel data are used, and the Johansen cointegration test and ordinary least squares (OLS) regression are applied.*

Sustainability Development through Green Economics
Contemporary Studies in Economic and Financial Analysis, Volume 114, 91–106

Published under exclusive licence by Emerald Publishing Limited
ISSN: 1569-3759/doi:10.1108/S1569-375920240000114006

Findings: *In the case of China and India, the null hypothesis has been rejected, which is depicted by the significant and high degree of relation between GHGs and the GDP of these two countries. The null hypothesis is also rejected for the USA and Germany, but it shows a significant and moderate degree of relationship between GHG and GDP. For Japan, the null hypothesis is accepted and reflects a negative relationship between GHG and GDP.*

Keywords: Green investment; green growth; sustainable development; green house gases; gross domestic product; decoupling; degrowth

JEL Codes: A11; A12; C01; C23; C31; G21; G23; G24; O16; Q50

INTRODUCTION

The concept of sustainable growth originated during the Rio20 conference in 2012 under the framework of environmental conservation. The summit concluded with the presentation of an agenda statement titled *The World We Want* (UN, 2012), which focussed on two primary objectives: promoting a 'green economy' and the achievement of 'sustained economic development'. Subsequently, prominent multinational corporations have accepted the theory of green growth, and it has become an integral component of environmental conservation strategies at both national and worldwide scales. The concept of green growth proposes that it is perfectly feasible to separate economic development from GHG emissions and resource utilisation (Hickel & Kallis, 2020). Humanity's tomorrow hinges on achieving rational development, necessitating the effective execution of policies to mitigate GHG emissions. GHG emissions, namely carbon dioxide (CO_2) emissions, are widely recognised as the primary obstacle to sustainable development (IPCC, 2014).

The conflict between economic progress and environmental preservation is evident in numerous environmental reports, climate change studies, and discussions on sustainable development. Furthermore, climate change is progressively intensifying, adversely affecting the overall economic progress, generating ecological disparities, and leading to unsustainable development. Undoubtedly, it is imperative for all governments, organisations, and enterprises to urgently seek solutions to climate change that facilitate the attainment of growth objectives while mitigating environmental effects. Companies must prioritise adopting green investments to foster green growth economies, including Vietnam's green growth policy. To eliminate the negative impacts of post-crisis and climate change, it is imperative to not only rely on the financial banking system to reorganise the financial system but also to undertake the reorganisation of the economy, which is crucial for enterprises (Eyraud et al., 2013).

The continuous patterns of economic development give rise to new challenges and responsibilities for the government in determining the path for future progress. Hence, it is imperative to address the concerns above to establish an economic, social, and ecological framework that can effectively accomplish the objectives and milestones of sustainable development (Vasylieva et al., 2019). As per the European Union's agenda, sustainable development is the primary focus for creating and implementing policies across all areas. This approach aims to enhance countries' competitiveness and create better conditions for companies and society (Dabyltayeva & Rakhymzhan, 2019; Dalevska et al., 2019). Hence, the European Union considers the attainment of sustainability through the utilisation of renewable resources as a means to mitigate both the adverse effects of climate change and to foster tangible economic advantages by diminishing reliance on imported fuel (Brożyna et al., 2017).

When countries face the choice between climate change and economic development, businesses play a crucial role in advancing green economic development. They do this by transitioning from a polluting economy to an environmentally friendly one through investments in projects that protect the environment (Mo et al., 2023). This shift promotes sustainable and socially responsible development. Green investment is an essential expenditure aimed at mitigating the impact of GHG emissions and air pollution while maintaining energy production and consumption levels and the production of non-energy items. Green Investment encompasses both public and private investment (Ozturk & Ullah, 2023).

Moreover, green investment can be broken down into three primary elements: low-emission energy supply encompasses nuclear power, biofuels, and renewable energy. Energy efficiency pertains to both energy supply and consumption. Carbon isolation involves deforestation and agriculture (IMF, 2011).

The upward trajectory of consumption and production activities, driven by heightened investment, leads to a surge in economic growth, resulting in increased CO_2 emissions. Therefore, investment in large-scale infrastructure projects has gained significant attention from authorities in Asian economies (Bhargave & Tandon, 2022; Gao et al., 2022; Ozturk & Ullah, 2022; Yerpude et al., 2023). The function of investment is increasingly pivotal in promoting or regulating CO_2 emissions. Based on an estimation, an investment of US$1.7 trillion on an annual basis, or a cumulative investment of US$26 trillion, is required to tackle the issues of poverty, promote economic growth effectively, and the challenges posed by climate change from 2016 to 2030 (Sachs et al., 2019). The power sector requires a total investment of US$14.7 trillion, the transportation sector needs an investment of US$8.4 trillion, US$2.3 trillion for the telecommunication sector, and US$800 billion for the water and sanitation sector (Puška et al., 2024; Wang et al., 2020; Yerpude et al., 2023).

Several policies, documents, and publications, like the one from the IPCC, operate under the assumption that economic growth will remain a fundamental aspect of prosperous future societies (Hickel & Kallis, 2020). Nevertheless, if the expansion of the economy coincides with escalating resource utilisation and emissions, it could jeopardise the prospects of achieving future sustainability transformation objectives and attaining objectives such as the SDGs (TWI2050, 2018; Azhgaliyeva et al., 2020). It demands eliminating GHG emissions by about 2050. It necessitates significant cutbacks in the consumption of resources, such as energy or materials, in many places across the globe. Net negative emissions can be obtained in many situations by promoting tree plantation and other land-based 'natural climate solutions' (Griscom et al., 2017) or technology that removes CO_2 from the atmosphere post-2050 is necessary to take action to restore the climate to the desired target level when it has exceeded the goals set for climate change mitigation. The necessity for 'negative emissions' arises in all situations if there is a failure to achieve adequate reductions in carbon emissions over the first half of the century (IPCC, 2018).

It is crucial to differentiate between resource decoupling, derived from GDP from energy consumption (Jackson & Victor, 2016), and effect decoupling, derived from GDP from GHG emissions. Reducing resource use will inevitably decrease impacts by minimising resource extraction, processing, and disposal. However, certain influences can be further reduced and redirected through technological advancements, such as flue gas cleaning or substituting low-carbon fuels for high-carbon fuels like oil and coal. These measures can be effective even if resource use itself is not reduced. Intensive research is being conducted on strategies for reducing GHG emissions, which may become more significant due to the development of carbon capture and sequestration (CCS) technology (Fuss et al., 2014). The emphasis on energy efficiency and demand-side initiatives is backed by IPCC assessments, which show that these approaches carry fewer risks and provide greater benefits to society than technology solutions (IPCC, 2014).

In light of the significance of maintaining a sustainable environment and promoting environmentally friendly economic growth, authorities are currently directing their attention on transitioning the energy sector from utilising non-renewable energy sources such as coal, gas, and oil to adopting renewable alternatives such as wind, solar, biofuel, and nuclear power (Sharma & Bajaj, 2023). The shift in energy structure primarily relies on implementing green financing and accurately valuing the external costs associated with energy production. More than merely implementing a pricing mechanism for emissions is required to address the challenge of environmental sustainability (Li & Ullah, 2022). The IMF also emphasised that only pricing the external costs may not address the challenge posed by global warming and climate change (Lagarde & Gaspar, 2019). Improved public investments in the form of green financing shall have a notable impact on carbon emissions control and the development of a more efficient energy system. Financial policies facilitate the mobilisation of private investment to accelerate the process of transitioning to a low-carbon economy (Ullah et al., 2021). To separate environmental pollution from economic growth, policymakers globally are depending on green investment to alleviate the impacts of environmental pollution and generate funding for transitioning countries from carbon-intensive to low-carbon economies. The increasing need for energy-efficient initiatives necessitates governments to undertake appropriate measures, such as adopting green bonds, a novel financial instrument that can effectively address the issue of climate emergency (Lei et al., 2022). In brief, green investment can be a vital and impactful technique for segregating economic progress from environmental degradation (Chen & Ma, 2021; Wang & Zhi, 2016).

GDP is the representative of the economic dimension, whereas GHGs are the representative of the environmental dimension. This chapter investigates the relationship between GDP growth and GHG emissions, with the underlying objective of understanding the Importance of green investment for sustainable economic development.

LITERATURE REVIEW

Green Investment

Wang et al. (2020) analyse the significance of climate-friendly investment. By employing advanced econometric techniques, the authors discovered that investing in green initiatives is beneficial for enhancing environmental quality and promoting sustainability. Furthermore, the authors contend that the provision of green investments specifically for the renewable sources industry is particularly advantageous in attaining the objectives of zero carbon emissions. Nevertheless, substantial funding is necessary to support the extensive investment initiatives in the renewable energy industry and fully capitalise on the advantages of renewable energy sources. David and Venkatachalam (2018) studied the impact of green investment on reducing CO_2 emissions. The authors contend that by utilising public–private partnerships, the beneficial effects of climate-friendly investments on the quality of the environment can be enhanced. However, to establish a public–private collaboration, it is essential to first focus on institutional development. Azhgaliyeva (2019) emphasises the importance of enhancing private investment to facilitate sustainable economic growth. The authors contend that the private sector can have a crucial impact on funding large-scale projects related to environmental quality. The study's findings indicate a strong connection between GDP, CO_2 emissions, energy consumption, and primary exergy intake. Recent research by Saidi and Hammami (2015) has examined the regional or national investigation of GHG emissions and their connection to economic growth. The findings indicate that economic expansion has a significant and beneficial influence on global energy consumption.

Gross Domestic Product

Recently, numerous academics have identified a correlation between GDP and GHG emissions (Lapinskiene et al., 2017). According Vasylieva et al. (2019), Ukraine has found a significant correlation between GDP and GHGs. Specifically, a per capita increase in GDP can facilitate the adoption of clean energy sources over the long run. The environmental kuznets curve hypothesis states that increasing economic development is the means via which environmental safety and quality of life metrics can be raised (Furkan et al., 2023). Therefore, emerging nations should adopt an economic growth strategy since it will ultimately enable them to attain eco-friendly and economic objectives. Simultaneously, government policy, exclusively prioritising environmental safety, hinders economic expansion. The theory can be visually represented by an inverted U-shaped curve (Webber & Allen, 2010).

Bozkurt and Yusuf (2014) analysed to ascertain the enduring effects of CO_2 emissions and consumption of energy on the GDP in Turkey between

1960 and 2010, and it was discovered that in the country Turkey, energy consumption has a beneficial influence on economic development, whereas carbon emissions have an adverse impact. In a separate study (Ozturk & Acaravci, 2010), the authors aimed to demonstrate the correlation between the use of energy, CO_2 emissions, and growth in Turkey's GDP. They discovered positive long-term correlation estimates of emissions in connection to energy consumption. Additionally, it was discovered that there is a positive correlation between the increase in GDP per capita and the increase in carbon emissions per capita. In Canada, there is a one-way causal relationship where the consumption of energy and economic growth lead to GHG emissions. This indicates a connection between economic expansion and GHG emissions (Hamit-Haggar, 2012; Kaur et al., 2023). A study conducted in Bangladesh demonstrated the correlation between the growth of the economy and CO_2 emissions. The author has determined a direct correlation between the increase in CO_2 emissions and the expansion of the GDP contribution from the industry and services sectors (Alam, 2014). A study conducted on 16 Asian countries revealed that there is a bidirectional Granger causality relationship between the consumption of energy, the GDP, and GHGs emissions.

Similarly, there is also a bidirectional Granger causation relationship among GDP, emissions of GHGs, and energy consumption (Lu, 2017). Research on CCS demonstrated that implementing CCS technology can result in a 54% reduction in CO_2 emissions inside the European Union and a 33% reduction globally by 2025. However, more than this decrease is needed to achieve climate stability. Consequently, it is necessary to enhance energy efficiency. The objective of this project is to develop a model that combines econometric and emission statistics for GHGs with supplementary information on understanding the rule of law, population size, and trade openness. The aim is to determine the most effective way to utilise economic growth to reduce emissions of GHGs (Stangeland, 2007). The trends in overall energy efficiency (measured by GDP/final energy) vary across countries and industries within countries. The primary factors driving gains in energy efficiency are the intensity and affluence effect (Cunha et al., 2018).

Green House Gases

The escalating trajectory of CO_2 emissions poses a grave risk to human existence on Earth (Yeoh et al., 2014). Green finance encompasses the realms of sustainable, environmental, carbon, and climate financing. Sustainable finance encompasses the areas of corporate governance and social responsibility, whereas environmental finance focusses on the protection of the environment. Carbon finance is specifically aimed at reducing carbon emissions, while green financing addresses the mitigation of and adaptation to climate-friendly change to attain a low-carbon economy (Noh, 2010). Huang et al. (2021) explores the significance of green investment and analyses the key elements that influence CO_2 emissions. According to the findings of the OECD, neither an environmental kuznets curve's association nor a natural relation between GDP and energy was discovered (Arango-Miranda et al., 2018). Increasing consumption typically leads to higher emissions, but decreases in emissions intensities somewhat offset this pattern (resulting in relative decoupling). Identifies increasing amounts of GHG emissions contained within products from developing countries (Kaur & Tanwar, 2024; Liu et al., 2019).

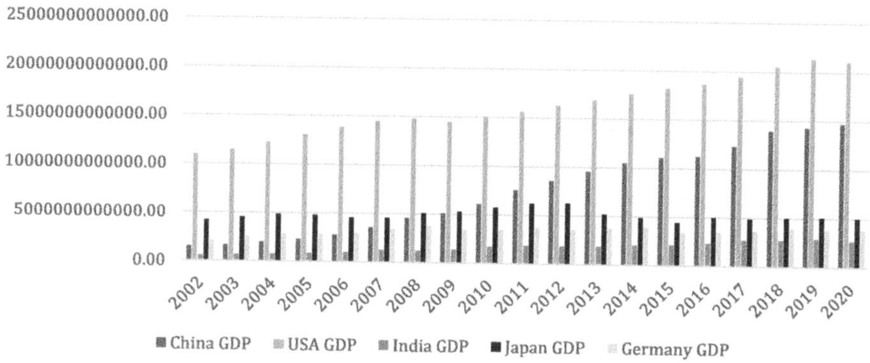

Fig. 6.1. Gross Domestic Product Trend. *Source*: World Bank Data (2023).

Fig. 6.1 depicts the GDP patterns of the USA, China, Germany, Japan, and India from 2002 to 2020. The *x*-axis denotes the chronological progression of years, while the *y*-axis signifies the monetary amount of GDP measured in current US$. The US exhibited an upward trend throughout the period, followed by China's GDP trend, which is remarkable and showing exponential growth over the years. Next to it is Germany, which maintains a consistent positive trend featuring steady growth. On the other hand, Japan shows a restrained growth pattern with periods of stagnation in the early 2000s. Lastly, India's data exhibit a notable and consistent increase, especially throughout the latter portion of the observed timeframe.

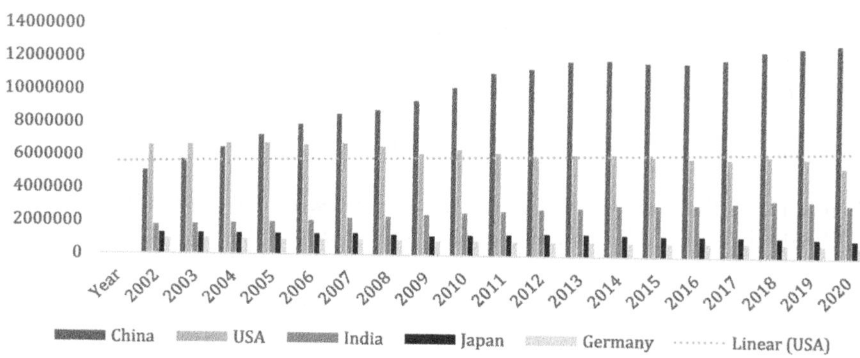

Fig. 6.2. Green House Gases Emission Trend. *Source*: World Bank Data (2023).

Fig. 6.2 depicts the GHG patterns of the USA, China, Germany, Japan, and India from 2002 to 2020. The *x*-axis denotes the chronological progression of years, while the *y*-axis signifies the monetary amount of GHG measured in kilo tons of CO_2 equivalent. The USA demonstrates a variable pattern in GHGs, whereas China's GHG emissions have shown a significant rising trend, strongly linked to its fast industrialisation and economic expansion. Germany's emissions have been decreasing, particularly in recent years. Contrary to this, Japan's emissions exhibit periodic changes but generally follow a consistent and stable pattern. Lastly, India's GHG emissions demonstrate a significant rising trajectory, corresponding to its economic growth.

DATA AND METHODOLOGY

For the analysis, the top five countries, the USA, China, Germany, Japan, and India, during 2002–2022 were chosen based on the world's largest economies in 2023, as per their GDP data (Table 6.1).

Hypothesis

H_0. There is no significant relationship between GHGs and GDP.

H_1. There is a significant relationship between GHGs and GDP.

For the analysis, the top five countries, the USA, China, Germany, Japan, and India, during 2002–2022 were chosen based on the world's largest economies in 2023, as per their GDP data (Forbes India, 2023).

For testing the hypothesis, the authors used data from the World Bank database with *GDP* (GDP is an acronym that stands for gross domestic product. It serves as an indicator of a nation's economic activity and overall well-being. GDP represents the aggregate monetary worth of all products and services generated and exchanged inside a nation within a specific timeframe. The duration of this time often spans one year) as *the dependent variable*, and *GHG* (GHGs are gaseous substances that can capture and retain heat, hence increasing the temperature of the Earth's atmosphere. It includes gases like CO_2, methane, nitrous oxide, and water vapour) as *the independent variable*.

For further analysis of the economic component of sustainable development, the authors used the following model:

$$\text{GDP} = m\text{GHG}+b$$

where GDP is the gross domestic product; m represents the impact of GHG on GDP; GHGs is the GHG emission, and b is the Y intercept.

Table 6.1. Top Five World Economies, 2023.

Rank	Country	GDP (US$ Billion)	GDP Per Capita (US$ Thousand)
1	USA	26,954	80.41
2	China	17,786	12.54
3	Germany	4,430	52.82
4	Japan	4,231	33.95
5	India	3,730	2.61

Source: IMF Data (as of 04 December 2023).

For the research, panel data of selected top five countries based on GDP and GHG have been analysed to study the impact of green investment, which has an indirect relation with GHGs and a direct relation with GDP on sustainable development. To test the hypotheses, the following tests were applied using EViews software: Johansen Cointegration Test (Johansen, 1991) to find out the association between independent variable (GHG) and dependent variable (GDP) and OLS regression (Davidson, 2000) which is widely used method for estimating the coefficients of linear regression equations that model the long-run connection between one or more independent quantitative variables and a dependent variable.

EMPIRICAL RESULTS

For USA

H_0. There is no significant correlation between GHGs and GDP.

H_1. There is a significant correlation between GHGs and GDP.

In Table 6.2, a high eigenvalue of 0.49 in the unrestricted cointegration rank test between GDP and GHG suggests a strong link over the long term. At the 0.05 level of significance, the critical value is 3.84, and at the 0.02 level of significance, it is 15.49. These crucial quantities are connected with *P*-values of 0.156 and 0.5126, respectively. The findings indicate a strong and statistically significant correlation between GDP and GHG emissions.

Table 6.3 reflects the *R*-value of 0.71 for the GHG and GDP connection in the least square's regression study, indicating a strong positive linear association. With an adjusted *R*-squared value of 0.69 (a statistic that considers the number of predictors in the model), GHG emissions explain around 69% of the variance in GDP. The regression model's overall significance is tested by the *F*-statistic, which is 42.17. The high *F*-statistic and the *P*-value of 0.00000 give substantial evidence that GHG emissions significantly impact GDP, rejecting the null hypothesis. In conclusion, the regression has statistical significance, and the model fits well, explaining a large percentage of the GDP variability.

Table 6.2. Johansen Cointegration Result of Eigen Value of USA.

Hypothesised Value	Eigen	Trace Value	Critical Value	*P*-value
None	0.49	12.00	15.49	0.15
At most 1	0.02	0.42	3.84	0.51

Source: Compiled by the authors.

Table 6.3. Least Square Results of USA.

R-square	Adjusted *R*-square	*F*-value	*P*-value
0.74	0.69	42.17	0.00006

Source: Compiled by the authors.

For China

H_0. There is no significant correlation between GHGs and GDP.

H_1. There is a significant correlation between GHGs and GDP.

Table 6.4 shows that both GDP and GHG have an eigenvalue of 0.46 in the unrestricted cointegration rank test and suggesting a moderate long-term association. We employ critical values at 0.033 (15.49) and 0.05 (3.84) to determine if something is statistically significant. The corresponding *P*-values for these crucial quantities are 0.20 and 0.44, respectively. According to the results, there is a moderately substantial correlation between GDP and GHG emissions.

In Table 6.5, the *R*-value of 0.89 in the least square's regression study shows that GHG emissions are positively and linearly related to GDP. The adjusted *R*-squared value of 0.88 indicates a strong model fit, meaning that the independent variables explain 88% of the variance in the GDP. The overall model significance provides evidence that the GHG variable strongly influences *the dependent variable*, indicated by the high *F*-statistic of 146.34 and the extremely low *P*-value of 0.00000. Statistical analysis confirms that the model explains a substantial amount of the GDP fluctuation and shows a good match.

For Germany

H_0. There is no significant correlation between GHGs and GDP.

H_1. There is a *significant* correlation between GHGs and GDP.

Table 6.6 shows an eigenvalue of 0.41 in the GDP and GHG unrestricted cointegration rank test, indicating a moderate long-term association. With a significance level of 0.32 and a threshold of 0.05, the critical values are 14.26 and 3.84, respectively. These crucial values are connected with *P*-values of 0.277 and 0.009. The results show that GDP and GHG emissions are cointegrating, statistically significant, but not very strong.

Table 6.4. Johansen Cointegration Result of Eigen Value of China.

Hypothesised Value	Eigen	Trace Value	Critical Value	*P*-value
None	0.46	11.16	15.49	0.20
At most 1	0.33	0.58	3.84	0.44

Source: Compiled by the authors.

Table 6.5. Least Square Results of China.

R-square	Adjusted *R*-square	*F*-value	*P*-value
0.89	0.88	146.34	0.0000

Source: Compiled by the authors.

Table 6.6. Johansen Cointegration Result of Eigen Value of Germany.

Hypothesised Value	Eigen	Trace Value	Critical Value	*P*-value
None	0.41	15.86	14.26	0.27
At most 1	0.32	6.75	3.84	0.01

Source: Compiled by the authors.

In Table 6.7, the *R*-value of 0.60 indicates a moderately positive linear relationship between the GDP and GHG in the least squares regression analysis. A satisfactory model fit is suggested by the adjusted *R*-squared value of 0.57, which implies that the independent variables explain about 57% of the variability in *the dependent variable*. The overall model significance is strongly supported by the considerable *F*-statistic of 25.67 and the extremely low *P*-value of 0.0000. This indicates that GHG has a meaningful influence on *the dependent variable*. The model is statistically significant and shows a decent fit, explaining a considerable percentage of *the dependent variable's* variability.

For Japan

H_0. There is no significant correlation between GHGs and GDP.

H_1. There is a significant correlation between GHGs and GDP.

Table 6.8 shows a robust long-term link between GDP and GHG is indicated by an eigenvalue of 0.55 in the unconstrained cointegration rank test. There are critical values of 15.49 at the 0.068 significance level and 3.84 at the 0.05 significance level. These critical values are related to *P*-values of 0.063 and 0.271, respectively. The findings point to a strong and statistically significant correlation between GDP and emissions of GHGs.

In Table 6.9, the *R*-value of 0.000694 indicates a very weak and nearly insignificant linear association between GHG and GDP in the least squares regression study. The model does not significantly outperform the basic mean

Table 6.7. Least Square Results of Germany.

R-square	Adjusted *R*-square	*F*-value	*P*-value
0.60	0.57	25.67	0.000

Source: Compiled by the authors.

Table 6.8. Johansen Cointegration Result of Eigen Value of Japan.

Hypothesised Value	Eigen	Trace Value	Critical Value	*P*-value
None	0.55	13.58	14.26	0.06
At most 1	0.06	1.20	3.84	0.27

Source: Compiled by the authors.

Table 6.9. Least Square Results of Japan.

R-square	Adjusted R-square	F-value	P-value
0.000694	−0.058	0.91	0.011

Source: Compiled by the authors.

($R^2 = -0.058$), and the negative value implies the possibility of overfitting. A high P-value of 0.91000 and a low F-statistic of 0.011 indicate that the total model does not meet the statistical criteria for significance. To sum up, the model is not statistically significant, has a weak correlation between GHG and GDP, and has limited explanatory ability.

For India

H_0. There is no *significant* correlation between GHGs and GDP.

H_1. There is a significant correlation between GHGs and GDP.

Table 6.10 shows a moderate and statistically significant long-term link between GDP and GHG is indicated by an eigenvalue of 0.32 in the unrestricted cointegration rank test. At the 0.181 level of significance, the critical value is 15.49, while at the 0.05 level of significance, it is 3.84. There is a 0.27 and a 0.065 probability linked with these crucial values. The results indicate that the correlation between GDP and GHG emissions is statistically insignificant.

In Table 6.11, the R-value of 0.97 indicates a very significant positive linear association between the GHG and GDP variables in the least squares regression study. An outstanding model fit is demonstrated by the corrected R-squared value of 0.97, which suggests that GHG accounts for an astounding 97% of the GDP variability. With a statistic of 0.00000 and an F-statistic of 630.34, the total model is statistically significant, indicating that GHG strongly impacts the GDP. To sum up, the model is very statistically significant, fits the data quite well, and accounts for most of the variation in the GDP variable.

Table 6.10. Johansen Cointegration Result of Eigen Value of India.

Hypothesised Value	Eigen	Trace Value	Critical Value	P-value
None	0.32	10.08	15.49	0.27
At most 1	0.18	3.40	3.84	0.06

Source: Compiled by the authors.

Table 6.11. Least Square Results of India.

R-square	Adjusted R-square	F-value	P-value
0.97	0.97	630.34	0.0000

Source: Compiled by the authors.

CONCLUSIONS

SDG 13 specifically targets climate action intricately connected to green investment. Green investments typically focus on initiatives that aim to diminish the release of GHGs, particularly through projects associated with renewable energy sources (such as solar, wind, and hydropower), energy efficiency enhancements, and low-carbon technologies. Investments in environmentally friendly initiatives can bolster infrastructure projects, agricultural methods, and water management systems that improve the ability to withstand climate-related difficulties. Green investments encompass endorsing carbon markets and financial instruments that incentivise reducing emissions. This research helps to attain climate objectives as described in SDG 13. Collaboration between governments, corporations, and financial institutions can be undertaken to make green investments to accomplish the targets outlined in SDG 13. Public–private partnerships can gather resources and specialised knowledge to expand sustainable enterprises.

SDG 13 urges nations to swiftly and decisively address the threat of global warming. The concept of green growth, which entails engaging in carbon-free economic activities, has emerged as the most viable solution to address the issue of global warming and to meet the need for sustainable development. Green investment has a significant role to play in this matter. Hence, the analysis seeks to investigate the impact of GHGs emissions on the growth rate denoted by GDP of the top five world economies in terms of GDP for the promotion of environmentally sustainable economic growth with a precise focus on green investment.

The results of the null hypothesis and interesting insights on the GHG and GDP relationship represented in Table 6.12 of five countries, that is, the USA, China, Germany, Japan, and India, are:

Table 6.12. Hypothesis Results.

Hypothesis	Null Hypothesis	Relation Between GHG (IV) and GDP (DV)
USA	Rejected (Statistically significant)	Moderate relation
China	Rejected (Statistically significant)	High degree of relation
Germany	Rejected (Statistically significant)	Moderate relation
Japan	Accepted (Statistically insignificant)	Negative relation
India	Rejected (Statistically significant)	High degree of relation

Source: Compiled by the authors.

- In the case of China and India, the null hypothesis has been rejected, which is depicted by the significant and high degree of relationship between GHG and GDP of these two countries. In the case of the USA and Germany, the null hypothesis is also rejected, but it shows a significant and moderate degree of relationship between GHG and GDP. This indicates that economic expansion is linked to a rise in carbon emissions. This research is a consequence of industrialisation, dependence on fossil fuels, and activities that need significant energy. To tackle this high degree of correlation, it is necessary to implement green investment, sustainable practices, and policies that can separate economic expansion from its environmental consequences.

- For Japan, the null hypothesis is accepted and reflects a negative relationship between GHG and GDP. Japan's inverse correlation between GHG emissions and GDP shows that its economic growth is detached from emissions, indicating a relative decoupling. These findings indicate that Japan has successfully boosted its GDP without a corresponding increase in carbon emissions, demonstrating advancements in adopting green investment in energy-efficient technologies and cleaner behaviours, contributing to sustainable development.

REFERENCES

Alam, J. (2014). On the relationship between economic growth and CO_2 emissions: The Bangladesh experience. *IOSR Journal of Economics and Finance (IOSR-JEF)*, *5*(6), 36–41.

Arango-Miranda, R., Hausler, R., Romero-Lopez, R., Glaus, M., & Ibarra-Zavaleta, S. P. (2018). Carbon dioxide emissions, energy consumption and economic growth: A comparative empirical study of selected developed and developing countries. "The role of exergy". *Energies*, *11*(10), 2668–2684.

Azhgaliyeva, D. (2019). Energy storage and renewable energy deployment: Empirical evidence from OECD countries. *Energy Procedia*, *158*, 3647–3651.

Azhgaliyeva, D., Kapoor, A., & Liu, Y. (2020). Green bonds for financing renewable energy and energy efficiency in South-East Asia: A review of policies. *Journal of Sustainable Finance & Investment*, *10*(2), 113–140.

Bhargave, H., & Tandon, D. (2022). A survey study impact of mergers on Indian banking industry. *ECS Transactions*, *107*(1), 8769–8776.

Bozkurt, C., & Yusuf, A. K. A. N. (2014). Economic growth, CO_2 emissions and energy consumption: The Turkish case. *International Journal of Energy Economics and Policy*, *4*(3), 484–494.

Brożyna, J., Mentel, G., & Szetela, B. (2017). Renewable energy and economic development in the European Union. *Acta Polytechnica Hungarica*, *14*(7), 11–34.

Chen, Y., & Ma, Y. (2021). Does green investment improve energy firm performance? *Energy Policy*, *153*(1), 112252–112263.

Cunha, J., Nunes, M. L., & Lima, F. (2018). Discerning the factors explaining the change in energy efficiency. *Environment, Development and Sustainability*, *20*, 163–179.

Dabyltayeva, N., & Rakhymzhan, G. (2019). The green economy development path: Overview of economic policy priorities. *Journal of Security & Sustainability Issues*, *8*(4), 643–651.

Dalevska, N., Khobta, V., Kwilinski, A., & Kravchenko, S. (2019). A model for estimating social and economic indicators of sustainable development. *Entrepreneurship and Sustainability Issues*, *6*(4), 1839.

David, D., & Venkatachalam, A. (2018). *A comparative study on the role of public-private partnerships and green investment banks in boosting low-carbon investments (No. 870)*. ADBI Working Paper.

Davidson, J. (2000). *Econometric Theory*. Wiley-Blackwell.

Eyraud, L., Clements, B., & Wane, A. (2013). Green investment: Trends and determinants. *Energy Policy*, *60*, 852–865.

Forbes India. (2023). *The top 10 largest economies in the world in 2024*. Retrieved December 10, 2023, from https://www.forbesindia.com/article/explainers/top-10-largest-economies-in-the-world/86159/1

Furkan, H. B., Rakibul Hasan, K. M., & Uddin, M. J. (2023). Greenhouse gas emission, GDP, tertiary education, and rule of law: A comparative study between high-income and lower-middle income countries. *Heliyon*, *9*(6), e16265.

Fuss, S., Canadell, J. G., Peters, G. P., Tavoni, M., Andrew, R. M., Ciais, P., & Yamagata, Y. (2014). Betting on negative emissions. *Nature Climate Change*, *4*(10), 850–853.

Gao, B., Ozturk, I., & Ullah, S. (2022). A new framework to the green economy: Asymmetric role of public–private partnership investment on environment in selected Asian economies. *Economic Research-Ekonomska Istraživanja*, *36*(1), 1960–1971.

Griscom, B. W., Adams, J., Ellis, P. W., Houghton, R. A., Lomax, G., Miteva, D. A., Schlesinger, W. S., Shoch, D., Siikamäki, J. V., Smith, P., Woodbury, P., Zganjar, C., Blackman, A., Campari, J., Conant, R. T., Delgado, C., Elias, P., Gopalakrishna, T., Hamsik, M. R., … Fargione, J. (2017). Natural climate solutions. *Proceedings of the National Academy of Sciences of the United States of America*, *114*, 11645–11650.

Hamit-Haggar, M. (2012). Greenhouse gas emissions, energy consumption and economic growth: A panel cointegration analysis from Canadian industrial sector perspective. *Energy Economics*, *34*(1), 358–364.

Hickel, J., & Kallis, G. (2020). Is green growth possible? *New Political Economy*, *25*(4), 469–486.

Huang, Y. M., Xue, L., & Khan, Z. (2021). What abates carbon emissions in China: Examining the impact of renewable energy and green investment. *Sustainable Development*, *29*, 823–834.

IMF. (2011). *IMF annual report 2011*. https://www.imf.org/external/pubs/ft/ar/2011/eng/

IPCC. (2014). *Climate change 2014, synthesis report*. IPCC. Retrieved June 17, 2019, from http://www.ipcc.ch/pdf/assessmentreport/ar5/syr/SYR_AR5_FINAL_full_wcover.pdf

IPCC. (2018). *Global Warming of 1.5°C*. Retrieved December 10, 2023, from https://www.ipcc.ch/sr15/

Jackson, T., & Victor, P. A. (2016). Does slow growth lead to rising inequality? Some theoretical reflections and numerical simulations. *Ecological Economics*, *121*(C), 206–219.

Johansen, S. (1991). Estimation and hypothesis testing of cointegration vectors in Gaussian vector autoregressive models. *Econometrica*, *59*(6), 1551–1580.

Kaur, A., & Tanwar, A. (2024). Adoption potential and challenges of artificial intelligence in banking. In S. Taneja (Ed.), *Sustainable investments in green finance* (pp. 271–293). IGI Global.

Kaur, A., Tanwar, A., Kaur, H., & Singh, J. (2023). A study on linkage between global warming indicators and climate change expenditure. *IOP Conference Series: Earth and Environmental Science*, *1110*(1), 12059–12077.

Lagarde, C., & Gaspar, V. (2019). *Getting real on meeting Paris climate change commitments* [IMF Blog]. Retrieved November 25, 2023, from https://www.imf.org/en/Blogs/Articles/2019/05/03/blog-getting-real-on-meeting-paris-climate-change-commitments

Lapinskiene, G., Peleckis, K., & Slavinskaite, N. (2017). Energy consumption, economic growth and greenhouse gas emissions in the European Union countries. *Journal of Business Economics and Management*, *18*(6), 1082–1097.

Lei, W., Ozturk, I., Muhammad, H., & Ullah, S. (2022). On the asymmetric effects of financial deepening on renewable and non-renewable energy consumption: Insights from China. *Economic Research-Ekonomska Istraživanja*, *35*(1), 3961–3978.

Li, X., & Ullah, S. (2022). Caring for the environment: How CO_2 emissions respond to human capital in BRICS economies? *Environmental Science and Pollution Research*, *29*(12), 18036–18046.

Liu, D., Guo, X., & Xiao, B. (2019). What causes growth of global greenhouse gas emissions? Evidence from 40 countries. *Science of the Total Environment*, *661*(3), 750–766.

Lu, W. C. (2017). Greenhouse gas emissions, energy consumption and economic growth: A panel cointegration analysis for 16 Asian countries. *International Journal of Environmental Research and Public Health*, *14*(11), 1436.

Mo, Y., Ullah, S., & Ozturk, I. (2023). Green investment and its influence on green growth in high polluted Asian economies: Do financial markets and institutions matter? *Economic Research-Ekonomska Istraživanja*, *36*(3), 1–11.

Noh, H. J. (2010). Financial strategy to accelerate innovation for green growth. *Korea capital market institute*, 2–3.

Ozturk, I., & Acaravci, A. (2010). CO_2 emissions, energy consumption and economic growth in Turkey. *Renewable and Sustainable Energy Reviews*, *14*(9), 3220–3225.

Ozturk, I., & Ullah, S. (2022). Does digital financial inclusion matter for economic growth and environmental sustainability in OBRI economies? An empirical analysis. *Resources, Conservation and Recycling*, *185*(3), 106489.

Puška, A., Hodžić, I., Štilić, A., & Murtič, S. (2024). Evaluating European Union countries on climate change management: A fuzzy MABAC approach to the climate change performance index. *Journal of Green Economy and Low-Carbon Development*, *3*(1), 15–25.

Sachs, J. D., Woo, W. T., Yoshino, N., & Taghizadeh-Hesary, F. (2019). Importance of green finance for achieving sustainable development goals and energy security. *Handbook of Green Finance: Energy Security and Sustainable Development*, *10*, 1–10.

Saidi, K., & Hammami, S. (2015). The impact of CO_2 emissions and economic growth on energy consumption in 58 countries. *Energy Reports*, *1*(C), 62–70.

Sharma, A., & Bajaj, S. (2023). 10 Impact of Sustainability and Green Finance on SMEs to Promote Green Growth. In K. Mehta & R. Sharma (Eds.), Sustainability, *Green Management, and Performance of SMEs* (pp.187–198). Walter de Gruyter GmBh.

Stangeland, A. (2007). A model for the CO_2 capture potential. *International Journal of Greenhouse Gas Control*, *1*(4), 418–429.

TWI2050. (2018). The world in 2050. *Transformations to achieve the sustainable development goals. Report prepared by e World in 2050 initiative*. International Institute for Applied Systems Analysis (IIASA). www.twi2050.org

Ullah, S., Ozturk, I., & Sohail, S. (2021). The asymmetric effects of fiscal and monetary policy instruments on Pakistan's environmental pollution. *Environmental Science and Pollution Research International*, *28*(6), 7450–7461.

UN. (2012). United Nations conference on sustainable development. *Rio+20*, *une*, 20–22.

Vasylieva, T, Lyulyov, O, Bilan, Y, & Streimikiene, D. (2019). Sustainable economic development and greenhouse gas emissions: The dynamic impact of renewable energy consumption, GDP, and corruption. *Energies*, *12*(17), 3289.

Wang, L., Su, C. W., Ali, S., & Chang, H. L. (2020). How China is fostering sustainable growth: The interplay of green investment and production-based emission. *Environmental Science and Pollution Research*, *27*(31), 39607–39618.

Wang, Y., & Zhi, Q. (2016). The role of green finance in environmental protection: Two aspects of market mechanism and policies. *Energy Procedia*, 1041(C), 311–316.

Webber, D. J., & Allen, D. O. (2010). Environmental Kuznets curves: Mess or meaning? *International Journal of Sustainable Development & World Ecology*, *17*(3), 198–207.

World Bank Data. (2023). *Data bank*. Retrieved November, 7, 2023, from http://databank.worldbank.org/

Yeoh, W. K., Ali, A., & Forney, C. F. (2014). Effects of ozone on major antioxidants and microbial populations of fresh-cut papaya. *Postharvest Biology and Technology*, *89*, 56–58.

Yerpude, S, Sood, K, & Grima, S. (2023). Blockchain-augmented digital supply chain management: A way to sustainable business. *Journal of Risk and Financial Management*, *16*(1), 7.

CHAPTER 7

IMPACT OF GREEN BANKING PRACTICES ON THE ENVIRONMENTAL PERFORMANCE OF BANKS: THE MEDIATING ROLE OF GREEN FINANCING IN SRI LANKA

Narayanage Jayantha Dewasiri[a], Mawarala Vitharanage Probodika Hanshani[a], Mananage Shanika Hansini Rathnasiri[a] and Simon Grima[b]

[a]*Faculty of Management Studies, Sabaragamuwa University of Sri Lanka, Sri Lanka*
[b]*Faculty of Economics Management and Accountancy, University of Malta, Malta*

ABSTRACT

Purpose: *This chapter examines the effect of green banking practices (GBPs) on environmental performance (EP), specifically focussing on the Sri Lankan banking industry. Additionally, the study explores the mediating impact of green finance in the association between GBPs and the EP of banks listed in the Colombo Stock Exchange in Sri Lanka.*

Methodology: *The survey included 233 banking employees from Sri Lanka, and data for this study were collected via questionnaires. The formulated hypotheses were tested employing a regression analysis.*

Sustainability Development through Green Economics
Contemporary Studies in Economic and Financial Analysis, Volume 114, 107–120

ISSN: 1569-3759/doi:10.1108/S1569-375920240000114007

Findings: *GBPs such as employee, customer, operation, and policy-related practices significantly predicted the banks' EP. Furthermore, the study highlights that green finance partially mediates the relationship between GBPs and banks' EP in Sri Lanka.*

Implications of the study: *The study's results indicate that banks should prioritise integrating GBPs in their organisations to enhance environmental and overall performance. Moreover, strategically utilising green financing techniques might be a substantial channel for banks to further strengthen their ecological dedication and influence.*

Originality: *This is the first study to investigate the impact of GBPs on banks' EP with the mediating effect of green finance in the Sri Lankan context.*

Keywords: Banks; green banking practices; environmental performance; employee-related practices; customer-related practices; green financing; Sri Lanka

JEL Codes: F64; F65; G21; G22; G28; Q1; Q56

1. INTRODUCTION

Green banking refers to a broad range of activities and policies to ensure the sustainability of banks in terms of the economy, environment, and society. The environment holds significant importance for both ethical banks and numerous conventional banks seeking to enhance their moral image or believe that implementing environmentally sustainable practices will benefit them (Mahale & Hebbar, 2023). According to banking experts, Biswas (2011) defines 'green banking' as a banking approach encompassing sustainability, ethical lending, conservation, and energy efficiency.

The advancement of green initiatives significantly contributes to environmental sustainability by effectively reducing carbon emissions (Jain et al., 2023; Jayarathne et al., 2023; Jayawardena et al., 2023; Muthusamy et al., 2023; Sun et al., 2023). The Sri Lankan banking industry has just begun implementing the concepts of 'environmental sustainability' and 'sustainable banking'. The regulatory authority overseeing the banking sector in the country is the Central Bank of Sri Lanka (CBSL). The banking system in Sri Lanka comprises 24 licenced commercial banks and six licenced specialised banks (Dewasiri, Pigera, et al., 2023). A commercial bank is a financial organisation that accepts deposits, provides investment services (such as certificates of deposit and savings accounts), offers various loan choices, and administers checking accounts, among other activities (Abutabenjeh & Jaradat, 2018; Dewasiri, Karunarathna, et al., 2023). As pioneers in adopting the 'green banking' notion, these organisations have prompted Sri Lanka's banking sector to prioritise environmental sustainability. Consequently, the industry is actively implementing measures to provide eco-friendly products and services by embracing the 'going green' ideology (Shameem & Haleem, 2021).

There is a lack of research and information on the association between GBP, the ecological performance of the banks, and green finance in Sri Lanka. It is crucial to study how green banking activities affect EP and whether green financing can mediate this association. Hence, this chapter investigates the impact of GBPs in the banking industry, specifically how these practices impact a bank's EP. The critical concern in this scenario is the extent of commercial impact on ecological performance. The effect of an organisation on the natural environment can be assessed through various indicators such as the use of eco-friendly products, implementation of paperless document flow, promotion of green products, reducing carbon emissions, improving energy-saving operations and equipment, and engaging in eco-oriented sponsorship and charity initiatives (Rana et al., 2022; Sharma & Choubey, 2022).

This study assesses GBP's impact on EP in the Sri Lankan banking industry. It also investigates the mediating effect of green financing. The findings of this study will provide a critical review of whether these GBPs influence the banks' ecological performance.

2. LITERATURE REVIEW

This section highlights different concepts that have been employed as the theoretical basis for the investigation. The study's theoretical implications primarily contribute to the existing knowledge on green banking, such as the 'Equator Principle' and other related theories. The Equator Principle, designed to assess, identify, and handle social and environmental risks in project financing, applies to examining green banking. The banking institutions have adopted the GBPs to mitigate ecological problems by conserving limited resources (Conley & Williams, 2011; Pareek et al., 2022).

A study by Lalon (2015) discovered that most private and foreign banks in Bangladesh have implemented GBPs, unlike state-owned commercial and specialised development banks. Implementing GBPs, such as reducing paper consumption, has been demonstrated to improve brand recognition and increase stakeholders' understanding of environmental concerns. Examples include solar technology, biogas, effluent treatment plants, hybrid Hoffman kilns, and other environmentally friendly solutions. Conversely, a study in China highlights the importance of sustainable GBPs in the banking industry and financial sector. The study emphasises that globalisation and the rise of emerging economies have made it imperative for banks to prioritise environmental and ecological considerations in their lending principles, including authorised investments in environmental management practices to promote sustainable development (Weber, 2016). Qi et al. (2014) discovered an association between ecological and financial performance in China.

A study on green finance reveals how several forms of green finance, including environmental, economic, and social aspects, enhance corporate social responsibility (CSR) in multiple ways. Wang et al. (2022) recommended that the banking industry allocate additional cash to improve their support for CSR attributes. Akomea-Frimpong et al. (2022) revealed that banking institutions' primary green finance services include green securities, insurance, investments, lending, and infrastructural bonds. The study elucidates key determinants impacting banks' green financing practices, including interest rates, ecological and climate change policies, social integration and justice, and banking regulations. The increasing adoption of the green transition in rich and emerging nations relies on green finance (Wang et al., 2021).

Desalegn and Tangl (2022) identified several key factors contributing to the green financing gap. These include insufficient funding, inadequate selection and management of green projects, the challenge of balancing risk and return tradeoffs, and a scarcity of expertise in assessing and evaluating the risks associated with green initiatives. Specifically, it has been observed that the primary hindrance to enhancing green financing is regulatory apprehensions. Moreover, Taneja and Özen (2023) found that the bank's environmental support strategies and policies substantially influence its ecological performance. The study's findings recommend that banks endorse sustainable environmental technologies, which are crucial for enhancing their performance and reputation among clients.

Fernando et al. (2023) highlighted that GBPs in Sri Lanka is in its early adoption. Most banks use green banking to improve their brand image and differentiate their products and services to stay competitive. Additionally, it calls for banks to adopt more environmentally sound ideas to their day-to-day operations, loan choices, and investment decisions. In addition, it involves instructing employees and customers about the advantages of green banking, enabling banks to enhance their environmental impact and build enduring corporate principles actively.

Researchers have extensively studied GBPs, their ramifications, and the banks' ecological performance and green financing worldwide and within individual countries. Conversely, numerous research studies analysed the various aspects of GBPs. However, limited empirical studies have examined the interconnected association between GBPs and banks' ecological performance. No prior research was conducted to explore the association between GBPs and the banks' ecological performance, explicitly considering the mediating impact of green finance from a national viewpoint. Hence, it is imperative to conduct a comprehensive analysis to examine the connotation between GBPs and banks' ecological performance, specifically in Sri Lanka. Therefore, this chapter addresses the existing empirical void in the literature by generating novel insights that contribute to the knowledge base of the country and the global community.

2.1. Development of Hypotheses

Many banks have adopted green banking methods as a strategic reaction to address the escalating environmental problems caused by a significant rise in carbon emissions (Khairunnessa et al., 2021). Banks that implemented environmentally friendly policies, such as engaging in sustainable lending and investing in renewable energy projects, observed decreased environmental risks associated with their portfolios. Furthermore, these banks demonstrated superior EP, as indicated by their diminished carbon footprint and compliance with environmental legislation. Integrating environmentally sustainable practices into banking operations not only helps to reduce environmental risks but also improves the overall ecological performance of banks (Asim Ali Bukhari et al., 2019).

Moreover, GBPs can enhance reputational advantages, appealing to investors and customers prioritising environmental sustainability. Banks that actively participate in environmentally friendly activities may attract favourable attention and support from stakeholders, which could result in higher investments and deposits. Furthermore, it has been observed that banks that incorporate environmental criteria into their lending and investment choices are inclined to allocate resources towards initiatives that have lesser ecological consequences, thus promoting a more sustainable economy (Scholtens & Kang, 2013). Therefore, the present study suggests that GBPs can benefit the banks' ecological performance.

H_1. GBPs significantly impact banks' EP.

Zhang et al. (2022) analysed the influence of GBPs on the banks' ecological performance. The study explored the fact that banks practising green banking demonstrated a higher ecological performance. Accordingly, green finance sources, such as investments in renewable energy projects and environmentally friendly activities, significantly influenced the connection between GBPs and banks' ecological performance. The results emphasise the crucial significance of green sources of financing in determining how GBPs lead to enhanced EP for banks. This research supports the idea that the sources of green funding mediate the connection between GBPs and banks' ecological performance.

H_2. The connection between GBPs and banks' EP is mediated by green financing.

3. METHODOLOGY

The study utilised a deductive research strategy, which aligned with the quantitative aspect of the examination. The study used an explanatory survey research design to investigate causal relationships, specifically examining the association between GBPs and banks' EP (Dewasiri et al., 2018). The primary data were obtained through a self-administered questionnaire circulated among banking personnel in Sri Lanka. The questionnaire included sections on demographic information, GBPs, banks' EP, and the mediating factor of green finance. The researchers collected 233 completed questionnaires using a simple random sampling technique during the designated data collection timeframe: July to August 2023. Regression analyses were employed to examine hypotheses regarding the drivers of the ecological performance of banks and the mediating impact of green funding. Furthermore, hierarchical regression analysis was used to investigate the mediation effect of green finance on the existing relationship.

4. RESULTS AND DISCUSSION

First, researchers ensured the validity and reliability of the concepts before conducting the inferential analysis. Based on the findings in Table 7.1, the composite reliability of all concepts ranged from 0.833 to 0.916, while the average variance extracted varied from 0.581 to 0.785. These results ensured the construct reliability of the study. Moreover, when the results exceed the required threshold of 0.7 for Cronbach's alpha, it signifies a high level of reliability in the construct (Hair et al., 2014). Alternatively, reliability levels that are considered acceptable are stated explicitly, as Cronbach's alpha values (CAV) are between 0.6 and 0.7 (Hajjar, 2018). CAVs for each construct in the study, as presented in Table 7.1, range from 0.690 to 0.863, showing that the multi-scale items are reliable and significantly contribute to the conceptualisation of the respective constructs. These CAV suggest that the study's reliability statistics are acceptable. Further, the composite reliability values ensured the internal consistency of the measurement items.

The Kaiser–Meyer–Olkin (KMO) test is employed to assess the sufficiency of the current sample. At the same time, Bartlett's test of sphericity (BTS) is utilised to measure the strength of the association between the study variables. All variables in the study exhibit KMO coefficients greater than 0.5, as evidenced by Table 7.2. Furthermore, none of the significant values of the variable exceeded 0.05. Instead,

Table 7.1. Reliability of the Measurement Properties.

Construct	No. of Items	Composite Reliability	Average Variance Extracted	Cronbach's Alpha
Bank's employee-related practices	3	0.833	0.627	0.690
Bank's operation-related practices	3	0.916	0.785	0.863
Bank's customer-related practices	4	0.847	0.581	0.760
Bank's policy-related practices	4	0.858	0.603	0.779
Bank's EP	4	0.881	0.651	0.818
Green financing	4	0.904	0.703	0.858

Source: Authors' compilation based on the SPSS output.

Table 7.2. Results of the KMO and BTS Tests.

Construct	KMO	BTS (Sig. Value)
Bank's employee-related practices	0.609	0.000
Bank's operation related practices	0.705	0.000
Bank's customer-related practices	0.741	0.000
Bank's policy related practices	0.778	0.000
Banks' EP	0.780	0.000

Source: Authors' compilation based on the SPSS output.

all significant values in this study were precisely 0.000, indicating strong correlations between the variables and that the sampling adequacy is considerable, allowing us to proceed with the investigation (Puška et al., 2024; Yerpude et al., 2022).

Furthermore, the item factor loading values on a high-quality measurement indicator must exceed 0.5 to ensure the validity of the measurement properties (Black & Babin, 2019). The factor loadings of 22 items are presented in Table 7.3. The indicator loadings in this investigation varied from 0.664 to 0.919. Hence, the study's construct validity was statistically ensured, as each indicator's factor loading exceeded 0.5.

Regression analysis involves a model that must satisfy certain multivariate assumptions, including linearity, statistical independence, homoscedasticity, normality, and multicollinearity (Shrestha, 2020). The Normal probability plots ensured a linear association between the concepts examined in this study.[1] The Durbin–Watson value obtained in the present investigation was 2.114. Thus, it may be inferred that the residuals do not display statistically significant autocorrelation, thereby ensuring their statistical independence. Parametric statistical tests rely on the fundamental assumption of homoscedasticity, which means that the variances are identical across the group. It is expected that the faults will continuously fluctuate. The residuals scatterplot is a valuable tool for assessing homoscedasticity. Fig. 7.1 demonstrates that the residual plots in this investigation do not exhibit any curved component and instead show a random pattern, ensuring homoscedasticity.

Table 7.3. Summary of Factor Loadings.

Construct	Item	Factor Loading
Bank's employee-related practices	BERP1	0.832
	BERP2	0.866
	BERP3	0.664
Bank's operation related practices	BORP1	0.839
	BORP2	0.919
	BORP3	0.899
Bank's customer-related practices	BCRP1	0.790
	BCRP2	0.769
	BCRP3	0.765
	BCRP4	0.725
Bank's policy related practices	BPRP1	0.791
	BPRP2	0.789
	BPRP3	0.759
	BPRP4	0.767
Banks' EP	BEP1	0.869
	BEP2	0.842
	BEP3	0.753
	BEP4	0.758
Green financing	GF1	0.839
	GF2	0.834
	GF3	0.844
	GF4	0.837

Source: Authors' compilation based on the SPSS output.

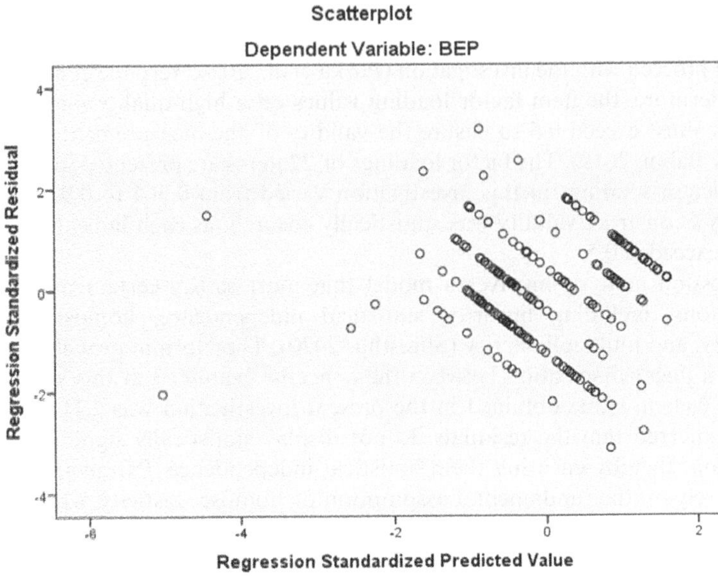

Fig. 7.1. Scatterplot. *Source*: Authors' compilation based on the SPSS output.

The data series in this investigation have a normal distribution, as evidenced by the Kolmogorov–Smirnov test.[2] The significant values for all concepts are more critical than 0.05. Furthermore, the skewness and kurtosis test outcomes lie between −1 and +1. Therefore, the study's dependent and independent variables exhibit a data set that follows a normal distribution.

Multicollinearity is another significant problem when a regression model correlates with two or more independent variables (Shrestha, 2020). Hence, detecting and resolving the multicollinearity issue is crucial before commencing the data modelling process. The method to locate it involves examining each independent variable's variance inflation factor (VIF) and tolerance. According to Table 7.4, all the independent variables in this investigation have tolerances greater than 0.1 and VIF values lower than ten, ensuring no multicollinearity issue.

We used a multiple linear regression analysis to examine the impact of GBPs on banks' ecological performance. In this study, the independent variable was defined as 'GBPs', which represents the constructs' composite value about the environmentally friendly practices of banks in Sri Lanka. Conversely, the

Table 7.4. Multicollinearity of the Constructs.

Construct	Tolerance Level	VIF
Banks' employee-related practices	0.550	1.820
Banks' operation-related practices	0.463	2.159
Banks' customer-related practices	0.338	2.954
Banks' policy-related practices	0.486	2.057

Source: Authors' compilation based on the SPSS output.

dependent variable was defined as the 'banks' EP'. GBPs encompass four measurements: employee-related, operation-related, customer-related, and policy-related practices. Adjusted R^2 of the regression represents the variance of the EP that the independent variables can explain. The results indicate that GBPs may explain 59.2% (Adjusted $R^2 = 0.592$) of the banks' EP variation. In other words, the created model in the current study accounts for 59.2% of the total variability of the EP. The ANOVA table is utilised to ascertain whether the entire model is a statistically significant predictor of the result variable. The results indicated that the calculated p-value is lower than the usual threshold of 0.05, ensuring the regression model's predictability in explaining the dependent variable.

The coefficients table displays the specific contribution of each predictor variable to the overall model. The coefficient Table 7.5 represents the outcome of the multiple linear regression. The dimensions of GBPs, including bank staff practices, bank operation practices, policy practices, and bank customer practices, are all significant in this model at the significance level of 0.05. All coefficients of GBPs have substantial values, positively impacting banks' EP. In addition, according to Table 7.5, the coefficient for the bank's employee-related practices dimension of green banking is 0.333, indicating that the bank's employee-related practices have the highest effect on the banks' EP in Sri Lanka.

This chapter investigates the mediating impact of green finance on the association between GBPs and banks' ecological performance. Hierarchical regression analysis was employed to analyse the mediation effect of green financing (Baron & Kenny, 1986).

Table 7.6 displays the outcomes of the mediation impact analysis of green financing obtained by hierarchical regression analysis. Accordingly, two stages of hierarchical regression analysis were carried out in line with two causal pathways that contribute to the outcome variable of banks' EP. The first pathway examines the influence of GBPs as a predictor (Path 1). In contrast, the second pathway investigates the impact of green financing as a mediator, including the interaction between these two factors (Path 2). Support for the mediator hypothesis is shown if the interaction is deemed substantial.

Our findings indicate that GBPs and green financing have a statistically significant impact, as their p-values were below the significance level of 0.05. The independent variables' coefficients decrease from 0.846 to 0.620 while enhancing the

Table 7.5. Coefficients of the Regression Model.

	Model	Unstandardised Coefficients		Standardised Coefficients	*T*	Sig.
		B	Std. Error	Beta		
1	(Constant)	0.589	0.210		2.802	0.006
	BERP	0.333	0.058	0.330	5.781	0.000
	BORP	0.123	0.053	0.145	2.333	0.021
	BCRP	0.241	0.070	0.251	3.448	0.001
	BPRP	0.172	0.059	0.177	2.925	0.004

Source: Authors' compilation based on the SPSS output.

Table 7.6. Results of the Hierarchical Regression Analysis.

Model		Unstandardised coefficients		Sig
		B	Std. Error	
1	(Constant)	0.670	0.208	0.001
	GBP	0.846	0.047	0.000
2	(Constant)	0.691	0.202	0.001
	GBP	0.620	0.075	0.000
	GF	0.223	0.059	0.000

Source: Authors' compilation based on the SPSS output.

adjusted R^2 in the second model. Thus, it may be inferred that green finance partially mediates the connection between GBPs and banks' ecological performance.

5. DISCUSSION

This chapter has elucidated the association between GBPS and the ecological performance of banks while focussing on the mediator impact of green financing. This work adds value to the current literature on sustainable banking and environmental accountability. The study found evidence supporting the hypothesised connection between GBPs and the banks' ecological performance, indicating a strong positive association. The substantial association can be attributed to the banking institutions' heightened concern for the environment, prompted by the ongoing environmental deterioration caused by human and organisational activity.

The findings demonstrate that the bank's employee-related, operation-related, customer-related, and policy-related practices positively and significantly impact the bank's ecological performance. In addition, our study found evidence of a partial mediation of green finance on the relationship between GBPs and banks' ecological performance, as determined using hierarchical regression analysis.

Assessing banks' EP has recently become a significant area, mainly due to the increasing importance of sustainability and environmental issues. Several studies have examined the influence of ecological practices in the banking industry on the overall EP. Some studies have focussed on green financing, sustainable investments, and CSR activities (Weber, 2016).

A significant distinguishing factor of this chapter is its investigation of the intermediary impact of green finance. Our study recognises the significance of financial operations and the distribution of funds towards eco-friendly projects as a mediator that impacts the connection between GBP and banks' EP. This contribution is significant because it goes beyond previous studies showing a favourable relationship between GBP and ecological performance. Instead, this research focusses on the precise financial routes that could potentially strengthen this connection. Furthermore, this study discovered that green finance mediates the relationship between GBPS and the banks' ecological performance (Zhang et al., 2022).

Nevertheless, while examining the current body of research, multiple studies have already confirmed a favourable relationship between GBPs and ecological performance. A recent study by Khan et al. (2020) emphasised that incorporating environmentally friendly practices into banking operations favours ecological performance, consistent with the present study's findings. Similarly, Aslam and Jawaid (2023) researched the significance of green banking adoption practices, commonly integrated into green banking, in enhancing the ecological performance of the banking industry in Pakistan. Similarly to our findings, Chen et al. (2022) also discovered that employee, operation, and policy-related practices significantly impact the ecological performance of Bangladeshi banks. However, contrary to our findings, Chen et al. (2022) showcase that customer-related practices do not affect the bank's EP.

Taneja and Özen (2023) focussed on the direct association between GBPs and ecological performance in India. However, our study focussed on the mediating role of green finance following Zhang et al.'s (2022) study, which discovered a mediating impact of green finance on the relationship between GBPs and banks' performance in Bangladesh. However, our study's noteworthy contribution lies in its emphasis on Sri Lanka and green financing as a mediator between GBPs and particularly ecological performance. This new study further clarifies the potential role of allocating funds to ecologically beneficial initiatives as a significant catalyst for enhancing banks' EP, building upon previous research that has already acknowledged the effect of green practices. The study highlights the importance of recognising this intermediary function, drawing attention to a more focussed strategy for banks to enhance their ecological performance.

6. CONCLUSIONS OF THE STUDY

This study is the first investigation in Sri Lanka that examines the effect of GBPs on the banks' ecological performance while considering the mediating role of green finance in the relationship between GBPs and banks' ecological performance. Our study concludes that the bank's employee-related, operation-related, customer-related, and policy-related practices positively affect the bank's EP. Further, this study concludes that green finance partially mediates the relationship between GBPs and banks' EP in Sri Lanka. In conclusion, introducing this intermediary element may stimulate additional research to investigate more complex financial mechanisms in green banking and their influence on environmental sustainability in the banking industry.

7. IMPLICATIONS OF THE STUDY

The study offers insight into the banking institutions that sustain their GBPs and those organisations' ability to cultivate and enhance such practices. The study's practical ramifications are evident in the immediate and extended periods since multiple stakeholders in the banking institutions have incorporated them. The study's findings indicate a notable and favourable connection between the implementation of GBPs and banks' ecological performance. Consequently, our study recommends that policymakers in the banking industry establish effective rules that prioritise GBPs, as they are regarded as a means to achieve environmental sustainability. Moreover, the use and implementation of green financing might be employed to enhance the banking industry. Furthermore, climate change is projected to endure indefinitely due to the escalating carbon footprint and environmental deterioration. Policymakers should establish educational programmes to foster ecological banking practices and mitigate the negative impact of banking activities on carbon emissions.

The study suggests that prioritising GBPs in day-to-day operations can enhance the EP of banks in Sri Lanka. It is recommended that banking institutions facilitate adopting these practices by providing convenience for their staff. Furthermore, to increase knowledge and enhance user-friendliness, banking institutions could strategise and implement employee and customer awareness initiatives and promotional activities to educate the public about their environmentally friendly banking practices. Moreover, given that the study demonstrates a substantial correlation between GBPs and the banks' EP, banking institutions must prioritise their staff members, who are responsible for implementing and upholding these policies. The results of this study could assist the strategists of banking organisations in improving their efforts towards green banking. Consequently, they can develop efficient and successful strategies promoting the bank's adoption of environmentally friendly banking practices.

Nevertheless, the banking institutions that have not yet implemented GBPs will benefit significantly from the study's findings. Consequently, they will have the capacity to formulate and execute appropriate strategic initiatives to adopt environmentally friendly banking practices.

The findings suggest that the government, management, shareholders, and other stakeholders of banking institutions such as the Central Bank of Sri Lanka formulate and execute pragmatic policies focussing on GBPs and green finance. Furthermore, anyone interested in this subject matter, such as readers and researchers, may find the present study valuable and informative.

NOTES

1. The results of the normal-probability plots are available on request.
2. The results of the Kolmogorov–Smirnov test are available on request.

REFERENCES

Abutabenjeh, S., & Jaradat, R. (2018). Clarification of research design, research methods, and research methodology: A guide for public administration researchers and practitioners. *Teaching Public Administration*, *36*(3), 237–258.

Akomea-Frimpong, I., Adeabah, D., Ofosu, D., & Tenakwah, E. J. (2022). A review of studies on green finance of banks, research gaps and future directions. *Journal of Sustainable Finance & Investment*, *12*(4), 1241–1264.

Asim Ali Bukhari, S., Hashim, F., & Amran, A. (2019). Determinants of green banking adoption: A theoretical framework. *KnE Social Sciences*, *3*(22), 1–14. https://doi.org/10.18502/kss.v3i22.50

Aslam, W., & Jawaid, S. T. (2023). Green banking adoption practices: Improving environmental, financial, and operational performance. *International Journal of Ethics and Systems*, *39*(4), 820–840.

Baron, R. M., & Kenny, D. A. (1986). The moderator–mediator variable distinction in social psychological research: Conceptual, strategic, and statistical considerations. *Journal of Personality and Social Psychology*, *51*(6), 1173.

Biswas, N. (2011). Sustainable green banking approach: The need of the hour. *Business Spectrum*, *1*(1), 32–38.

Black, W., & Babin, B. J. (2019). Multivariate data analysis: Its approach, evolution, and impact. In B. J. Babin & M. Sarstedt (Eds.), *The great facilitator: Reflections on the contributions of Joseph F. Hair, Jr. to marketing and business research* (pp. 121–130). Springer International Publishing.

Chen, J., Siddik, A. B., Zheng, G. W., Masukujjaman, M., & Bekhzod, S. (2022). The effect of green banking practices on banks' environmental performance and green financing: An empirical study. *Energies*, *15*(4), 1292.

Conley, J. M., & Williams, C. A. (2011). Global banks as global sustainability regulators? The equator principles. *Law & Policy*, *33*(4), 542–575.

Desalegn, G., & Tangl, A. (2022). Enhancing green finance for inclusive green growth: A systematic approach. *Sustainability*, *14*(12), 7416.

Dewasiri, N. J., Karunarathna, K. S. S. N., Rathnasiri, M. S. H., Sood, K., & Saini, A. (2023), The role of health-related perceptions on mobile payment adoption: Evidence from the mobile banking industry in Sri Lanka. In K. Sood, B. Balusamy, & S. Grima, (Eds.), *Digital transformation, strategic resilience, cyber security and risk management* (Contemporary Studies in Economic and Financial Analysis, Vol. 111C, pp. 67–86). Emerald Publishing Limited. https://doi.org/10.1108/S1569-37592023000111C004

Dewasiri, N. J., Pigera, A. K. M., Karunarathne, K. S. S. N., & Rathnasiri, M. S. H. (2023), Financial services employee engagement and attitude toward artificial intelligence: Evidence from Sri Lanka, In A. Saini, & V. Garg, (Eds.). *Transformation for sustainable business and management practices: Exploring the spectrum of industry 5.0* (pp. 231–245). Emerald Publishing Limited. https://doi.org/10.1108/978-1-80262-277-520231017

Dewasiri, N. J., Weerakoon, Y. K. B., & Azeez, A. A. (2018). Mixed methods in finance research: The rationale and research designs. *International Journal of Qualitative Methods*, *17*(1), 1–17.

Fernando, K. D. U. D., Tharanga, T. M. N., Dewasiri, N. J., Sood, K., Grima, S., & Thalassinos, E. (2023). Insurance penetration and institutional spillover on economic growth: A dynamic spatial econometric approach on the Asian and Europe region. *Journal of Risk and Financial Management*, *16*(8), 1–21.

Hair, J. F., Black, W. C., Babin, B. J., & Anderson, R. E. (2014). *Multivariate data analysis: Pearson new international edition, 1*(2). Pearson Education Limited.

Hajjar, S. T. (2018). Statistical analysis: Internal consistency reliability and construct validity. *International Journal of Quantitative and Qualitative Research Methods*, *6*(1), 27–38.

Jain, R., Kumar, S., Sood, K., Grima, S., & Rupeika-Apoga, R. (2023). A systematic literature review of the risk landscape in fintech. *Risks*, *11*(2), 1–16.

Jayarathne, P. G. S. A., Chathuranga, B. T. K., Dewasiri, N. J., & Rana, S. (2023). Motives of mobile payment adoption during COVID-19 pandemic in Sri Lanka: A holistic approach of both customers' and retailers' perspectives. *South Asian Journal of Marketing*, *4*(1), 51–73. https://doi.org/10.1108/SAJM-03-2022-0013

Jayawardena, N. S., Quach, S., Perera, C. H., Thaichon, P., & Dewasiri, N. J. (2023). Luxury marketing and sustainability in the South Asian context. In P. Thaichon & S. Quach (Eds.), *Luxury marketing, sustainability and technology* (pp. 1–14). Routledge.

Khairunnessa, F., Vazquez-Brust, D. A., & Yakovleva, N. (2021). A review of the recent developments of green banking in Bangladesh. *Sustainability*, *13*(4), 1904.

Khan, H. Z., Bose, S., & Johns, R. (2020). Regulatory influences on CSR practices within banks in an emerging economy: Do banks merely comply? *Critical Perspectives on Accounting*, *71*, 1–20.

Lalon, R. M. (2015). Green banking: Going green. *International Journal of Economics, Finance and Management Sciences*, *3*(1), 34–42.

Mahale, P., & Hebbar, C. (2023). Green banking awareness: A study with special reference to State Bank of India. *International Research Journal of Modernization in Engineering Technology and Science*, *5*(2), 14–17.

Muthusamy, V., Dewasiri, N. J., Lankanatha, K. M. R. C., Sood, K., & Grima, S. (2023), Financial soundness of general insurance industry in Sri Lanka: A CARAMELS approach, In S. Grima, E. Thalassinos, M. Cristea, M. Kadłubek, D. Maditinos, & L. Peiseniece, (Eds.). *Digital transformation, strategic resilience, cyber security and risk management* (Contemporary Studies in Economic and Financial Analysis, Vol. 111A, pp. 231–242). Emerald Publishing Limited. https://doi.org/10.1108/S1569-37592023000111A016

Pareek, T., Sood, K., & Grima, S. (2022). The impact of big data technology on the advancement of the insurance industry, In K. Sood, B. Balusamy, S. Grima, & P. Marano, (Eds.). *Big data analytics in the insurance market (emerald studies in finance, insurance, and risk management)* (pp. 221–239). Emerald Publishing Limited. https://doi.org/10.1108/978-1-80262-637-720221012

Puška, A., Hodžić, I., Štilić, A., & Murtič, S. (2024). Evaluating European Union countries on climate change management: A fuzzy MABAC approach to the climate change performance index. *Journal of Green Economy and Low-Carbon Development, 3*(1), 15–25.

Qi, G. Y., Zeng, S. X., Shi, J. J., Meng, X. H., Lin, H., & Yang, Q. X. (2014). Revisiting the relationship between environmental and financial performance in Chinese industry. *Journal of Environmental Management, 145*, 349–356.

Rana, S., Udunuwara, M., Dewasiri, N. J., Kashif, M., & Rathnasiri, M. S. H. (2022). Editorial: Is South Asia ready for the next universe – metaverse? Arguments and suggestions for further research. *South Asian Journal of Marketing, 3*(2), 77–81. https://doi.org/10.1108/SAJM-10-2022-141

Scholtens, B., & Kang, F. C. (2013). Corporate social responsibility and earnings management: Evidence from Asian economies. *Corporate Social Responsibility and Environmental Management, 20*(2), 95–112.

Shameem, A. L. M. A., & Haleem, A. (2021). A study on green banking practices in the banking industry: Sri Lankan context. *Journal of Contemporary Issues in Business and Government, 27*(1), 490–505.

Sharma, M., & Choubey, A. (2022). Green banking initiatives: A qualitative study on the Indian banking sector. *Environment, Development and Sustainability, 24*(1), 293–319.

Shrestha, N. (2020). Detecting multicollinearity in regression analysis. *American Journal of Applied Mathematics and Statistics, 8*(2), 39–42.

Sun, G., Li, G., Dilanchiev, A., & Kazimova, A. (2023). Promotion of green financing: Role of renewable energy and energy transition in China. *Renewable Energy, 210*, 769–775.

Taneja, S., & Özen, E. (2023). To analyse the relationship between a bank's green financing and environmental performance. *International Journal of Electronic Finance, 12*(2), 163–175.

Wang, C., Li, X. W., Wen, H. X., & Nie, P. Y. (2021). Order financing for promoting green transition. *Journal of Cleaner Production, 283*, 125415.

Wang, Z., Shahid, M. S., Binh An, N., Shahzad, M., & Abdul-Samad, Z. (2022). Does green finance facilitate firms in achieving corporate social responsibility goals? *Economic Research-Ekonomska Istraživanja, 35*(1), 5400–5419.

Weber, O. (2016). The impact of green banking guidelines on the sustainability performance of banks: The Chinese case. *CIGI Policy Brief, 79*, 1–8.

Yerpude, S., Sood, K., & Grima, S. (2022). Blockchain-augmented digital supply chain management: A way to sustainable business. *Journal of Risk and Financial Management, 16*(1), 7.

Zhang, X., Wang, Z., Zhong, X., Yang, S., & Siddik, A. B. (2022). Do green banking activities improve the banks' environmental performance? The mediating effect of green financing. *Sustainability, 14*(2), 989–998.

CHAPTER 8

GREEN HRM: REDESIGNING WORK AND GREEN JOB STRUCTURES FOR ORGANISATIONAL SUSTAINABILITY

Tanya Chouhan[a] and Arjita Singh[b]

[a]*Galgotias College of Engineering and Technology, Greater Noida, India*
[b]*Raj Kumar Goel Institute of Technology, Ghaziabad, India*

ABSTRACT

Purpose: *The study is focussed on redesigning work and green job structures for organisational sustainability. The contribution of this chapter is two-fold: HR practices can be redesigned to incorporate eco-friendly principles into job roles and explore green human resource management (HRM) as innovative approaches that organisations can adopt to promote environmental responsibility and sustainable practices within their workforce.*

Need of study: *The study on green HRM and job redesign is crucial for organisations to align operations with environmental sustainability. It addresses the need for practical guidelines and strategies for implementing sustainable practices. With increasing emphasis on corporate social responsibility and stakeholder demand, this study is essential for organisations to enhance their reputation, attract environmentally conscious talent, and positively impact society and the environment.*

Sustainability Development through Green Economics
Contemporary Studies in Economic and Financial Analysis, Volume 114, 121–133

ISSN: 1569-3759/doi:10.1108/S1569-375920240000114008

Methodology: *The chapter is conceptually oriented; the data utilised in this study will primarily rely on secondary sources.*

Findings: *The findings demonstrated that adopting green HRM practices can help businesses improve their environmental performance and employee satisfaction. These procedures also allow the organisation to remain sustainable, guaranteeing its long-term success.*

Practical implications: *Humans know that redesigned work and job structures in green HRM can allow staff members to learn new sustainability-related skills and knowledge, boosting their professional growth and future employability. Redesigning work structures and implementing green HRM practices can also increase employee pride and loyalty to the company by integrating them into a mission-driven, sustainability-focussed workforce.*

Keywords: HRM practices; sustainability; green HRM; organisation redesigning; job restructuring; organisational development; HRM initiatives

JEL Codes: M00; M20; M16; M14; M12

INTRODUCTION

Jabbour and de Sousa Jabbour (2016) emphasise how the 1990s saw an increase in the number of greening studies conducted in organisations, and they tie this increase to the expansion of EMS and, in particular, the introduction of ISO 14001. Since organisational greening studies have become more popular since the 1990s, it has become clear that implementing green practices in businesses requires the support of HR procedures, including performance reviews, training, and reward systems.

The foundation of green HRM is a multifaceted strategy that combines ideas and practices from the psychological, economic, sociological, and management disciplines. The broad structure of green HRM studies encompasses all issues about the adoption, understanding, and execution of HR practices that impact sustainability (Benevene & Buonomo, 2020).

Similarly, this study aims to explore the concept of green HRM and examine the redesign of work and job structures to enhance organisational sustainability.

In the current phase, there is a significant emphasis on adopting the concept of green business and implementing environmentally friendly practices worldwide. Green business refers to an approach where organisations strive to conduct their operations to minimise or eliminate adverse impacts on the environment.

This concept has gained prominence due to its pragmatic nature and the increasing global concern for sustainability. Organisations actively seek ways to align their practices with green principles and mitigate their environmental footprint.

Moreover, organisations increasingly recognise the importance of integrating environmental considerations into their strategies and operations. They are actively seeking opportunities to pursue sustainability initiatives and mitigate the impact of environmental degradation. As a result, a competitive landscape has emerged where organisations strive to adopt practices promoting environmental protection and sustainability. This shift in focus reflects a growing awareness of the need to address ecological concerns and embrace environmentally responsible practices to maintain market competitiveness.

Green HRM plays a significant role in reducing organisations' carbon footprint. By adopting environmentally friendly practices, such as reducing paper usage and implementing sustainable resource management strategies, organisations can contribute to a more sustainable future. Green HRM is a crucial strategy for organisations to align their operations with sustainability principles and ensure the responsible use of resources. Organisations can effectively contribute to environmental conservation and promote long-term sustainability by incorporating green practices into HRM processes. Green HRM ensures employees are informed and engaged in sustainable practices and initiatives. Various studies have revealed that business and non-business organisations have taken proactive measures to transform their operations and protect the environment from potential harm. These organisations consciously try to incorporate green practices into their strategies and promote sustainability as a core value.

Additionally, the concept of green business prioritises preserving environmental quality, acknowledging its critical role in preventing further harm to the planet. Extensive research has underscored the significance of this matter, revealing that green businesses actively formulate strategies and implement proactive measures to safeguard the Earth from hazardous and detrimental impacts. Consequently, green organisations are better equipped to address environmental challenges and establish improved physical settings that prioritise eco-friendliness without compromising profitability. To ensure the long-term sustainability of organisations, it is crucial to effectively utilise environmental resources while preserving the Earth's natural resources.

This can be achieved by adopting a green business strategy and implementing green HRM practices, which are instrumental in promoting sustainable environmental performance within the organisation. Recognising the interconnectedness of business operations with people, society, and the environment, it becomes imperative to conduct business in an environmentally responsible manner. Green HRM is pivotal in driving this transformation by implementing policies and practices that align with sustainable principles. By embracing green HRM, organisations can transition into eco-friendly entities and establish themselves as leaders in sustainable business practices. The time is ripe for organisations to prioritise and implement proper green HRM policies, thereby creating environmentally responsible organisations and fostering the development of sustainable businesses.

BACKGROUND AND RATIONALE

Environmental Responsibility in Organisations

Environmental sustainability has become a pressing concern for organisations worldwide. The detrimental impact of human activities on the environment, such as carbon emissions, deforestation, and pollution, has necessitated a shift towards more sustainable practices. Stakeholders, including customers, employees, investors, and regulatory bodies, increasingly demand that organisations operate environmentally responsibly. Failure to address these concerns can result in reputational damage, loss of market share, and legal repercussions. Consequently, organisations recognise the need to integrate sustainability into their core operations and strategic decision-making processes.

The Role of HRM in Promoting Sustainability

Traditionally focussed on managing human capital and supporting organisational goals, HRM significantly promotes sustainability within organisations. Green HRM involves adopting environmentally friendly approaches in HR processes to support and enhance sustainability initiatives. By incorporating sustainability principles into HR practices, organisations can align their workforce with environmental goals, nurture an environmentally conscious culture, and contribute to overall organisational sustainability.

Redesigning Work and Job Structures for Sustainability

One crucial aspect of green HRM is redesigning work and job structures to incorporate sustainable practices. Traditional job roles and work structures may need to adequately address organisations' environmental challenges. Organisations can integrate eco-friendly principles into job roles and responsibilities by reimagining work and job structures through a sustainability lens. This approach can encompass various aspects, such as incorporating green skills, promoting eco-innovation, and developing environmentally conscious competencies within employees.

This study aims to comprehensively understand green HRM, including its definition, principles, and role in promoting environmental responsibility within organisations. By examining the existing literature and case studies, this research seeks to identify critical components and best practices of green HRM. This study investigates how work and job structures can be redesigned to incorporate sustainable practices. By analysing successful examples and innovative approaches, the research will identify strategies for integrating environmental responsibilities into job roles, enhancing employee engagement, and fostering a green workforce. This study investigates how work and job structures can be redesigned to incorporate sustainable practices. By analysing successful examples and innovative approaches, the research will identify strategies for integrating environmental responsibilities into job roles, enhancing employee engagement, and fostering a green workforce.

LITERATURE REVIEW

Green HR practices encourage the green staffing process to promote green HR practices globally. It also transforms aspirations and good intentions into everyday behaviour and attitudes of the employees in the business organisation. Green staffing entailed hiring people with organisational sustainability, strong technical and managerial skills, and solid knowledge of environmental issues. This raised awareness among other employees and converted regular workers into green employees through training that improved morale and attitudes towards the sustainability of the organisation, individuals, the community, and the environment (Sharma & Gupta, 2015). By leveraging the skills and expertise of green HRM in organisational processes, change management, and culture stewardship, HRM can contribute to the development and implementation of sustainable business strategies throughout the entire organisation. Although green HRM is still in its nascent stages in India, this study outlines how green HRM and HR professionals can tap into a growing body of knowledge to assist them on their journey towards organisational sustainability (Das & Singh, 2016).

In a study conducted by Kaur (2011), the correlation between HR factors and employees' perceived environmental performance in different business organisations was investigated. The study's findings suggest that companies should engage in activities such as conducting energy audits, transitioning to paperless operations, recycling, and motivating their employees to participate in environmentally friendly initiatives, all of which contribute to organisational sustainability. Green HR is a valuable tool, as it can help reduce costs.

According to a study by Gill (2012), implementing green HR practices is expected to enhance employee well-being within the workplace. These practices improve the working environment, cater to the needs of an environmentally conscious workforce, and positively impact employee and organisational performance, aligning to achieve corporate sustainability.

Following the findings of Sharma and Gupta (2015), environment management plays a crucial role in training and development initiatives within green HRM. The focus should be on enhancing employees' skills, knowledge, attitudes, and behaviour related to environmental conservation and environmental initiatives. Training activities should encompass methods for conserving energy, minimising waste, fostering environmental awareness, and engaging employees in solving environmental issues.

By incorporating such training, employees' capacity to adopt proactive attitudes towards organisational sustainability is also expected to be enhanced, as Carter and Dresner (2001) suggested.

Daily and Huang (2001) stated that several factors are crucial in successfully implementing environmental management activities. These factors include the support of top management, environment training and development programmes, teamwork, empowerment of employees, and an effective reward system. For encouraging employee involvement and participation, one significant approach is to identify and foster eco-entrepreneurs within the organisation who possess a social or ecological orientation.

In Shafaei et al.'s (2020) research, the authors sought to shed light on the causes and effects of green HRM at both the organisational and individual levels. Additionally, it aimed to investigate how employing green HRM might benefit workers. It was found that green HRM favourably correlates with an organisation's environmental performance at the organisational level and that corporate environmental culture is strongly associated with green HRM. Green HRM favourably affects employees' job satisfaction individually and meaningful work is a potent mediating factor in this relationship.

In a study by Faisal (2023), the concept of green HRM was explored, encompassing a range of organisational policies, practices, and processes aimed at promoting environmentally friendly methods that benefit individuals, businesses, and the environment. The study involved a systematic review of empirical articles gathered from Scopus, analysing 31 studies published since 2010. The primary objective of this research was to identify various factors and measuring tools associated with green HRM, utilising the ability–motivation–opportunity theory and the review methodology. Several factors were identified: green recruitment and selection, green training and development, green compensation management, green performance management, green employee empowerment and participation, and green employee relations. The study sheds light on these factors and presents new opportunities for future research in the field. Additionally, it offers different perspectives and suggestions for future studies that can aid in integrating sustainability initiatives into the organisational agenda.

Jirawuttinunt and Limsuwan (2019) examined the relationship between green HRM practices, intellectual capital, and environmental performance. They identified four dimensions of green HRM: green recruitment and selection, green training and development, green compensation and rewards, and green performance management. The study findings demonstrate that these dimensions directly impact organisational performance. Furthermore, the results indicate that organisational performance is associated with green intellectual capital and environmental performance. The researchers also found that employee motivation is crucial in driving green organisational performance.

Saeed et al. (2018) conducted a study to investigate the influence of green HRM practices on employees' pro-environmental behaviour. The findings revealed a positive impact of green HRM practices on pro-environmental behaviour, with this relationship being mediated by pro-environmental psychological capital.

Similarly, Shen et al. (2018) found that perceived green HRM affects non-green employee workplace outcomes through motivational, social, and psychological processes. The study also highlighted the moderating effect of perceived organisational support on the relationship between green HRM and employee workplace outcomes.

Chaudhary (2019) discovered that green HRM significantly predicts task-related and voluntary employee green behaviours. The study emphasises the vital role of HRM in achieving environmental sustainability and stresses the importance of incorporating sustainability dimensions into HR practices.

Moreover, Yuriev and Sierra-Baron (2020) concentrated on the antecedent beliefs that underlie green workplace practices across cultural boundaries. Semi-directed interviews were performed with non-academic staff members of Canadian and Colombian universities to find out how they felt about two behaviours being studied: taking an alternate route to school and bringing up environmental suggestions at work. The study's findings show that cultural and contextual differences significantly impact employees' intentions to adopt environmentally friendly workplace practices. Only transcripts from one nation included certain elements that either encouraged or hindered the intention to engage in the behaviours under study.

The objectives of this study are:

(1) To explore the concept of green HRM.
(2) To examine the redesign of work and job structures for sustainability.
(3) To identify facilitators for successful implementation.

Research question:

(1) What is the concept of green HRM, and how does it align with environmental sustainability goals?
(2) How can work and job structures be redesigned to incorporate sustainable practices and promote organisational sustainability?

METHODOLOGY

This study adopts a conceptually oriented approach, primarily relying on secondary sources. The data will be gathered through an extensive review of scholarly articles, books, case studies, and reports on green HRM and redesigning work and job structures for sustainability. This will provide a comprehensive understanding of green HRM practices' theoretical foundations, practical implications, and real-world applications.

Aim of Study

This study aims to explore the concept of green HRM and examine the redesign of work and job structures to enhance organisational sustainability. By investigating the integration of environmentally friendly principles into HR practices and the redesign of work structures, this research seeks to contribute to developing strategies and guidelines for creating a green workforce. The study aims to identify the critical components of green HRM, understand how work and job structures can be redesigned to incorporate sustainable practices and identify the facilitators for successful implementation. The ultimate goal is to provide practical insights and recommendations for HR professionals and managers, enabling them to align their HR practices with environmental goals and contribute to a more sustainable future.

To Explore the Concept of Green HRM

Green HRM

In the present day, organisations place greater emphasis on and prioritise the implementation of green HRM policies. Green HRM refers to integrating environmental management principles into HRM processes. It portrays a positive image to society and offers a competitive advantage. Specific functions need to be followed to make organisations sustainable and prosperous through green HRM practices. Numerous researchers have explored various functions of green HRM, identifying key components such as green job design, green HR planning, green recruitment, green health, and safety management. Green selection, training, and development functions collectively contribute to establishing environmentally conscious practices within organisations.

Green Job Design

Job design is a process that enhances employee motivation and productivity by creating a more engaging and focussed work environment. Some organisations incorporate job design elements that prioritise environmental protection. These organisations assign environmental-based duties and responsibilities to employees to foster a more eco-friendly workplace. By emphasising environmental dimensions in job tasks and responsibilities, organisations can practice green HRM and contribute to their overall sustainability.

Green HR Planning

In contemporary times, many organisations have prioritised recruiting environmentally conscious and eco-friendly individuals. It is possible to strategically plan and execute recruitment efforts to attract more environmentally conscious individuals to the organisation.

Green Recruitment and Selection

Organisations that embrace green HRM practices typically have unique recruitment and selection policies. Each organisation may have its own strategy for the hiring process. Organisations adopt environmentally focussed approaches in green recruitment and target candidates with environmental orientations. Organisations demonstrate their commitment to environmentally friendly practices by incorporating environmental issues into recruitment advertisements. Employing the best green recruitment practices is crucial for attracting ecologically conscious individuals to fill job vacancies. During candidate selection, evaluating and assessing candidates on environment-related issues and questions in interviews or examinations becomes essential (Crosbie & Knight, 1995).

Green Training and Development

Employee training and development are integral functions for enhancing organisational effectiveness and efficiency. Proper training boosts company productivity and enhances employees' knowledge and skills. Similarly, organisations should provide environmental training to their workforce to promote ecological awareness and understanding among employees. Environmental training supports the organisation by minimising negative environmental impacts and encouraging practices such as recycling and waste management (Jackson et al., 2011). Presently, organisations offer opportunities for employees to receive training on environmental aspects and develop their skills and knowledge in greening practices, thereby ensuring effective environmental management and organisational sustainability.

Green Performance and Reward Management

Organisations evaluate employee performance based on their environmental contributions. Establishing an environmental management information system and conducting ecological audits are essential for effective performance management. To assess employee performance, managers should set green targets, goals, and responsibilities within job roles (Renwick et al., 2013). Evaluating green performance is a critical function of green HRM, as it ensures holistic environmental performance. Regular feedback and good management practices are crucial to success in this area.

Green reward management is closely tied to the evaluation of green performance. Performance management is crucial for organisational profitability and sustainability, and employee satisfaction is pivotal for corporate sustainability. Rewards can be financial and non-financial, with monetary rewards as a motivating factor (Govindarajulu & Daily, 2004). Non-financial rewards such as awards, recognition, leaves, gifts, and publicity are also effective (Renwick et al., 2008). Extrinsic rewards like admiration and acknowledgment can be given to employees for their environmental efforts (Opatha & Arulrajah, 2014). Providing performance feedback motivates employees to perform better in their roles.

Green Safety Management and Employee Relations

An organisation's performance, productivity, and profitability depend on the efforts of its employees. Therefore, ensuring a safe and healthy workplace and fostering good employee relations are crucial. Employees require a safe and supportive environment, which promotes job satisfaction and interest in working for an organisation. A green workplace, designed with environmental considerations, is attractive to employees who appreciate nature. Construction, garments, and manufacturing companies often develop strategies and policies to address employee health concerns. Additionally, it is essential to provide employees with opportunities for growth, skills utilisation, decision-making participation, and problem-solving involvement. Building green relations with employees and involving them in environmental matters contribute to smooth organisational operations and sustainability.

Green Business

The number of green businesses has steadily increased, with approximately 5% growth over the past three years (Mandip, 2011). Green business entails various procedures and activities aimed at reducing negative environmental impacts. It involves eco-friendly practices to prevent and minimise waste and consideration for employees and society. Green businesses aim to reduce harmful environmental effects, and this can be achieved through the '4Rs': reduction, reuse, recycling, and recovery (Wossen Kassaye, 2001). Numerous green activities contribute to this goal, such as utilising natural and renewable products, implementing green building practices, reducing plastic usage, minimising power waste, and practising green HRM. By adopting green practices, organisations become more environmentally conscious, which earns them recognition and loyalty from stakeholders. Embracing environmentally friendly approaches helps protect the Earth and contributes to organisational sustainability.

2.9 Organisational Sustainability

Organisational sustainability refers to the long-term viability of a business. It involves future-proofing the organisation by achieving success without compromising the needs of future generations (Boudreau & Ramstad, 2005). HRs are crucial in implementing environmental policies and ensuring organisational sustainability (Govindarajulu & Daily, 2004). Green HRM facilitates the integration of environmental sustainability into HR functions such as staffing, selection, training, development, performance appraisal, and reward management (Renwick et al., 2008). Green HRM promotes organisational and environmental sustainability by fostering a culture of greening among employees and employers (Wehrmeyer, 2017). To ensure corporate sustainability, it is necessary to establish a green business approach and align it with green HRM practices, as both are indispensable for creating a sustainable organisation.

Ribeiro et al. (2022) investigated how green HRM affected employees' eco-friendly behaviour and organisational identity. They also examined how organisational identity acted as a mediator in the relationship between eco-friendly behaviour and HRM. Consequently, it was discovered that the effects of green HRM policies can only be beneficial and offer long-term competitive advantages for the growth and development of the business if they are well-received by staff members, particularly by those who share the organisation's goals.

Therefore, companies should acquire leaders with a more environmentally conscious mindset. These leaders should support openness in processes, the value of close relationships, effective communication, and attending to the socio-emotional needs of workers. Therefore, companies should acquire leaders with a more environmentally conscious mindset. These leaders should support openness in processes, the value of close relationships, effective communication, and attending to the socio-emotional needs of workers.

Several facilitators contribute to the successful implementation of green HRM practices. These facilitators are crucial for organisations to adopt and integrate sustainable HR practices effectively. The following are some key facilitators, along with existing references:

Employee involvement: Engaging employees in implementing green HRM practices is essential. Employees who feel involved and empowered are more likely to embrace and support sustainable initiatives. Their participation can range from suggesting ideas for environmental improvements to actively participating in green projects and initiatives.

Training and development: Providing training and development opportunities on environmental sustainability is crucial. This helps employees develop the necessary knowledge, skills, and attitudes to embrace and implement green HRM practices effectively. Training programmes can focus on environmental awareness, energy conservation, waste reduction, and sustainable practices (Jackson et al., 2011).

Performance Measurement and Feedback: Establishing performance metrics and providing feedback related to environmental sustainability can drive the successful implementation of green HRM. Regular performance evaluations that include ecological objectives and targets help monitor progress and motivate employees to achieve sustainability goals (Renwick et al., 2008).

Integration with organisational strategy: Aligning green HRM practices with the overall organisational strategy is essential. When sustainability goals are integrated into the core business objectives, it reinforces the importance of environmental responsibility and ensures that green HRM is embedded in all aspects of the organisation (Renwick et al., 2008).

RESULTS AND INTERPRETATION

The study's findings highlight several key factors contributing to the successful implementation of green HRM practices. The results emphasise the importance of leadership support, employee involvement, effective communication, training and development, performance measurement, and integration with the organisational strategy.

Leadership support emerged as a critical facilitator, as it creates a culture of environmental responsibility within the organisation. When leaders demonstrate their commitment to sustainability and actively promote green initiatives, it inspires employees to embrace and support sustainable practices.

Employee involvement was identified as another crucial facilitator. Engaging employees in the implementation of green HRM practices fosters a sense of ownership and responsibility. It encourages active participation in green initiatives, leading to a collective commitment to environmental sustainability.

Effective communication plays a vital role in successful implementation. Open and transparent communication channels raise awareness about sustainability goals, benefits, and progress. Regular communication ensures that employees are well-informed and engaged in green initiatives, strengthening their commitment to environmental responsibility.

Training and development programmes were found to be facilitators for enhancing employees' knowledge and skills related to environmental sustainability. Providing training opportunities on green practices equips employees with the necessary competencies to implement green HRM initiatives effectively.

Performance measurement and feedback systems are essential for monitoring and motivating employees' environmental performance. By establishing performance metrics and providing regular feedback on sustainability goals, employees stay accountable and motivated to achieve desired outcomes.

Integration of green HRM practices with the organisational strategy emerged as a critical factor. When sustainability goals are embedded into the core business objectives, it ensures that environmental responsibility is considered in all aspects of the organisation's operations, contributing to long-term sustainability.

CONCLUSION

In conclusion, the study emphasises the significance of green HRM in promoting environmental sustainability within organisations. The results indicate that leadership support, employee involvement, effective communication, training and development, performance measurement, and integration with the organisational strategy are critical facilitators for successful implementation.

By embracing green HRM practices, organisations can create a sustainable workforce that actively participates in environmental initiatives. This has various benefits, including improved environmental performance, employee satisfaction, and overall organisational sustainability. The findings have practical implications for HR professionals and managers seeking to integrate sustainable practices into their HRM processes.

Further research is needed to explore green HRM practices' specific impacts and outcomes on organisational performance, employee engagement, and environmental sustainability. Future studies can investigate measuring and evaluating green HRM initiatives and their long-term effects on corporate success and ecological preservation.

REFERENCES

Benevene, P., & Buonomo, I. (2020). Green human resource management: An evidence-based systematic literature review. *Sustainability*, *12*(15), 1–25.

Boudreau, J. W., & Ramstad, P. M. (2005). Talentship, talent segmentation, and sustainability: A new HR decision science paradigm for a new strategy definition. *Wiley Inter Science*, *44*(2), 129–136.

Carter, C. R., & Dresner, M. (2001). Purchasing's role in environmental management: Cross-functional development of grounded theory. *Journal of Supply Chain Management*, *37*(2), 12–27.

Chaudhary, R. (2019). Green human resource management and employee green behavior: An empirical analysis. *Corporate Social Responsibility and Environmental Management*, *27*(2), 1–12.

Crosbie, L., & Knight, K. (1995). *Strategy for sustainable business: Environmental opportunity and strategic choice*. (Henley Management Series,. pp. 1–270). McGraw-Hill.

Daily, B. F., & Huang, S. (2001). Achieving sustainability through attention to human resource factors in environmental management. *International Journal of Operations & Production Management*, *21*(12), 1539–1552.

Das, S. C., & Singh, R. K. (2016). Green HRM and organizational sustainability: An empirical review. *Kegees Journal of Social Science*, *8*(1), 227–236.

Faisal, S. (2023). Green human resource management—A synthesis. *Sustainability*, *15*, 2259. https://doi.org/10.3390/su15032259

Gill, M. (2012). Green HRM: People management commitment to environmental sustainability. *Research Journal of Recent Sciences*, *1*, 244–252. https://doi.org/10.1128/MCB.24.6.2444

Govindarajulu, N., & Daily, B. F. (2004). Motivating employees for environmental improvement. *Industrial Management & Data Systems*, *104*(4), 364–372.

Jabbour, C. J. C., & de Sousa Jabbour, A. B. L. (2016). Green human resource management and green supply chain management: Linking two emerging agendas. *Journal of Cleaner Production*, *112*(3), 1824–1833. https://doi.org/10.1016/ j.jclepro.2015.01.052

Jackson, S. E., Renwick, D. W., Jabbour, C. J., & Muller-Camen, M. (2011). State-of-the-art and future directions for green human resource management. *German Journal of Human Resource Management*, *25*(2), 99–116.

Jirawuttinunt, S., & Limsuwan, K. (2019). The effect of green human resource management on the performance of certified ISO 14000 businesses in Thailand. *UTCC International Journal of Business and Economics*, *11*(1), 168–185. http://ijbejournal.com/images/files/11875455535cc6cf80bff3b.pdf

Kaur, H. (2011). Impact human resource factors on perceived environmental performance: An empirical analysis of a sample of ISO) EMS companies in Malaysia. *Journal of Sustainable Development*, *4*(1), 211–223.

Mandip, G. (2011) Green HRM: People management commitment to environmental sustainability. *Research Journal of Recent Sciences*, *1*, 244–252. https://doi.org/10.1128/MCB.24.6.2444

Opatha, H. H., & Arulrajah, A. A. (2014). Green human resource management: Simplified general reflections. *International Business Research*, *7*, 101–112.

Renwick, D. W., Redman, T., & Maguire, S. (2008). Green HRM: A review, process model, and research agenda. *The International Journal of Human Resource Management*, *19*(5), 883–902.

Renwick, D. W., Redman, T., & Maguire, S. (2013). Green human resource management: A review and research agenda. *International Journal of Management Reviews*, *15*(1), 1–14.

Ribeiro, N., Gomes, D. R., Ortega, E., Gomes, G. P., & Semedo, A. S. (2022). *The impact of green HRM on employees' eco-friendly behavior: The mediator role of organizational identification*. https://www.mdpi.com/2071-1050/14/5/2897

Saeed, B. B., Afsar, B., Hafeez, S., Khan, I., Tahir, M., & Afridi, M. A. (2018). Promoting employee's pro-environmental behavior through green human resource management practices. *Corporate Social Responsibility and Environmental Management*, *26*, 424–438.

Shafaei, A., Nejati, M., & Yusoff, Y. M. (2020). Green human resource management: A two-study investigation of antecedents and outcomes. *International Journal of Manpower*, *41*(7), 1041–1060.

Sharma, R., & Gupta, N. (2015). Green HRM: An innovative approach to environmental sustainability. In *Proceeding of the twelfth AIMS international conference on management* (pp. 2–5). http://www.aims-international.org/aims12/12A-CD/PDF/K723-final.pdf

Shen, J., Dumont, J., & Deng, X. (2018). Employees' perceptions of green HRM and non-green employee work outcomes: The social identity and stakeholder perspectives. *Group & Organization Management*, *43*, 594–622.

Wossen Kassaye, W. (2001). Green dilemma. *Marketing Intelligence & Planning*, *19*(6), 444–455.

Wehrmeyer, W. (2017). *Greening people: Human resources and environmental management*. Routledge.

Yuriev, A., & Sierra-Baron, W. (2020). Exploring sustainability cross-culturally: Employees' beliefs on green behaviors. *Sustainable Development*, *28*, 1199–207.

CHAPTER 9

A QUANTITATIVE STUDY ON ENVIRONMENTAL SUSTAINABILITY IN ECOTOURISM: THE NEED FOR ECO-SMART TECHNOLOGY INTEGRATION IN MARKETING DYNAMICS

Bhakti Pawar[a], Arnab Chakraborty[a], Deepali Gala[b], Bhaskar Vijayrao Patil[c], Bhavesh P. Joshi[a] and Kirti Khanna[a]

[a]*School of Leadership and Management, Manav Rachna Educational Institutions, MRIIRS, Faridabad, Haryana, India*
[b]*Department of Management, Bharati Vidyapeeth (Deemed to be University) Institute of Management, Kolhapur, Maharashtra, India*
[c]*Department of Computers, Bharati Vidyapeeth (Deemed to be University), Institute of Management, Kolhapur, Maharashtra, India*

ABSTRACT

Introduction: *'Ecotourism' refers to tourism that promotes and preserves a site's eco-heritage to make tourists aware of the cultural past and protect the environment at the same time. The elementary impression behind ecotourism*

Sustainability Development through Green Economics
Contemporary Studies in Economic and Financial Analysis, Volume 114, 135–156

Published under exclusive licence by Emerald Publishing Limited
ISSN: 1569-3759/doi:10.1108/S1569-375920240000114009

is that it signifies an appealing alternative to the mass tourism paradigm, significantly altering the natural and social circumstances of tourist destinations worldwide.

Purpose: *To study the various factors responsible for the prospects and development of ecotourism, including marketing strategies, which necessitates and deliberates for society's well-being and the safeguarding of the landscape.*

Need for the study: *This research provides perceptions into the economic, environmental, and social factors and the marketing tools that influence the sustainable development of ecotourism and to address the historical neglect or minimal consideration of environmental impacts associated with tourism practices.*

Methodology: *The study involved quantitative analysis gathering primary data from 100 respondents and inclusion of secondary data sourced from journals and articles. The collected data underwent testing and analysis, employing descriptive statistical analysis, analysis of variance (ANOVA), correlation analysis, and structural equation modelling (SEM). These analyses successfully established relationships among the variables under investigation.*

Findings: *The study recommends a futuristic plan to boost the sustainable growth of ecotourism on the basis of the findings of the study.*

Practical implication: *The research underscores the pivotal role of local community engagement, education, enhanced visitor experiences, and strategic promotion facilitated by eco-smart technologies in fostering the sustainable growth of ecotourism destinations.*

Keywords: Ecotourism; environmental sustainability; marketing strategy; eco-smart technology; economic and social development; responsible travel; policy and management

JEL Codes: O13; O31; Q43; Q56; Z32

1. INTRODUCTION

Conceptual background – 'Ecotourism' denotes a traveller's interest in a region's natural potential. Ecological tourism, ecotourism, or nature tourism offer the chance to observe the surrounding environment. The notion of ecotourism has progressed over the last few decades with a motive to reduce the adverse effects of the mass tourism that expanded extensively from the coastal resorts and urban areas, which often neglected or least considered the environmental impacts. Thus, ecotourism means travel to natural areas; the concept emerged to maintain economic and environmental sustainability.

Evolution of ecotourism – The term 'eco-tours' was initially mentioned by Canada's government agency in the 1960s, and the country-maintained prominence in heritage tourism and ecotourism. Nevertheless, the eco-friendly designs of ecotourism were specialised by a Mexican architect named Lascurian in 1983 (Saidmamatov et al., 2020). Later, in 1990, The International Ecotourism Society (TIES) was established to envision and voice out the principles and concepts of ecotourism across the globe. The definition of ecotourism, as given by TIES, is the conservation of the environment by visiting the natural areas, thereby enhancing the welfare of the local communities. Thus, ecotourism is an approach that protects and conserves the environment. In addition, ecotourism can improve economic development, which various studies have identified (Ismail et al., 2021). Since the emergence of ecotourism, more destinations have become aware of it and the United Nations designated 2002 as the International Year of Ecotourism (Kalaitan et al., 2021). This initiative and growth have greatly influenced society and similar conceptions have developed with various names like responsible tourism, green tourism, geo-tourism, indigenous tourism, adventure travel, low-impact tourism, alternative tourism, and village tourism.

Importance of ecotourism and environmental sustainability – Ecotourism aims to protect ecosystems and engage with the environment sustainably and kindly in response to the global climate catastrophe. Ecotourism's primary focus is environmental sustainability and personal and societal growth through responsible travel to places where the cultural heritage, fauna, and flora are the major attractions. In the same manner, ecotourism also fosters the tourists about the appreciation of natural habitats and also provides insights into the impacts imposed upon the environment by human beings. Thus, ecotourism encourages environmental sustainability and is less harmful to the environment. The value of ecotourism is recognised and its scope is universally appreciated. Ecotourism development can provide financial rewards to nearby local communities. Ecotourism contributes to the decline of poverty and the progress of sustainable development in these eco-destinations by assisting small establishments and generating jobs in the tourism industry.

Key challenges and opportunities in ecotourism – The adaptability of ecotourism needs to be clarified as various economic, environmental, and social factors affect its sustainability. Moreover, the ecotourism industry needs marketing of certain factors. In this context, ecolabels are vital as they offer labelling and performance certification. Eco-labels also help identify environmentally safe services (Notohamijoyo et al., 2020). These certifications, the potential tool in marketing, provide the mark of authenticity and quality to the products. However, most certification programmes need more customer recognition as they operate regionally (Chi, 2021). Hence, ecotourism businesses help maximise their marketing value to compensate for the lack of a brand name. Thus, ecotourism marketing still requires considerable planning as many of its processes and principles are still developing with the growth of ecotourism.

As a result, this research study examines the problems and variables related to the sustainability and promotion of ecotourism. Additionally, it offers insights into potential future developments.

Objectives

The objectives of the research are as follows:

To identify the factors that help in the sustainable development of ecotourism.

To find if marketing strategy influences the sustainability and development of ecotourism.

To propose a futuristic approach for sustainable ecotourism focussing on the need for eco-smart technology integration in marketing dynamics.

Paper Organisation

Section 1 is the introductory part that outlines the concepts of ecotourism, Section 2 is the literature review that presents the existing literature on the chosen context of the study and identifies the research gaps of the existing literature, Section 3 is the methodology part that briefs about the data collection and sampling, Section 4 is the data analysis part that presents the analysis of the collected data and its interpretations, Section 5 provides the implications of result and futuristic model, Section 6 provides the limitations of the study and Section 7 is the conclusion part that summarises the research work.

2. LITERATURE REVIEW

The literature review covers the fundamental topics viz.; the role of local communities, institutions, policies, connecting variables, government, and the function of authority. It also clarifies the significance of marketing and green labels. The literature review analyses the factors and marketing strategies in line with the purpose and established objectives that impact ecotourism's long-term expansion and sustainability.

Factors Helping Sustainable Development of Ecotourism

A study focusses on the changes in the development of ecotourism practices that paved the way for the importance of the participation of local communities and it thus remains a contributing factor in sustainable development. The study also emphasised the importance of community initiatives by local authorities with the government's joint effort on ecotourism development, as they are the significant players in this business (Puri et al., 2019).

The local authorities and the government are expected to follow proper guidelines in line with local traditions and the environment to maintain the sustainable development of ecotourism. The study highlighted the needs of these authorities as it was found that they frequently have direct control over planning and promotion (Hameed & Khalid, 2018).

Either way, the government is responsible for revising and implementing procedures to enhance the development of ecotourism.

The interconnection among ecological sustainability, economic growth, and participation has been identified to emphasise sustainability in ecotourism (Brandt & Buckley, 2018).

It has also been affirmed and analysed in other studies (Mtapuri & Giampiccoli, 2019) that cultural and social sustainability would ensure the sustainable development of ecotourism as the development is compatible with the maintenance of biological resources, biodiversity, and ecological processes. Thus, the broad scope of interconnectivity would ensure ecotourism sustainability in the long run.

Another research emphasises integrating precision marketing with advanced Big Data technology. It highlights successful applications of precision marketing in improving customer engagement and personalised experiences. Addressing challenges and ethical considerations, the paper guides effective practitioners to leverage precision marketing for effective results (Saluja et al., 2023).

Further, yet another study emphasised revising the institutions and policies of ecotourism and identified the gaps in the policies' guidelines. It has been discovered that the presence of various sanctioning authorities in the policies of ecotourism and the absence of specific indicators for institutional support and regulations were the main gaps that created the need for the revision of the policies (Poyyamoli, 2018).

Further, one of the studies investigates the impact of marketing on self-help groups (SHGs), emphasising the importance of product acceptability and sustainability for the social-economic well-being of group members. Addressing the research gap, the study suggests enhancing SHG functionality by focussing on market accessibility, intermediary roles, and government financial support. By empowering SHGs with effective marketing techniques and emphasising good manufacturing processes, these groups can overcome vulnerabilities to global market competition, contributing significantly to economic and social development, including women empowerment, employment generation, and improved living standards for the marginalised poor (Chakraborty et al., 2022).

Numerous research studies have proposed the development of multistage methodologies for evaluating the sustainability of ecotourism and quantitative and qualitative analysis has validated the methods. One such study examined the ecotourism sustainability model's applicability given determining the environmental and other factors related to biodiversity that negatively impact the business at present and in the future. This evaluation pinpointed several management problems, such as increased tourist traffic, lack of infrastructure, cooperation between local governments, NGOs, and other organisations, a lack of effective policies, and a disregard for indigenous knowledge. Likewise, the study identified 20 issues that would inform stakeholders about an alternative approach. Further, the study concluded that observed implications of the work, if properly addressed, would create more sustainability in the ecotourism business when considered in line with the model. However, the study did not consider societal difficulties, the significance of marketing, or other relevant issues (Ashok et al., 2019).

Role of Marketing Strategies in Influencing Ecotourism

The role of marketing in ecotourism development has been proven vital through various studies, such as in the Baikal region, where various measures for sustainable ecotourism are created through the involvement of local communities. In this study, the author emphasises the role of the local community in ecotourism through economic development and preserving the Baikal region's cultural heritage. This work contains a model for ecological development by marketing strategies to help the local communities to get economic support and preserve the heritage. This model is based on five sectors, viz., the involvement of local citizens, scientists, the travel industry, tourists, and government. The role of marketing in ecotourism development has been proven essential through various studies. One such study looked at the idea of marketing ecotourism and the necessary adjustments to marketing strategy. For the same, the study examined the marketing-related problems in Baikal Lake. Employee motivation, for example, has been discovered to impact internal marketing and marketing strategy significantly. In addition, other areas of marketing strategy were recognised, such as expanding and maintaining current markets to include new customers and locations, reducing the impact of seasonality on demand, and finding and establishing new markets. Additionally, studies have emphasised using digital marketing as one of the most attractive ecotourism marketing tactics (Dayneko & Dayneko, 2018).

Another study focusses on using ecolabels to improve credibility. However, the availability of plenty of similar labels in the market must be clarified for customers, weakening the trust and credibility of ecotourism development. Concerning the same, it has been found that limiting the number of labels and regulating and harmonising the procedure is more important, ultimately reducing the administrative burden on producers. Moreover, eco-labelling could provide economic incentives for better long-term stewardship and availability of natural resources necessary for national economic welfare. It has been found that ecolabelling awareness promotion activities need to spread in all geographic areas in Bangladesh (rural, suburban, and urban) to achieve sustainable goals (Russel & Robidas, 2019).

Ecotourism has been identified as the instrument that promotes sustainable environmental and human development (Xu et al., 2023). This study analysed and identified the positive impacts and the challenges associated with ecotourism. Given that Indian ecotourism was critical to comprehend, the study did not concentrate on any specific population group. It has been determined that understanding the causes of the failures in Indian ecotourism was essential. However, it has been found that widespread ecotourism has narrowed local poverty and ecological deterioration.

The participation of local communities will also be the foremost attention of economic development, according to one more research study. Additionally, it has been revealed that local populations' means of subsistence enhanced as a result of their participation. As a result, the study's findings suggest that the ecotourism policy should be revised to recognise the contribution of local communities to the industry's sustainable growth since they may share their cultural legacy through strategies for economic development (Cabral & Dhar, 2020).

In one of the research articles, the author has focussed on the means of new stages of popularising China's scenic beauties and whole tourist tourism through the application of technologies like artificial intelligence (AI) and blockchain. The government of China has introduced marketing activities to obtain a perfect tourism system with the inclusion of marketing experts, celebrities, and professionals. A tourist information marketing database is one such step taken to identify the needs of a tourist, which factors attracted them the most, and scientifically classify the needs of tourists, which will help in understanding the needs and decide changes accordingly and strategically create a bond with the tourist for future visits. The author has also focussed on strengthening the integrated information communication channel to have a practical appeal to visitors (Zhang, 2021).

Further, one of the research studies reflected on the implications of information and communication technologies (ICTs) in rural areas and communities, although quite promising, is less explored. The focus is on the type of environments, and more specifically on the role of ICT, which can help in the protection of valuable ecosystems that are forming the ground for ecotourism development (Katsoni & Dologlou, 2017; Puška et al., 2024; Yerpude et al., 2022).

Research Gaps

According to the review, only a limited number of research studies have identified all of the various factors that provide backing to the sustainability of ecotourism. Moreover, more work is needed to address sustainability, marketing, and promotion difficulties. Hence, this research will fill this information gap by considering the economic, environmental, and social factors and marketing policies that can significantly impact sustainable development. Further, this study offers a futuristic approach and resourceful description of ecotourism sustainability as there is the identified gap in existing research lies in the limited utilisation of ICT and the absence of integrated eco-smart technology in marketing dynamics within the realm of ecotourism, prompting the need for this study to explore and address these critical aspects for a more sustainable future in the field.

3. RESEARCH METHODOLOGY

The methodology of the research is explained in the below section.

Aim of the Study

This research aimed to analyse the issues associated with the sustainability and marketing of ecotourism in India. The research also provided insights into the future aspects of model development with the inference from the study's results.

Research Questions

What are the factors that assist in sustainable ecotourism development?

What are the impacts of marketing strategy on sustainability ecotourism development?

Hypothesis

The hypothesis is based on the objectives of the study, which are mentioned below:

H11. There is a significant relationship between the economic, environmental, and social factors and sustainable ecotourism.

H10. There is no significant relationship between the economic, environmental, and social factors and sustainable ecotourism.

H21. Marketing strategies create a significant impact on sustainable ecotourism development.

H20. Marketing strategies do not significantly impact sustainable ecotourism development.

Research Design

This study looks at marketing and sustainability challenges related to the growth of ecotourism. It is founded on descriptive and empirical research since it offers core knowledge about the ecotourism factors and variables in chosen locations and uses evidence to arrive at the research outcome. The study's information was gathered randomly from nine districts and eco-destinations in two divisions of Western Maharashtra, viz. Pune and South Konkan. Eco-destinations of the Pune division include Pune, Satara, Sangli, Kolhapur, and Solapur, whereas eco-destinations of the South Konkan division include Sindhudurg, Ratnagiri, Raigad, and Thane. The primary justification for choosing these eco-destinations is given below:

The biodiversity present in Wester Maharashtra – natural parks, wildlife sanctuary, and reserved forest.

Natural landscape – hills, valleys, rivers, waterfalls, and opportunities for adventure activities like trekking, hiking, and nature photography.

Agrotourism – farm visits, fruit picking, organic farming practices, vineyards, and spice plantation.

Historical and cultural significance – history, culture, architecture, and heritage of temples, forts, and dotting landscapes.

Sustainable tourism initiatives by the Maharashtra Government and local communities – preservation of natural habitat, promoting responsible tourism, and economic benefits to the stakeholders.

Accessibility – there is good travel connectivity both domestically and internationally.

Due to the combination mentioned above, the study sheds light on ecotourism's sustainability and marketing concerns to protect and exhibit ecological heritage. The leading information was gathered from 100 respondents using a structured and closed-ended online questionnaire. The Likert scale survey was also followed in the study. These respondents are the contact points that provide ecotourism services. Here, the term 'contact points' refers to the single organisational representative for a given task; in this case, the points of contact for ecotourism in particular geographic regions have been focussed. The study considers the participants/contact points' ages, years of experience working in the ecotourism industry, positions held, and contributions to the various ecotourism levels. These contact points were targeted to get valuable insights on decision-making, marketing strategies, visitor experience, and sustainability efforts.

Also, the secondary data were gathered from various bases like journals, newspapers, articles, and magazines from 2018 to the date. The collected data were analysed and tested using SPSS software. The hypothesis based on the research objectives using correlation, ANOVA, and SEM was made to determine the association between the selected variables of the study. The process of the research can be seen in Fig. 9.1.

Variables Used in the Study

The dependent and independent variables used in the study are as follows. The dependent variables are sustainability, marketing, and development, while the independent variables are categorised into three factors: economic, environmental, and social. The economic factors consist of the employment of the local community, usage of ecolabels, and certification. The environmental factor is biodiversity conservation and the social factor is the infrastructure system, institutions, and policies.

Data Analysis Method

The collected data were analysed using MS Excel and SPSS software. The distribution of frequency is provided in the table and chart. Further ANOVA, correlation analysis, and SEM were done to test the hypotheses. The three levels of data analysis are as follows:

Level-1: Collection of information. The data are collected using a convenient sampling method to collect information from respondents working at different levels at different eco-destinations as they are most accessible.

The demographic information from the acquired data was examined in MS Excel and the frequency distribution is explained in the study.

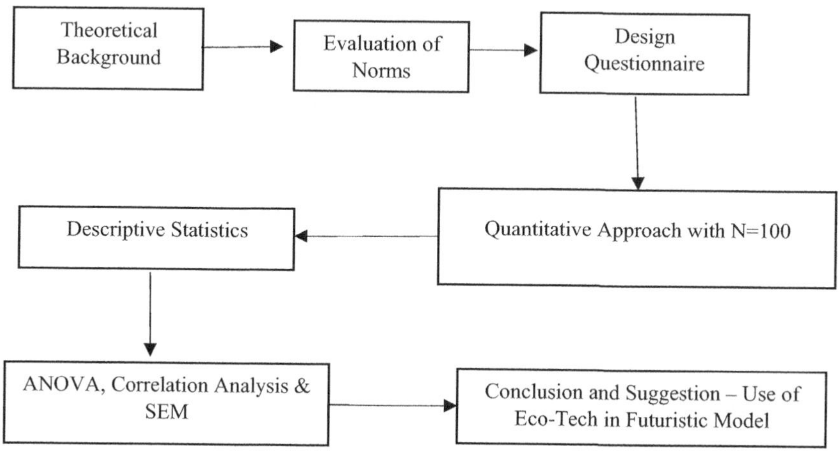

Fig. 9.1. Flow of Research Design. *Source*: Author's work.

Level-2: Statistical analysis with SPSS. The statistical analysis was performed with the SPSS software to find the mean and standard deviation values of the variables used in the study.

Level-3: Testing of hypothesis. The hypotheses were tested with ANOVA, correlation analysis, and SEM.

4. RESULTS AND DISCUSSION

This section presents the data analysis and pertinent interpretations for each test during the current investigation. Using MS Excel and IBM SPSS software, all the variables have been examined using frequency distribution charts, table descriptive statistics, ANOVA, and correlation analysis.

It can be understood from Table 9.1 that a majority of the respondents of 26% belonged to Sindhudurg, 22% of them belonged to Kolhapur, 12% of them belonged to Pune, 10% respondents are from Ratnagiri, 8% of them belonged to Raigad & Satara, 6% of them belonged to Solapur & Thane, and 2% of them belonged to Sangli. These respondents are taken into consideration for the study as the contact points to know the sustainability and Marketing issues of ecotourism. The emphasis is on a higher or lower frequency of respondents, which is vital to understanding, controlling, and regulating the ecotourism potentials in their areas.

It can be inferred from Fig. 9.2 that a majority of the respondents who provided ecotourism services belong to 35–40 years of age with a total percentage of 28%, whereas 26% of the respondents belong to 25–35 years of age while 24% of the respondents belong to 20–25 years of age and 22% of the respondents belong to 40–60 years of age. Fig. 9.3 indicates that out of 100 respondents, 50% of the respondents have 0–5 years of experience in the ecotourism field, while 34% of the respondents belong to the group of experience between 6 and 10 years,

Table 9.1. Frequency Distribution of the Respondents Working in the Ecotourism Sector.

		Eco-destinations			
		Frequency	Per cent	Valid Per cent	Cumulative Per cent
Valid	Ratnagiri	10	10.0	10.0	10.0
	Thane	6	6.0	6.0	16.0
	Sindhudurg	26	26.0	26.0	42.0
	Solapur	6	6.0	6.0	48.0
	Raigad	8	8.0	8.0	56.0
	Kolhapur	22	22.0	22.0	78.0
	Sangli	2	2.0	2.0	80.0
	Satara	8	8.0	8.0	88.0
	Pune	12	12.0	12.0	100.0
	Total	100	100.0	100.0	

Source: Author's calculations.

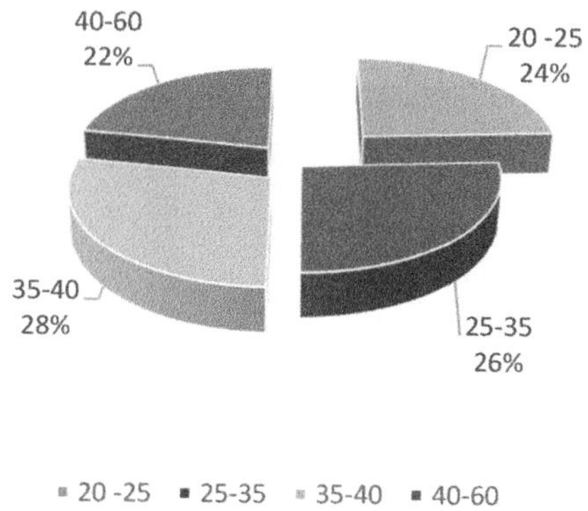

Fig. 9.2. Age-wise Distribution. *Source*: Author's calculations and graph.

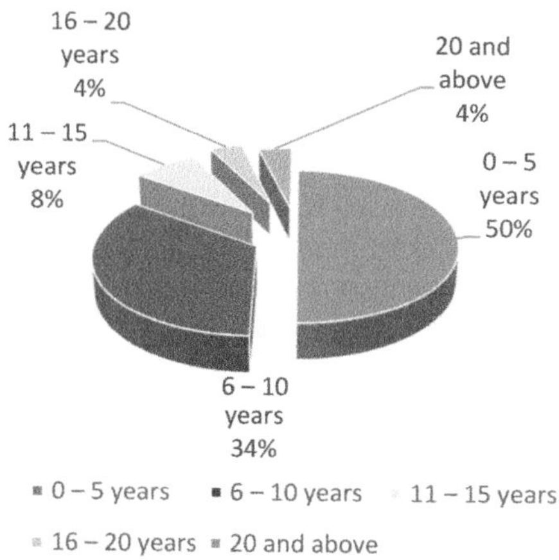

Fig. 9.3. Years of Experience in Ecotourism. *Source*: Author's calculations and graph.

8% of the respondents have a total experience of 11–15, 4% of the respondents who have a total experience of 16–20 years, and 4% of the respondents who have a total experience of 20 years and above.

Fig. 9.4 shows that out of 100 respondents, only four (4%) were business owners and 28 (27%) were destination managers. In contrast, 20 of the respondents (19%) were marketing managers, 32 of them (31%) were sales managers, and 20 of them (19%) were volunteers coordinating ecotourism. Further, it can be interpreted from Fig. 9.5 that 56 of the respondents (56%) worked for internal/local ecotourism services, while 12 of them (12%) contributed to international ecotourism services and 32 of them (32%) provided ecotourism services at the national level.

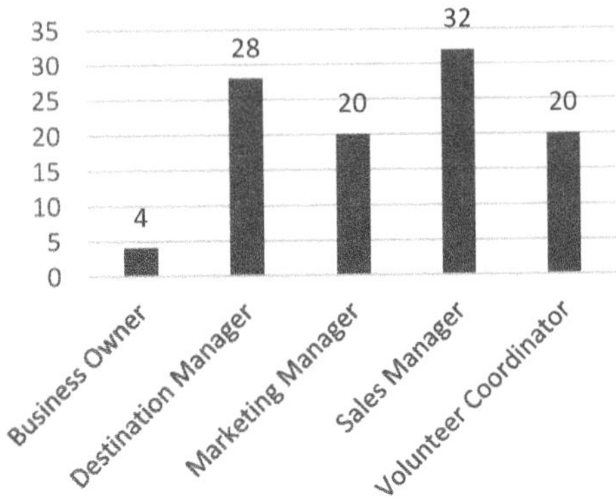

Fig. 9.4. Designation of Respondents. *Source*: Author's calculations and graph.

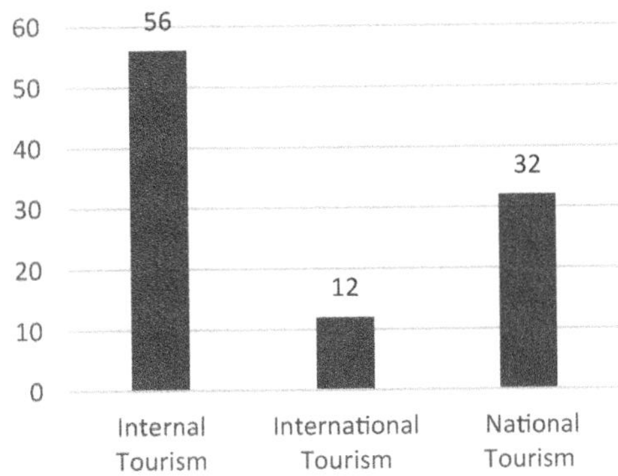

Fig. 9.5. Type of Tourism Provided. *Source*: Author's calculations and graph.

The descriptive statistical analysis includes various aspects that help promote ecotourism marketing and support sustainable development.

It can be seen from the above descriptive statistical analysis in Table 9.2 that the mean values of the variables are positive and the highest mean value in the above table is 1.92. Hence, the variable with the mean value of 1.92 is the most required phenomenon and it impacts the development of the industry. In addition, the value of standard deviation, skewness, and kurtosis are higher than the significant value of 0.05, indicating a positive effect in the study.

Further, an ANOVA has been used to evaluate the impact of employing the resident in ecotourism development, protection of biodiversity, and the role and responsibilities of institutions and policies that hold ecotourism and sustainable development practices. A statistical technique, ANOVA, is used to compare the means of several groups to determine if there are significant differences.

It is evident from Table 9.3 that ANOVA analysis of the economic factor shows that the significant value is lower than 0.05. It shows the rejection of the null hypothesis and the acceptance of the alternate hypothesis. It can also be

Table 9.2. Descriptive Statistical Analysis.

	N	Mean	Std. Deviation	Skewness		Kurtosis	
	Statistic	Statistic	Statistic	Statistic	Std. Error	Statistic	Std. Error
Promoting offers in branding	100	1.36	0.482	0.592	0.241	1.683	0.478
Usage of new marketing strategies	100	1.06	0.239	1.762	0.241	6.401	0.478
Marketing strategy helping in sustainable development	100	1.19	0.394	1.605	0.241	0.586	0.478
Sustainability orientation of eco-centre	100	1.92	0.837	0.153	0.241	4.560	0.478
Use of eco-labels	100	1.49	2.120	1.327	0.241	0.909	0.478
Eco-labels will improve marketing	100	1.15	0.557	1.051	0.241	29.156	0.478
COVID-19 affected the sustainability and marketing of ecotourism	100	1.13	0.597	1.759	0.241	4.998	0.478
Institutions and Policies play a role in sustainability	100	1.15	0.609	1.383	0.241	1.418	0.478
Employing local communities will improve sustainability	100	1.47	0.822	2.046	0.241	3.770	0.478
Conservation can promote sustainability	100	1.10	0.461	1.444	0.241	1.275	0.478
Better infrastructure can improve the industry development	100	1.12	0.537	1.892	0.241	2.757	0.478
Ecotourism certificates are an efficient marketing tool	100	1.10	0.461	1.444	0.241	3.275	0.478
Valid *N* (list-wise)	100						

Source: Author's calculations.

confirmed that there is a noteworthy relationship between the economic factor and the sustainable development of ecotourism, which means that employment of local communities would enhance sustainability.

Table 9.3. ANOVA Analysis of Economic Factor.

ANOVA					
Employing Local Communities Will Improve Sustainability					
	Sum of Squares	Df	Mean Square	*F*	Sig.
Between groups	68.247	1	44.247	24.363	0.000
Within groups	66.663	98	0.680		
Total	66.910	99			

Source: Author's calculations.

It can be seen in Table 9.4 that the significant value of the analysis of the environmental factor is below 0.05. It shows the acceptance of the alternate hypothesis and rejection of the null hypothesis. It can also be confirmed that there is a noteworthy relationship between the environmental factor and the sustainable development of ecotourism, which means that conserving the environment more cautiously can enhance the industry's sustainable development.

It is evident from Table 9.5 that the ANOVA analysis of the social factor shows that the significant value is below 0.05. It rejects the null hypothesis and accepts the alternate hypothesis. Also, there is a noteworthy relationship between social factors and the sustainable development of ecotourism, which means that a transformation in institutions and policies and improved set-up can potentially augment the sustainability of ecotourism.

Table 9.4. ANOVA Analysis of Environmental Factor.

ANOVA					
Conservation Can Promote Sustainability					
	Sum of Squares	df	Mean Square	*F*	Sig.
Between groups	32.064	1	51.064	31.299	0.000
Within groups	20.936	98	0.214		
Total	21.000	99			

Source: Author's calculations.

Table 9.5. ANOVA Analysis of Social Factor.

ANOVA						
		Sum of Squares	df	Mean Square	*F*	Sig.
Institutions and policies play a role in sustainability	Between groups	36.144	1	16.144	65.384	0.003
	Within groups	36.606	98	0.374		
	Total	36.750	99			
Better infrastructure can improve the industry development	Between groups	28.092	1	31.092	44.316	0.000
	Within groups	28.468	98	0.290		
	Total	28.560	99			

Source: Author's calculations.

For many reasons, including effective communication, competitive advantage, increasing environmental awareness, promoting accountability, and leveraging market demand for sustainable tourism service, the relationship between advancements in marketing tools and ecolabels is significant in this study. Considering the same advantage, ecotourism development may build meaningful relationships with customers and become more responsible to help ensure a more sustainable future.

The Pearson correlation in Table 9.6 shows that the correlation coefficient value is 0.774 between the improvements of marketing tools and ecolabels. It is also observed that the value of both variables increases to one, which illustrates a positive relation between the variables. Thus, it can be realised that marketing strategies significantly impact the sustainable development of ecotourism.

SEM, a comprehensive framework, is used to analyse data further to understand the direct and indirect effects of variables on each other. The precision and dependability of the SEM results provide a better comprehension of the study. Fig. 9.6 depicts the same.

It can be seen from Fig. 9.6 that the employment of local communities, which is the economic factor, was positive with the sustainability with β value of 0.336. Similarly, the conservation of the environmental factor was also positively related to sustainability, with a β value of 0.113. Likewise, infrastructure, institutions, and policies, the social factors, were positively related with β values of 0.219 and 0.248, respectively. The ecolabels and ecotourism certificates positively related to the promotion of marketing, with β values of 0.562 and 0.0103, respectively. Further, the inclusion of marketing strategies showed a positive relation to the sustainability of ecotourism with a 0.326 β value.

From Table 9.7, it can be understood that economic, environmental, and social factors, as well as marketing strategies, have a significant relationship with the sustainability of ecotourism, with all having a significant value of p lower than 0.05.

The study found that the integration of ICT or eco tech integration has been notably scarce in the selected area. This deficiency hampers the sector's potential

Table 9.6. Correlation Analysis.

Correlations			
		Eco-labels Will Improve Marketing	Ecotourism Certificates Are an Efficient Marketing Tool
Eco-labels will improve marketing	Pearson correlation	1	0.774
	Sig. (2-tailed)	0.000	0.000
	N	100	100
Ecotourism certificates are an efficient marketing tool	Pearson correlation	0.774	1
	Sig. (2-tailed)	0.000	0.000
	N	100	100

Source: Author's calculations.

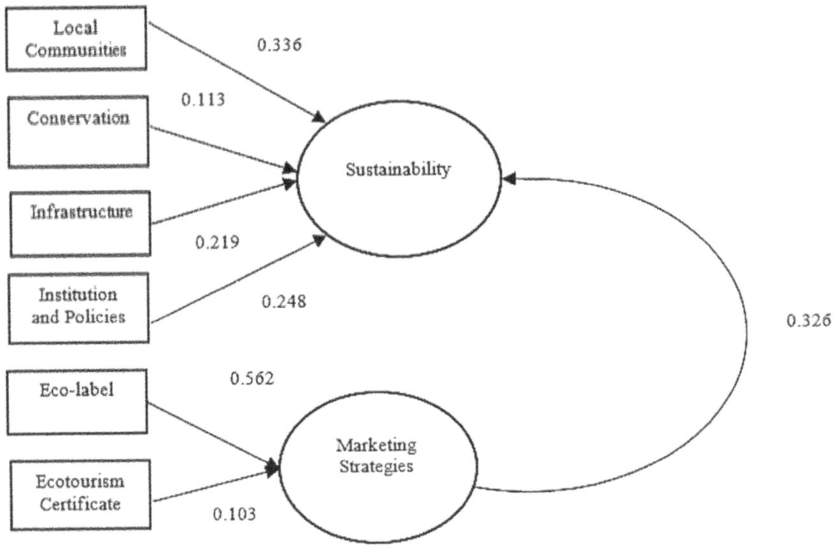

Fig. 9.6. Result of SEM (N=100). *Source*: Author's calculations.

Table 9.7. Result of SEM (N= 100).

Model	Standardised Coefficients β	T	Sig.
Employing local communities will improve sustainability – economic factor	0.336	22.316	0.000
Conservation can promote sustainability – environmental factor	0.113	16.030	0.001
Better infrastructure can improve industry development - social factor	0.219	10.177	0.006
Institutions and policies play a role in sustainability – social factor	0.248	26.350	0.001
Eco-labels will improve marketing – marketing strategy	0.562	10.489	0.000
Ecotourism certificates are efficient marketing tools – marketing strategy	0.103	11.000	0.002
Marketing strategy helped in sustainable development	0.326	8.252	0.001

Source: Author's calculations.
$R^2 = 0.74$, dF = 92, $p < 0.05$, β – regression coefficient.

for growth and sustainability. The underutilisation of ICT limits the efficiency of marketing strategies, visitor engagement, and overall management, hindering the state's ecotourism initiatives from reaching their full technological and ecological capacities.

5. IMPLICATIONS AND FUTURISTIC APPROACH

Implications of Economic, Environmental, and Social Factors

Sustainable ecotourism development leads to careful consideration of the economic viability of tourism activities, conservation, resilience, and adaptive changes to climate change impacts. Also, it ensures the long-term viability of natural resources and ecosystems. Ecotourism helps to restrain the outflow of tourism revenue by promoting local sourcing, community engagement and empowerment, preservation of socio-cultural heritage, supporting local ecotourism initiatives, and fostering linkages between tourism and other sectors of the local economy.

From the results of the above study, it is evident that economic, social, and environmental factors help in the sustainable development of ecotourism in India and all the factors show a positive impact. Hence, concentrating on upgrading factors and revising institutional policies, provision of improved infrastructure, and appropriate marketing strategies can boost the sustainability of the ecotourism industry.

Futuristic Approach

With the above implications, specific futuristic approaches can be recommended, keeping simplicity, sustainability, and integrity in mind.

Simplicity: It includes the practice of keeping ecotourism initiatives simple, less intrusive, more mindful, uncomplicated, and aligned with the core principles of sustainability, focussing on minimal ecological footprints.

Sustainability: It emphasises long-term viability by balancing the needs of visitors, the environment, and host communities. It promotes eco-friendly practices that lead to the provision of educational and enriching experiences for tourists.

Integrity: In ecotourism, integrity entails protecting the pristine natural environments while respecting and preserving local communities' unique cultural traditions and practices. Maintaining integrity in ecotourism involves careful planning, responsible management, and adherence to sustainable practices.

Like the initiative taken in the Thenmala ecotourism project, an effective marketing strategy for ecotourism should align with the values of sustainability, authenticity, and responsible tourism practices. At Thenmala, it collectively aims to provide immersive and educational experiences while ensuring the protection and conservation of the natural environment, waste management, and the well-being of local communities.

The following approaches help resolve sustainability and marketing issues in ecotourism.

Ecotourism Policy and Management

It is necessary to frame preferential policies for enduring and steady investment, particularly for plans with ubiquitous outcomes from the ecotourism business to other industries. Also, to contribute to the sustainable development of ecotourism, it is necessary to increase the efficacy of the state's management of ecotourism. It is also imperative to introduce constructive policies and mechanisms by the government authorities so that ample investment will be made to improve facilities and infrastructure.

Infrastructure

Infrastructure in the ecotourism industry denotes the tourists' infrastructure and transportation facilities. Hence, an all-inclusive improvement of the travel infrastructure and transportation facility, including airways, waterways, and roadways, will endorse the progress and sustainability of ecotourism, in addition to these concentrations on infrastructure investment like ecotourism accommodations and other supplementary services that include technological services, eco-friendly entertainment venues, and local food facility to the tourist.

Community Involvement

Conserving biodiversity in ecotourism is another factor that can be improved by adequately inspecting the artistic heritages and historical and cultural sites by the service provider conjointly government initiatives. Therefore, approachable local community involvement in the ecotourism service at the site will dynamically support this kind of initiative through environmentally friendly practices. Hence, the government authorities and the service providers intend to seek and encourage the support of the local communities so that their active participation will add to the sustainable development of ecotourism. It will also stabilise the economy of the local communities, simultaneously developing safe and friendly ecotourism for visitors.

Marketing Strategy

In addition to the above, marketing strategies and tools play a significant role in the sustainability of ecotourism. Hence, ecotourism's marketing plan must be more substantial to maintain sustainability. It should include developing and implementing targeted plans, identifying target markets, unique selling propositions, storytelling, authenticity, user-friendly technology, content marketing, networking, and ecolabels for branding, partnership, and collaborations.

Eco-smart Technology Integration

The eco-destinations in Pune and South Konkan divisions of Western Maharashtra present immense potential for sustainable ecotourism. To fully unlock this potential, the strategic integration of ICT, e-commerce platforms, networking and interconnection technologies, AI, geographic information systems (GIS), and peer-to-peer (P2P) systems is crucial. These technologies can enhance marketing dynamics by providing real-time information to tourists.

E-commerce

Online booking and reservations: Develop user-friendly websites and mobile apps that allow tourists to book eco-friendly accommodations, tours, and activities online.

Payment systems: Implement secure online payment gateways for seamless transactions, ensuring the financial security of both tourists and ecotourism providers.

Marketplace for eco-friendly products: Create online marketplaces for eco-friendly products and souvenirs, encouraging local artisans and promoting sustainable goods.

Networking and Interconnection Technologies

Collaborative platforms: Establish online platforms where ecotourism businesses, local communities, and tourists can collaborate, share ideas, and plan initiatives collectively.

Social media integration: Leverage social media networks to create communities interested in ecotourism, enabling real-time sharing of experiences and recommendations.

Artificial Intelligence

Personalised recommendations: Use AI algorithms to analyse tourists' preferences and behaviour, providing personalised recommendations for eco-friendly destinations, activities, and accommodations.

Chatbots and virtual assistants: Implement AI-powered chatbots on websites and apps to provide instant assistance, answer queries, and enhance the overall user experience.

Geographic Information Systems

Interactive maps: Develop interactive maps that showcase eco-friendly destinations, hiking trails, wildlife sanctuaries, and other points of interest. Include information on conservation efforts, local flora, and fauna.

Environmental impact assessment: Use GIS to assess and monitor the environmental impact of ecotourism activities, ensuring the conservation of natural habitats.

P2P Systems

Local experience sharing: Create P2P platforms where local guides and community members can offer unique, eco-conscious experiences to tourists, promoting cultural exchange and supporting local economies.

Homestays and community-based tourism: Facilitate P2P accommodation services, connecting tourists with local families willing to host guests, promoting cultural immersion and sustainable income for host communities.

By implementing these innovations, the ecotourism sector can attract more visitors and ensure responsible tourism practices, thereby preserving the natural and cultural heritage of these regions for future generations.

6. LIMITATIONS

The study's primary limitation is that it was conducted with 100 respondents from eco-destinations in Western Maharashtra that were accessible to the researcher. Hence, expanding data collection to almost all the ecotourism places in India would be more significant. Due to time constraints, this study restricts providing insights into the dynamics of visitors' experience, attitude, and behaviour. A study systematically attempts to reach a concrete conclusion using suitable methods. Certain limitations may compromise the conclusion's validity due to sample errors, skewed perspectives, and a lack of accuracy and completeness in secondary data.

7. CONCLUSION

The study results revealed that few chosen eco-destinations have received appropriate attention when it comes to the growth of ecotourism, while other eco-destinations still require attention. The respondents' ages and professional backgrounds provide insight into their contributions to the growth of ecotourism. Almost all the respondents who work and own centres in ecotourism were very concerned about sustainable development through ecotourism. Their suggestions were considered for the long-term strategy for sustainably expanding ecotourism. According to the study and the tested hypothesis, marketing strategies, branding, environmental labels, certification, institutional policies, local community involvement, and improved infrastructure can have a reliable impact on the progress of ecotourism. There is a strong correlation between economic, social, and environmental considerations that leads to meaningful influence in the long-term growth of ecotourism. It was observed from the descriptive analysis that COVID-19 also harmed the industry's marketing and sustainability. Thus, the research study helps make a substantial contribution to the sustainable development of ecotourism in various eco-potential areas.

Moreover, it helps to understand that ecotourism initiatives can be successfully provided if eco-friendly activities are implemented with proper marketing strategies that keep the futuristic approach simple, sustainable, and integrated. Policymakers are crucial in framing comprehensive ecotourism policies and formulating clear guidelines and regulations that promote sustainable practices. There is a strong need for ample resources that help strengthen enforcement and monitor those regulations by fostering PPP – public private partnership. The role of ecotourism operators is also significant in adopting sustainable infrastructure and engaging and empowering local communities by involving them in ecotourism planning, decision-making, and revenue-sharing mechanisms. Educating tourists about responsible behaviour at various eco-destinations is also essential. For further fruitful developments in ecotourism, we can also involve other stakeholders, viz.: NGOs, educational institutions, media organisations, and volunteers to promote awareness of sustainable ecotourism. There are certain possible avenues for forthcoming research, which include actual environmental impact assessment, the study of visitor conducts and activities, awareness, impetus, innovative financing models, and integration of eco-smart technologies. The advancements in eco-smart technologies can aid in minimising the ecological footprint of tourism, ensuring the preservation of natural habitats and wildlife for future generations. Investigating these areas will provide valuable insights and knowledge, which will lead to guiding, developing, and managing sustainable ecotourism initiatives, ensuring their long-term viability.

REFERENCES

Ashok, S., Behera, M. D., & Tewari, H. R. (2019). Evaluating the applicability of the ESM (Ecotourism Sustainability Maximization) model to assess, monitor, and manage ecotourism sustainability in the mountain ecosystem (Mt. Kangchendzonga Base Camp Trek, India). *Environmental Monitoring and Assessment, 191*(S3), 801. https://doi.org/10.1007/s10661-019-7702-y

Brandt, J. S., & Buckley, R. C. (2018). A global systematic review of empirical evidence of ecotourism impacts on forests in biodiversity hotspots. *Current Opinion in Environmental Sustainability, 32*, 112–118. https://doi.org/10.1016/j.cosust.2018.04.004

Cabral, C., & Dhar, R. L. (2020). Ecotourism research in India: From an integrative literature review to a future research framework. *Journal of Ecotourism, 19*(1), 23–49. https://doi.org/10.1080/14724049.2019.1625359

Chakraborty, A., Kumar, N., Kaur, G., Kathuria, G., & Chakraborty, D. (2022). Vulnerability of self-help groups in marketing their products – Identification of the key factors for enhanced market reach and profitability. *Indian Journal of Agricultural Economics, 77*(1), 179–193.

Chi, N. T. K. (2021). Understanding the effects of ecolabel, eco-brand, and social media on green consumption intention in ecotourism destinations. *Journal of Cleaner Production, 321*, 128995. https://doi.org/10.1016/j.jclepro.2021.128995

Dayneko, D. V., & Dayneko, V. V. (2018). Development and marketing of ecotourism in the Baikal region. *IOP Conference Series: Earth and Environmental Science, 190*, 012004. https://doi.org/10.1088/1755-1315/190/1/012004

Hameed, B., & Khalid, A. (2018). Impact of ecotourism in ensuring the sustainable development of tourism. *Industry in India, 5*(2), 46–50.

Ismail, F., Imran, A., Khan, N., & Qureshi, M. I. (2021). Past, present and future of ecotourism: A systematic literature review from last decade. *Studies in Applied Economics, 39*(4), 1–13. https://doi.org/10.25115/eea.v39i4.4592

Kalaitan, T. V., Stybel, V., Gutyj, B., Hrymak, O., Kushnir, L., Yaroshevych, N., Vovk, M., & Kindrat, O. (2021). Ecotourism and sustainable development. Prospects for Ukraine.*Ukrainian Journal of Ecology, 11*(1), 373–383. https://doi.org/10.15421/2021_55

Katsoni, V., & Dologlou, N. (2017). ICT applications in smart ecotourism environments. In A. Stratigea, E. Kyriakides, & C. Nicolaides (Eds.), *Smart Cities in the Mediterranean* (pp. 225–244). Springer International Publishing. https://doi.org/10.1007/978-3-319-54558-5_11

Mtapuri, O., & Giampiccoli, A. (2019). Tourism, community-based tourism and Ecotourism: A definitional problem. *South African Geographical Journal, 101*(1), 22–35. https://doi.org/10.1080/03736245.2018.1522598

Notohamijoyo, A., Abdul Hakim, A., Billah, M., & Setya Wiyata, A. (2020). Integration of ecolabelling and ecotourism schemes: A case study of forest honey in Indonesia. *E3S Web of Conferences, 211*, 01010. https://doi.org/10.1051/e3sconf/202021101010

Poyyamoli, G. (2018). Ecotourism policy in India: Rhetoric and reality. *Grassroots Journal of Natural Resources, 1*(1), 46–61. https://doi.org/10.33002/nr2581.6853.01015

Puri, M., Karanth, K. K., & Thapa, B. (2019). Trends and pathways for ecotourism research in India. *Journal of Ecotourism, 18*(2), 122–141. https://doi.org/10.1080/14724049.2018.1474885

Puška, A., Hodžić, I., Štilić, A., & Murtič, S. (2024). Evaluating European Union countries on climate change management: A fuzzy MABAC approach to the climate change performance index. *Journal of Green Economy and Low-Carbon Development, 3*(1), 15–25.

Russel, A. H., & Robidas, L. C. (2019). Opportunities and challenges of ecolabel practices in Bangladesh for promoting environmentally conscious consumers. *European Journal of Business and Management Research, 4*(6), 1–7. https://doi.org/10.24018/ejbmr.2019.4.6.158

Saidmamatov, O., Matyakubov, U., Rudenko, I., Filimonau, V., Day, J., & Luthe, T. (2020). Employing ecotourism opportunities for sustainability in the Aral sea region: Prospects and challenges. *Sustainability, 12*(21), 9249. https://doi.org/10.3390/su12219249

Saluja, A., Dharam Soth, R. K., Pawar, B. R., Pasunoori, V., Mungi, A., & Faldu, R. (2023). Precision marketing strategy for E-Commerce by using big data technology. *Journal of Informatics Education and Research*, *3*(2), 2554–2560. https://doi.org/10.52783/jier.v3i2.433

Xu, L., Ao, C., Liu, B., & Cai, Z. (2023). Ecotourism and sustainable development: A scientometric review of global research trends. *Environmental Development and Sustainability*, *25*(4), 2977–3003. https://doi.org/10.1007/s10668-022-02190-0

Yerpude, S., Sood, K., & Grima, S. (2022). Blockchain-Augmented digital supply chain management: A way to sustainable business. *Journal of Risk and Financial Management*, *16*(1), 7.

Zhang, H. (2021). Exploration and analysis of tourism marketing management innovation based on big data. *Journal of Physics: Conference Series*, *1744*(3), 32086. https://doi.org/10.1088/1742-6596/1744/3/032086

CHAPTER 10

A LITERATURE REVIEW ON ESG SCORE AND ITS IMPACT ON FIRM PERFORMANCE

Ayşegül Gürsoy and Gökçe Sinem Erbuğa

Dokuz Eylul University, Faculty of Economics and Administrative Sciences, İzmir, Turkey

ABSTRACT

Introduction: *The global financial crisis has affected the financial markets and has had social consequences in addition to economic ones. The concept of 'sustainability' concerns firms reaching their main corporate goals. So, to maximise corporate financial performance (FINP), firms pay attention to non-financial data, such as elements of governance, social, and environmental concerns (henceforth referred to as ESG). Therefore, non-financial information provided by EGS factors measured by the ESG score has a crucial role in incorporating strategy and firm performance.*

Purpose: *This chapter looks at how ESG scores affect the performance of firms. The term 'ESG' describes how corporate operations include ESG principles. The ESG score is a novel way to gauge a company's sustainability.*

Methodology: *ESG practices are a current phenomenon that has taken the attention of researchers in the last decades. Besides the amount of research conducted, researchers still need consensus regarding its impact. This chapter implements a systematic literature review to compile the research on ESG performance (ESGP) and how it affects business performance.*

Findings: *Businesses can incorporate sustainability practices into their operations with the help of ESG reports. ESG reports and scores provide*

Sustainability Development through Green Economics
Contemporary Studies in Economic and Financial Analysis, Volume 114, 157–171

Published under exclusive licence by Emerald Publishing Limited
ISSN: 1569-3759/doi:10.1108/S1569-375920240000114010

non-financial information, which is crucial for businesses to achieve sustainability in their activities and attract more investors. The chapter contributes to the literature by creating value through a comprehensive and theoretical literature review.

Keywords: ESG score; sustainability; firm performance; SDG; ESG disclosure; ESG; sustainable development

JEL Codes: E01; H32; O44

INTRODUCTION

The global financial crisis has affected the financial markets and has had social consequences in addition to economic ones. Concerns have arisen about ethical behaviour, risk management, non-financial information, and financial statements.

The rising awareness regarding the fast-paced environment and changes in the world is triggered by the pandemic. After the pandemic, global warming, climate change, increasing population, and urbanisation have attracted individuals' and institutions' attention (Aydoğmuş et al., 2022).

The concept of 'sustainability' is centred on firms reaching their main corporate goals. So, to maximise corporate FINP, firms focus on non-financial information such as ESG aspects.

ESG elements are those that are not included in standard financial statements but have a direct effect on the organisation's dangers and opportunities. Therefore, non-financial information provided by the ESG factors measured by ESG score has a crucial role in corporate strategy and firm performance (Halid et al., 2023).

The ESG score is an innovative technique used as an intermediary for the operations of an organisation. Even though ESG is not a mandatory factor in financial statements, an increasing number of companies share their ESG reports to indicate the advancement in corporate sustainability (Serban et al., 2022).

The hyperlink between ESG and corporate achievement is still up for debate among academia, which is why the subject is actively being explored. While some researchers show no correlation at all or a negative effect, others discover a favourable link between business financial success and ESG. Consequently, this work's goal is to conduct a comprehensive literature study and create a theoretical framework based on past research.

THEORETICAL BACKGROUND

The Sustainability Phenomenon

Today, many reasons, such as rapid increases in the world population, the development of technology and industry, difficulties in accessing food and clean water, irresponsible and unconscious consumption of scarce resources, global warming, and also climate change, have led to the development of the understanding of sustainability. Sustainability, in its simplest form, is expressed as the idea that the elements within the ecosystem will continue their activities for an unlimited future without undermining the functioning system and causing depletion of the system's essential resources (Gilman, 1992).

As the 20th century came to an end, there was a general realisation that there wouldn't be enough resources to fulfill the needs and desires of the world's growing populace. Since the Brundtland Report was published by the United Nations-affiliated World Commission on Environment and Development in 1987, sustainability has gained significant attention in both the public at large and the corporate world. The idea of sustainability based on development was covered in the aforementioned paper. The paper claims that sustainable development encompasses more than just a nation's environmental sustainability policies. But it's also a phenomenon whose social and economic aspects ought to be taken into account and used (Tüm, 2014, p. 59).

Sustainable development evaluates economic, environmental, and social factors together in order for both businesses and countries to carry out balanced decision-making processes that will bring healthy, rational, and optimal results in the long term (Garriga & Mele, 2004, p. 61). Thus, in order to fulfill the goal of leaving future generations with a more liveable, equitable, and fair world, the notion of sustainable development intrinsically necessitates the assessment of economic, environmental, and social variables (Sarıkaya & Kara, 2007, p. 221). It is possible to define the phenomenon of sustainable development simply as the efforts and process of achieving human development in a fair, equal, safe, healthy, and caring manner without leaving anyone behind (Gladwin & Kennelly, 1995, p. 876).

In order to maintain sustainability and raise living standards, we must abandon our fast-paced, consumerism-based lifestyle and join the global solidarity movement by balancing the needs of the social, economic, and environmental spheres. In this regard, it is stated that sustainability consists of three main components. It is impossible to consider these three elements, which can be expressed as economy, environment, and society, separately from each other within the scope of sustainability. In other words, sustainability is the intersection of the economy, environment, and society. Fig. 10.1 shows the components of sustainability. If one of these three elements is missing, talking about sustainability will not be possible (Özmehmet, 2008, p. 1855).

What Is ESG?

From an economic perspective, the most basic production factors are nature, labour, capital, and the entrepreneur. Over the years, nature has been destroyed due to increasing competition and the aim of obtaining maximum profit at minimum cost. It has been concluded that when the destruction of natural resources reaches a point of no return, production, growth, and development will be disrupted.

In this context, sustainable development was defined and passed on to future generations. Environmental, social, and economic factors are the most fundamental elements for sustainable development. However, considering only environmental, social, and economic factors is not considered a sufficient effort today.

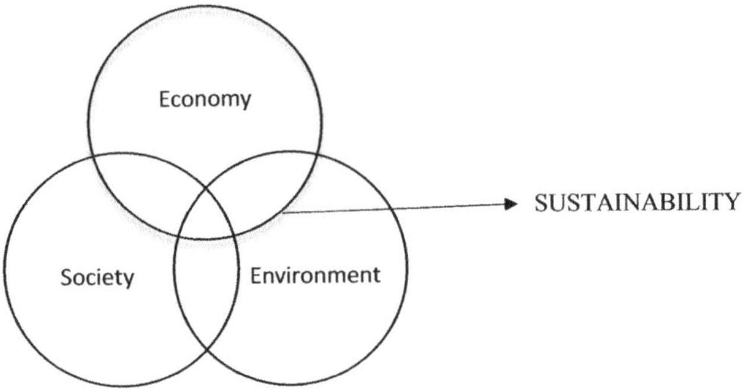

Fig. 10.1. Components of Sustainability. *Source*: Özmehmet (2008).

The interactions and relationships of these factors with the macro and micro variables of the countries are also a critical concern today. They are being investigated as a subject of study by many researchers. Also, according to the universally accepted view, the power of technology is needed to support these factors.

The emergence of ESG dates back to the 1970s. A group of investors who pay attention to the social and environmental aspects of the companies they have invested in resulted in the introduction of ESG concepts (Richardson, 2009).

The ESG is supported by two eminent organisations. UN Secretary-General Kofi Annan invited some of the largest institutional investors in the world to take part in the lengthy task of creating the Principles for Responsible Investment in 2005. The Principles for Responsible Investment (PRI) were first introduced by the United Nations in 2006. Ever since its establishment, it has consistently expanded. Nearly 4,000 signatories worldwide as of 2021 represent US$130 trillion in invested capital under control (UN PRI, 2023).

So, as to corporate ESG issues in investment, UN PRI has six principles:

- *Principle 1:* We will incorporate ESG issues into investment analysis and decision-making processes.
- *Principle 2:* We will be active owners and incorporate ESG issues into our ownership policies and practices.
- *Principle 3:* We will seek appropriate disclosure on ESG issues by the entities we invest in.
- *Principle 4:* We will promote acceptance and implementation of the principles within the investment industry.
- *Principle 5*: We will work together to enhance our effectiveness in implementing the principles.
- *Principle 6:* We will each report on our activities and progress towards implementing the principles.

UN PRI's list of priority environmental concerns includes plastics, water, fracking, methane, biodiversity, sustainable land use, and the circular economy. Conversely, social issues include labour rights, inclusion, diversity, equity, and decent job opportunities. Examples of governance-related issues include tax equity, moral political engagement, cyber security, executive remuneration, company mission, anti-corruption, whistle-blowers, and director nominations.

The second entity that has an influence on ESG and business sustainability is the Global Reporting Initiative (GRI), which started out in 2001 in conjunction with the Tellus Institute, the Coalition of Environmentally Responsible Economies, and the United Nations Environmental Program. Its goal is to ensure that companies respond to issues pertaining to society, the environment, and the government.

The first worldwide methodology/foundation for sustainability reporting was established in 2000 with the release of the GRI Guidelines (G1). The second iteration of the Guidelines (G2) was introduced in 2002. In response to growing organisational knowledge and demand, the Guidelines were revised to G3 in 2006 and G4 in 2013. In 2016, GRI produced the first global GRI standards, which serve as requirements for sustainability reporting (GRI, 2023).

LITERATURE REVIEW

In the last few decades, the number of researches about ESG has risen. The relationship between a company's FINP and its ESG scores is a topic that has been the focus of numerous studies in the literature, but it has long been recognised as a significant area for research. These studies were conducted mainly before 2015, and almost all chose to analyse the association among ESGP and cost of capital, share performance, and operational efficiency as the focus of their inquiry (Whelan et al., 2021).

Whelan et al.'s (2021) research assessed the findings of over 1,000 studies regarding the connection, as measured spanning 2015 through 2020, among the economy's performance and ESG accomplishments. A same-directional association between business FINP and ESG was found in 58% of the research that was done. The study's conclusions, which evaluate the connection between ESG and FINP at the business and investment performance levels (assess the relationship between ESG and FINP at two fundamental levels: corporate FINP and investment performance), support this assertion.

A definitive conclusion on the character of the collaborative relationship within ESGP (with the ESG score serving as the most reliable indicator of ESGP) and FINP is unfeasible in light of other research that has already been conducted. Some research appears to support the adverse association between the two determinants (Brammer et al., 2006; Branco & Rodrigues, 2008; Lee et al., 2009), despite the majority of studies (Cahan et al., 2015; Eccles et al., 2014; Fatemi et al., 2015; Filbeck et al., 2009; Lo & Sheu, 2007) showing a positive relationship between the variables. According to certain experts in this field (Galema et al., 2008; Horváthová, 2010; Orlitzky et al., 2003; Statman, 2006), there is no connection between the two (Puška et al., 2024; Yerpude et al., 2022).

Meuer et al. (2020) included a striking finding in their study on the ESG–FINP relationship. According to Meuer et al., there are more than 30 definitions of corporate sustainability currently used in the literature, which may cause companies to make different measurements by taking different definitions as a reference to measure their corporate sustainability (Douglas et al., 2017). It will not be possible to accurately compare the sustainability scores different companies offer due to different measurements. Therefore, it is vital to eliminate existing terminology differences to make a fair measurement (Meuer et al., 2020).

Conversely, some research focuses on the macro-level effects of ESG. Shaikh (2022), for instance, examines the hyperlink between uncertain policy and investments that are sustainable. The Dow Jones Sustainability Indexes (DJSIUS) and the economic and political landscape from 2000 until 2017 are among the primary topics of the study. The outcomes show that noteworthy catastrophes like the Lehman crisis, stock market boom, and monetary struggles have significantly harmed the DJSIUS. Furthermore, Ahsan and Qureshi (2021) investigate the interaction between sustainability disclosure, the performance of businesses, and policy uncertainty in Europe. The empirical study's observations show that organisations' ESG disclosure strengthens their reputation and reduces policy uncertainty.

The effect of social responsibility and business governance on Tobin's *Q* during a 13-year period in 40 countries has been investigated by Borghesi et al. (2019). Empirical data show that in times of economic uncertainty, the effectiveness of board and executive members' actions is restricted by shareholder-centric corporate governance procedures. From 2010 to 2018, Zhao et al. (2021) investigated the results of corporate social responsibility (CSR) and economic policy uncertainty in Chinese enterprises.

Many academics concentrate on volatility and capital market returns as they relate to ESG concerns. In the Chinese capital markets, for example, Dai (2020) examines the relationship between portfolio diversification and ESG investing. Deng et al. (2022) conducted an empirical examination of the connection between capital market liberalisation and business ESGP using the Shanghai-Hong Kong Stock Connect mechanism. Results show that the Shanghai-Hong Kong Stock Connect mechanism raises knowledge of ESG and organisational ESGP. The dataset spans the years 2011–2019. Brandon et al. (2021) examine the causal connection between stock performance and disagreements in ESG ratings for a sample of companies that were traded in the S&P 500 Index between 2010 and 2017. Findings indicate that stock performance and ESG rating disagreements are positively correlated.

On the other hand, it is important to remember that the number of studies dealing with the ESG–FINP relationship on a theoretical basis is considerable in the literature. In his study, Freeman (1984) emphasises that the studies performed in the literature are predicated mainly on stakeholder theory. This shows that while stakeholder theory has continued to guide studies in the last 30 years, other theories can. Considering these studies, they are mainly based on stakeholder theory, shared value theory, legitimacy theory, and resource-based view theories (Meuer et al., 2020).

Stakeholder theory-oriented studies broadly reveal that a favourable correlation exists among ESGP and FINP) (Barnett & Salomon, 2006; Godfrey et al., 2009).

In addition, some of the studies that proved that the relationship in question was positive and revealed the results used the meta-analysis research method (Wu, 2006); in certain research, evidence that the relationship is positive is presented through a review of the available literature (Beurden & Goessling, 2008; Margolis & Walsh, 2003).

Stakeholder Theory

The stakeholder term represents an approach that concerns many sub-fields under the management discipline, from finance, organisational behaviour, and marketing to strategic management, and is considered the starting point for many studies in these areas.

The foundations of the stakeholder concept, which has found its place in the literature as an essential research topic, especially in recent years, can be traced back to Adam Smith. Although businesses are designed as open structures under the dominance of free trade today, Smith evaluated businesses as a closed system in his works 'The Theory of Moral Sentiments' and 'The Wealth of Nations', which he wrote in the 1700s. He assumed businesses do not interact with their environment because they are closed to the outside world. However, by the 1950s, this approach put forward by Smith began to lose its validity, and the idea that businesses should actually be considered open systems and, therefore, be affected by their external environment by interacting with them began to be accepted. Within the framework of this acceptance, the notion of CSR has been included in the literature (Garriga & Domenec, 2004, p. 55). This concept has formed the basis of many theories (Ertuğrul, 2008, p. 200).

Stakeholder theory, developed in line with this understanding, does not evaluate companies alone but considers the company and its environment. In this context, companies not only try to maximise their shareholders' welfare but also consider the welfare and demands of their non-shareholder actors. On the other hand, this approach guides companies in determining which stakeholders they should consider more carefully (Mitchell et al., 1997, p. 853–854). With this advantage provided by the approach, businesses can manage their resources more optimally, efficiently, and effectively, thus preventing resource waste (Ertuğrul, 2008, p. 205).

Stakeholders are described as people or groups that have the potential to influence or be impacted by a firm's operations based on the sustainability of the firm (Freeman, 1984). Freeman (1984) classifies internal and external stakeholders and emphasises that the interests of various stakeholder groups impact an organisation's performance. As a contemporary issue, sustainable performance, or sustainable disclosure is assumed to be an indicator of firm performance.

Moreover, according to Hamdi et al. (2022), when a company has enough cash due to its activities, the cash generated is invested in ESG activities.

ESG scores and ratings measure firm performance and stakeholders' expectations. The empirical analysis is implemented in terms of risk management (Li et al., 2022) and cost of capital (Chen & Yang, 2020; Hamrouni et al., 2019; Kaiser & Welters, 2019).

Although many studies evaluate ESGP within the scope of stakeholder theory, these studies investigate the relationship in question with different dimensions in different samples, using different research and measurement methods. However, the fact that a generally accepted theoretical framework for value creation on a global scale has yet to be established causes researchers to reach different results, leading to a lack of consensus on the subject. In this regard, Kumar (2023), who summarised the literature currently available to researchers on value creation, discussed sustainability with the revisions he made to grounded theory and investigated how effective ESGP is in creating value for company stakeholders. In another study conducted by Hörisch et al. (2014), a sustainable business approach was covered in relation to the stakeholder theory framework. In the research conducted by Garvare and Johansson (2010), the main point of using stakeholder theory was to reveal the possible connection and relationship between global and organisational sustainability.

Institutional Theory

Three main theories are associated with ESG factors. The first is the institutional theory, which focuses on how the social and cultural environment affects the organisations (DiMaggio & Powell, 1983). Moreover, Scott and Meyer (1994) emphasise the importance of cultural issues, such as beliefs and expectations, in organisational structures. Organisations align with these expectations instead of quantitative factors such as optimal input and output.

Academics have looked into institutional theory through empirical study. Galbreath (2013), for instance, employed institutional theory prediction to support an evaluation of the ESG disclosure of 300 listed firms on the Australian Securities Exchange (ASX) spanning the time period from 2002 to 2009. According to the investigation, it turns out that high-impact companies performed better when it came to practices related to sustainability than impact. Additionally, Orsato et al. (2015) conducted a survey of sustainability indices and spoke with executives from corporations about their plans to join indices of sustainability (such as ISE, Brazil). According to their survey, which backs up the institutional theory, organisations that voluntarily disclose non-financial information develop new skills, improve their reputation, and disseminate knowledge more effectively. These firms are seen as sustainability practice and ESG compliant.

Agency Theory

Agency theory focuses on governance practices such as the efficiency of internal control, independent boards, and various committees regarding audit and risk. According to Setiadi et al. (2017), good governance practices protect minorities within the corporation and eliminate conflicts of interest among shareholders. All these practices result in better financial and non-financial reporting that creates value in the long term for all stakeholders.

Based on the research that was done by Ferrell et al. (2016), a clear answer has yet to be reached due to the assessment of the success of companies in ESG activities according to agency or stakeholder theories. In the literature, the

ESG activities of companies are still a matter of great debate based on theories. Therefore, there are still unanswered questions and unclarified points regarding the subject.

Within the framework of agency theory, Cheng et al. (2013) state in their study that they benefit from the individual benefits provided by investing in sustainability activities and, therefore, ESG and they emphasise that this situation is precisely parallel to the basic logic on which agency theory is based. On the other hand, in contrast to agency theory, some studies in the literature support stakeholder theory. In these studies, addressing the ESG phenomenon from the stakeholder theory perspective, it is seen that the involvement/participation of company employees in ESG activities increases their motivation and, therefore, company productivity and efficiency (Baron, 2008).

In addition, studies show that carrying out ESG activities and taking an active part in these activities causes employees to act more consciously and responsibly regarding both the use of materials as well as energy (Qi et al., 2014). In addition, some studies conducted while evaluating ESG activities within the scope of agency theory reveal that ESG activities lead to establishing and maintaining healthy and good relationships and connections with employees and third parties (actors) outside the company (Hou, 2019).

ESG Disclosure and Firm Performance

Today's economies want to be included in the race by reinventing themselves to become sustainable. In this regard, both national economies and companies must carry out their activities to maximise the welfare of social stakeholders, the environment, and the entire ecosystem. For this reason, sustainable development goals (SDGs) and ESG concerns created within this framework show their impact on the daily activities of businesses. Additionally, ESG disclosure is regarded as essential to business sustainability.

However, as stated by Khan (2022) in his study, despite the importance mentioned earlier of ESG, it is still seen that disclosures still need to be carried out in a regular and standard manner by all businesses. The fact that a standard ESGP measurement cannot be made and the measurement can be carried out by many different companies with very different methods (Huber & Comstock, 2017) does not make it possible to talk about a stable index as an ESGP measure (Matos et al., 2020). This situation prevents existing and potential investors from carrying out their decision-making processes healthily and undermines the process of measuring companies' ESGPs realistically and healthily (Lokuwaduge & Heenetigala, 2017).

Cohen et al. (2012) investigated the way the 50 publicly traded companies from five different industries disclosed non-financial information on their economic performance and sustainability in 2004. The results show that there is a need for increased industry and firm size indicator uniformity. It is stressed how crucial integrated reporting and assurance services are.

ESG disclosure's impact and company performance on the companies included and evaluated in the Egyptian Corporate Responsibility Index from 2007 to 2016 are examined by Aboud and Diab (2018). Tobin's Q has been employed in the research as a stand-in for business performance. Higher ESG rankings possess a favourable connection with business performance, in accordance with the empirical study's findings.

According to Malik (2015), the vast majority of the most recent studies indicate that CSR initiatives have a big impact on business performance.

According to Wasiuzzaman et al. (2022), there is a substantial inverse link between the factors and ESG disclosure's effect on a company's FINP. In a similar vein, P and Busru (2021) discovered a negative correlation between 386 Indian companies listed in the BSE 500 Index and firm performance over a 10-year period from 2006 to 2017. A negative trend is triggered by social and environmental disclosure, according to empirical investigation.

ESG Score and Firm Performance

The overwhelming majority of study results indicate that an organisation's financial achievement and ESG are positively correlated. Nonetheless, the results vary depending on the area or duration of the dataset examined. Li et al. (2022) investigated how Chinese stock returns during COVID-19 were impacted by ESGP. The event study's empirical findings show that ESGP increases abnormal returns for businesses. Van Linh et al. (2022) examine the connection between company success as determined by Tobin's *Q* and sustainability reporting. The report includes the GRI standards of 360 firms from 2015 to 2019. There is a correlation identified between company performance and sustainability reporting that is positive.

From 2005 to 2019, Chouaibi et al. (2022) examined the impact of ESG practices on business performance in a sample of 115 UK and 90 German companies. Research demonstrates that the performance of an organisation improves with the strength it possesses in ESG practices. The impact of an ESG rating on firm performance—which is determined by ROA, ROE, share price, market capitalisation, firm size, PBDIT, and Tobin's *Q* – is examined by Sinha Ray and Goel (2023). An empirical study conducted from 2011 to 2019 on 48 Indian enterprises demonstrates the importance of the ESG score for corporate performance.

Furthermore, rather than emphasising ESG aspects, some research concentrates on ESG factors independently. In comparison to the social and environmental components, the governance factor has the greatest effect on FINP, according to the findings of Xie et al. (2019) and Velte (2017).

Additionally, Setiadi et al. (2017) assess that board independence and environmental disclosure have a beneficial impact on business value. The paper's conclusions validate the core tenets of corporate governance. Haninun et al. (2018) discovered that FINP is considerably impacted by environmental performance and disclosure. The results corroborate the conclusions of Purnomo and Widianingsih (2012). According to the study, firm performance is unaffected by CSR disclosure, whereas FINP is positively impacted by environmental performance.

According to Atan et al. (2018), there is no discernible correlation between the individual and combined ESG components and the profitability of Malaysian companies in terms of ROE and Tobin's *Q*. The effect of ESG parameters on the FINP of 65 Indian companies listed on the NSE 100 ESG Index has been examined by Dalal and Thaker (2019). The empirical study's outcomes demonstrate how the ESG score has a favourable impact on financial success, as determined by the return on asset and Tobin's *Q*.

Garcia and Orsato (2020) conducted an empirical investigation of 2,165 corporations in both advanced and developing countries. The results of the study illustrate an encouraging connection between corporate FINP and ESGP. On the other hand, ESG and the corporate of emerging market business enterprises have an inverse relationship.

Saygili et al. (2022) investigated the impact of ESGP on the FINP of listed companies in Türkiye between 2007 and 2017. ESG disclosures have mixed effects on corporate firm performance. For instance, environmental disclosure has a negative relationship with firm performance, while stockholder participation in management has a positive impact from a social perspective. Shareholder rights and the board of directors, which are used as a proxy for the governance dimension, positively impact FINP.

Using data from 1,042 corporations throughout the years 2010 and 2019, Naeem et al. (2022) evaluated the consequences of ESG variables on FINP in markets that are emerging. Results demonstrate that both individual and aggregate ESG scores have a favourable impact on business value as determined by the return on assets and Tobin's *Q*.

The impact of ESG scores on the FINP of Norwegian-listed companies was examined by Giannopoulos et al. (2022) between 2010 and 2019. ESG scores have a negative correlation with profitability as a return on asset and a positive correlation with company value as measured by Tobin's *Q*.

CONCLUSIONS

As a result of the scarcity of resources in our world becoming less and less accessible, especially in recent years, the understanding of sustainability has become the dominant thought movement of today. It has caused businesses to reshape all their activities in line with their understanding of this phenomenon and with this concern. Today, nations and companies want to be included in the race, so they reinvent themselves to become sustainable. In this regard, both national economies and companies must carry out their activities to maximise their environmental and social benefits and economic profit.

For this reason, both sustainability and sustainable development concepts are precious. So much so that scientific research proves that the trend is in this direction and is numerous. For example, as seen in the research conducted by Whelan et al. (2021) at the New York University (NYU) Stern Center for Sustainable Business, there were more than 1,000 scientific studies between 2015 and 2020 aimed solely at determining and measuring the impact of sustainability on FINP.

When the studies on the subject in the literature are evaluated, it is seen that they aim to evaluate the relationship between ESG, which is an important criterion and also an indicator of sustainability and many different essential variables and determinants to measure the size of this relationship. A variety of studies exploring the relationships between ESG and financial success show that the two factors have a positive association. Conversely, a small number of research studies support the claim that there is either no connection anyhow or a negative relationship among both of these variables. Considering the studies that reveal the ESG–FINP relationship, both positive and negative way, it is seen that although they are numerous, they are quite insufficient to explain the underlying reasons for this relationship (Whelan et al., 2021).

According to another determination regarding the existing studies in the literature, there is no commonly agreed definition of terminology, especially in the definitions of frequently used concepts. Therefore, companies using different definitions measure their ESGPs using different measurements, which prevents the healthy comparability of their ESGPs.

On the other hand, very few studies in the literature focus on the ESG disclosure issue, and it is not easy to find studies on determining the relationship between ESG disclosure and FINP (Khan, 2022). In addition, during the evaluation of the studies, the fact that the sample sizes were generally relatively small- and the time horizon was limited revealed the need for studies on a larger scale and covering long periods.

REFERENCES

Aboud, A., & Diab, A. (2018). The impact of social, environmental and corporate governance disclosures on firm value: Evidence from Egypt. *Journal of Accounting in Emerging Economies*, *8*(4), 442–458.

Ahsan, T., & Qureshi, M. A. (2021). The nexus between policy uncertainty, sustainability disclosure, and firm performance. *Applied Economics*, *53*(4), 441–453.

Atan, R., Alam, M. M., Said, J., & Zamri, M. (2018). The impacts of environmental, social, and governance factors on firm performance: Panel study of Malaysian companies. *Management of Environmental Quality*, *29*(2), 182–194.

Aydoğmuş, M., Gülay, G., & Ergun, K. (2022). Impact of ESG performance on firm value and profitability. *Borsa Istanbul Review*, *22*(2), 119–127.

Barnett, M. L., & Salomon, R. M. (2006). Beyond dichotomy: The curvilinear relationship between social responsibility and financial performance. *Strategic Management Journal*, *27*(11), 1101–1122.

Baron, D. P. (2008). Managerial contracting and corporate social responsibility. *Journal of Public Economics*, *92*(1), 268–288.

Beurden, P., & Goessling, T. (2008). The worth of values – A literature review on the relation between corporate social and financial performance. *Journal of Business Ethics*, *82*(2), 407–424.

Borghesi, R., Chang, K., & Li, Y. (2019). Firm value in commonly uncertain times: The divergent effects of corporate governance and CSR. *Applied Economics*, *51*(43), 4726–4741.

Brammer, S., Brooks, C., & Pavelin, S. (2006). Corporate social performance and stock returns: UK evidence from disaggregate measures. *Financial Management*, *35*(3), 97–116.

Branco, M. C., & Rodrigues, L. L. (2008). Social responsibility disclosure: A study of proxies for the public visibility of Portuguese banks. *The British Accounting Review*, *40*(2), 161–181.

Brandon, R. G., Krueger, P., & Schmidt, P. S. (2021). ESG rating disagreement and stock returns. *Financial Analysts Journal*, *77*(4), 104–127.

Cahan, S. F., Chen, C., Chen, L., & Nguyen, N. H. (2015). Corporate social responsibility and media coverage. *Journal of Banking & Finance*, *59*, 409–422.

Chen, H. Y., & Yang, S. S. (2020). Do investors exaggerate corporate ESG information? Evidence of the ESG momentum effect in the Taiwanese market. *Pacific-Basin Finance Journal*, *63*, 101407.

Cheng, I. H., Hong, H., & Shue, K. (2013). *Do managers do good with other peoples' money?* [Working paper, Dartmouth College, Princeton University, and University of Chicago].

Cohen, J. R., Holder-Webb, L. L., Nath, L., & Wood, D. (2012). Corporate reporting of non-financial leading indicators of economic performance and sustainability. *Accounting Horizons*, *26*(1), 65–90.

Dai, Y. (2020). Can ESG Investing beat the market and improve portfolio diversification? Evidence from China. *The Chinese Economy*, *54*(4), 272–285.

Dalal, K. K., & Thaker, N. (2019). ESG and corporate financial performance: A panel study of Indian companies. *Journal of Corporate Governance*, *18*, 44–59.

Deng, P., Wen, J., Wei, H., Chen, Y.-E., & Wang, Y.-P. (2022). Capital market opening and ESG performance. *Emerging Markets Finance and Trade*, *59*(13), 3866–3876.

DiMaggio, P. J., & Powell, W. W. (1983). The iron cage revisited: Institutional isomorphism and collective rationality in organizational fields. *American Sociological Review*, *48*(2), 147–160.

Douglas, E., Van Holt, T., & Whelan, T. (2017). Responsible investing: Guide to ESG data providers and relevant trends. *The Journal of Environmental Investing*, *8*(1), 92–114.

Eccles, R. G., Ioannou, I., & Serafeim, G. (2014). The impact of corporate sustainability on organizational process, *60*(11), 2835–2857.

Ertuğrul, F. (2008). Paydaş teorisi ve işletmelerin paydaşlari ile ilişkilerinin yönetimi. *Erciyes Üniversitesi İktisadi ve İdari Bilimler Fakültesi Dergisi*, *31*, 199–223.

Fatemi, A., Fooladi, I., & Tehranian, H. (2015). Valuation effects of corporate social responsibility. *Journal of Banking & Finance*, *59*, 182–192.

Ferrell, A., Liang, H., & Renneboog, L. (2016). Socially responsible firms. *Journal of Financial Economics*, *122*(3), 585–606.

Filbeck, G., Gorman, R., & Zhao, X. (2009). The "Best Corporate Citizens": Are they good for their shareholders? *Financial Review*, *44*(2), 239–262.

Freeman, R. E. (1984). *Strategic management: A stakeholder approach*. Pitman.

Galbreath, J. (2013). ESG in focus: The Australian evidence. *Journal of Business Ethics*, *118*(3), 529–541.

Galema, R., Plantinga, A., & Scholtens, B. (2008). The stocks at stake: Return and risk in socially responsible investment. *Journal of Banking & Finance*, *32*(12), 2646–2654.

Garcia, A. S., & Orsato, R. J. (2020). Testing the institutional difference hypothesis: A study about environmental, social, governance, and financial performance. *Business Strategy and the Environment*, *29*(8), 3261–3272.

Garriga, E., & Mele, D. (2004). Corporate social responsibility theories: Mapping the territory. *Journal of Business Ethics*, *53*, 51–71.

Garvare, R., & Johansson, P. (2010). Management for sustainability – A stakeholder theory. *Total Quality Management*, *21*(7), 737–744.

Gilman, R. (1992). *Sustainability by Robert Gilman from the 1992 UIA/AIA call for sustainable community solutions*. Retrieved June 3, 2023, from http://www.context.org

Giannopoulos, G., Fagernes, R. V. K., Elmarzouky, M., & Hossain, K. A. B. M. A. (2022). The ESG disclosure and the financial performance of Norwegian listed firms. *Journal of Risk and Financial Management*, *15*(6), 237.

Gladwin, N., & Kennelly, J. (1995). Shifting paradigms for sustainable development: Implications for management theory and research. *Academy of Management Review*, *20*(4), 874–904.

Godfrey, P. C., Merrill, C. B., & Hansen, J. M. (2009). The relationship between corporate social responsibility and shareholder value: An empirical test of the risk management hypothesis. *Strategic Management Journal*, *30*(4), 425–455.

GRI. (2023, May 28). https://www.globalreporting.org/about-gri/mission-history/

Halid, S., Rahman, R. A., Mahmud, R., Mansor, N., & Wahab, R. A. (2023). A literature review on ESG score and its impact on firm performance. *International Journal of Academic Research in Accounting Finance and Management Sciences*, *13*(1), 272–282.

Hamdi, K., Guenich, H., & Ben Saada, M. (2022). Does corporate financial performance promote ESG: Evidence from US firms. *Cogent Business & Management*, *9*(1), 2154053.

Hamrouni, A., Boussaada, R., & Toumi, N. B. F. (2019). Corporate social responsibility disclosure and debt financing. *Journal of Applied Accounting Research*, *20*(4), 394–415.

Haninun, H., Lindrianasari, L., & Denziana, A. (2018). The effect of environmental performance and disclosure on financial performance. *International Journal Trade and Global Markets*, *11*(1/2), 138–148.

Hörisch, J., Freeman, R. E., & Schaltegger, S. (2014). Applying stakeholder theory in sustainability management: Links, similarities, dissimilarities, and a conceptual framework. *Organization & Environment*, *27*(4), 328–346.

Hou, T. C. T. (2019). The relationship between corporate social responsibility and sustainable financial performance: Firm-level evidence from Taiwan. *Corporate Social Responsibility and Environmental Management*, *26*(1), 19–28.

Horváthová, E. (2010). Does environmental performance affect financial performance? A meta-analysis. *Ecological Economics*, *70*(1), 52–59.

Huber, B. M., Comstock, M., 2017. ESG reports and ratings: What they are, why they matter? Oversight role: A practical guide. *Corporate Governance Advisory Services*, *25*(5), 1–12.

Kaiser, L., & Welters, J. (2019). Risk-mitigating effect of ESG on momentum portfolios. *Journal of Risk Finance*, *20*(5), 542–555.

Khan, M. A. (2022). ESG disclosure and firm performance: A bibliometric and meta-analysis. *Research in International Business and Finance*, *61*, 1–19.

Kumar, S. (2023). A review ESG performance as a measure of stakeholders theory. *Academy of Marketing Studies Journal*, *27*(S3).

Lee, D. D., Faf, R. W., & Langfeld-Smith, K. (2009). Revisiting the vexing question: Does superior corporate social performance lead to improved financial performance? *Australian Journal of Management*, *34*(1), 21–49.

Li, Z., Feng, L., Pan, Z., & Sohail, H. M. (2022). ESG performance and stock prices: Evidence from the COVID-19 outbreak in China. *Humanities and Social Sciences Communications*, *9*(1), 1–10.

Lo, S., & Sheu, H. (2007). Is corporate sustainability a value-increasing strategy for business? *Corporate Governance: An International Review*, *15*(2), 345–358.

Lokuwaduge, C. S. D. S., & Heenetigala, K., 2017. Integrating environmental, social and governance (ESG) disclosure for a sustainable development: An Australian study. *Business Strategy and the Environment*, *26*(4), 438–450.

Malik, M. (2015). Value-enhancing capabilities of CSR: A brief review of contemporary literature. *Journal of Business Ethics*, *127*(2), 419–438.

Margolis, J. D., & Walsh, J. P. (2003). Misery loves companies: Rethinking social initiatives by business. *Administrative Science Quarterly*, *48*(2), 268–305.

Matos, P. V., Barros, V., Sarmento, J. M. (2020). Does ESG affect the stability of dividend policies in Europe? *Sustainability*, *12*(21), 1–15.

Meuer, J., Koelbel, J., & Hoffmann, V. H. (2020). On the nature of corporate sustainability. *Organization & Environment*, *33*(3), 319–341.

Mitchell, R. K., Agle, B. R., & Wood, D. J. (1997). Toward a theory of stakeholder identification and salience: Defining the principle of who and what really counts. *Academy of Management Review*, *22*(4), 853–886.

Naeem, M., Ullah, H., Shahid, J., & Kakakhel, S. J. (2022). The impact of ESG practices on firm performance: Evidence from emerging countries. *Indian Journal of Economics and Business*, *20*(1), 731–750.

Orsato, R. J., Garcia, A., Mendes-Da-Silva, W., Simonetti, R., & Monzoni, M. (2015). Sustainability indexes: Why join in? A study of the "Corporate Sustainability Index (ISE)" in Brazil. *Journal of Cleaner Production*, *96*, 161–170.

Özmehmet, E. (2008). Dünyada ve Tükiye Sürdürülebilir Kalkinma Yaklaşimlari. *Yaşar Üniversitesi E-Dergisi*, *3*(12), 1853–1876.

Purnomo, P. K., & Widianingsih, L. P. (2012). The influence of environmental performance on financial performance with corporate social responsibility (CSR) disclosure as a moderating variable: Evidence from listed companies in Indonesia. *Review of Integrative Business and Economics Research*, *1*(1), 57–69.

Puška, A., Hodžić, I., Štilić, A., & Murtič, S. (2024). Evaluating European Union countries on climate change management: A fuzzy MABAC approach to the climate change performance index. *Journal of Green Economy and Low-Carbon Development*, *3*(1), 15–25.

Qi, G. Y., Zeng, S. X., Shi, J. J., Meng, X. H., Lin, H., & Yang, Q. X. (2014). Revisiting the relationship between environmental and financial performance in Chinese industry. *Journal of Environmental Management*, *145*, 349–356.

Richardson, B. J. (2009). Keeping ethical investment ethical: Regulatory issues for investing for sustainability. *Journal of Business Ethics*, *87*, 555–572.

Sarıkaya, M., & Kara, Z. F. (2007). Sürdürülebilir Kalkınmada İşletmenin Rolü: Kurumsal Vatandaşlık. *Yönetim ve Ekonomi Dergisi*, *14*(2), 221–233.

Saygili, E., Arslan, S., & Birkan, A. O. (2022). ESG practices and corporate financial performance: Evidence from Borsa Istanbul. *Borsa Istanbul Review*, *22*(3), 525–533.

Scott, R. W., & Meyer, J. W. (1994). *Institutional environments and organizations*. Sage.

Serban, R.-A., Mihaiu, D. M., & Tichindelean, M. (2022). Environment, social, and governance score and value-added impacts on market capitalization: A sectoral-based approach. *Sustainability*, *14*(4), 2069.

Setiadi, I., Rahmawati Suhardjanto, D., & Djuminah. (2017). Board independence, environmental disclosure, and firm value. *Review of Integrative Business and Economics Research*, *6*(4), 409–417.

Sinha Ray, R., & Goel, S. (2023). Impact of ESG score on financial performance of Indian firms: Static and dynamic panel regression analyses. *Applied Economics*, *55*(15), 1742–1755.

Shaikh, I. (2022). On the relationship between policy uncertainty and sustainable investing. *Journal of Modelling in Management*, *17*(4), 1504–1523.

Statman, M. (2006). Socially responsible indexes: Composition, performance, and tracking error. *Journal of Portfolio Management*, *32*(3), 100–109.

Tüm, K. (2014). Kurumsal sürdürülebilirlik ve muhasebeye yansımaları: Sürdürülebilirlik muhasebesi. *Akademik Yaklaşımlar Dergisi*, *5*(1), 51.

UN PRI. (2023, May 14). https://www.unpri.org/about-us/about-the-pri

Van Linh, N., Hung, D. N., Binh, T. Q., & McMillan, D. (2022). Relationship between sustainability reporting and firm's value: Evidence from Vietnam. *Cogent Business & Management*, *9*(1), 2082014.

Velte, P. (2017). Does ESG performance have an impact on financial performance? Evidence from Germany. *Journal of Global Responsibility*, *8*(2), 169–178.

Wasiuzzaman, S., Ibrahim, S. A., & Kawi, F. (2022). Environmental, social and governance (ESG) disclosure and firm performance: Does national culture matter? *Meditari Accountancy Research*, *31*(5), 1239–1265.

Whelan, T., Atz, U., Van Holt, T., & Clark, C. (2021). *Uncovering the relationship by aggregating evidence from 1,000 plus studies published between 2015–2020*. https://sri360.com/wp-content/uploads/2022/10/NYU-RAM_ESG-Paper_2021-2.pdf

Wu, M. L. (2006). Corporate social performance, corporate financial performance, and firm size: A meta-analysis. *The Journal of American Academy of Business*, *8*(1), 163–171.

Xie, J., Nozawa, W., Yagi, M., Fujii, H., & Managi, S. (2019). Do environmental, social, and governance activities improve corporate financial performance? *Business Strategy Environment*, *28*(2), 286–300.

Yerpude, S., Sood, K., & Grima, S. (2022). Blockchain-augmented digital supply chain management: A way to sustainable business. *Journal of Risk and Financial Management*, *16*(1), 7.

Zhao, T., Xiao, X., & Zhang, B. (2021). Economic policy uncertainty and corporate social responsibility performance: Evidence from China. *Sustainability Accounting, Management and Policy Journal*, *12*(5), 1003–1026.

CHAPTER 11

THE IMPACT OF THE TRANSITION TO THE CIRCULAR ECONOMY IMPLEMENTATIONS IN THE FINANCIAL INDUSTRY: RECOMMENDATIONS FOR GOOD PRACTICE

Lethiwe Nzama-Sithole[a] and Sezer Bozkus Kahyaoglu[a,b]

[a]*Department of Commercial Accounting, College of Business & Economics, University of Johannesburg, South Africa*
[b]*Izmir Bakircay University, Management Department, Turkey*

ABSTRACT

Introduction: *The circular economy is observed as a good sustainability practice that has gained importance recently. The effects of this practice specific to the financial industry are examined in the context of green accounting, finance, and sustainability reporting standards and needs.*

Purpose: *This chapter aims to analyse the impact of the circular economy on the finance industry based on three research questions: (1) What benefits and challenges does the circular economy bring to the financial industry? (2) What should be the financial industry's strategic roadmap and business model for transitioning from a linear economy to a circular economy? (3) What are the differentiating aspects of ecosystem accounting and environmental accounting in its structure and use in the financial industry?*

Sustainability Development through Green Economics
Contemporary Studies in Economic and Financial Analysis, Volume 114, 173–189

Published under exclusive licence by Emerald Publishing Limited
ISSN: 1569-3759/doi:10.1108/S1569-375920240000114011

Methodology: *The method of our work is based on a 'strategic road map for circular economy' implementation and a 'sustainability business model framework' relevant to the finance industry. Thus, we systematically present the 'value generation process' considering the industry trends and dynamics and regulatory challenges regarding 'green business model' management with a strategic approach.*

Findings: *To coordinate the transition to a circular economy based on systematic knowledge about the state of ecosystems and their interactions with society, it is necessary to design monitoring, accounting and reporting systems that adapt to the new business operating environment. This chapter provides recommendations from the perspective of the financial sector.*

Keywords: Circular economy; linear economy; sharing economy; sustainable finance; green accounting; value hill; green blockchain; green business model for finance industry

JEL Codes: G10; Q50

INTRODUCTION

This study aims to analyse the effects of the circular economy, which has recently become a priority issue in the financial industry. The financial industry's structure is more complex than that of other sectors (ING, 2015). The main reason for this is that the financial industry has a structure that is affected by external factors and, accordingly, is subject to strict supervision based on internal, external, and even global financial standards (Bozkus Kahyaglu & Kurt, 2020; EY, 2015). The basic information regarding the application of these standards becomes visible through financial statements shared with the public.

It is a fact that many areas of change and innovation have emerged recently. These areas of change and innovation are also reflected in international financial accounting and reporting standards to monitor and harmonise their effects in financial statements. New standards, renewed accounting policies, and principles are emerging to find solutions to inadequate adaptation to such developments (CCA (Coalition Circular Accounting), 2022; EY, 2015). While some of these areas of change and innovation are optional, some are necessary. This study examines the situation of innovations and changes in the financial industry in the context of circular economy, sustainability, and ecosystem accounting practices. In particular, opportunities and threats arising from change and innovation are presented. The motivation of our work focusses on three main issues based on the below research questions:

1. What benefits and challenges does the circular economy bring to the financial industry?
2. What should be the financial industry's strategic roadmap and business model for transitioning from a linear economy to a circular economy?

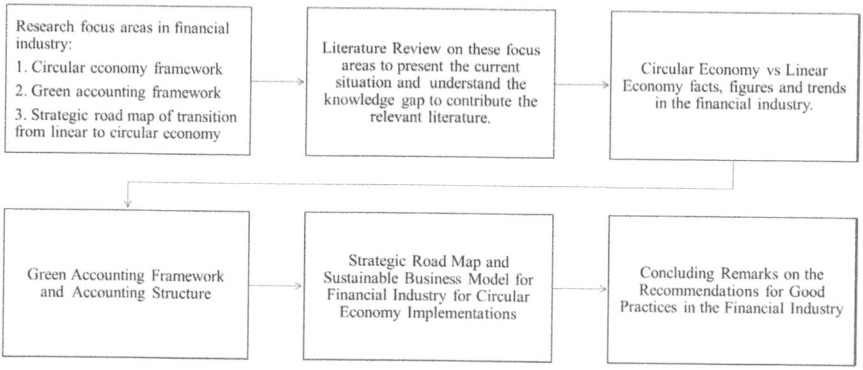

Fig. 11.1. The Flow of the Work Plan. *Source*: Prepared by the authors.

3. What are the differentiating aspects of ecosystem accounting and environmental accounting in its structure and use in the financial industry?

Based on this, the flow of the work plan is given as follows (Fig. 11.1).

LITERATURE REVIEW

To our knowledge, there is no clear and generally accepted definition of circular economy yet. Pearce and Turner (1989) first put forward the circular economy. According to these authors, there is interdependence between the economy and the environment. This interdependence is proposed based on the first law of thermodynamics (Zohuri, 2018). This law states that energy and natural resources cannot be destroyed and can only be transformed into different forms (Gonçalves et al., 2022; Zohuri, 2018).

The essence of the circular economy is to achieve a sustainable structure that encourages the reuse of waste materials. This approach offers a permanent solution, unlike the disposal of used material waste in the linear economy (CCA, 2022). For the circular economy to be fully implemented, a comprehensive change of perspective is required in production, consumption and all types of uses. The general view of the circular economy structure and the 'Value Hill as a Business Strategy Tool' is similar for all sectors and is shown in Fig. 11.2. Since there is such a general view and approach that includes all sectors in the circular economy, an interdisciplinary study is required. The basis of the circular economy and the prominent source of inspiration in the literature are based on nature and the ecosystem (CCA, 2016, 2022). In other words, there is a chain process in which the input of one product is the waste or output of another (Ellen MacArthur Foundation, 2015).

Businesses that offer products and services based on a circular economy approach generally design a product to preserve its added value for as long as possible. Therefore, in the context of 'Value Hill' for a product or service, value is added in the 'uphill' direction. Thus, through the circular business model

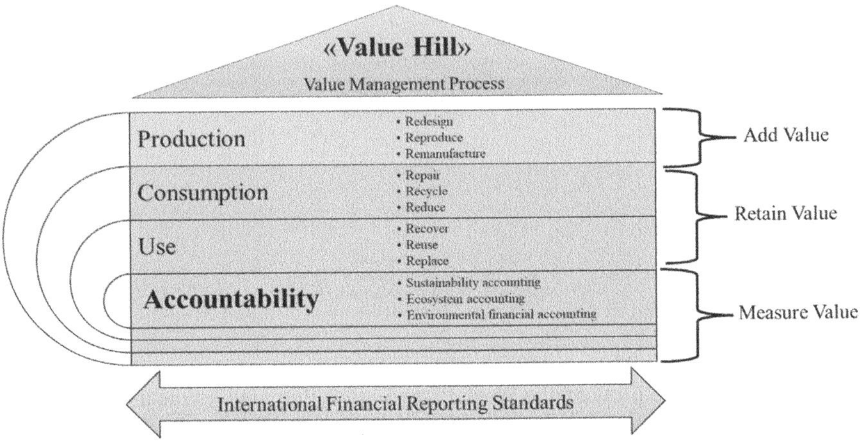

Fig. 11.2. The Structure of Circular Economy and the Value Hill.
Sources: Adapted from CCA (2022), Ozili and Opene (2021), and CCA (2016).

strategies applied in developing the product or service in question, efforts are made to keep the product or service at the highest value (at the top of the value hill) for as long as possible. Since the products are designed to be long-lasting and suitable for maintenance and repair, welding cycles are slowed (Bocken et al., 2016), and the product's life is extended. When a product is ready to begin its downhill process, it is done as slowly as possible so that its valuable resources can continue to serve others.

According to a forecast by the World Economic Forum (WEF, 2022), ecosystems and circular economy activities are gaining importance across all sectors, with their ability to create up to $100 trillion in value to drive business and societal benefits over the next decade. As evidence and a result of this situation, many interdisciplinary works have been produced in the literature. As seen in Table 11.1, when we look at the literature, we see that publications addressing the circular economy in different dimensions are based on a wide range of scientific fields.

Table 11.1. Publications on Circular Economy.

Field of Study	Number of Publications	%
Environmental Sciences	45	25
Business, Management and Accounting	32	18
Energy	26	14
Engineering	24	13
Social Sciences	19	10
Economy, Econometrics, and Finance	15	8
Computer Science	5	3
Others	15	8

Source: Web of Science (2023).

Considering the recent publications in indexed journals summarised in Table 11.1 in line with Fig. 11.2, although they are all about the circular economy and green, sustainability, ecosystem, and environmental accounting,[1] they were published in reputable and indexed journals that stand out in different scientific fields. The field that constitutes the research subject of this study is the second most published in the ranking and has a share of 18%. In addition, when we look at the total publications, including the social sciences, economics, econometrics, and finance, which form a part of our research in the sub-topics, it was determined that this rate reached 36%. Although there is a wide variety of studies on circular economy in the literature, it has been determined that few studies directly address the subject's relationship with finance. The main reason may be that publications on these topics in the literature increased significantly in 2015 and after and have not yet been entirely consumed by researchers in a short period (Camón & Celma, 2020; Dewick & Joseph, 2023; Gonçalves et al., 2022; Goyal et al., 2021; Sassanelli et al., 2019).

A circular economy has generally been examined within the theoretical framework of two approaches. In the first theoretical approach, engineers and environmental scientists work to carry out technical investigations on circular economy. These scientists have carried out studies focussing on environmental research problems in the context of production, such as technical issues such as biochemicals, new materials to increase the efficiency of production processes, metals, plastics, and food processing (Alcalde-Calonge et al., 2022). Even though there are valuable applications and contributions to the literature obtained through this approach, it does not consider the situation from the strategic management perspective of businesses since it examines the subject only from a technical perspective (see Kuhlmann et al., 2022; UNEP, 2020). There has been a need to consider the circular economy, which constitutes the second theoretical approach on this subject, from the perspective of strategic business management, environmental, financial management, and ecosystem accounting implementations (Ahmad et al., 2023; Alcalde-Calonge et al., 2022; CCA, 2022). This study is designed to contribute to the second theoretical approach. In this context, it aims to reveal the cooperation areas based on good practice so businesses can effectively use the circular strategy, circular business model, circular process control, ecosystem accounting, and integrated reporting infrastructure required to transition from a linear economy to a circular economy.

In making the circular economy functional, the macro policies followed by countries and the approach of the financial industry that will support the financing of this transformation are important (Aboulamer et al., 2020). Regarding measurement and reporting standards for the circular economy, there appears to be no generally accepted way to measure at either the micro or macro level (Kristensen & Mosgaard, 2020). Additionally, it is argued that most indicators used to measure the circular economy pay less attention to environmental and social aspects (CCA, 2022; Luis & Celma, 2020).

The circular economy is rapidly expanding its scope. While it was described with 3R in its first definition, it is followed by 6R in the second stage and 9R in the last stage. These activities, starting with R's, are essentially used to describe a phase within the circular economy. The current list of 9R activities has been published by UNEP (2020) and is given in Fig. 11.2.

The United Nations (UNEP) has taken an important initiative to meet this deficiency, most notably the needs of the business world. This major initiative, launched in 2013 by the 'United Nations System of Environmental-Economic Accounting' (SEEA), offers an essential tool for achieving sustainable development goals. In other words, SEEA is authorised to design monitoring, accounting, and reporting systems that will adapt to the global work environment through international cooperation and coordination based on implementations of ecosystem accounting standards.

To fully ensure the transition to a circular economy and become a good practice, businesses must review their corporate risks, cash flow management processes, and stakeholder relationships (UNEP, 2020). The financial industry and the approach of finance professionals, in general, will need to adapt to these changes to deliver the tools and services that businesses will need. When evaluated from this perspective, defining, measuring, accounting for, monitoring the development of sustainability-related activities, environmental issues, and the circular economy is necessary. Determining and implementing circular economy topics is strategically vital for the finance sector and many sectors. This study aims to contribute to disseminating good practices in the financial industry.

As a well-known general acceptance, the financial industry is ready to finance any project and customer it finds profitable as long as there are no legal restrictions or prohibitions. The relevant project or issue must be measurable for the finance industry to make quick decisions and provide financial support (Aboulamer et al., 2020; CCA, 2022). In this context, details are presented below to determine the advantages and disadvantages of the circular economy and to decide by making a cost-benefit analysis within the framework of the approach of the finance industry and finance professionals.

ADVANTAGES AND DISADVANTAGES OF CIRCULAR ECONOMY WITHIN THE FINANCIAL INDUSTRY PERSPECTIVE

While approaches addressing the advantages and disadvantages of globalisation were important in the recent past, it is observed that there is a need for new performance indicators compatible with global sustainable development goals within the framework of rapid technological developments and digital transformation that emerged after the pandemic (Aboulamer et al., 2020; Baldarelli et al., 2017). A different perspective is needed to guide companies' strategic business decisions, enriched with other essential elements such as non-financial issues based on expected benefits, collaborations, and social responsibilities concerning sustainability perspective, rather than the competition of sectors. This need necessitates closely monitoring, protecting, and using environmental variables, which are critical for the depletion of natural resources and the survival of companies and the planet and for the right purposes (Baldarelli et al., 2017).

When evaluated from this perspective, environmental variables are beginning to be considered as increasing opportunities for both businesses and countries globally regarding socio-economic benefits beyond being associated only with the physical environment or cost elements that burden companies. This situation forces all businesses and countries to meet on the same ground and act responsibly and jointly due to the scarcity of natural resources in an intensely competitive business environment (Baldarelli et al., 2017). This can be possible by transitioning from a linear economy to a circular economy based on international collaborations on a global scale and within the framework of international financial reporting standards based on environmental, social, ethical, and economic perspectives to achieve a value-added approach (Fig. 11.2).

It is a fact that deciding to abandon the linear economy and transition to a circular economy is not an easy decision for organisations and instead, it should be treated as a basic 'necessity'. Therefore, it would be appropriate for organisations to include this issue in their strategic business plans in the new era and accelerate the transition process. At this stage, the finance industry and professionals play an essential role in financing and correctly managing the transition to a circular economy. In this study, we try to contribute through recommendations for good practice and the establishment of a strategic road map that may be needed in the creation of the infrastructure by revealing the issues that need to be taken into consideration in carrying out the role expected from the finance industry and finance professionals. Based on this, in the first stage, the differences between circular and linear economies should be determined and a good understanding of why the transition is necessary should be ensured. For this purpose, the main features of the two economic approaches are briefly compared concerning characterisation, business model, and the impact on the environment, employment, energy consumption, accountability, and technological advancements, respectively. This is presented as a summary table in Appendix 1. Within the framework of comparing linear and circular economy systems in Appendix 1, the data obtained from their impacts on the environment, employment, and business processes are sufficient to understand why this change and transformation should be rapid. As the following steps, the benefits, and criticised aspects of the circular economy, specifically in the financial industry, are given below with a balanced and objective approach.

Advantages of the Circular Economy

Among the benefits of the circular economy, the most important one that we can associate with the financial industry is the diversification of the loan portfolio. Thus, new sectoral gains may emerge, allowing the financial industry to transfer funds and resources. This approach also offers a win-win model to the parties within the scope of responsible investing and finance (Ozili & Opene, 2021).

Since the perception of the financial industry in general and bankers in particular in the eyes of customers and society is not very positive, there is an opportunity to change this perception positively within the framework of responsible finance. Whichever company and sector we consider, they will all need external funds, resources, and financing. Therefore, if the finance industry supports and prioritises green financing, it can increase the effectiveness and scope of a sustainable business environment, especially green entrepreneurship (Aranda-Usón et al., 2019; Ellen MacArthur Foundation, 2015).

Within the framework of research conducted in the literature, evidence shows that organisations that are leaders in sustainability implementations are more innovative, achieve better financial performance and ethical decision-making with a responsible management approach and have better credit scores. Therefore, this information is strategically important regarding the finance industry's credit portfolio and risk management. Namely, for banks, directing more assets and capital into sustainable businesses is essential to building a healthy portfolio and helps facilitate the transition to a low-carbon economy. As a result, every sustainability-related financing request is now a business opportunity for the financial industry (ING, 2015).

Disadvantages of the Circular Economy

The difficulties faced by the circular economy transition process and the shortcomings in its implementation arise from the imbalance between risk and return when evaluated from the financial industry's perspective (UNEP, 2020). Considering the fact that the transition to a circular economy is much more complex than the linear economy for organisations and the constraints of a trained workforce to manage this process, a situation arises that increases the portfolio risks of the finance industry and shows their perception as risky when making decisions for green financing and credit risk assessment. The situations that trigger this increase in risk perception can be summarised as follows: Firstly, the business model for the circular economy is more complex and although the needs for financing this process are high, the return cannot be fully predicted. Secondly, the linear economy is perceived as less risky in the current financial industry and they are more familiar with and accustomed to the business model. Thirdly, there is the inability to fully know and measure the value of physical risks due to environmental and climate impacts and the deficiencies in reporting (UNEP, 2020).

While listing the advantages of the implementation of a circular economy, it should not be forgotten that these are long-term, that they must be supported by a long-term investment strategy within the framework of a strategic management approach and that a business cannot achieve this goal alone and must cooperate with their stakeholders. This situation causes criticism and disadvantages to emerge during the transition to a circular economy.

Recycling all the materials used in the circular economy may not be possible, or the cost may be too high. This situation is at the forefront of the difficulties encountered in practice and causes criticism. Government support and financing are required to realise a comprehensive circular economy. When evaluated from this perspective, difficulties may arise in these businesses in accessing this support and financing. At the same time, the circular economy is not an application that can only be initiated by changing the system infrastructure. Cultural change is also imperative. This can be a challenging goal to achieve if there are disruptions in business management. As a general trend in the world, most of the population migrates to cities and wants to work in cities to live in better conditions instead of living in rural areas. Even though this situation brings about high-income levels and economic growth, it also causes sustainability-related issues to gain importance within the framework of environmental pollution and social problems. In this respect, it is necessary to be able to implement the circular economy fully. This is necessary because developed countries create more waste, which is not sustainable (UNEP, 2020).

The Sharing Economy and Green Blockchain-based Implementations

It can be stated that the 'sharing economy' defines the savings that need to be made today to equalise the living level between generations and ensure the survival of the next generations within the framework of the sustainability of world resources. In this context, the necessity of using usable and consumable goods for consumption is at the forefront. When evaluated from this perspective, ensuring the transfer of goods that can be used and create the same benefit when used between individuals in the economy stands out as an essential tool (Fig. 11.3).

The process in question can also be evaluated in terms of production processes. At this point, transferring consumption not only prevents the use of new resources but can also be a source of savings that will enable the transfer of said resources to a cleaner environment, energy, and similar areas. In this respect, the sharing economy is gaining importance as a primary tool. However, for this practice to go beyond being a dream, it depends on the habitual consumption culture and consent to change, especially on those who decide to consume. Hence, this is a significant difficulty. The measures to be taken to ensure this transformation are not only economic but also sociological and psychological.

One of the critical issues here is establishing a 'trust-based' infrastructure to increase social benefits in the sharing economy. Blockchain technology makes this possible (Bakarich et al., 2020; Esmaeilian et al., 2020). Although blockchain technology has many advantages concerning the sharing economy and circular economy, it is not easy to achieve this in a short time since all system users must transform the system infrastructure (Puška et al., 2024; Yerpude et al., 2022).

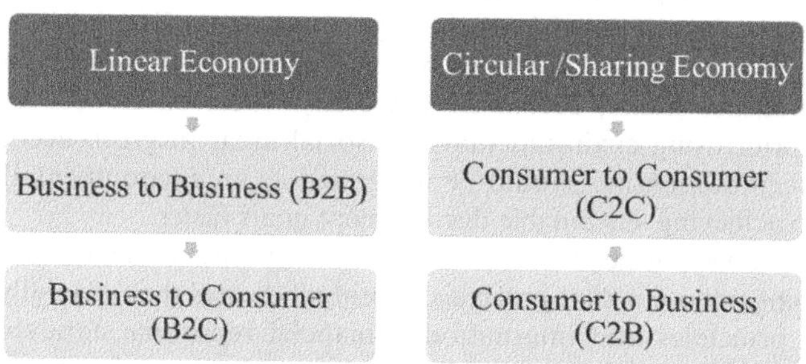

Fig. 11.3. The Segments of Linear Economy Versus Circular/Sharing Economy. *Source*: Prepared by the authors by adapting from ING (2015).

Blockchain technology is a disruptive innovation in the financial sector due to cryptocurrencies (Parmentola et al., 2022). However, it offers a reliable system infrastructure and intelligent contract approach-based applications that can be used for the financial sector and all sectors. In this context, it has a significant potential to expand the scope of sustainability practices, which is a prominent issue. It contributes to the sharing economy, which is the application area of sustainable development goals, and is expected to gain even more importance in the future (Bellucci et al., 2022; Lu, 2018; Parmentola et al., 2022). If the opportunities offered by blockchain technologies are considered within the sustainability framework, they are expected to provide benefits in three main areas. These are, respectively, (1) determination of resource rights, (2) monitoring the origin of products, and (3) monitoring behaviours and incentives based on a reliable and unchangeable recording system (Bakarich et al., 2020; Hughes et al., 2019; Parmentola et al., 2022). Recently, priority has been given to reducing carbon emissions and energy consumption through approaches referred to as green blockchain implementations, thereby ensuring the use of the 'green blockchain' in an environmentally sustainable manner (Alzoubi & Mishra, 2023).

To implement the sharing and circular economy fully and effectively in businesses, it is necessary to integrate it with the system infrastructure required for accounting and financial reporting (Bonsón & Bednárová, 2019; Cai, 2021). This necessitates restructuring accounting and finance practices, which we can generally refer to as 'green accounting', with an interdisciplinary approach (Bellucci et al., 2022; Kokina et al., 2017).

THE GREEN ACCOUNTING FRAMEWORK

In accounting standards, the definition of green has begun to be used as a general and inclusive expression, and as seen in Fig. 11.4, accounting standards are created to serve the same purpose from different perspectives. In this context, it is observed that there are institutions and platforms within the UNEP (2020) that try to ensure international policy coordination to increase the effectiveness of application standards.

The emergence of green accounting solves problems arising from deficiencies in the current accounting and financial reporting system. The green accounting types in Fig. 11.4 have been developed within the framework of different environmental approaches (Lako, 2018a; UNEP, 2020). These differences in approach arise from prioritising environmental and social areas in green accounting. In all cases, green accounting should be integrated as an environmentally friendly approach to achieving sustainable development goals faster.

This study does not need to explain accounting types in detail. However, the essential point to note is that green accounting indicates that generally accepted accounting principles and international financial reporting standards (IFRS) reporting activities are no longer sufficient in measuring and reporting performance related to sustainability and circular economy (Gallhofer & Haslam, 1997; Lako, 2018b). The significant differences between IFRS and Green Accounting

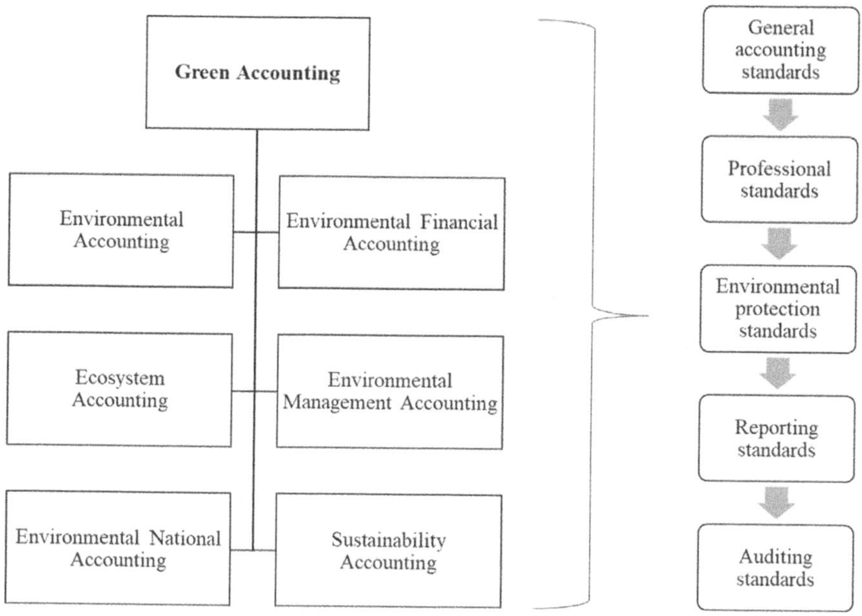

Fig. 11.4. Green Accounting Framework. *Source*: Prepared by the authors by adapting from Cui and Chen (2022), UNEP (2020), and Lako (2018b).

are explained in Appendix 2. In this respect, it is necessary to accept that it has become a profession that requires those working in accounting and finance processes to have technical knowledge in statistics, mathematics, data analytics, geographical information systems and environmental issues or that requires interdisciplinary cooperation. In the new era, finance professionals need to be prepared for a new learning process concerning sustainability issues and climate-related risks. It is essential to increase their competence in the basic requirements of changing accounting and financial reporting standards. This situation becomes even more critical for the finance industry, which finances change and transformation of the global economy in this regard and is one of the leading sectors due to its structure.

THE ROLE OF THE FINANCIAL INDUSTRY IN THE TRANSITION TO A CIRCULAR ECONOMY

Within the framework of the finance initiative launched by the UNEP (2023) for financial institutions, the green business model, strategic goals about sustainability, and what needs to be done in the transition to a circular economy are recommended. The highlights for financial institutions that support compliance with this are summarised as follows:

1. Compliance: it is necessary to determine the international, regional, or national policy frameworks with which the institution generally complies in relation to the green finance approach.
2. Baseline: It is necessary to define, measure, and monitor the baseline and current compliance level for the indicators determined within the framework of strategic objectives based on green accounting and reporting standards.
3. SMART goals (including green key performance indicators [KPIs]): defining, implementing, and reporting a detailed set of goals and KPIs are necessary to monitor progress towards achieving the strategic goals set by the institution concerning the sustainable development goals (SDGs).
4. Action plan: It is necessary to define, implement, and report the basic green business model, green business plans, and critical 'responsible', 'sustainable', and 'green' actions that the institution defines to achieve its smart goals.

The finance industry has a vital role as a leader in the circular economy and as a lender to the circular economy. In this transition process, technology will be a crucial enabler towards a circular economy, as it can reduce waste, reuse resources, and increase efficiency. Financial institutions, specifically banks, have a critical position in this transition plan and can do many beneficial things, as indicated in Fig. 11.5.

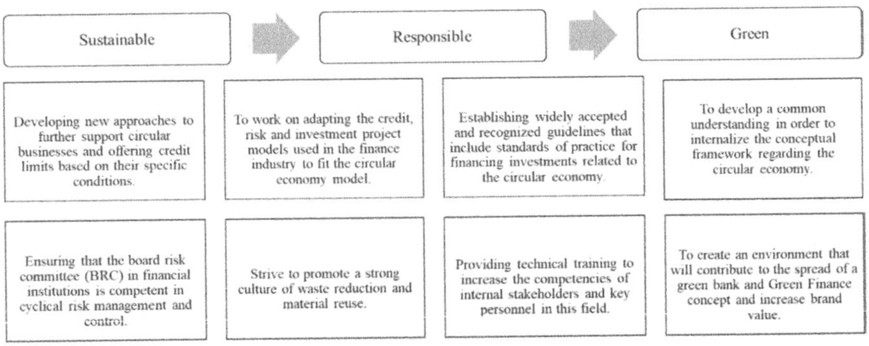

Fig. 11.5. The Role of Financial Institutions in the Transition to the Circular Economy. *Source*: Prepared by the authors based on information in Transition Plan Taskforce (TPT, 2023).

CONCLUDING REMARKS AND RECOMMENDATIONS FOR FUTURE WORK

This study focusses on the basic requirements and emerging challenges in transitioning to a circular economy from the financial industry perspective. Based on this, needs are put forward that will form the basis for practices that will enable our planet to live in a healthier and fairer environment for new generations.

Within the scope of sustainability, a circular economy will gain importance as a necessity. In this context, expanding and implementing a green economy in applications to reduce carbon dioxide emissions has become necessary. Considering these practices, measures should be taken to change the habits of decision-making units in the economy, especially consumers, towards this practice and to create behavioural tendencies.

Observations are that there is an avoidance of behaviour towards circular economy in developing countries. In this respect, it may be recommended to take measures to implement a dissemination strategy based on public consent beyond coercion. It is generally known that more than one tool is used to create an economic structure for this circular economy. Using these tools disconnected and separate from each other may lead to increased implementation costs. Therefore, it is necessary to take measures to share this cost. In this respect, the transition to a circular economy will bring about a financing problem. It also reveals a structural change in all finance-related executive reporting and accounting infrastructures. Finding this financing source also remains a global problem for all related parties. The most important feature distinguishing the finance industry from other sectors is that it contributes to providing services for itself and society and constitutes an essential element in the value chain. At the same time, since it operates in a regulated market, it is more likely to comply with standards and be an example of good practice.

It is an essential achievement that financial institutions with a responsible, sustainable, and green financial approach are given priority in bringing together those in need of funds and those with surplus funds. Finance professionals must internalise the cultural change required within the circular economy to initiate and lead this. Once this is achieved, it may be possible to realise sustainable development goals more systematically and quickly.

NOTE

1. It should be noted that green accounting, sustainability accounting, ecosystem accounting, and environmental accounting are similar terms in nature, and for this reason, the authors use these terms interchangeably.

REFERENCES

Aboulamer, A., Soufani, K., & Esposito, M. (2020). Financing the circular economic model. *Thunderbird International Business Review*, *62*(6), 641–646.

Ahmad, F., Bask, A., Laari, S., & Robinson, C. V. (2023). Business management perspectives on the circular economy: Present state and future directions. *Technological Forecasting and Social Change*, *187*, 122182. https://doi.org/10.1016/j.techfore.2022.122182

Alcalde-Calonge, A., Sáez-Martínez, F. J., & Ruiz-Palomino, P. (2022). Evolution of research on circular economy and related trends and topics. A thirteen-year review. *Ecological Informatics*, *70*, 101716. https://doi.org/10.1016/j.ecoinf.2022.101716

Alzoubi, Y. I., & Mishra, A. (2023). Green blockchain–A move towards sustainability. *Journal of Cleaner Production*, *430*, 139541.

Aranda-Usón, A., Portillo-Tarragona, P., Marín-Vinuesa, L. M., & Scarpellini, S. (2019). Financial resources for the circular economy: A perspective from businesses. *Sustainability*, *11*(3), 888. https://doi.org/10.3390/su11030888

Bakarich, K. M., Castonguay, J. J., & O'Brien, P. E. (2020). The use of blockchains to enhance sustainability reporting and assurance. *Accounting Perspectives*, *19*(4), 389–412.

Baldarelli, M. G., Del Baldo, M., Nesheva-Kiosseva, N., Baldarelli, M. G., Matacena, A., & Pascari, L. (2017). New Challenges for the enterprise in the age of "sustainable modernity". *Environmental Accounting and Reporting: Theory and Practice*, 1–34. https://doi.org/10.1007/978-3-319-50918-1_1

Bellucci, M., Cesa Bianchi, D., & Manetti, G. (2022). Blockchain in accounting practice and research: Systematic literature review. *Meditari Accountancy Research*, *30*(7), 121–146. https://doi.org/10.1108/MEDAR-10-2021-1477

Blomsma, F., & Tennant, M. (2020). Circular economy: Preserving materials or products?*Introducing the Resource States framework. Resources, Conservation and Recycling*, *156*, 104–698.

Bocken, N. M. P., De Pauw, I., Bakker, C., & Van Der Grinten, B. (2016). Product design and business model strategies for a circular economy. *Journal of Industrial and Production Engineering*, *33*(5), 308–320. https://doi.org/10.1080/21681015.2016.1172124

Bonsón, E., & Bednárová, M. (2019). Blockchain and its implications for accounting and auditing. *Meditari Accountancy Research*, *27*(5), 725–740.

Bozkus Kahyaglu, S., & Kurt, G. (2020). Future expectations in banking risk management. *Journal of Accounting & Finance/Muhasebe ve Finansman Dergisi*, *Spring*(86), 267–287.

Cai, C. W. (2021). Triple-entry accounting with blockchain: How far have we come? *Accounting & Finance*, *61*(1), 71–93.

Camón Luis, E., & Celma, D., (2020). Circular Economy. A Review and Bibliometric Analysis. *Sustainability*, *12*, 6381. https://doi.org/10.3390/su12166381

CCA. (2016). Create a Financeable Circular Business in 10 steps. *Finance White Paper*. Retrieved December 23, 2023 from https://assets-global.website-files.com/5d26d80e8836af2d12ed1269/5dea753a5293546f4dc60c37_finance-white-paper-20161207-EN.pdf

CCA (Coalition Circular Accounting). (2022). *Financial accounting in the circular economy: Redefining value, impact and risk to accelerate the circular transition*. Retrieved December 30, 2023, from https://www.circle-economy.com/resources/financial-accounting-in-the-circular-economy-redefining-value-impact-and-risk-to-accelerate-the-circular-transition

Cui, C., & Chen, D. (2022). The ımplementation measures of environmental accounting in heavy pollution ındustry in the context of sustainable development. *Mobile Information Systems*, *2022*(2), 1–11, https://doi.org/10.1155/2022/3614435

Dewick, P., & Joseph, S. (2023). Investment opportunities for a sustainable and circular economy. *Amplify*, *36*(10), 2023. Retrieved December 30, 2023, from https://www.cutter.com/journal/investment-opportunities-sustainable-circular-economy

Ellen MacArthur Foundation. (2015). *Towards a circular economy: Business rationale for an accelerated transition*. Retrieved December 30, 2023, from https://kidv.nl/media/rapportages/towards_a_circular_economy.pdf?1.2.1

Esmaeilian, B., Sarkis, J., Lewis, K., & Behdad, S. (2020). Blockchain for the future of sustainable supply chain management in ındustry 4.0. *Resources, Conservation and Recycling*, *163*, 105064. https://doi.org/10.1016/j.resconrec.2020.105064; Retrieved December 30, 2023, from https://www.sciencedirect.com/science/article/abs/pii/S0921344920303815?via%3Dihub

EY. (2015). *Rethinking risk management banks focus on non-financial risks and accountability, 2015 risk management survey of major financial institutions* [online]. Retrieved December 30, 2023, from http://www.ey.com/Publication/vwLUAssets/EY-rethinking-riskmanagement/$FILE/EY-rethinking-risk-management.pdf

Gallhofer, S., & Haslam, J. (1997). The direction of green accounting policy: Critical reflections. *Accounting, Auditing & Accountability Journal*, *10*(2), 148–174.

Ghisellini, P., Cialani, C., & Ulgiati, S. (2016). A review on circular economy: The expected transition to a balanced interplay of environmental and economic systems. *Journal of Cleaner Production*, *114*, 11–32. https://doi.org/10.1016/j.jclepro.2015.09.007

Gonçalves, B. D. S. M., Carvalho, F. L. D., & Fiorini, P. D. C. (2022). Circular economy and financial aspects: A systematic review of the literature. *Sustainability*, *14*(5), 3023. https://doi.org/10.3390/su14053023

Goyal, S., Chauhan, S., & Mishra, P. (2021). Circular economy research: A bibliometric analysis (2000–2019) and future research insights. *Journal of cleaner production*, *287*, 125011.

Hughes, L., Dwivedi, Y. K., Misra, S. K., Rana, N. P., Raghavan, V., & Akella, V. (2019). Blockchain research, practice and policy: Applications, benefits, limitations, emerging research themes and research agenda. *International Journal of İnformation Management*, *49*, 114–129. https://doi.org/10.1016/j.ijinfomgt.2019.02.005

ING. (2015, May). *Rethinking finance in a circular economy, report of economics department*. Retrieved December 30, 2023, from https://www.ing.com/MediaEditPage/Financing-the-Circular-Economy.htm

Kokina, J., Mancha, R., & Pachamanova, D. (2017). Blockchain: Emergent industry adoption and implications for accounting. *Journal of Emerging Technologies in Accounting*, *14*(2), 91–100.

Kristensen, H. S., & Mosgaard, M. A. (2020). A review of micro level indicators for a circular economy–moving away from the three dimensions of sustainability? *Journal of Cleaner Production*, *243*, 118–531.

Kuhlmann, M., Bening, C. R., & Hoffmann, V. H. (2022). How incumbents realize disruptive circular innovation—Overcoming the innovator's dilemma for a circular economy. *Business Strategy and the Environment*, *32*(3), 1106–1121. https://doi.org/10.1002/bse.3109

Lako, A. (2018a, April–June). *The green accounting conceptual framework* (pp. 60–66). AKUNTAN INDONESIA.

Lako, A. (2018b). Conceptual framework of green accounting. *Accounting*, 60–66. Retrieved December 30, 2023, from https://www.researchgate.net/profile/Andreas-Lako/publication/333384989_Conceptual_Framework_of_Green_Accounting/links/5cea10ac92851c4eabbf18b0/Conceptual-Framework-of-Green-Accounting.pdf

Lu, Y. (2018). Blockchain and the related issues: A review of current research topics. *Journal of Management Analytics*, *5*(4), 231–255.

Luis, E. C., & Celma, D. (2020). Circular economy. A review and bibliometric analysis. *Sustainability*, *12*(16), 6381.

Ozili, P. K. (2021). Circular economy, banks and other financial institutions: what's in it for them?. https://mpra.ub.uni-muenchen.de/107397/

Ozili, P. K. & Opene, F. U. (2021). The role of banks in the circular economy. *World Journal of Science, Technology and Sustainable Development*.

Parmentola, A., Petrillo, A., Tutore, I., & De Felice, F. (2022). Is blockchain able to enhance environmental sustainability? A systematic review and research agenda from the perspective of Sustainable Development Goals (SDGs). *Business Strategy and the Environment*, *31*(1), 194–217. https://doi.org/10.1002/bse.2882

Pearce, D. W., & Turner, R. K. (1989). *Economics of natural resources and the environment*. Johns Hopkins University Press.

Puška, A., Hodžić, I., Štilić, A., & Murtič, S. (2024). Evaluating European Union countries on climate change management: A fuzzy MABAC approach to the climate change performance ındex. *Journal Green Economy Low-Carbon Development*, *3*(1), 15–25.

Sassanelli, C., Rosa, P., Rocca, R., & Terzi, S. (2019). Circular economy performance assessment methods: A systematic literature review. *Journal of Cleaner Production*, *229*, 440–453.

Sauvé, S., Bernard, S., & Sloan, P. (2016). Environmental sciences, sustainable development and circular economy: Alternative concepts for trans-disciplinary research. *Environmental Development*, *17*, 48–56.

Transition Plan Taskforce (TPT). (2023). *TPT disclosure framework*. Retrieved December 30, 2023, from https://transitiontaskforce.net/wp-content/uploads/2023/10/TPT_Disclosure-framework-2023.pdf

UNEP. (2020). *Financing circularity: October 2020 demystifying finance for circular economies*. Retrieved December 30, 2023, from https://www.unep.org/news-and-stories/press-release/new-unep-report-lights-way-financial-institutions-shift-more

UNEP. (2023). *Principles for responsible banking: Guidance for banks*. Retrieved December 30, 2023, from https://www.unepfi.org/wordpress/wp-content/uploads/2023/11/PRB-Nature-Target-Setting-Guidance_2023.pdf

Web of Science. (2023). *Cited Refernce Serach*. https://webofscience.help.clarivate.com/en-us/Content/cited-reference-search.htm

World Economic Forum (WEF). (2022). *Global risk report*. Retrieved December 30, 2023, from https://www3.weforum.org/docs/WEF_The_Global_Risks_Report_2022.pdf

Yerpude, S., Sood, K., & Grima, S. (2022). Blockchain-augmented digital supply chain management: A way to sustainable business. *Journal of Risk and Financial Management*, *16*(1), 7.

Zohuri, B. (2018). *First law of thermodynamics an ultralow temperature phenomenon*. Elsevier Publications. https://doi.org/10.1016/C2017-0-01796-2

APPENDIX 1. THE COMPARISON OF THE LINEAR ECONOMY AND CIRCULAR ECONOMY

Topic	Linear Economy	Circular Economy
Characterisation	An economic system based on a 'take-make-dispose' approach (Goyal et al., 2021) Money is the dominant value of this approach	An economic system promotes efficiency by 'eliminating waste and the continuous use of resources' (Ghisellini et al., 2016; Sauvé et al., 2016) In addition to money, social and environmental values are considered in the approach
Business model	(i) 'From production to consumption' (ii) 'From consumption to waste' (iii) 'From waste to the destruction of waste material'	(i) 'From production to waste' (ii) 'Waste is then recycled as raw material for reuse'
Impact on environment	The waste is disposed of at the end of the process and serves no other purpose after that. For this reason, environmentally harmful waste increases	At the end of the process, waste materials are shared, reused, or recycled as raw materials for other uses with innovative methods, ensuring continuity Thus, it contributes to the environmental protection
Impact on energy consumption	More resources and energy are needed to produce new goods	Less resources and energy are required to produce new goods
Impact on employment	Using the same business lines in society is sufficient; new jobs are not created. Only the same jobs are created	New and unique jobs can be created to participate in waste recycling processes. In addition, it could lead to the creation of a new industry, such as the recycling industry
Impact on accountability	Linear economy is the economic model that is most widely adopted in many countries of the world Financial indicators and cost-benefit analysis measure the success of the system	A circular economy is an economic model that is less adopted globally and has recently gained awareness within the framework of sustainable development goals The system's success is measured by financial and non-financial indicators and cost-benefit analysis, including all the stakeholders and society
Impact on technological advancements	Linear economy has been implemented since the Industrial Revolution in the 1800s Technological advances previously appeared within the context of seemingly unlimited natural resources. However, this becomes challenging for organisations since the linear economic model ends in waste, leading to various unsustainability issues related to biodiversity loss, environmental pollution, deforestation, and material depletion	In the new era, a new economic paradigm of 'reduce, reuse and recycle' is needed, and thus, the circular economy aims to solve this challenge by combining income with social impact with the help of technological innovations Examples of technological innovations that force the linear economy to change and transform into a circular economy: nanotechnology, the Internet of Things, renewable energy, smart devices and contracts, and blockchain

Sources: Adapted from Ozili (2021) and Blomsma and Tennant (2020).

APPENDIX 2. THE DIFFERENCES BETWEEN IFRS AND GREEN ACCOUNTING

Topic	IFRS	Green Accounting
The scope of information	Financial and economic issues are addressed in the accounting information. It is argued that the information produced during the accounting and reporting process and disclosed to the public through financial statements for evaluation and decision-making purposes is predominantly financial, partial, and incomplete. Since non-financial information is not fully included, it is considered less relevant, reliable and misleading	Accounting information is based on all phenomena, namely, 'objects', 'actions', or 'transactions' that are inherent or occur in the planet and business environment. The major assumption is that human behaviour as a representative of society and any corporation has reciprocal relations with the planet. In this respect, social, financial/economic and environmental accounting become part of Green Accounting issues. Accounting for all nature, that is, land, plants, forests, water, air, atmosphere, sea, carbon, waste, corporate, social, and environmental responsibility (CSR) is also part of Green Accounting
The scope of reporting	It is criticised for presenting a reporting approach based on financial information (quantitative information) and is inadequate in informing the public	In reporting, in addition to financial information (quantitative information), presentations are made based on social and environmental information (qualitative information)
	IFRS Reporting is used	Integrated reporting is used based on IFRS, Social Reporting, Environmental Reporting, and Sustainability Reporting
The scope of elements	The elements are in line with the IFRS. The key elements are asset, liability, owner's equity, income, expense, and profit	The elements are in line with the IFRS. The key elements are asset, liability, owner's equity, income, expense, and profit. In addition, there are sub-elements to determine natural resource assets, social and environmental investments, intangible assets, and contingent social and environmental liabilities
The scope of reporting horizon	It is prepared annually within the framework of the conventional reporting period	In addition to the annual presentation given in conventional reporting, the organisation's future expectations, targets, and commitments on environmental and social issues valid within the scope of sustainable development goals are revealed in the short, medium, and long term

Sources: Adapted from UNEP (2020) and Lako (2018b).

CHAPTER 12

ECONOMIC POLICIES FOR SUSTAINABLE HEALTHCARE: A COMPARATIVE ANALYSIS OF TELEMEDICINE IN EUROPE

Adriana AnaMaria Davidescu[a,b], Eduard Mihai Manta[c] and Ioana Birlan[d]

[a]*Faculty of Statistics and Econometrics, The Bucharest University of Economic Studies, Bucharest, Romania*
[b]*National Scientific Research Institute for Labour and Social Protection, Bucharest, Romania*
[c]*Doctoral School of Cybernetics and Statistics, Bucharest University of Economic Studies, Bucharest, Romania*
[d]*Master of Applied Statistics and Data Science, Bucharest University of Economic Studies, Bucharest, Romania*

ABSTRACT

Purpose: *This study investigates the role of telemedicine in sustaining healthcare systems in Europe, during the COVID-19 pandemic. It focusses on how telemedicine serves as a strategic response to modern healthcare challenges, emphasising its efficiency, accessibility, and patient-centred nature.*

Need for the study: *The need for this study arises from the escalating demands on healthcare systems, especially during the COVID-19 pandemic. It aims to understand the adoption of telemedicine practices across European Union (EU) countries and their impact on healthcare sustainability.*

Methodology: *This study employs hierarchical and K-Means clustering to analyse EU citizens' attitudes towards teleconsultations during COVID-19.*

Sustainability Development through Green Economics
Contemporary Studies in Economic and Financial Analysis, Volume 114, 191–217

Published under exclusive licence by Emerald Publishing Limited
ISSN: 1569-3759/doi:10.1108/S1569-375920240000114012

Principal component analysis (PCA) is used for data compression and insight extraction. Data is sourced from Eurofound's 2020 and 2021 surveys, involving extensive participant responses across the EU.

Findings: *The study's findings reveal significant shifts towards digital healthcare solutions, such as an increase in online consultations and prescriptions. It identifies different patterns of telemedicine use across EU countries, influenced by socioeconomic and geographical factors. These findings offer insights into future healthcare policy and strategy development.*

Practical implications: *The findings provide valuable insights into the shifts in telemedicine adoption in the EU, highlighting the significance of economic and sociological factors in healthcare trends. This study stresses the importance of customising healthcare strategies to suit the unique needs and digital capabilities of different countries.*

Keywords: Telemedicine; healthcare sustainability; economic policies; digital healthcare; COVID-19 pandemic; European Union; cluster analysis;

JEL Codes: I11; I12; I18; L86

INTRODUCTION

Telemedicine in Europe has emerged as a cornerstone in the pursuit of sustainable healthcare, reflecting a shift towards more efficient, accessible, and patient-centred medical services. This innovative approach to healthcare delivery harnesses the power of digital technology to bridge geographical gaps, bringing specialised care to remote areas and underserved populations. In countries like Sweden and Spain, telemedicine initiatives have significantly reduced the need for physical consultations, thereby decreasing healthcare costs and minimising environmental impacts associated with travel. Moreover, the adoption of telemedicine across Europe is increasingly viewed as a key strategy in managing chronic diseases and ageing populations, offering continuous, real-time monitoring and care without the need for frequent hospital visits. This not only enhances the quality of life for patients but also alleviates the strain on healthcare systems. As European nations continue to navigate the challenges of healthcare sustainability, telemedicine stands out as a transformative solution, integrating technological advancements with the fundamental goal of providing equitable and effective healthcare for all.

Economic policies surrounding telemedicine have become pivotal in shaping healthcare landscapes across the globe. These policies often focus on funding models, reimbursement strategies, and regulatory frameworks that support the integration of telemedicine into mainstream healthcare systems. Governments and healthcare organisations are increasingly recognising the cost-effectiveness of telemedicine, leading to policies that incentivise its adoption. For instance, many countries have introduced reimbursement schemes that cover telemedicine consultations, making them financially viable for both healthcare providers and patients. Additionally, investments in digital infrastructure and technology are crucial aspects of these policies, ensuring that telemedicine services are accessible and reliable. Regulatory policies also play a significant role, in addressing issues like data privacy, cross-border healthcare provision, and telemedicine standards to maintain the quality and security of digital healthcare services. These economic policies not only support the financial sustainability of telemedicine initiatives but also foster innovation and scalability in the healthcare sector.

As countries grapple with the escalating demands of modern healthcare, the integration of telemedicine emerges as a pivotal strategy in sustaining health systems. This chapter delves into the economic policies that underpin telemedicine in Europe, offering a comparative analysis of its implementation across various nations. The chapter explores the multifaceted impact of these policies on healthcare sustainability, examining how telemedicine is reshaping patient care, reducing healthcare disparities, and driving innovation in medical practices. Through this analysis, the main aim is to highlight the lessons learned and the future pathways for telemedicine, positioning it as a cornerstone for sustainable healthcare in Europe.

The motivation of this chapter is to respond to the following research questions: *RQ1*: Did the pandemic significantly influence the adoption of telemedicine practices across the EU countries? *RQ2*: How did specific countries within the EU cluster in terms of healthcare practices during the pandemic? *RQ3*: What factors influence the clustering of countries in terms of their healthcare response to the pandemic? *RQ4*: How has the adoption of telemedicine varied across EU countries during the pandemic? *RQ5*: Which EU countries adopted digitalisation measures during the pandemic? *RQ6*: What are the implications of these healthcare trends for future policy and strategy development in the EU?

This chapter is divided into five sections. The first section is devoted to briefly introducing and demonstrating the topic's importance. The second section is devoted to the theoretical framework and the literature review of telemedicine. The third section presents the data and the working methods, while the fourth section concentrates on the empirical results. The key conclusions are presented at the end of the study.

LITERATURE REVIEW

Digitalisation and telehealth represent transformative forces in contemporary healthcare, offering new and innovative pathways for medical service delivery. As pivotal elements in modern society, they not only promise to enhance existing healthcare systems but also usher in a new era of accessibility and efficiency in medical care.

In May 2018, the member states of the World Health Organization unanimously endorsed the World Health Assembly Resolution on digital health. This resolution acknowledged the potential value of digital technologies in achieving universal health coverage (UHC) and the health-related goals of the United Nations Sustainable Development Goals (VO, 2023).

The World Health Organization defines digital health as the field of knowledge and practice associated with the development and use of digital technologies to improve health. It is a broad umbrella term that encompasses eHealth and emerging areas, such as the use of advanced informatics sciences in big data, genomics, and artificial intelligence (World Health Organization, 2021). All these means are encompassed by the concept of e-health, defined as all communication technologies that provide medical support and information.

Understanding public health as a concept that spans all societal facets, including health policy, education, and the environment, lays the groundwork for a broader discussion. This comprehensive view, as outlined by Odone et al. (2019), underscores the multifaceted nature of healthcare, extending beyond treatment to encompass prevention and care pathways. Building on this holistic perspective, Dvoryadkina and Fechina (2021) highlight how digital transformation transcends healthcare, influencing every sector of the economy, society, and industry. This transformation, driven by new technologies and innovations, not only fosters the development of new products and services but also marks a significant societal shift, heralding the onset of the fourth industrial revolution. The link between public health's broad scope and the pervasive impact of digital advancements illustrates the interconnectedness of these domains.

The evolving landscape of digitalisation, as Dijmărescu (2021) points out, now permeates a broad spectrum of fields and activities, often linked with disruptive technologies that aim to revolutionise traditional practices, including those in the medical field. This evolution in healthcare digitalisation goes beyond basic computer and database usage, embracing more intricate technologies like robotics, automation, the Internet of Things (IoT), artificial intelligence, and collaborative platforms. Such advancements hold the potential to significantly reduce the costs associated with managing chronic diseases. As Rayan et al. (2021) note, an array of technological innovations, ranging from health monitoring gadgets to automated medication administration systems, are gaining traction.

Seamlessly transitioning into the broader implications of these developments, the concept of the IoT emerges as a pivotal element in this technological revolution. As Al-Mahmud et al. (2020) describe, IoT encompasses an array of integrated sensors and software devices capable of autonomous data collection and exchange. In the realm of medicine, the IoT is not just a tool for enhancing patient care; it's a strategic innovation aimed at maintaining public health and reducing healthcare costs in the future. This interconnected network of devices and platforms illustrates a significant shift towards a more integrated, efficient, and patient-centred approach to healthcare delivery.

The benefits of digital systems, especially in the context of public health, have been significantly highlighted during the COVID-19 pandemic. The IoT, as a case in point, demonstrates remarkable capabilities in data collection and analysis. This technology not only aids in predicting and diagnosing certain health conditions but also plays a crucial role in the treatment and monitoring of patients, both in outpatient settings and within hospital environments. Dijmărescu (2021) particularly underlines the value of extensive data sets in identifying varied disease patterns, which is essential for advancing medical knowledge and practice.

Despite these advantages, the widespread adoption of such technologies faces challenges, primarily due to a lack of public awareness and concerns over data security and privacy. These issues pose significant barriers to fully leveraging the potential of large-scale data analysis in healthcare.

Further emphasising the critical role of digitalisation in healthcare, the digital transformation of medical systems is identified as vital for delivering reliable information to the public, which is indispensable for promoting preventive measures and early diagnosis. As Odone et al. (2019) suggest, this transformation facilitates a more straightforward interaction between doctors and patients, contributing to a healthcare system that is not only more patient-centric but also more efficient, safer, and cost-effective. The shift towards digitalisation in healthcare is thus presented as a promising development, offering a multitude of benefits that align with the overarching goals of public health, particularly in terms of prevention and patient-centred care.

Building on the theme of digital innovation in healthcare, Cohen et al. (2021), showcases the practical application of digital tools in healthcare analytics. The study reveals a significant correlation between Google Trends search volumes for hand osteoarthritis and the actual patient volumes suffering from the condition. By leveraging data from Google Trends, these professionals can better anticipate procedural volumes, enabling more effective staffing and resource allocation. The predictive power of such digital tools extends beyond immediate healthcare needs, allowing for more informed planning and resource management to meet future demands. This exemplifies the broader impact of digitalisation in healthcare, where data analytics becomes a pivotal tool in enhancing patient care and operational efficiency.

In the context of technological advancements, it's crucial to integrate the principles of sustainability, which aims to fulfil the needs of the populace. Sakalasooriya (2021) aptly notes that sustainability is an ongoing process, not a final goal. The World Commission on Environment and Development's definition of sustainable development (EUR-Lex, 1987), focussing on using resources and the environment to meet current needs without compromising future generations' ability, underscores the necessity of incorporating economic, social, and environmental factors into long-term planning. Such an approach ensures that future generations inherit a world where they can thrive and prosper.

Echoing these sentiments, Momete (2016) argues for a reformed healthcare approach in the EU, where the focus is on delivering value and quality-driven results. The challenges confronting the EU's healthcare system are multifaceted, encompassing the ageing population, economic strains, chronic disease management, and the health impacts of environmental degradation. The demographic shift towards an older population demands more resources and specialised care, exacerbating the pressure on healthcare systems. Despite increased healthcare funding by governments, issues like reduced affordability and access to medical services persist. Additionally, environmental factors are increasingly influencing public health, contributing to the rise in chronic diseases. This scenario highlights the urgent need for a holistic, sustainable approach in healthcare that addresses immediate challenges while paving the way for future generations wellbeing.

However, as Moore et al. (2017) highlight, the path towards this sustainable healthcare system is challenged by the lack of a standard, universally accepted definition of sustainability. The varied terminology used in the literature creates obstacles in operationalising and measuring sustainability, impeding research advancement, and risking repetitive efforts. This scenario calls for a clear, unified understanding of sustainability to effectively guide the development of healthcare policies and practices.

Cravo Oliveira Hashiguchi (2020) highlights that the economic costs of telemedicine are context-specific, influenced by factors like cost accuracy, specialty area, and the healthcare system. These costs encompass both direct expenses like equipment and personnel and indirect ones such as travel time and productivity loss. Additionally, sustainability in telemedicine hinges on factors like perceived effectiveness, patient tailoring, communication, process organisation, and technology quality. Addressing access and literacy inequalities is crucial for making telemedicine more equitable and effective (Puška et al., 2024; Yerpude et al., 2022).

Oliveira et al. (2013) found that teleconsultations significantly reduce travel distances and emissions, highlighting the environmental benefits of remote care services. Their study showed a 95% reduction in travel and emissions, suggesting that the integration of telemedicine could play a role in economic evaluations and technology assessments, especially in the context of global efforts to reduce carbon footprints.

M. V. et al. (2022) present a case for the pivotal role of policy intervention in achieving UHC, essential for sustainable healthcare and integral to meeting the United Nations' Sustainable Development Goal 3.8. The authors argue for an increase in healthcare spending relative to GDP and a strategic focus on the economic aspects of UHC, highlighting the complexities of healthcare cost management and the nuanced role of federal funding in global healthcare systems. They advocate for enhancing healthcare financing through a combination of individual and government contributions. Emphasising the importance of preventive primary healthcare, the chapter suggests a shift in focus from tertiary curative interventions to preventive measures, addressing the 'preventive paradox' and promoting a more cost-effective approach to health management. This strategy entails adequate funding across preventive, curative, and rehabilitative healthcare services to successfully implement UHC. The chapter also underscores UHC's critical role in the development of human capital, crucial for economic growth and poverty reduction, and notes the significant contribution of the healthcare sector to the global economy, particularly with its predominantly female workforce.

DATA AND METHODOLOGY

The purpose of this analysis is to examine the differences in the perceptions of citizens across the EU between 2020 and 2021 regarding their willingness to use teleconsultations and their need for various medical services during the COVID-19 pandemic. The study employs hierarchical clustering to identify the optimal number of clusters for grouping countries, followed by the application of K-Means clustering to characterise each cluster based on the variables most significantly influencing the grouping. Additionally, clustering methods will enable us to ascertain Romania's position and its similarities with other countries. PCA will aid in visualising the data in a reduced-dimension space, compressing the data into a few principal components for an in-depth analysis of the most influential variables in component formation. Finally, the study will compare the differences between the two years using insights from the PCA, to discern if there were notable changes in the behaviours of EU countries.

According to Kettenring (2006), clustering methods have emerged as one of the most significant techniques in multivariate analysis due to their utility. Cluster analysis, as described by Blashfield and Aldenderfer (1978), is an exploratory technique primarily focussed on identifying similarities or differences between the objects being examined. Its main objective is to divide multiple units into several mutually exclusive, relatively homogeneous subsets known as clusters. The foundation of cluster analysis is categorisation, encompassing two basic approaches: hierarchical clustering and non-hierarchical clustering. Hierarchical clustering is based on the use of already formed clusters, which are then utilised to create other clusters from the remaining database. This process continues until all elements are part of a cluster. Non-hierarchical clustering, on the other hand, operates on the principle of minimising the difference from the mean. This procedure is advantageous only if the number of clusters to be formed is predetermined, which can become a significant limitation in subsequent research, as pointed out by Majerova and Nevima (2017).

The principle behind Ward's method is not optimisation but the minimisation of heterogeneity, aiming to find the highest similarity (Strauss & von Maltitz, 2017). Squared Euclidean distance is used in Ward's method, which focusses on optimising the homogeneity of clusters based on a specific criterion – minimising the increase in the sum of squared deviations from the centroid points of the cluster (Murtagh & Legendre, 2014). This squared sum is calculated for every possible pair of connecting aggregates at each stage of the analysis, combining those clusters that result in the minimal increase in the sum of squared errors.

Let X^{ijk} denote the value for variable k in observation j belonging to cluster i.

The Euclidian distance between the observation and the centroid:

$$d(j,\overline{x}_i)=\sqrt{\sum_{K}^{k=1}(X_{jk}-\overline{x}_{ik})^2}$$

Error sum of squares:

$$\text{ESS}=\sum_i\sum_j\sum_k |X_{ijk}-\overline{x}_{i\cdot k}|^2$$

Total sum of squares:

$$\text{TSS}=\sum_i\sum_j\sum_k |X_{ijk}-\overline{x}_{i\cdot\cdot k}|^2$$

R-square:

$$r^2 = \frac{TSS - ESS}{TSS}$$

R-square is the proportion of variation explained by a particular clustering of the observations (14.7 – Ward's Method | STAT 505, n.d.). A higher r^2 indicates that the clustering explains a larger proportion of the total variance.

The motivation and advantage of using Ward's method is its tendency to eliminate small groups, thus forming clusters of approximately the same size. Since this method minimises intra-cluster dispersion, leading to more precise research of the examined objects, it was the best choice for the study's purposes.

K-Means clustering follows an easy method of classifying a given data set into a certain number of clusters (assumed *k* clusters) fixed a priori. It requires specifying the number of clusters at the outset (Syakur et al., 2018). To achieve satisfactory clustering results, it often necessitates several iterations where the algorithm is executed with different values of *k*. In the K-Means algorithm, the criterion is to minimise the distortion of clusters, so the evaluation function takes this parameter into account. In K-Means clustering, a cluster's distortion is a function of the data population and the distance between objects and the cluster centre. Each cluster is represented by its distortion and its impact on the entire data set is evaluated through its contribution to the sum of all distortions (Pham et al., 2005).

A cluster that has a small WCSS (Within Cluster Sum of Squares) is more compact and indicates that the data points are as close as possible to the centroids of their respective clusters, implying tighter and well-defined clusters:

$$WCSS = \sum_{i=1}^{K} \sum_{j \epsilon C_i} \| x_j - u_i \|^2$$

where K is the number of clusters, C_i is the set of points in cluster i, x_j is the jth data point in cluster C_i, μ_i is the centroid of points in cluster C_i and $\|x_j - \mu_i\|$ is the Euclidean distance between x_j and the centroid μ_i.

The PCA methodology starts with the standardisation of data which ensures that each variable contributes equally to the analysis. Given PCA's sensitivity to the variances of initial variables, standardisation is crucial. After that, the covariance matrix is computed to understand how variables vary from the mean relative to each other.

The covariance matrix Σ is given by:

$$\Sigma = \frac{1}{n-1} X^T X$$

where n is the number of observations and X^T is the transpose of X

The third step involves computing eigenvectors and eigenvalues from the covariance matrix to identify the principal components of the data. The eigen decomposition where Σ is the covariance matrix, λ is an eigenvalue and v is the corresponding eigenvector is:

$$\Sigma v = \lambda v$$

Principal components are new variables constructed as linear combinations of the initial variables (Jaadi, 2019). They are designed to be uncorrelated and encompass most of the information from the original variables. The eigenvectors indicate the direction of maximum variance, while eigenvalues determine the variance's magnitude. By ranking eigenvectors in order of their corresponding eigenvalues the principal components can be prioritised in terms of their significance. Once the eigenvectors are ordered, the next decision is whether to keep all components or discard the less significant ones. This choice forms the feature vector, a matrix comprising the chosen eigenvectors. This step is critical as it marks the transition towards dimensionality reduction – choosing fewer eigenvectors means reducing the number of dimensions in the final dataset. The final step involves reorienting the data from its original axes to those represented by the principal components. This transformation is achieved by multiplying the transpose of the original dataset by the transpose of the feature vector. This reorientation allows the data to be expressed in terms of the new, uncorrelated principal components, enhancing the visibility and interpretability of the data.

An initial hypothesis might be that countries will cluster based on their geographical location. However, the willingness to adopt new technologies like telemedicine is influenced not only by a country's economic situation or technological development but also by its perception of new medical technologies. Therefore, this research also requires incorporating sociological arguments to fully understand the factors driving telemedicine adoption across different nations. Thus, analysing the results of a survey can provide valuable insights.

In the analysis, the chapter examined data from 27 EU countries. The database was sourced from Eurofound (European Foundation for the Improvement of Living and Working Conditions), specifically from the section Quality of Public Services during COVID-19.

Eurofound's electronic survey, conducted in two distinct time phases, aimed to study the impact of the pandemic on people's lives across the EU. These phases were specifically chosen to represent different stages of the pandemic and to observe its immediate economic and social impacts on EU countries. The first phase was conducted in 2020, a period marked by the gradual reopening of economies. The second round was conducted in 2021, amidst new COVID-19 waves and the implementation of vaccination plans.

The survey was completed by 24,123 individuals in 2020 and by 46,800 individuals in 2021. Fig. 12.1 illustrates the respondent distribution across various countries for the year 2020, highlighting that the majority of responses originated from Ireland, Portugal, and Hungary. The target population consisted of people over 18 years old living in an EU count. The survey was distributed online using snowball sampling.

The individual-level data in the study were aggregated to create country and EU-level averages. To achieve this, individual responses were reweighted to be representative of each respondent's country's demographics. The data were adjusted based on a combination of age and gender (in 12 age-sex combinations), urbanisation level (2 categories), and education level (2 categories). This weighting was done using the anesrake R package for each country and then the resultant weights

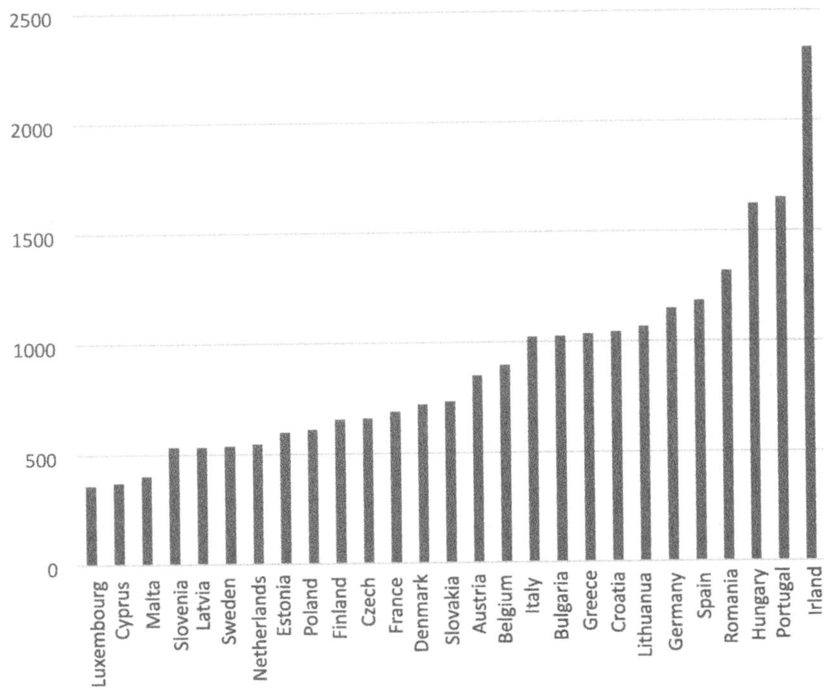

Fig. 12.1. Number of Respondents by Country for 2020. *Source*: Authors' selection from survey database.

were scaled up to match the population size. Extreme weights were trimmed using the trim weights function of the R package (Eurofound, 2020).

Eurofound's (2020) study methodology specifies minimum thresholds for sample size. The effective sample size is calculated using the Kish formula (1965), which considers the number of respondents for a specific question but also adjusts for survey composition by considering the design effect due to weighting.

According to Eurofound's (2020) methodology, the minimum thresholds are: results are not reported if the effective sample size is less than 100, the results are marked with an asterisk (*) to indicate low data confidence if the effective sample size is between 100 and 200 and also the results are reported normally if the effective sample size is 200 or more.

In 2020, countries with low data confidence were Cyprus, Latvia, Luxembourg, and Malta. In 2021, Luxembourg was the only country with low data confidence. The variables included in the analysis encompass the following aspects: the percentage of individuals who received prescriptions online or via phone, the percentage of individuals who had an online or telephonic consultation, the percentage of individuals who utilised emergency services (ambulance or emergency department), the percentage of individuals who had a consultation with a general practitioner, family doctor, or at a health centre, the percentage of individuals who had a consultation at a hospital or with a medical specialist and the percentage of individuals with unmet medical needs. The six variables analysed are quantitative and measured in the same unit (percentages).

From Table 12.1, the variables with a coefficient of variation greater than 30% are the utilisation of emergency services and individuals with unmet medical needs. This indicates that for these variables, the standard deviation is relatively large compared to the mean, suggesting low homogeneity for these variables and will require standardisation.

As shown in Figs. 12.12 and 12.13, the use of online or telephonic prescriptions are correlated positively with medical consultations effectuated online or by telephone for both years. However, the correlation is stronger between the two in 2021 (0.59 vs 0.66). Another noticeable change is that for 2021, there is a stronger positive correlation between the respondents that effectuated medical consultations online or by telephone and those that needed emergency healthcare (0.56).

EMPIRICAL RESULTS – TELEMEDICINE TRENDS IN EUROPE: A COMPREHENSIVE CLUSTERING STUDY WITH A DEEP DIVE INTO ROMANIA'S PROGRESS

A Comparative Analysis of Hierarchical Clustering for Periods 2020 and 2021

Ward's method was employed to identify the optimal number of clusters for categorising countries. The dendrograms were generated for both years.

Table 12.1. Descriptive Statistics.

Variable	Min	Mean	Median	Max	Standard Deviation	Coefficient of Variation
'Prescriptions online or by telephone' by country	17.8	45.1	47.6	65.5	12.31628	27.30883
'Medical consultation online or by telephone' by country	16.6	31.87037	31.8	48.2	7.762376	24.35609
Emergency healthcare (such as ambulance or emergency department)	2.9	6.533333	6.2	12.1	2.06956	31.67693
'Consultation at the GP, family doctor or health centre premises' by country	18.1	34.11852	31.3	51.2	9.169432	26.87524
'Consultation at the hospital or a medical specialist premises' by country	15.4	24.48519	23.5	37.3	5.69012	23.23903
'Unmet need for healthcare' by country	12.4	21.93704	20.4	38.2	7.792854	35.52373

Source: Authors' calculations.

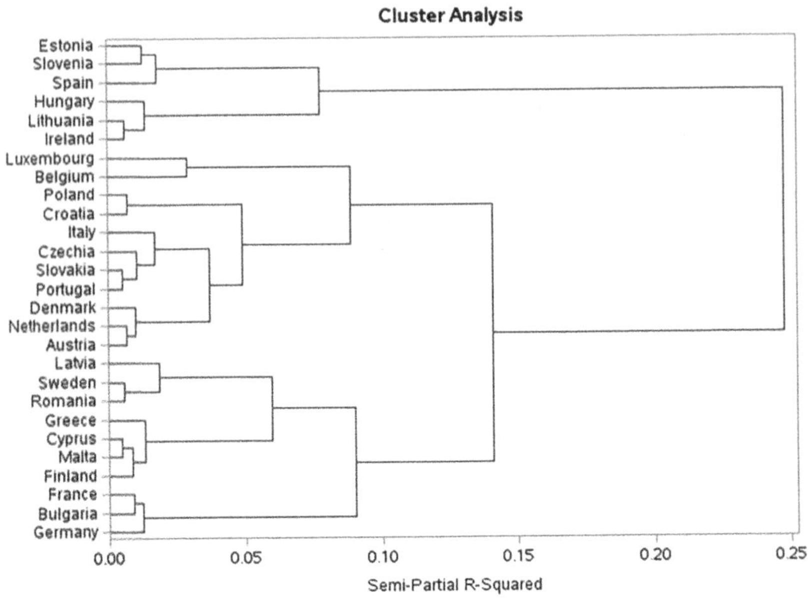

Fig. 12.2. The Dendogram for 2020. *Source*: Generated by the authors.

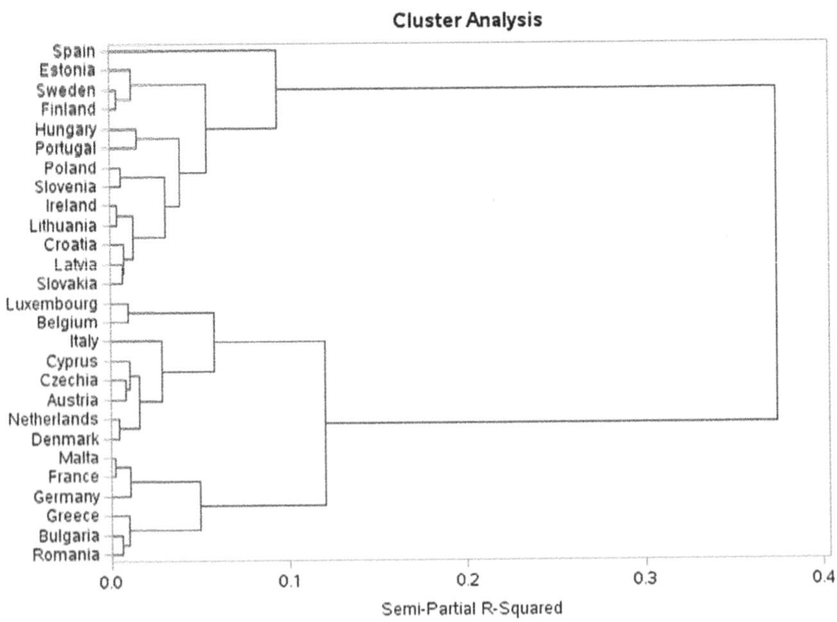

Fig. 12.3. The Dendogram for 2021. *Source*: Generated by the authors.

For 2020, the dendrogram (Fig. 12.2) suggests that the appropriate number of clusters is 5. Additionally, the Cluster History output, as displayed in Table 12.3, indicates significant differences among the groups when five clusters are considered, with an *R*-square value of 0.567. The R-square represents the proportion of the total variance that is accounted for by the clustering. A higher *R*-square value indicates that the clustering explains more variance. For 2021, the dendrogram (Fig. 12.3) generated suggested that the ideal number of clusters is three and that was the conclusion from the cluster history output, as displayed in Table 12.4, with significative differences at three clusters (*R*-square =0.516). To verify that there are significant differences between these clusters in terms of their features, the Kruskal-Wallis test was used since not all of the features were normally distributed. For each feature, the means across different clusters were compared.

As shown in Table 12.2, all features show statistically significant differences among the clusters. The magnitude of these differences (as indicated by the *F*-values) varies more greatly, with 'Medical consultation online or by telephone by country 2021' showing the most pronounced differences. These results suggest that the clusters are well-differentiated based on these healthcare-related metrics for the year 2021.

A Comparative Analysis of K-Means Clustering

In this subsection, the K-Means clustering method was applied to segment countries based on specific criteria derived from the dataset. The results for 2020 delineate a fascinating geographical and possibly socio-economic patterning of European countries into five distinct clusters:

Table 12.2. Kruskal–Wallis Test.

Variable	Statistic 2020	*p*-value 2020	Statistic 2021	*p*-value 2021
Prescriptions online or by telephone by country 2021	12.58	0.014*	15.89	0.000***
Medical consultation online or by telephone by country 2021	16.96	0.002**	15.91	0.000***
Emergency healthcare such as ambulance or emergency department 2021	7.64	0.105	11.09	0.003**
Consultation at the GP family doctor or health centre premises by country 2021	15.89	0.003**	13.19	0.001***
Consultation at the hospital or a medical specialist premises by country 2021	16.51	0.002**	12.91	0.001***
Unmet need for healthcare by country 2021	12.95	0.012*	9.93	0.006**

Source: Authors' calculations.
Notes: $*p<0.1$, $**p<0.05$, $***p<0.01$.

- *Cluster 1: Low adoption of telemedicine* – This cluster comprises six countries: Germany, Greece, Bulgaria, France, Cyprus, and Malta. This cluster is characterised by high values for general practitioner consultations but the lowest for online consultations and receiving prescriptions online or by telephone. These countries also have the fewest unmet medical needs.
- *Cluster 2: Leaders in family doctor consultations* – Belgium and Denmark fall into this category. These are the countries with the highest number of family doctor consultations.
- *Cluster 3: High adoption of telemedicine with unmet medical needs* – This group includes Ireland, Hungary, Lithuania, and Latvia. These countries have the highest percentage of receiving online or telephone prescriptions and conducting medical consultations online or by phone. However, these countries have the least use of emergency services at the pandemic's onset and the highest level of unmet medical needs.
- *Cluster 4: Telemedicine and responsive emergency services* – Comprising Finland, Spain, Luxembourg, Slovenia, and Estonia, this cluster is diverse in terms of geography and culture. Compared to Cluster 3, these countries have more frequent use of emergency services and a lower level of unmet medical needs.
- *Cluster 5: Varied healthcare approaches* – The largest cluster, encompasses 10 countries: Austria, Portugal, Italy, Croatia, Slovakia, Romania, Sweden, Czech Republic, Poland, and the Netherlands. These are countries with high values for receiving prescriptions online or by telephone (second only to Cluster 3). However, this cluster has low values for conducting online or telephone medical consultations and using emergency services, with a moderate level of unmet medical needs.

In 2020, Ireland, Hungary, Lithuania, and Latvia were the countries where citizens most frequently used telemedicine for medical consultations and receiving prescriptions online or by telephone. Romania, part of Cluster 5, belonged to the group of countries with fewer online or telephone medical consultations but a high level of online or telephone prescription services. The most influential variable in cluster grouping is 'Prescriptions online or by telephone' with an R-square of 0.65, followed by 'Emergency Healthcare' (R-square $= 0.62$) and 'Unmet need for healthcare' (R-square $= 0.61$). These three variables most significantly differentiate the five country groups. The least impactful is 'Consultation at the hospital or a medical specialist on-premises' with an R-square of 0.423. R-square measures how distinct they formed clusters are from each other based on the respective variable.

The results for the year 2021 (Fig. 12.5) revealed the presence of three clusters this time, compared with 2020 (Fig. 12.4) with the following explanations:

- *Cluster 1: Diverse healthcare approaches* – encompasses 12 countries: Slovakia, Portugal, Hungary, Finland, Sweden, Latvia, Lithuania, Slovenia, Czech Republic, Croatia, Poland, and Ireland. This cluster is characterised by moderate values for online consultations but the lowest for family doctor consultations at a centre.

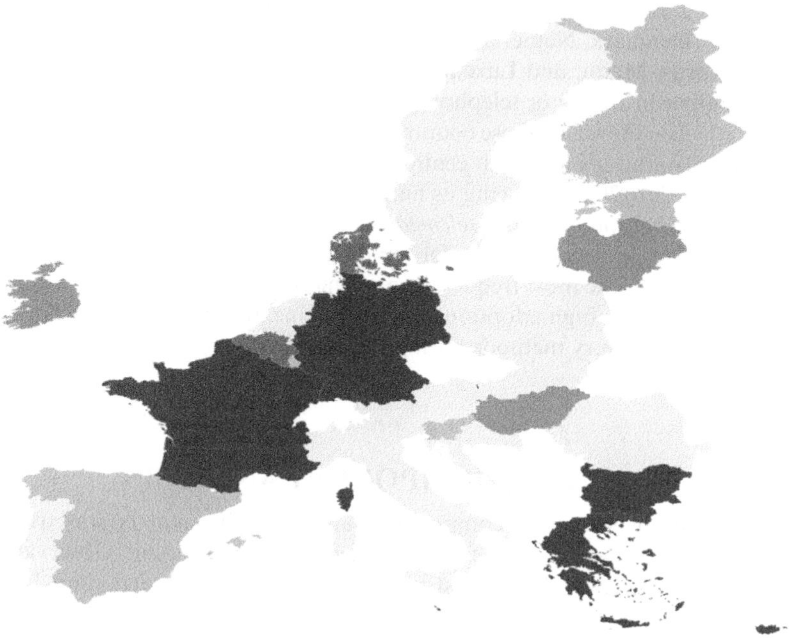

Fig. 12.4. Visual Representation of the Clusters for 2020. *Source*: Generated by the authors.

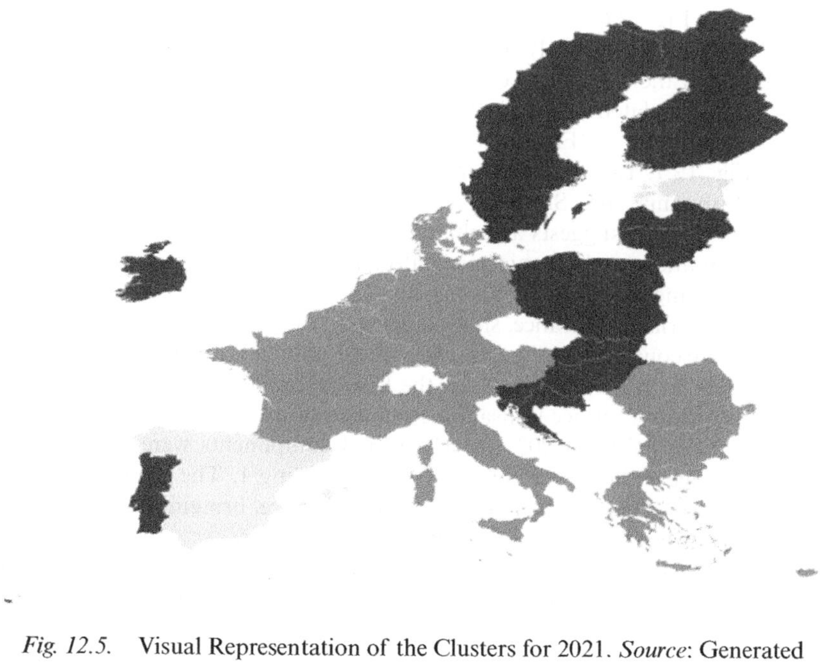

Fig. 12.5. Visual Representation of the Clusters for 2021. *Source*: Generated by the authors.

- *Cluster 2: Limited online consultations* – comprising 13 countries – Romania, Germany, Denmark, Netherlands, Greece, Austria, Belgium, Bulgaria, France, Italy, Cyprus, Malta, and Luxembourg. This group is notable for having the least number of online or telephonic consultations and the least use of emergency services. However, these countries recorded the highest values for family doctor consultations at health centres. Romania, part of this cluster, showed a shift from July 2020, reducing its number of online medical consultations.
- *Cluster 3: High adoption of telemedicine* – containing Spain and Estonia, records the highest percentages for conducting medical consultations online or by phone and the most frequent use of emergency services. These countries stand out for their high adoption of telemedicine, reflecting a significant shift in healthcare delivery methods during the pandemic.

PRINCIPAL COMPONENT ANALYSIS

In the analysis of principal components, an eigenvalue matrix was used to determine the optimal number of principal components to retain. Observations for 2020 revealed that only the first two eigenvalues were greater than 1, suggesting the presence of two principal components. The first value accounted for slightly more than two variables, contributing to preserving 43% of the total variance. The second value represented about one variable, adding 22.2% to the total variance. Cumulatively, these two components explained 65.56% of the total variability.

As shown in Fig. 12.6, 'Unmet needs', 'Prescriptions online', and 'Medical consultations online' are positively correlated and positively determine component 1. 'Consultation at the GP' and 'Consultation at the hospital or medical specialist' are positively correlated and negatively influence component 1. Component 2 is positively determined by 'Emergency healthcare' and 'Consultation at the GP'.

From Fig. 12.7, Luxembourg emerged as an outlier. Additionally, Ireland, Hungary, Lithuania, and Slovenia – exhibited high values for the first principal component. This suggests a higher percentage of citizens in these countries engaged in online or telephonic medical consultations, received prescriptions through these mediums, and experienced unmet medical needs. Conversely, Germany, Bulgaria, and France, showed negative values for the first component, indicating these countries had the lowest levels of unmet medical needs. Romania, did not exhibit high or low values for the first component, implying a different pattern in healthcare service utilisation compared to the other groups.

Analysing the PCA for 2021, two principal components were identified, as the first two eigenvalues were the only ones exceeding 1. The second principal component accounted for 20.55% of the total variance, bringing the cumulative explanatory power of the total variability to 69.67%.

It was noted that all analysed variables positively influenced the first principal component, except for 'Consultation at the GP' and 'Consultation at the

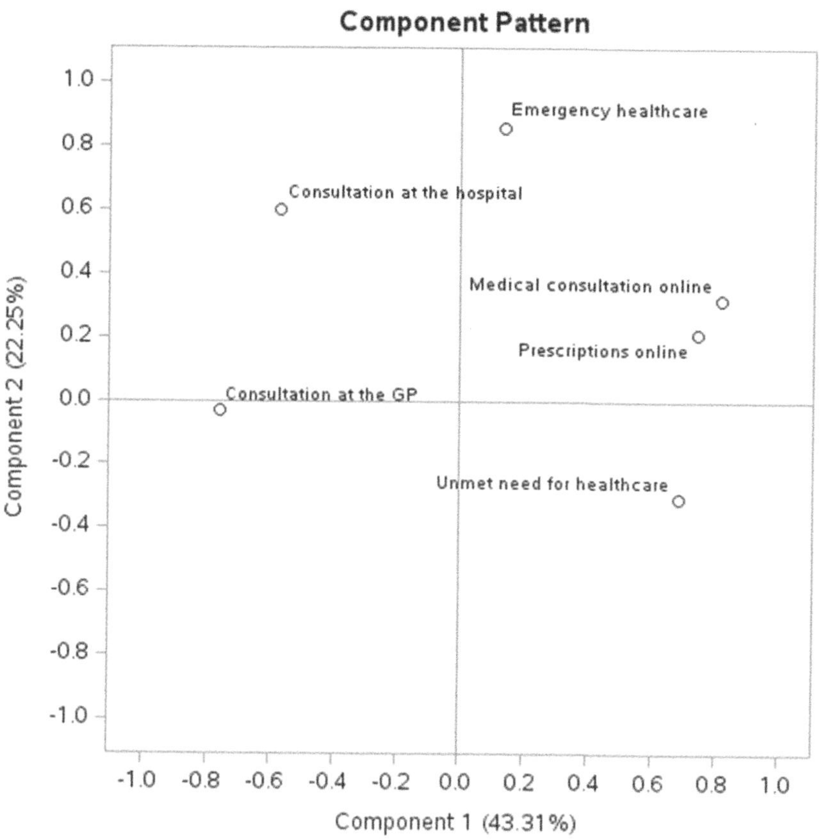

Fig. 12.6. PCA Components. *Source*: Generated by the authors.

Hospital'. 'Emergency healthcare' and 'Consultation at the hospital or a medical specialist premises' positively influenced the second component. In contrast, 'Unmet needs' negatively impacted the second component. This analysis provides a nuanced understanding of the factors influencing healthcare behaviours and needs during the study period.

As shown in Fig. 12.8, Spain emerged as a clear outlier. From the cluster analysis, Cluster three consists of countries with the highest percentage of citizens receiving prescriptions online or by telephone and participating in online or telephonic consultations. These countries are positioned positively in both components 1 and 2 of the PCA. Furthermore, Romania is observed to be situated on the negative side of component 2, indicating that its respondents less frequently used emergency services and family doctor consultations. Additionally, the Romanian respondents showed a higher percentage of unmet medical needs, a conclusion consistent with the findings from 2020.

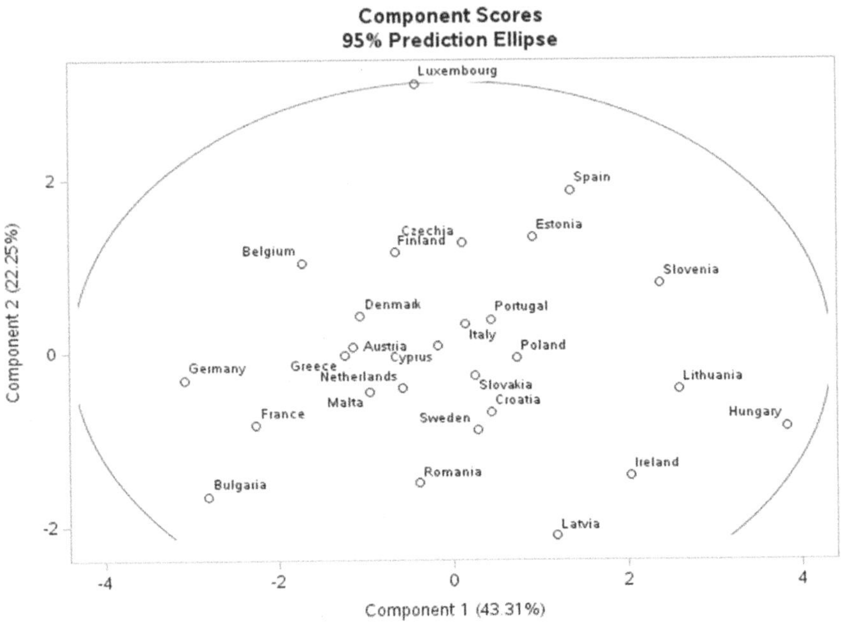

Fig. 12.7. Component Scores Country Representation. *Source*: Generated by the authors.

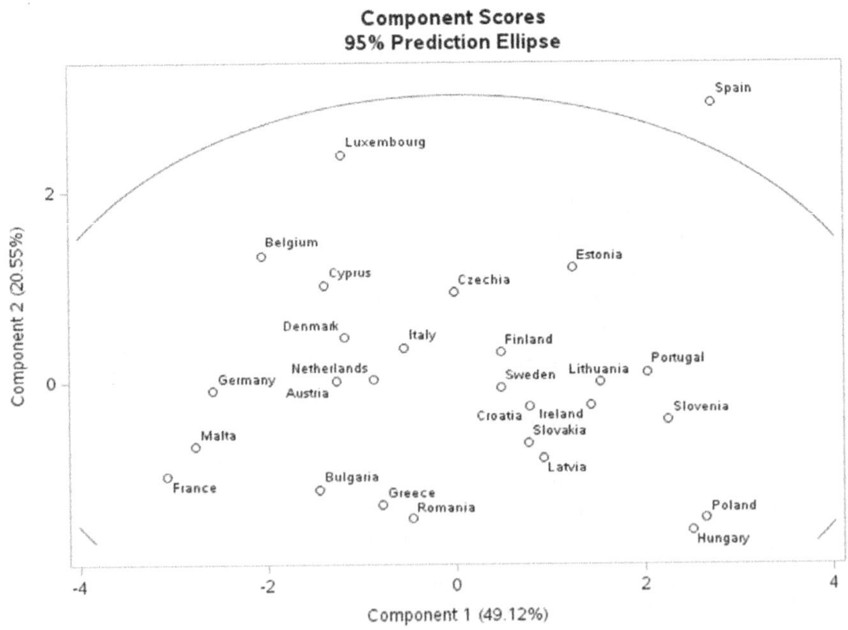

Fig. 12.8. Component Scores. *Source*: Generated by the authors.

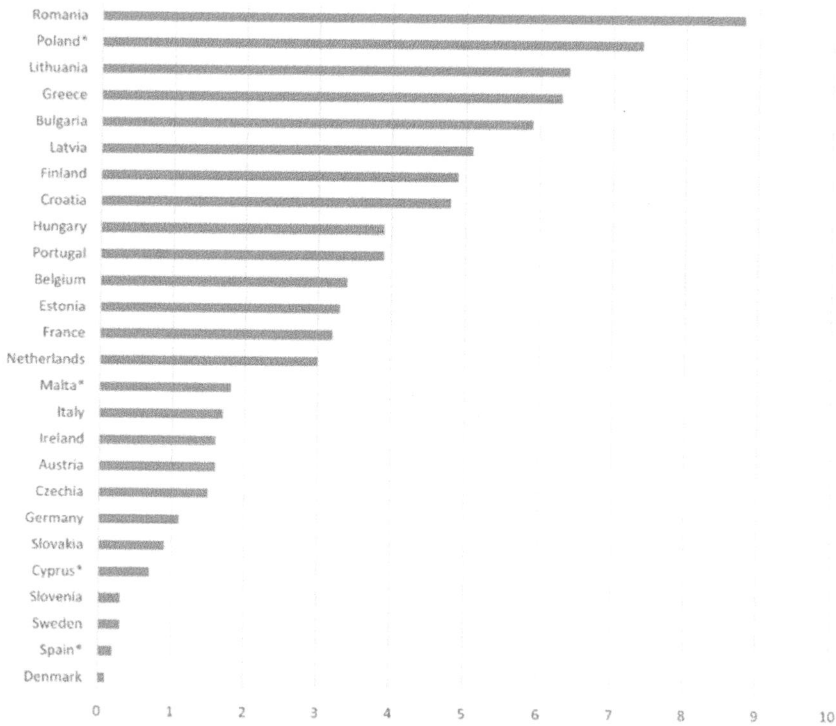

Fig. 12.9. Reason for Not Using Telemedicine. *Source*: Authors' selection from survey database.

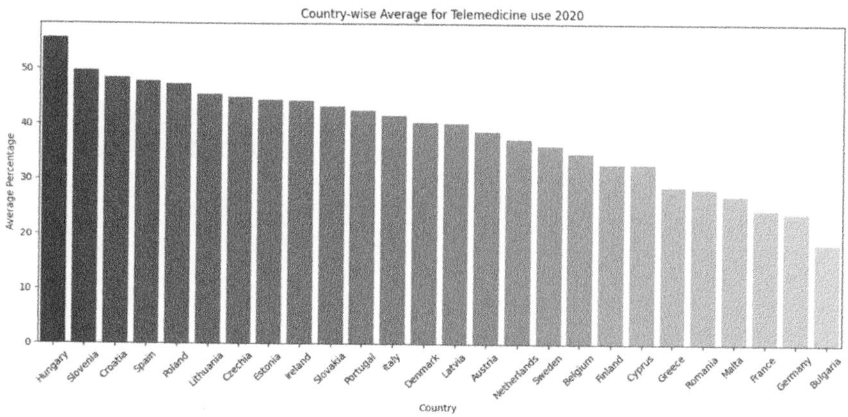

Fig. 12.10. Telemedicine Use in 2020. *Source*: Authors' selection from survey database. *Notes*. According to Eurofound's (2020) methodology, the results are not reported if the effective sample size is less than 100, the results are marked with an asterisk (*) to indicate low data confidence if the effective sample size is between 100–200 and also the results are reported normally if the effective sample size is 200 or more.

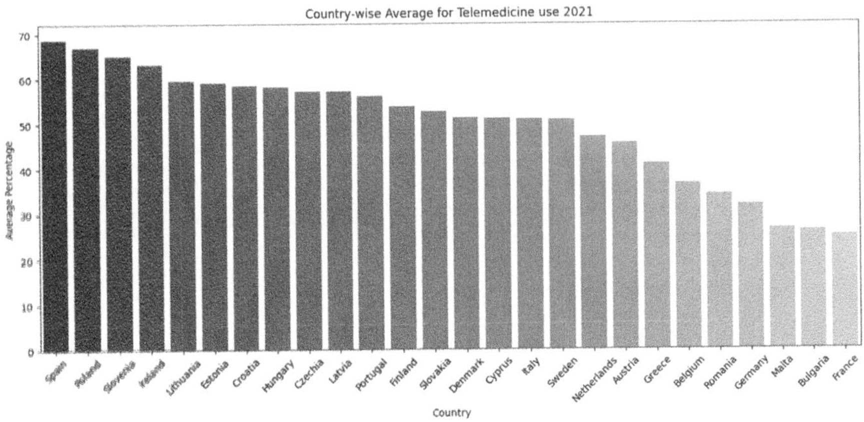

Fig. 12.11. Telemedicine Use in 2021. *Source*: Authors' selection from survey database.

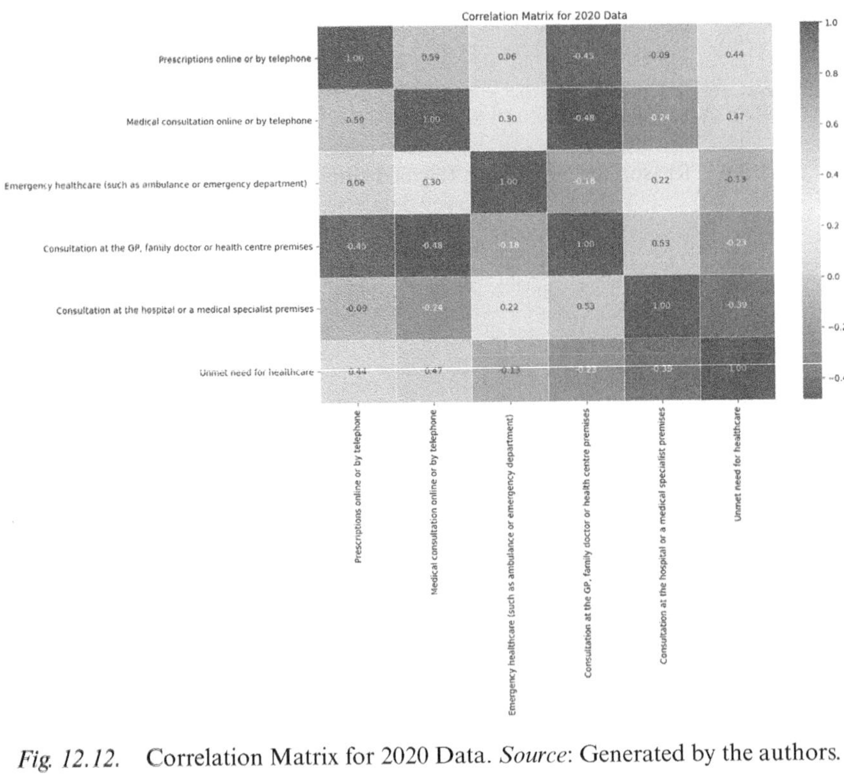

Fig. 12.12. Correlation Matrix for 2020 Data. *Source*: Generated by the authors.

For the 2021 survey, the respondents were also asked why they did not try an online or telephonic medical consultation.

As shown in Fig. 12.14, the primary reason why most Romanians, according to the Eurofound survey, did not participate in an online consultation was that they did not need a medical consultation (50.7%). Over a quarter (26.3%) stated a preference for face-to-face consultations (Fig. 12.15), and 17.8% indicated that their issue could only be addressed through an in-person visit (Fig. 12.16).

Applying K-Means clustering to the motivations for not using telemedicine places Romania in the same cluster with countries like Finland, Lithuania, Croatia, Greece, and Poland. The variables that most distinctly differentiated the clusters were 'not needing a consultation' (*R*-square = 0.66) and 'unable to afford an online consultation' (*R*-square = 0.7). Romania is among the countries with the highest values for variables such as 'unable to afford' (shown in Fig. 12.9), 'too difficult to use', and 'these services are not available in my country'. Notably, Romania recorded the highest percentage (8.8%) of respondents citing cost as a reason for not using telemedicine in 2021. This data reflects the varying accessibility and perception of telemedicine across different European countries, with economic factors playing a significant role.

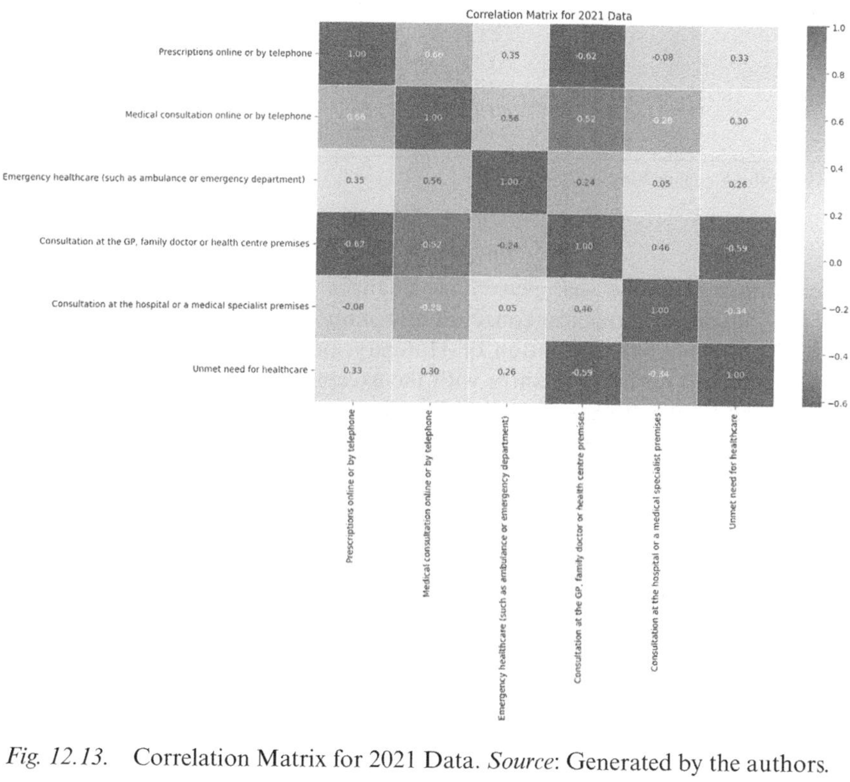

Fig. 12.13. Correlation Matrix for 2021 Data. *Source*: Generated by the authors.

Table 12.3. Cluster History for 2020.

Number of Clusters	Clusters Joined		Freq	Semipartial R-square	R-square
26	Malta	Cyprus	2	0.0048	0.995
25	Portugal	Slovakia	2	0.0052	0.99
24	Romania	Sweden	2	0.006	0.984
23	Ireland	Lithuania	2	0.0061	0.978
22	Austria	Netherlands	2	0.0066	0.971
21	Croatia	Poland	2	0.0071	0.964
20	Finland	CL26	3	0.0085	0.956
19	Bulgaria	France	2	0.0093	0.946
18	CL22	Denmark	3	0.0099	0.936
17	CL25	Czechia	3	0.0105	0.926
16	Germany	CL19	3	0.0123	0.914
15	Slovenia	Estonia	2	0.0128	0.901
14	CL20	Greece	4	0.0134	0.888
13	CL23	Hungary	3	0.0139	0.874
12	CL17	Italy	4	0.0173	0.856
11	Spain	CL15	3	0.0183	0.838
10	CL24	Latvia	3	0.0184	0.82
9	Belgium	Luxembourg	2	0.0289	0.791
8	CL18	CL12	7	0.0373	0.753
7	CL8	CL21	9	0.0492	0.704
6	CL14	CL10	7	0.0596	0.645
5	CL13	CL11	6	0.0777	0.567
4	CL7	CL9	11	0.0885	0.479
3	CL16	CL6	10	0.0899	0.389
2	CL3	CL4	21	0.1409	0.248
1	CL2	CL5	27	0.2477	0

Source: Authors' calculations.

Comparative Analysis

Visualising the year-to-year percentage changes as shown in Figs. 12.10 and 12.11, highlights that medical consultations online or by telephone increased for every country with the exception of Hungary, prescriptions online or by telephone increased for every country with the exception of France and Malta and unmet need for healthcare increased for Germany, Finland, Greece, Portugal, Spain, Bulgaria, Slovakia, Romania, Slovenia, and Estonia in 2021.

The principal components from the PCA revealed significant trends in healthcare service utilisation across Europe between 2020 and 2021. The analysis shows noteworthy shifts in how different countries have adapted their healthcare approaches, particularly in telemedicine.

There was a notable increase in the percentage of Romanians engaging in online consultations and receiving prescriptions online or by telephone. Concurrently, there was a decrease in the use of emergency services and in-person consultations with family doctors and specialists. Impressively, the percentage of people with unmet medical needs in Romania decreased by nearly 6%.

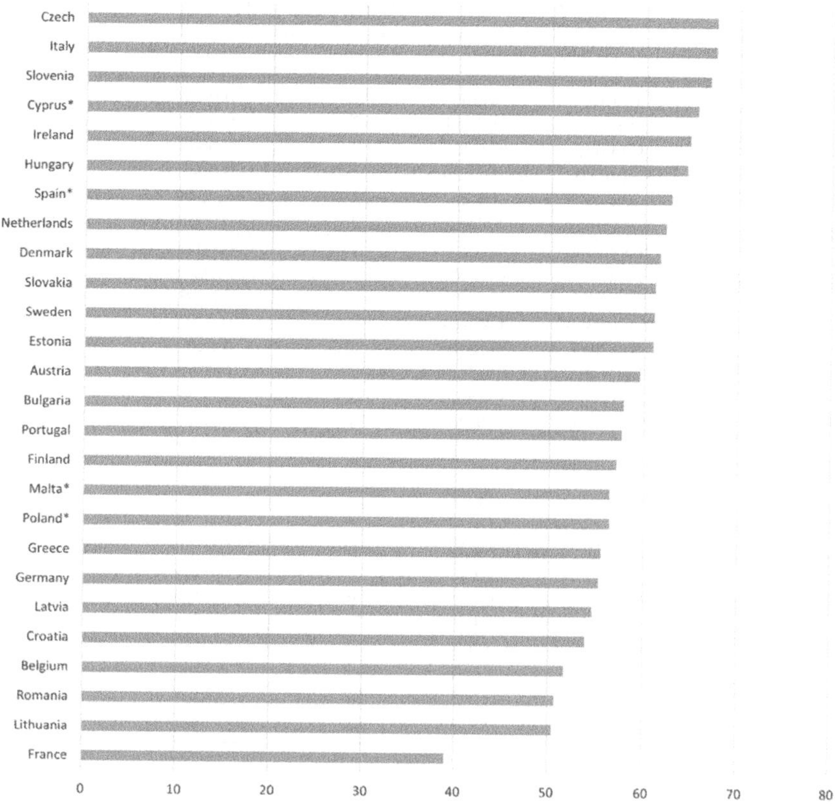

Fig. 12.14. Percentage of Respondents Who Did Not Need Medical Consultations. *Source*: Authors' selection from survey database.

Estonia and Spain experienced a significant increase in all six variables, indicating a robust adoption of telemedicine. Contrarily, France saw a decrease in almost all healthcare variables in 2021 compared to 2020, except for family doctor and specialist consultations.

Portugal, Poland, Hungary, and Slovenia experienced a decrease in family doctor visits, but an increase in the number of consultations and prescriptions issued online or by telephone.

These findings highlight the dynamic nature of healthcare service utilisation across different European countries, particularly the growing inclination towards telemedicine and the varying degrees of reliance on traditional healthcare services during the pandemic period.

The data suggests a growing trend towards digital health solutions, reflecting a pivotal change in healthcare delivery during the pandemic. This analysis not only provides a snapshot of the current state but also offers insights for future healthcare strategies and policies.

Table 12.4. Cluster History for 2021.

Number of Clusters	Clusters Joined		Freq	Semipartial *R*-square	*R*-square
26	France	Malta	2	0.0028	0.997
25	Lithuania	Ireland	2	0.0038	0.993
24	Finland	Sweden	2	0.0044	0.989
23	Denmark	Netherlands	2	0.0047	0.984
22	Latvia	CL25	3	0.0057	0.979
21	Slovenia	Poland	2	0.0058	0.973
20	Romania	Greece	2	0.0061	0.967
19	Austria	Czechia	2	0.008	0.959
18	Slovakia	Croatia	2	0.0091	0.95
17	CL23	Cyprus	3	0.0101	0.939
16	CL20	Bulgaria	3	0.0107	0.929
15	Belgium	Luxembourg	2	0.0116	0.917
14	CL24	Estonia	3	0.0117	0.905
13	Germany	CL26	3	0.0117	0.894
12	CL18	CL22	5	0.0131	0.881
11	Portugal	Hungary	2	0.0133	0.867
10	CL19	Italy	3	0.016	0.851
9	CL12	CL14	8	0.0275	0.824
8	CL17	CL10	6	0.0314	0.793
7	CL11	CL21	4	0.0339	0.759
6	CL16	CL13	6	0.0519	0.707
5	CL8	CL15	8	0.0565	0.65
4	CL9	CL7	12	0.0639	0.586
3	CL4	Spain	13	0.0702	0.516
2	CL6	CL5	14	0.1308	0.385
1	CL2	CL3	27	0.3853	0

Source: Authors' calculations.

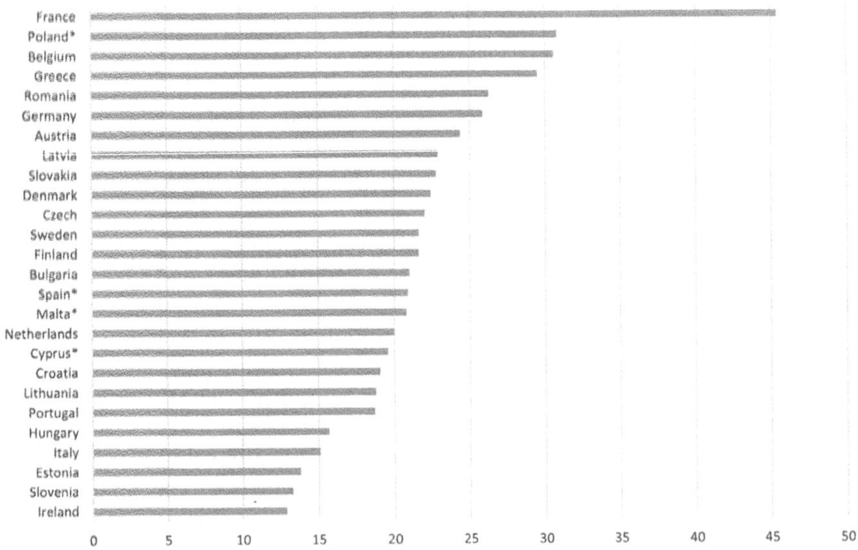

Fig. 12.15. Percentage of Respondents Who Prefer Having Consultations Face-to-Face. *Source*: Generated by the authors.

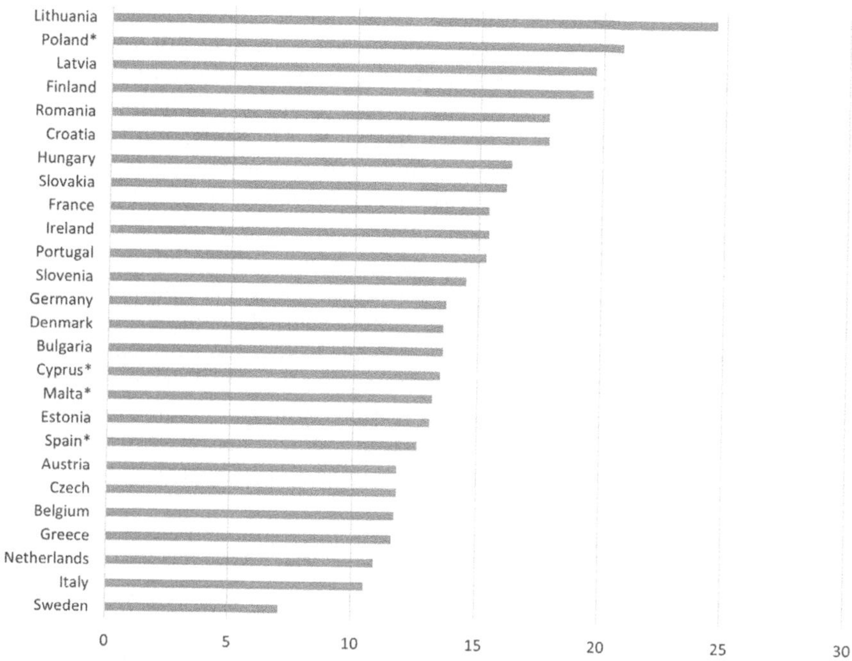

Fig. 12.16. Percentage of Respondents Whose Problem Could Only Be Solved Face-to-Face. *Source*: Generated by the authors.

DISCUSSIONS AND CONCLUSIONS

The analysis identifies distinct clusters of countries exhibiting varied patterns in telemedicine use, emergency service reliance, and in-person medical consultations. Notably, the study highlights significant shifts towards digital healthcare solutions, including a marked increase in online consultations and prescriptions. The findings also reveal variations in the adoption of telemedicine and traditional healthcare services, influenced by socioeconomic and geographical factors.

The chapter explores the underlying reasons for these shifts, analysing variables such as the necessity of medical consultations, the preference for face-to-face interactions, and economic considerations. The clustering results demonstrate commonalities and differences among EU countries, offering insights into the broader implications for healthcare policy and strategy development in a post-pandemic landscape.

This study contributes to the understanding of how European healthcare systems have adapted during a crisis and provides a basis for informed policymaking aimed at enhancing healthcare delivery and meeting emerging challenges in the future.

The dendrogram analysis for 2020 and 2021 revealed an optimal grouping of countries into five and three clusters, respectively, highlighting the shifting landscape in healthcare. This change in clustering patterns reflects significant year-to-year transformations in healthcare dynamics and priorities. Notably, the marked increase in 'Medical consultation online or by telephone' across both years exemplifies these shifts, indicating a growing trend towards digital health solutions.

The empirical results of the k-mean clustering analysis revealed that countries such as Belgium and Denmark were the leaders in terms of family doctors' consultations, while countries such as Ireland, Hungary, Lithuania, and Latvia had the highest percentage of online prescriptions and conductions of medical services. However, in 2021, countries such as Spain and Estonia recorded the highest percentages for conducting medical consultations online or by phone.

The PCA from 2020 and 2021 underscores a substantial shift in Europe's healthcare utilisation, notably the swift rise of telemedicine, evidenced by the adoption trends in countries like Estonia and Spain. Romania experienced a notable increase in online healthcare services, while France saw a decrease in these services, showing the differing approaches to telemedicine in Europe. The PCA highlights the need for country-specific healthcare strategies, acknowledging the unique challenges and digital adoption levels in different nations, from Portugal and Hungary's move towards online services to Germany's consistent management of unmet medical needs.

In terms of limitations, the study relies on data from a Eurofound survey. Therefore, gaps in the data could affect the author's findings. The analysis is specific to the COVID-19 pandemic period. It may not reflect long-term trends or post-pandemic developments in healthcare practices. The study primarily uses quantitative data, which may miss out on qualitative aspects of healthcare experiences and attitudes towards telemedicine and digital health services. There may be other unexamined factors influencing healthcare practices during the pandemic, such as government policies, public health initiatives, or individual healthcare provider decisions.

REFERENCES

Al-Mahmud, O., Khan, K., Roy, R., & Mashuque Alamgir, F. (2020). Internet of things (IoT) based smart health care medical box for elderly people. In *2020 International conference for emerging technology (INCET)*. https://doi.org/10.1109/incet49848.2020.9153994

Blashfield, R. K., & Aldenderfer, M. S. (1978). The literature on cluster analysis. *Multivariate Behavioral Research*, *13*(3), 271–295. https://doi.org/10.1207/s15327906mbr1303_2

Cohen, S. A., Zhuang, T., Xiao, M., Michaud, J. B., Shapiro, L., & Kamal, R. N. (2021, March 9). Using Google Trends data to track healthcare use for hand osteoarthritis. *Cureus*, *13*(3), Article e13786. https://doi.org/10.7759/cureus.13786

Dijmărescu, I. (2021). Some characteristics of entrepreneurship in medicine. The digitalization of the medical system in Romania. *Romanian Journal of Pediatrics*, *70*(2), 99–102. https://doi.org/10.37897/rjp.2021.2.2

Dvoryadkina, E., & Fechina, A. (2021). Defining "telemedicine services" in the context of large-scale digitalization. *In E3S Web of Conferences*, *296*, Article 08021. https://doi.org/10.1051/e3sconf/202129608021

EUR-Lex. (1987). *Sustainable development – EN*. EUR-Lex. Retrieved December 15, 2023, from https://eur-lex.europa.eu/EN/legal-content/glossary/sustainable-development.html

European Foundation for the Improvement of Living and Working Conditions. (n.d.). *Living, working and COVID-19 e-survey*. Retrieved December 1, 2023, from https://www.eurofound.europa.eu/en/data-catalogue/living-working-and-covid-19-e-survey-1

Eurofound. (n.d.). *Living, working and COVID-19*. Retrieved December 1, 2023, from https://www.eurofound.europa.eu/publications/report/2020/living-working-and-covid-19#wp-101863

Jaadi, Z. (2019). A step by step explanation of principal component analysis. Built In. Retrieved December 1, 2023, from https://builtin.com/data-science/step-step-explanation-principal-component-analysis

Kettenring, J. R. (2006). The practice of cluster analysis. *Journal of Classification*, *23*(1), 3–30. https://doi.org/10.1007/s00357-006-0002-6

Majerova, I., & Nevima, J. (2017). The measurement of human development using the Ward method of cluster analysis. *Journal of International Studies*, *10*(2), 239–257. https://doi.org/10.14254/2071-8330.2017/10-2/17

Momete, D. C. (2016). Building a sustainable healthcare model: A cross-country analysis. *Sustainability*, *8*(9), 836. https://doi.org/10.3390/su8090836

Moore, J. E., Mascarenhas, A., Bain, J., & Sharon, E. S. (2017). Developing a comprehensive definition of sustainability. *Implementation Science*, *12*, Article 110. https://doi.org/10.1186/s13012-017-0637-1

Murtagh, F., & Legendre, P. (2014). Ward's hierarchical agglomerative clustering method: Which algorithms implement Ward's criterion? *Journal of Classification*, *31*(3), 274–295. https://doi.org/10.1007/s00357-014-9161-z

Odone, A., Buttigieg, S., Ricciardi, W., Azzopardi-Muscat, N., & Staines, A. (2019). Public health digitalization in Europe EUPHA vision, action and role in digital public health. *European Journal of Public Health*, *29*(Supplement_3), 28–35. https://doi.org/10.1093/eurpub/ckz161

Oliveira Hashiguchi, T. (2020). Bringing health care to the patient: An overview of the use of telemedicine in OECD countries. *OECD Health Working Papers*, *116*, OECD Publishing. https://doi.org/10.1787/8e56ede7-en

Oliveira, T. C., Barlow, J., Gonçalves, L., & Bayer, S. (2013). Teleconsultations reduce greenhouse gas emissions. *Journal of Health Services Research & Policy*, *18*(4), 209–214. https://doi.org/10.1177/1355819613492717

Pham, D. T., Dimov, S. S., & Nguyen, C. D. (2005). Selection of K in K-means clustering. *Proceedings of the Institution of Mechanical Engineers, Part C: Journal of Mechanical Engineering Science*, *219*(1), 103–119. https://doi.org/10.1243/095440605x8298

Puška, A., Hodžić, I., Štilić, A., & Murtič, S. (2024). Evaluating European Union countries on climate change management: A fuzzy MABAC approach to the climate change performance index. *Journal of Green Economy and Low-Carbon Development*, *3*(1), 15–25.

PennState: Statistics Online Courses. (n.d.). *Ward's method | STAT 505* (19 December 2007). https://online.stat.psu.edu/stat505/lesson/14/14.7

Rayan, R. A., Tsagkaris, C., & Iryna, R. B. (2021). The internet of things for healthcare: Applications, selected cases and challenges. In G. Marques, A. K. Bhoi, V. H. C. de Albuquerque, & K. S. Hareesha (Eds.). *IoT in healthcare and ambient assisted living* (Vol. 933, pp. 1–15). Springer. https://doi.org/10.1007/978-981-15-9897-5_1

Sakalasooriya, N. (2021). Conceptual analysis of sustainability and sustainable development. *Open Journal of Social Sciences*, *9*(3), 396–414. https://doi.org/10.4236/jss.2021.93026

Strauss, T., & von Maltitz, M. J. (2017). Generalising ward's method for use with Manhattan distances. *PloS One*, *12*(1), e0168288. https://doi.org/10.1371/journal.pone.0168288

Syakur, M. A., Khotimah, B. K., Rochman, E. M. S., & Satoto, B. D. (2018). Integration K-Means clustering method and elbow method for identification of the best customer profile cluster. *IOP Conference Series: Materials Science and Engineering*, *336*, 012017. https://doi.org/10.1088/1757-899x/336/1/012017

Vo, J. (2023, December 11). UN Sustainable Development Goal 3: Achieving Universal Health Coverage Through Digital Transformation. *Public Health Insight*. https://thepublichealthinsight.com/un-sustainable-development-goal-3-achieving-universal-health-coverage-through-digital-transformation-2/

World Health Organization (WHO). (2021). *Global strategy on digital health 2020–2025*. https://www.who.int/docs/default-source/documents/gs4dhdaa2a9f352b0445bafbc79ca799dce4d.pdf

World Health Organization. (2023, December 11). UN Sustainable Development Goal 3: Achieving Universal Health Coverage Through Digital Transformation. *Public Health Insight*. https://thepublichealthinsight.com/un-sustainable-development-goal-3-achieving-universal-health-coverage-through-digital-transformation-2/

Yerpude, S., Sood, K., & Grima, S. (2022). Blockchain-augmented digital supply chain management: A way to sustainable business. *Journal of Risk and Financial Management*, *16*(1), 7.

CHAPTER 13

THE QUESTION OF JOB LOSSES IN THE FOSSIL FUEL ECONOMIES DURING ENERGY TRANSITION: LOSSES AND GAINS

Paiman Ahmad[a], Alhamzah Alnoor[b] and Twana N. Mohamad Khan[c]

[a] *Law Department, University of Raparin, Ranya, Kurdistan Region, Iraq*
[b] *Management Technical College, Southern Technical University, Basrah, Iraq*
[c] *Ministry of Higher Education and Scientific Research, Erbil-Kurdistan Region, Iraq*

ABSTRACT

Introduction: *The notion of job losses during energy transition phases and their influences on fossil fuel economies have been debated in various aspects. Meanwhile, unemployment and poverty have been critical economic challenges for many developing countries, even the resource-rich countries in the Middle East. Concurrently, no country so far is poverty-free and has not entirely fulfilled Sustainable Development Goals (SDG) Nos. 1 and 8, as many resource-rich countries account for the significant global poverty and unemployment, such as Nigeria, Iraq, Yemen, and Venezuela.*

Purpose: *The issue of green transition has created new fears for the job market in the fossil fuel economies, where the lives of many people could be mainly affected. This study investigates the macroeconomic challenges of green transition and the macroeconomic consequences that fossil fuel economies will deal with.*

Sustainability Development through Green Economics
Contemporary Studies in Economic and Financial Analysis, Volume 114, 219–229

Published under exclusive licence by Emerald Publishing Limited
ISSN: 1569-3759/doi:10.1108/S1569-375920240000114013

Methodology: *This study follows content analysis and a desk-search review of job loss during the green transition in the context of fossil fuel economies. In addition, the descriptive analysis is just a clear understanding of the fundamental review of the topic that will lead to another cross-country analysis study based on in-depth knowledge and analysing data.*

Findings: *The European Green Deal (EGD) will have profound economic, social, and political implications for fossil fuel-dependent economies for various reasons. First, fossil fuel economies are less diversified; the economy depends on a single commodity; the systems must be developed and people must prepare for a quick economic transition.*

Keywords: Energy transition; fossil fuel economies; European green deal; job losses; poverty; SDGs; Middle East

JEL Codes: P28; Q49; NEP-ENE; Q42; Q40

INTRODUCTION

This chapter overviews how energy transition affects jobs in the context of fossil fuel economies in the Middle East. The green transition will directly affect the labour market and workers in the fossil fuel economies. The energy transition phases are already underway in many countries around the world. Whistle, the rapid transition to renewable energy will not fit the fossil fuel economies very soon. A faster transition towards a green economy may result in conflict between economic development, socially acceptable transition, and iconological sustainability. Meanwhile, moving to a greener, low-carbon economy means re-directing all sectors and actors towards economic growth in a sustainable and inclusive direction, even though energy and development are intertwined (Blum & Legey, 2012; Braga & Ernst, 2023; Lamperti et al., 2019).

A just transition during the energy transition can help people, communities, states, and stakeholders worldwide. Therefore, a similar action plan for fossil fuel phase-out is required, as developing a phase-out plan for fossil fuels will gradually drive the fossil fuel economies to the right track, even at the late stage. It's the same as Germany's planned transition of coal phase-out by 2038 (Elliott, 2019). Indeed, the green transition should be lined up with Agenda 2030, the SDGs, in particular goal no. 1, 'leaving no one behind' and SDG no. 8, decent jobs for all, as the green transition poses severe challenges to the labour market and workers in the fossil fuel economies.

Full employment and job creation in the fossil fuel industries have always been limited and the sectors are known as foreign labour intense, with few job opportunities for the locals. This means the energy transition's effect on the general public regarding jobs will be smooth while it will be costly for the government.

It is vital to remember that fossil fuel economies have a few peculiarities, not only employment-centred but also associated with other aspects of their resources. In the context of fossil fuel economies, an energy transition might protect the resource-abundant countries from resource curse and Dutch disease. It is estimated that it is not the resource wealth that curses the mineral-rich countries but their chosen ownership structure. Besides, a strong growth performance is based on wise investments in oil revenues in the other sectors of the economy, which leads to successful economic diversification (Arezki et al., 2012).

The existing economic infrastructure is fragile, as even during price shocks, governments hardly adjust fiscal policy, while the exchange rate also affects public spending. In addition to capital flow and trade balance, which will be directly affected during the energy transition, a reduction in foreign direct investment in the fossil fuel sectors will affect net capital inflows (Graham et al., 2005).

Calculating the spillovers of energy transition could mean drastic structural economic change in the fossil fuel economies, in which the question of recovery needs an efficient response. Another severe challenge is the resource curse and the failure of fossil fuel states to benefit from natural resources properly. Thus, a just transition might help resource-abundant countries lift the resource curse, steer to better economic development and achieve the SDG targets. More importantly, natural resources have killed other sectors, such as agriculture, industry, and services, resulting in decline and job losses. Another aspect is commodity prices and their influence on producers, where in many fossil fuel economies, there is a lack of stabilisation funds or commodity agreements. Energy exporters confront climate change, which is a severe challenge on the global scale (Auty, 2002; Humphreys et al., 2007; Lederman & Maloney, 2007; Shaffer & Ziyadov, 2012).

Yet, the transition can create economic opportunities for the fossil fuel economies in the Middle East, such as developing renewable energy sources that can create new jobs and are climate-friendly. The possibility of creating more jobs than losing can be possible in the long run. However, based on the initial indications, achieving a just transition could not be possible in the fossil fuel economies in the first few decades of green transition since job losses will be in the coal, oil, and gas sectors that are the primary sources of the economy in the fossil fuel countries. Job creation will be in other countries, with an estimated 10.3 million net new jobs globally by 2030 and a loss of 2.7 million jobs in the fossil fuel sectors (World Energy Outlook, 2021). However, no accurate global or country-based estimations regarding job losses in the fossil fuel economies have been given. The numbers given are different based on the sources of the information. It is suggested that at least 13–30 million clean-energy-related jobs can be created by 2030, while five million job losses are expected in the fossil fuel industries. Yet, renewable job creation depends on specific geographical locations (IRENA & ILO, 2023).

Progress in achieving sustainable development and action response in favour of climate change in most fossil fuel economies lag behind the other regions. Developing countries, typically fossil fuel producers, have suffered from economic and political conflicts; therefore, economic policies and economic development have been short-term oriented to meet the pressing needs of the people. Thus, developing countries are left behind in the race for economic growth and better climate change mitigation (Puška et al., 2024; Yerpude et al., 2022).

The economic implications of the energy transition will affect poverty and job security in many fossil fuel economies. There are expected economic challenges awaiting fossil fuel producers, as the landscape of green transition is neither aligned with sustainable development nor with the financial well-being of fossil fuel producers. Considering the economic conditions of fossil fuel producers in the phase of the energy transition, severe economic implications can be felt in terms of job creation, poverty, and unemployment for two main reasons. First, the fossil fuel-producing countries are single commodity-dependent economies, which are depleted commodities that are volatile and non-renewable. More visible, the green transition has created fear among the fossil fuel economies, as achieving a just transition might be impossible if all countries do not take decisive action together as a shared responsibility.

THE NEXUS BETWEEN LEAVING NO ONE BEHIND AND POVERTY DURING ENERGY TRANSITION

Leaving no one behind and focussing on our shared future as a global responsibility has been reflected since 1987 in 'Our Common Future'. Sustainable development has been addressed as 'development that meets the needs of the present without compromising the ability of future generations to meet their own needs' (OECD, 2021). Meeting the three main pillars of sustainable development, social, environmental, and economic, aligns with ecological concerns. Paragraph 4 of the 2030 Agenda states, 'As we embark on this incredible collective journey', we pledge that no one will be left behind. Considering the dignity of the human person as fundamental, I wish to see all goals and targets met for all nations and peoples and all segments of society (Asefa, 2005). The *Guidelines for a Just Transition Towards Environmentally Sustainable Economies and Societies for All*, which were published by the International Labour Organization (ILO, 2015), envisioned the necessary pillars align with green transition, including sustainable development, a sharing common global purpose, ensuring a just transition, poverty eradication, and decent work.

The recent shift in energy transition has influenced many economies to think of decarbonising their economies positioned with climate change and sustainable development initiatives. Gradually, the transition to green energy results in the decline of demand for fossil fuels as many European countries have already shifted some segments of their economy to clean energies with low emissions to meet the targets set in EGD. During the energy transition, fossil fuel producers will encounter a few challenges, similar to the previous energy price shocks, such as the recent price decline during the COVID-19 pandemic. Based on current observations, fossil fuel producers keep on the same economic rhythm while necessary change is required to adjust to global changes.

In a regional context of rising poverty and income inequality parallel to the green transition journey, the serious question is who is left behind or who will be left behind? Recognising who is in poor status and where they are and differentiating them from the upcoming expected job losses due to the green transition can help all people being included in response policies to mitigate the risks of the green transition. In essence, focussing on leaving no country behind emphasises countries that are the most in need. In line, the pledge for a just transition could mean the same equal opportunities for all during the green transition. Fulfilling a just transition needs transforming policies and approaches, which assess how those left behind can be reached and monitor the progress of these people while enabling equality of opportunities. There are a few crucial challenges regarding climate change and energy transition. First, there is no global energy policy for mitigating climate change and there needs to be more collaboration between the government, the private sector, and the people. Moreover, more climate mitigation agreements between developed and developing countries must exist (Marhold, 2016; OECD, 2018).

In the early 1980s, oil and gas contributed to the economic growth and development of most oil and gas producers in the Middle East. The economic benefits differ for each country, as some economies are performing very well, while some economies in the Middle East are fragile and unsustainable. Resource dependency has sometimes created weak economic conditions, such as in Iraq. The economic regime needs to be stronger, based on the pursuit of short-term policies that sap the financial strength, leaving little room for resilience against external shocks (Auty, 2002).

The energy transition will directly shift fossil fuel-producing countries towards fossil fuel phase-out. The primary economic challenges are first job losses, which the fossil fuel phase-out will cause. However, the actual scenario is not the job losses many scholars suggest but revenue losses. There are many reasons why fossil fuels will affect job losses. Meanwhile, suppose the fossil fuel producers step towards energy transition as soon as possible. In that case, the job losses will be compensated by developing renewable energy and alternative new jobs will be created. Otherwise, revenue losses will directly affect the public, as in fossil fuel economies, the public sector has the most significant share of employment.

The fuel sector has never created enough jobs and benefits for the people based on the implications of the paradox of plenty or the poverty paradox. This refers to many resource-abundant countries' failures to benefit from their natural wealth fully. Meanwhile, jobs in the fossil fuel sector are mainly concentrated on foreign knowledge and labour and fossil fuel producers must develop the knowledge and skills needed to adapt to green transition and localise the necessary changes. The energy transition story's actual phase is a green transition, which will result in better economic conditions for the rest of the world. Hence, fossil fuel-dependent economies must mitigate the green transition's economic, social, and environmental effects before being late. As time has gone on the resource curse side, citizen expectations concerning renewable energy resources are relatively similar, as people in resource-rich countries have never fully benefitted from their existing natural wealth (Auty, 2002; Gelb, 1988; Karl, 1997).

THE ECONOMIC RELATION BETWEEN SUSTAINABLE DEVELOPMENT AND ENERGY TRANSITION IN THE CASE OF FOSSIL FUEL PRODUCERS

A just transition must be considered when it comes to green transition, as the benefits of energy transition for advanced economies should not harm the fossil fuel economies. Ensuring a just transition during the energy transition needs regional and global cooperation to mitigate the adverse effects on fossil fuel economies. Economic changes can vary based on the country's context, economic well-being, infrastructure, and human resources because green transition causes job losses in specific geographical areas. In contrast, green jobs might be instead created in other locations. Furthermore, job relocations and substitution expectedly can take time due to the requirements of the skills that green technologies need. As noted, the brown jobs are a small portion of the employment pool and will be mainly concentrated in the fossil fuel economies. However, jobs require higher skills than other jobs, which may create complications in relocating workers from fossil fuel sectors to green energy industries.

Moreover, the labour market impacts of green transition will affect sectors, countries, and communities differently as no one-size policy fits all. As has been experienced in the fossil fuel economies, during oil price declines and global financial crises such as 2008, 2015, and 2020, many jobs in the fossil fuel sectors, especially oil, have declined, while the economic recovery in the post-crisis has never created new employment. In this regard, fossil fuel employment has always had challenges; thus, the green transition will not be the first shock for the labour market (OECD, 2018; Transition Report 2023–2024, 2023, Chapter 3; Vandeplas et al., 2022).

Approaching a green economy means achieving economic profitability and environmental sustainability. The United Nations Environment Programme (UNEP) identified a green economy as an economy 'that results in improved human well-being and social equity while reducing environmental risks and ecological scarcity'.[1] Whistle, a Just Transition means 'greening the economy which is fair and inclusive to everyone concerned, creating decent work opportunities and leaving no one behind' (ILO, 2015). Green transition encamps green jobs, sectors, and skills, which will all be environmentally friendly and fair to all.

The energy transition is estimated to create more jobs in general, but it is suggested that job losses in the fossil fuel economies will be high; Iraq is on the front line for encountering this challenge and the other prevailing challenges. Similarly, the climate change effects have already started and climate migration from some parts has been on the rise due to extreme heat, droughts, climate change, and lack of water resources, especially in the Marshes (al-Ahwar) in the south (UNDP, 2021).

Unfortunately, Iraq is very slow in addressing climate change and the challenges with concrete policies to reduce the general effects on the public and economy. Based on the current evidence in Iraq, many fossil fuel economies need to handle transition and climate change according to the Paris Agreement, which demands countries do more than the agreement. On the natural ground, Iraq must catch up in targeting carbon emissions and a net-neutral economy. It has been working on increasing fossil fuel production annually since 2005. Considering the current situations and constituencies in many fossil fuel countries, severe macroeconomic concerns about the consequences of the green transition push many people away from being integrated with the change. Economic consequences such as job losses may be encountered in some cities with the decline of fossil fuel production and the decline in global demand for fossil fuel commodities soon.

Another crucial factor in fossil fuel-dependent economies is culture, as people are used to cheap energy and access costs that are less than renewable energy resources, which are cost-competitive. Thus, changing the mentality and consumer attitude will take time for many people. Hence, this will be another central challenge for accelerating the transition in the fossil fuel economies in the Middle East. Despite the recent call for the green transition, the call for more employment has been lined up with the previous economic recovery plans after the 2014 conflict. Iraq had a target to increase 10 million new jobs by 2030, but in developing the fossil fuel sectors and related value-added industries. The World Bank (2014) has supported the Government of Iraq in developing its national energy strategy.

According to the data from the Iraq Labor Force Survey 2021, before encountering the challenges created by the green transition, Iraq as a fossil fuel economy already suffered from high unemployment of men, women, and youth; 'the combined rate of unemployment and time-related underemployment was 24.0 percent of the labor force, significantly higher than the unemployment rate'. Based on the data, Iraq has a potential young labour force, which can contribute if it is appropriately utilised if diversification is undertaken; if not, the effects of the green transition will be doubled since the unemployment rate is already alarming.

Suppose the status of jobs in the fossil fuel sectors in the producing countries is considered. In that case, real macroeconomic challenges can be expected because the employment dimensions of the transition should be observed and studied based on the country's context and economic situation. If fossil fuel countries intend to benefit from green transition, then more employment and jobs will be created in the renewable sector. Therefore, urgent investment is required not just in the renewable sector but also in the other sectors of each economy that are fossil fuel-based.

Strategic steps should be taken as soon as possible, such as reskilling some workers from the fossil fuel sectors, as some technicians and labour force can be reskilled easily with less cost and time. Accordingly, many workers in the traditional energy industries have experiences that can help them integrate into renewable energy development in different aspects of the energy transition. Therefore, job losses will also influence the renewable energy companies in finding talented and qualified workers to fill the new positions; thus, reskilling will be the best-fit strategy. In case of job losses, data prove that jobs in the fossil fuel sectors are very concentrated and the number of people working in the other sectors is more than in the fossil fuel sector. In Saudi Arabia, a leading fossil fuel economy, only 4.8% of the population is employed in the energy industry.

In contrast, almost half of the GDP is derived from the fossil fuel sector (Cozzi & Motherway, 2021). In the *Guidelines for a Just Transition Towards*

Environmentally Sustainable Economies and Societies for All, which was published by the ILO (2015), the guideline emphasises a few key issues, including reskilling some workers who will be affected by the transition and providing initial learning in green business practices and fintech knowledge. Despite some of the current initiatives towards energy transition, the future demand and the Iraqi capacity to increase oil production, like some other countries, indicate a regressive attempt towards developing and replacing fossil fuels with renewables soon (International Energy Agency, 2023), as Fig. 13.1 show:

In comparing the labour force in the traditional energy sector to renewable, the gaps to be highlighted include the employment structure, the skills required, the requirement of higher-level qualifications, and knowledge in renewable energies, which may lead to a shift in the labour market and energy transition can create more jobs and even better qualified and decent ones (Dominish et al., 2019, Chapter 10; Ram et al., 2022).

Besides, social awareness is required as workers in the fossil fuel sector should be warned about the transition and the consequences so they are better prepared for the risks and challenges. Decision-making regarding transition should be collective; government, people, civil society, and foreign stakeholders should all be involved to mitigate the risks and challenges for the best of all. However, similar to state behaviour, the attitude and commitment of buyers concerning green products and reducing purchases of fossil-fuel products could not be easily achieved in fossil-fuel economies. Moreover, a transition of the population from traditional to modern markets will significantly influence the nature of policy changes in the energy industries, which could be economic and social (Pandey, 2002). Moreover, the financial security of fossil fuel economies will be gradually affected by the energy transition and no-producing economies, as energy is the economic contributor that influences welfare, social priorities, employment, etc. (Ram et al., 2022).

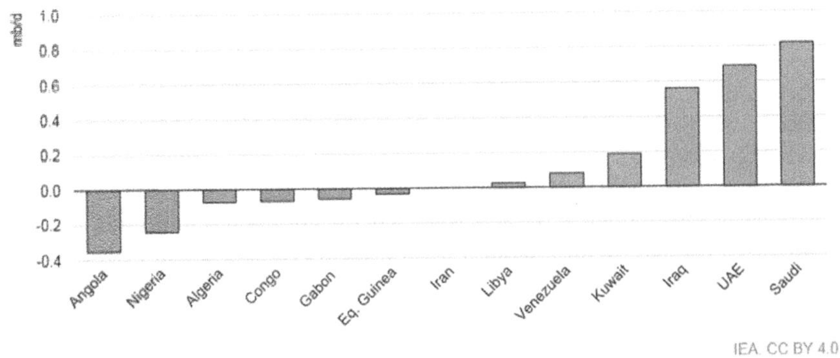

Note: Assumes Iran remains under sanctions.

Fig. 13.1. OPEC Crude Oil Production Capacity Change 2023–2028. *Source*: International Energy Agency (2023).]

CONCLUSIONS

The green transition will pose challenges and opportunities for many of the fossil fuel economies in the Middle East, similar to the other resource-abundant regions. However, it is too early to make clear conclusions before making statistical country analyses on the potential and promises that green transition could have for fossil fuel economies. Notably, many national and subnational governments have deployed transition plans to provide the necessary means for revitalising local economies, combining investment and education strategies (Cozzi & Motherway, 2021).

In the context of fossil fuel economies, the dead-end question is, can a just transition be achieved, and can the transition be people-centred? It has been estimated that six in 10 workers need the required training by 2027, while a limited number of workers have access to adequate training opportunities. Therefore, governments should consider increasing decent and equal opportunities for more workers to fit the changes requiring high-tech skills. In addition, getting well-prepared for the long term involves education and training policies aligned with the future new skill demands. Adequate training helps workers to switch from declining to emerging sectors. Besides, green jobs can facilitate achieving SDG 8, where complete and productive employment and decent work for all are the primary targets (Kruse et al., 2017).

As the literature indicates, Middle Eastern countries have the potential to develop renewables, especially solar and wind. In contrast, many countries must overcome challenges such as creating better investment opportunities, enforcing financial necessities, and coping means such as technologies and a skilled labour force. Developing renewables helps Iraq, as a fossil fuel economy, reduce dependence on oil and gas and makes the economy relatively accessible from foreign rents (Ersoy & Pfaff, 2021). To this end, energy transition and climate change complexities increase the challenges for countries and regions; therefore, proper solutions lie in building international collaborations that target a just transition (Keskes & Haytayan, 2023).

Bearing that the green transition needs social awareness and stakeholder contribution, the transition can be converted to fruitful opportunities, especially for creating green jobs and reducing the environmental impacts of fossil fuels. Moreover, a just transition can be the only promising means that supports employing more people in the renewable sectors soon.

POLICY RECOMMENDATIONS

The history of the labour market has been full of stories where, at times, many jobs have been either lost or created. Meanwhile, globalisation and technological development have created thousands of jobs, incredibly high-tech skilled-based jobs, and whistle-changes in the labour markets that affect different segments of the population based on the economic foundation and context of the country. As the development of fossil fuel sectors in the past has created many jobs for locals and foreigners, the time has come to close these sectors gradually. Therefore, available jobs in these sectors will be limited in the future.

It is suggested that fossil fuel economies prepare for the transition and adapt to necessary adjustments, which can reduce risks and challenges and benefit the economy in the long run. To catch up with the rest of the world, the fossil fuel economies need to get either support from the United Nations Green Climate Fund, IMF, or country-based specific funds for supporting green transition and compensating for the effects in advance. Furthermore, fossil fuel economies should align policies with transition efforts, such as financial investment, to mitigate the impact of transition on workers and communities and build social dialogue among all stakeholders to achieve better outcomes (Cozzi & Motherway, 2021).

As suggested, reinforcing the social safety net and letting market forces work. The emphasis should be given to unemployment insurance, where people are compensated for losing jobs for no fault. This policy helps people who lose jobs to get substantial income, typically in the first months of displacement (Hanson, 2023).

The green transition will create a gap in the availability of the skills and talents required for the new jobs that are supposed to be made in the renewable energy sectors. Skills shortages could be filled with reskilling and training the labour force from the fossil fuel sectors to acquire the necessary skills for enhancing the employability and productivity of the workers in their newly assigned positions.

In addition, governments, foreign companies, and stakeholders must bear their responsibilities in contributing to the green transition to reduce the main burden on the labour force and communities. Indeed, the transition to green economies needs a just transition to support fossil fuel economies and other economies to smoothly transform into a green economy, mitigate the effect of climate change, and provide decent jobs for the public.

NOTE

1. https://www.unep.org/regions/asia-and-pacific/regional-initiatives/supporting-resource-efficiency/green-economy

REFERENCES

Arezki, R., Pattillo, C. A., Quintyn, M. G., & Zhu, M. (2012). *Commodity price volatility and inclusive growth in low-income countries.* International Monetary Fund. Retrieved October 24, 2012, from https://www.elibrary.imf.org/display/book/9781616353797/9781616353797.xml

Asefa, S. (2005). *The economics of sustainable development*. W.E. Upjohn Institute for Employment Research.

Auty, R. M. (2002). *Sustaining development in mineral economics*. Routledge.

Blum, H., & Legey, L. F. L. (2012). The challenging economics of energy security: Ensuring energy benefits in support to sustainable development. *Energy Economics*, *34*(6), 1982–1989.

Braga, J. P., & Ernst, E. (2023). We are financing the green transition. The role of macro-economic policies in ensuring a just transition. *Frontiers in Climate*, *5*(5), 1192706. https://doi.org/10.3389/fclim.2023.1192706

Cozzi, L., & Motherway, B. (2021, July6). *The importance of focusing on jobs and fairness in clean energy transitions*. IEA. https://www.iea.org/commentaries/the-importance-of-focusing-on-jobs-and-fairness-in-clean-energy-transitions

Dominish, E., Briggs, C., Teske, S., & Mey, F. (2019). Just transition: Employment projections for the 2.0 °C and 1.5 °C scenarios. In S. Teske (Ed.), *Achieving the Parish Climate Agreement goals* (pp. 413–436). Springer Nature.

Elliott, C. (2019, March25). *Planning for a "just transition": Leaving no worker behind in shifting to a low carbon future*. World Resource Institute. https://www.wri.org/insights/planning-just-transition-leaving-no-worker-behind-shifting-low-carbon-future

Energy Transitions Commission Report. (2023, November). *Fossil fuels in transition: Committing to the phase-down of all fossil fuels*. https://www.energy-transitions.org/wp-content/uploads/2023/11/ETC-Fossil-Fuels-MainReport.pdf

Ersoy, S. R., & Pfaff, J. T. (2021, May). *Sustainable transformation of Iraq's energy system* (p. 34). Friedrich Ebert Stiftung, Climate Change, Energy and Development.

Gelb, A. H. (1988). *Oil windfalls: Blessing or curse?*Oxford University Press/The World Bank.

Graham, E. M., Oding, N., & Welfens, P. J. (2005). *Internationalization and economic policy reforms in transition countries*. Springer.

Hanson, G. (2023, January). *Local labor market impact of the energy transition: Prospects and policies* [Faculty Research Working Paper Series RWP23-005, No. 30871, Harvard Kennedy School].

Humphreys, M., Sachs, D. J., & Stiglitz, J. E. (2007). *Escaping the resource curse*. Columbia University Press.

International Energy Agency. (2023). *World Energy Outlook*. IEA.

International Labour Organization. (2015). *Guidelines for a just transition towards environmentally sustainable economies and societies* (pp. 1–14). ILO.

IRENA & ILO. (2023). *Renewable energy and jobs: Annual review 2023*. International Renewable Energy Agency, Abu Dhabi and International Labour Organization.

Karl, T. L. (1997). *The paradox of plenty: Oil booms and petro-states*. University of California Press.

Keskes, H., & Haytayan, L. (2023, November). *Energy transition in the Middle East and North Africa: The Road to COP28* (pp. 1–17). National Resource Governance Institute.

Kruse, T., Dellink, R., & Chateau, J. (2017, June). *Employment implications of green growth: Linking jobs, growth, and green policies* [OECD Report for the G7 Environment Ministries, OECD Publishing].

Lamperti, F., Mazzucato, M., Roventini, A., & Semieniuk, G. (2019). The green transition: Public policy, finance and the role of the state. *Vierteljahrshefte zur Wirtschaftsforschung, DIW Berlin, 88*(2), 73–88.

Lederman, D., & Maloney, W. F. (2007). *Natural resources neither curse nor destiny*. Stanford University Press. https://doi.org/10.1596/978-0-8213-6545-8

Marhold, A. A. (2016). *The nexus between the WTO and the Energy Charter Treaty in sustainable global energy governance: Analysis and policy implications* [Issue Paper No. 7, pp. 1–40]. Global Economic Policy and Institutions/ICTSD. Retrieved March 1, 2016, from https://research.tilburguniversity.edu/en/publications/the-nexus-between-the-wto-and-the-energy-charter-treaty-in-global

OECD. (2018). *Development cooperation report 2018: Joining forces to leave no one behind*. OECD Publishing.

OECD. (2021). The DAC guidelines strategies for sustainable development: Guideline for development cooperation. OECD Publishing.

Pandey, R. (2002, January). Energy policy modelling: Agenda for developing countries. *Energy Policy, 30*(2), 97–106.

Ram, M., Osorio-Aravena, J., Aghahosseini, A., & Bogdanov, D. (2022, January). Job creation during a climate-compliant global energy transition across the power, heat, transport, and desalination sectors by 2050, *Energy, 238*, Part A, 121690.

Shaffer, B., & Ziyadov, T. (2012). *Beyond the resource curse*. University of Pennsylvania Press.

The World Bank. (2014, May 6). *Beyond conflict: Iraq's energy sector targets jobs and prosperity*. https://www.worldbank.org/en/news/feature/2014/05/06/beyond-conflict-iraqs-energy-sector-targets-jobs-and-prosperity

Transition Report 2023–2024. (2023). Transitions big and small, Chapter 3. Labor markets in the green transition, European Bank for Reconstruction and Development. Available at https://2023.tr-ebrd.com. (Accessed on April 26, 2024).

UNDP. (2021 March 28). *Ahwari women, the beating heart of the Iraqi Marshes*. United Nations Development Programme (undp.org).

Vandeplas, A., Vanyolos, I., Vigani, M., & Vogel, L. (2022, December). *The possible implications of green transition for the E.U. labor market* [Discussion paper 176, European Commission]. https://ec.europa.eu/info/publications/economic-and-financial-affairs-publications_en

Yerpude, S., Sood, K., & Grima, S. (2022). Blockchain-Augmented digital supply chain management: A way to sustainable business. *Journal of Risk and Financial Management, 16*(1), 7.

World Energy Outlook. (2021, October). *People-centered transitions*. International Energy Agency.

CHAPTER 14

GREEN FINANCING IN THE WAY OF SUSTAINABLE DEVELOPMENT

Md. Shajedul Islam[a], Md. Motahar Hossain[b] and Nitin Pathak[c]

[a]*Department of Business Studies, North Bengal International University, Rajshahi, Bangladesh*
[b]*Department of Business Management, University School of Business, Chandigarh University, Mohali, Punjab, India*
[c]*Department of Commerce, University School of Business, Chandigarh University, Mohali, Punjab, India*

ABSTRACT

Purpose: *The book chapter seeks to investigate the numerous green finance measures already taken by various banks in the direction of Bangladesh's sustainable development. The chapter also demonstrates the extent to which banks in the nation will use green finance between 2019 and 2022.*

Need for the study: *This study indicated that practically all banks participated in green finance initiatives to promote sustainable economic growth. Private commercial banks (PCBs) and foreign commercial banks (FCBs) have taken more measures than the other banks, although their efforts still fall short. Therefore, it will be better for the environment and sustainable growth if the financial industry adopts more green finance projects.*

Methodology: *The study mostly relied on secondary data and information gathered from Bangladesh Bank annual reports, numerous studies on green financing, and the websites of several institutions. Microsoft Excel has been used to examine the data. Data have been presented using tables, graphs, and charts.*

Sustainability Development through Green Economics
Contemporary Studies in Economic and Financial Analysis, Volume 114, 231–241

ISSN: 1569-3759/doi:10.1108/S1569-375920240000114014

Findings: *Green financing is now the demand of the time because the whole world, especially Bangladesh, is facing adverse impacts from global warming and climate change. So environmental issues have become the main concern of the government, Bangladesh Bank, stakeholders, and society, and they wish to know about the initiatives towards green financing taken by the various banks to reduce the impact of global warming.*

Implications: *Policymakers, governments, private and public organisations, banking industries, and their stakeholders will benefit from the book chapter.*

Keywords: Green financing; green banking; green initiatives; global warming; climate change; sustainable development

JEL Codes: G32; G21; Q54; Q01

1. INTRODUCTION

Global warming and climate change, which have a significant impact on the weather all over the world, have recently emerged as the most urgent and hotly debated topics. Moreover, the most complicated issue the world is currently dealing with is climate change. The world's eco-system occasionally struggles to practically adjust to the abrupt climate change brought on by global warming. This change has already hurt Bangladesh's air quality, water resources, land, agriculture, forestry, fisheries, livestock, biodiversity, and human health (Ullah, 2020). The frequency and severity of earthquakes, storms, floods, cyclones, and droughts have already increased. There have been ongoing efforts to assess and lessen the threat of climate change resulting from human activity. Numerous countries have made significant commitments to slowing climate change. To decrease the devastating effects of climate change and global warming, Bangladesh has likewise committed to reducing the nation's carbon intensity. Bangladesh has some of the greatest climate change and global warming effects, despite being one of the countries with the lowest carbon emissions. Environmental concerns have recently received a lot of attention in this context and the banking industry is under pressure to create 'green' programmes. Although customers do not primarily choose banks based on their use of green financing, growing customer awareness of environmental issues is pushing certain banks to adopt green practices. As socially conscious business people, Bangladesh's banking industry has a crucial obligation to support government initiatives to significantly reduce carbon emissions. Since their own 'internal' operations do not significantly harm the environment, banks are often regarded as being environmentally beneficial (Sahoo & Nayak, 2007). But occasionally, what their clients do has a substantial 'external' effect on the environment. Pharmaceuticals, chemicals, fertilisers, ready-to-wear apparel, textiles, paper, cement, and power are just a few of the businesses that produce the most carbon emissions and one of their main funding sources is the banking sector (Hoque et al., 2019). To assist environmentally sustainable and socially responsible investment, the banking industry can therefore act as a link between economic, social, and environmental development.

Banks are equipped to adopt and start providing green funding for sustainable development. A significant contribution is being made to the green economy and industry as a result of green banking, which is a crucial element of sustainable growth. Rashid and Uddin (2018) found that using grant, debt, and equity formats, green finance comprises providing or supporting financing for initiatives that benefit the environment. Green financing is the act of carrying out financial operations in settings and ways that permit a general decline in both internal and external carbon emissions (Meena, 2013). The concept of green finance is linked to the concept of sustainable development goals, which have significant practical implications for the sustainable development of a country by prioritising investment in environmentally friendly projects (Zheng et al., 2021). Banks ought to promote the financing of green technology and pollution-reduction initiatives to help reduce external carbon emissions. Although there is no link between the banking industry and pollution, the current scope of banking activities has greatly increased the carbon footprint as they consume considerable energy (such as high paper consumption, lighting, air conditioning, IT, a lack of green buildings, electronic equipment, etc.). As a result, banks should adopt strategies, procedures, and products that enable them to drastically cut their carbon footprint and build a sustainable business. Therefore, green financing and banking have advanced significantly in recent years because banks, as financiers, have a significant impact on funding projects undertaken by industries. According to Sachs et al. (2019), green banking is merely the standard banking procedure where all activities are subject to the same regulations with an added emphasis on environmental sustainability. Bhardwaj and Malhotra (2013) defined green banking as a bank initiative to support the expansion of ecologically friendly businesses and, as a result, restore the environment. Masukujjaman and Akhtar (2013) also defined green banking as the use of eco- or environment-friendly financial practices to halt environmental degradation and improve the habitability of this planet. Banks evaluate a project's environmental benefits and potential long-term repercussions before financing it to safeguard the environment. Green finance includes sustainable banking and investment, which makes lending and investment decisions based on risk assessment and environmental screening to meet sustainability criteria that protect against environmental and climate risks (Islam, 2014). For many industrial projects, including those involving chemicals, power, textiles, steel, fertilisers, paper, cement, etc., with potentially serious negative social or environmental repercussions, banking institutions serve as the principal source of financing (Azad & Islam, 2022). In actuality, green finance works to save the earth from environmental deterioration and promote sustainable economic growth. By balancing long-term social, financial, and environmental well-being while preserving long-term cultural, economic, and environmental health, sustainable development, on the other hand, ensures the development of the nation. Alternatively, sustainable development is the capacity of the present generation to achieve its requirements without compromising the capacity of the future generation (Brundtland, 1987). To preserve the environment and support long-term sustainable growth in Bangladesh, the banking sector invests in green initiatives through green finance (Puška et al., 2024; Yerpude et al., 2022).

2. PROBLEM STATEMENT

The concept of green financing evolved in developed countries, that is, western countries, and the 21st century, it spread to most developing countries like Bangladesh (Islam & Das, 2013). But concerning promoting green financing, financial institutions as well as the banking sector in Bangladesh are lagging behind their global counterparts (Akhter et al., 2021). As a result, the impact of global warming and climate change decreases the quality of human life and the quantity of natural resources. In this situation, the banking sector needs to act as a socially responsible citizen and implement green financing to ensure sustainable development. In this regard, the banking sector in developed countries is properly implementing green financing. As a result, the majority of research on green financing has been done so far in industrialised nations. There isn't much research on Bangladesh's green financing practices because the idea of green financing is still relatively new in developing nations like ours. Therefore, it has been stated that it is crucial to understand green funding methods in developing nations due to their varied socioeconomic contexts. Therefore, the current study's goal is to learn more about how Bangladesh Bank created its green financing policy and how it was implemented by the various banks that operate there, including PCBs, state-owned commercial banks (SCBs), state-owned development banks (SDBs), and FCBs.

3. LITERATURE REVIEW

Academics, researchers, and professionals are becoming more and more interested in themes such as green finance, green banking, and sustainable economic growth. Green financing is a notion that is just beginning to gain support to transform the financial sector and develop new sustainable business models. The management of environmental issues is integrated with banking activities. A company will only be granted a loan if all environmental safety standards have been met (Bihari, 2010). For sustainable development, banks can engage in green banking projects and practices to preserve nature and natural resources. Volz (2016) reported on the Asian Development Bank's (ADB) annual general meeting with a focus on the financial sector's crucial role in the green revolution. A researcher provided thoughts on green investment in Asia as well as a summary of green financial governance initiatives across Asian countries in his discussion of the need to green the financial system. The paper also identified market trends for green finance and highlighted the necessity of adopting sound monetary policies to remove obstacles to green lending and investment (Volz, 2016).

In a study, Hoshen et al. (2017) showed the trend of green products in Bangladesh Bank refinancing projects. According to this report, PCBs sponsor green initiatives more frequently and have a rising desire to reinvest in them. This paper recommends changing the regulations governing green financing to support Bangladesh's transition to sustainable development. Islam (2014) examined the green activities of five banks. Based on main and secondary data, the study found that none of the sample banks are engaged in green finance. Ullah (2013) compared different bank types, including SCBs, SDBs, PCBs, and FCBs, and examined the backdrop of green banking practices. The purpose of the study was to ascertain whether banks had adopted the guidelines for green banking created by Bangladesh Bank. In some green products, the study found that only PCBs and FCBs are carefully following laws and financing, while other contributions are hardly noticeable (Ullah, 2013). Shakil et al. (2014) investigated the green banking practices of PCBs, SCBs, SDBs, and FCBs in Bangladesh. The study found that the budget allocation and usage for SCBs and SDBs are insufficient. The ATM and Internet banking services provided by SCBs and SDBs are also substandard. It also identified a rising tendency in the bank's loan disbursements towards green initiatives.

According to the aforementioned literature, it is evident that the majority of studies have concentrated on the green financing of PCBs, with a small number of studies concentrating on SCBs and certain PCBs. In other words, a small number of studies centred on the banking sector as a whole have been carried out. The current study looks at green finance activities carried out by Bangladesh-based PCBs, SCBs, SDBs, and FCBs to overcome this gap.

4. OBJECTIVES

The study has been conducted:

(1) to analyse green financing initiatives taken by various banks to ensure the sustainable development of Bangladesh and
(2) to assess how PCBs, SCBs, SDBs, and FCBs in Bangladesh differ in their use of green finance.

5. METHODOLOGY

This study on green financing practices in Bangladesh's banking industry is descriptive. This research is exploratory. Thus, secondary data provide the bulk of the study's foundation. The data were acquired through periodicals, newspapers, publications from Bangladesh Bank, and the bank's website. To increase the public's understanding of specialised topics, several books and related articles from a variety of sources are used. The population of the study consists of all scheduled commercial banks operating in Bangladesh. A total of 61 banks are currently active in Bangladesh (Bangladesh Bank, 2022). These Bangladeshi banks are divided into four categories based on how they operate: PCBs, SCBs, SDBs, and FCBs. All scheduled banks in Bangladesh, including PCBs, SCBs, SDBs, and FCBs, have been chosen for this study based on the possibility that the data are accurate. For this study, data from the previous four years (2019–2022) were taken into account. Microsoft Excel was used to examine the data. Data are presented using tables, graphs, and charts.

6. DATA ANALYSIS AND DISCUSSION

6.1. Green Financing Practices of the Banking Sector

Commercial banks took the initiative to go green according to Bangladesh Bank guidelines. Currently, 61 scheduled banks are governed and overseen by the Bangladesh Bank (Hossain et al., 2013). The schemes for green financing that banks are undertaking between 2019 and 2022 are listed in this section, which also gives an overview of the situation of green finance in Bangladesh during the past several years. The information was gathered from the banks' annual reports. Details of Bangladesh's banking sector's annual allocation of green financing during the last four years are shown in Tables 14.1–14.5. The details are as follows:

6.1.1. Green Financing Practices of PCBs

Table 14.1 summarises green money by category throughout the previous four years, from 2019 to 2022. The study's conclusions showed that PCBs disbursed a total of 301,332.4 million BDT (Bangladeshi Taka) in green finance during the previous four fiscal years (2019–2022). The four financial years' largest and lowest disbursements, respectively, occurred in 2022 and 2020. The amounts were 96,393.73 million BDT and 61,593.37 million BDT, respectively.

Table 14.1. Category-wise Green Financing of PCBs.

Areas of Expenditure	2019 (Million BDT)	2020 (Million BDT)	2021 (Million BDT)	2022 (Million BDT)
Renewable energy	1,721.6	2,633.02	2,054.82	4,407.89
Energy efficiency	4,112.67	9,870	12,100.96	20,692.3
Alternative energy	88.84	38.37	43.84	45.4
Waste management	11,960.92	8,472.88	3,655.67	16,907.94
Recycling and manufacturing of recyclable goods	8,144.61	11,965.86	4,152.87	7,680.45
Environment-friendly brick production	12,241.74	8,097.72	2,526.35	3,216.83
Green/environment-friendly establishments	24,192.84	34,683.06	35,916.1	38,302.89
Green agriculture			332.14	1,387.32
Green CMSME			609.61	2,239.07
Green SRF			201.01	1,513.64
Miscellaneous	3,931.51	1,009.65		
Total	**66,574.73**	**76,770.56**	**61,593.37**	**96,393.73**

Source: Authors' compilation based on Bangladesh Bank Annual Report (2019–2022).

6.1.2. Green Financing Practices of SCBs

Table 14.2 shows the trend of green finance over the previous four years, from 2019 to 2022. According to the study's findings, SCBs disbursed a total of 22,684.74 million BDT in green finance throughout the last four financial years (2019–2022). The four financial years' largest and lowest disbursements, respectively, occurred in 2022 and 2019. 9,647.9 million BDT and 1,283.16 million BDT, respectively, were the sums. Among the four fiscal years, 2022 saw the largest disbursement and 2019 the lowest. The amounts were 9,647.9 million BDT and 1,283.16 million BDT, respectively.

6.1.3. Green Financing Practices of SDBs

Table 14.3 displays direct green financing by category for the previous four years, from 2019 to 2022. The study's conclusions showed that SDBs disbursed a total of 48.49 million BDT in green financing during the previous four fiscal years (2019–2022). The four financial years' largest and lowest disbursements, respectively, occurred in 2021 and 2020. The amounts were 23.98 million BDT and 6.34 million BDT, respectively.

Table 14.2. Category-wise Green Financing of SCBs.

Areas of Expenditure	2019 (Million BDT)	2020 (Million BDT)	2021 (Million BDT)	2022 (Million BDT)
Renewable energy	9.32	6.95	1,846.64	21.75
Energy efficiency	0	214.82	78.46	204.19
Alternative energy	0	0	0	131.45
Liquid waste management	416.25	743.86	154.8	
Solid waste management		0	119.13	4,684.1
Recycling and manufacturing of recyclable goods	361.47	887.54	148.49	196.31
Environment-friendly brick production	490.25	496.82	136.58	315.9
Green/environment-friendly establishments		5,984.71	259.24	3,378.82
Green agriculture			609.48	7.77
Green CMSME			19.71	706.61
Green SRF			0.15	0
Miscellaneous	5.87	46.98		
Total	**1,283.16**	**8,381.0**	**3,372.68**	**9,647.9**

Source: Authors' compilation based on Bangladesh Bank Annual Report (2019–2022).

Table 14.3. Category-wise Green Financing of SDBs.

Areas of Expenditure	2019 (Million BDT)	2020 (Million BDT)	2021 (Million BDT)	2022 (Million BDT)
Renewable energy	6.98	4.69	7.41	5.29
Green agriculture	0	0	4.32	2.18
Green CMSME	0	0	0.25	1.32
Miscellaneous	1.39	1.65	0	0
Total	**8.38**	**6.34**	**23.98**	**9.79**

Source: Authors' compilation based on Bangladesh Bank Annual Report (2019–2022).

6.1.4. Green Financing Practices of FCBs

Table 14.4 displays green money by category throughout the previous four years, from 2019 to 2022. The study's conclusions showed that banks in Bangladesh disbursed a total of 301,332.4 million BDT in green financing throughout the previous four fiscal years (2019–2022). The four financial years' largest and lowest disbursements, respectively, occurred in 2020 and 2022. The amounts were 30,132.66 million BDT and 1,621.2 million BDT, respectively.

6.1.5. Green Financing Practices of the Banking Sector in Bangladesh

Table 14.5 shows the trend of green financing by the banking sector in Bangladesh from 2019 to 2022. According to the findings of the study, the banking sector

Table 14.4 Category-wise Green Financing of FCBs.

Areas of Expenditure	2019 (Million BDT)	2020 (Million BDT)	2021 (Million BDT)	2022 (Million BDT)
Renewable energy	515.49	187.48	3	0
Energy efficiency	304.09	382.77	1,031.97	0
Alternative energy	0	0	8	0
Waste management	188.34	218.31	660.08	0
Recycling and manufacturing of recyclable goods	0	0	6.5	0
Green/environment-friendly establishments	36,047.84	2,865 4.12	7,381.95	619.24
Green agriculture			223.14	297.66
Green CMSME			560.2	744.3
Miscellaneous	35.59	685.38	0	
Total	**37,091.35**	**30,132.66**	**9,874.84**	**1,621.2**

Source: Authors' compilation based on Bangladesh Bank Annual Report (2019–2022).

Table 14.5 Category-wise Green Financing of Banking Sector in Bangladesh (2018–2022).

Areas of Expenditure	2019 (Million BDT)	2020 (Million BDT)	2021 (Million BDT)	2022 (Million BDT)	Total
Renewable energy	2,253.39	2,832.14	6,261.94	4,434.93	**15,782.4**
Energy efficiency	4,416.76	10,467.59	20,770.76	20,896.49	**56,551.6**
Alternative energy	88.84	38.37	45.4	176.85	**349.46**
Waste management	12,565.52	9,435.05	17,181.87	21,593.04	**59,082.61**
Manufacturing of recyclable goods	8,506.08	12,858	7,829.94	7,877.76	**37,071.78**
Environment-friendly brick production	12,911.99	8,535.05	3,364.41	3,532.73	**28,344.18**
Environment-friendly establishments	60,240.68	8,594.54	39,181.37	42,300.95	**15,0317**
Green agriculture			1,709.01	1,694.93	**3,403.94**
Green CMSME			3,593.1	3,691.3	**7,284.4**
Green SRF			1,513.79	1,513.64	**3,027.43**
Miscellaneous	3,974.36	1,743.66			**5,718.02**
Total	**104,957.6**	**115,291.2**	**101,451.6**	**107,712.6**	**209,164.2**

Source: Authors' compilation based on Bangladesh Bank Annual Report (2019–2022).

disbursed a total of 209,164.2 million BDT in green finance during the last four fiscal years (2019–2022). Over the four financial years, 2020 had the greatest disbursement and 2021 the lowest. It came to 115,291.2 million BDT and 101,451.6 million BDT, respectively.

6.1.6. Sector-wise Green Financing During 2018–2022

Fig. 14.1 demonstrates that over the past four years (2018–2022), the banking industry has given more than 41% of its funding to the sector of environmentally friendly businesses. The waste management sector is second with 16%, followed by energy efficiency at 15% and the manufacturing of recyclable goods at 10%. Therefore, waste management, energy efficiency, environmentally friendly businesses, and the production of recyclable goods are the areas where the banking industry invests the most. Environmentally friendly brick production, renewable energy, and green CMSME all receive nominal banking sector financing.

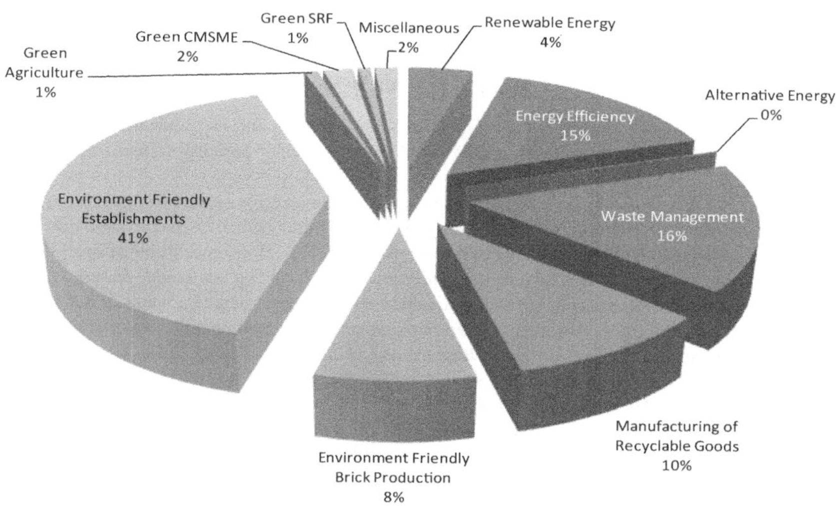

Fig. 14.1 Green Financing of Banking Sector in Bangladesh (2018–2022). *Source*: Authors' calculation based on Annual Report of Bangladesh Bank (2022) and authors' own work based on Bangladesh Bank Annual Report (2018–2022).

7. CONCLUSION

Bangladesh is one of the nations most at risk from climate change in the current era of globalisation because of the effects of global industrialisation. For sustainable development to take place in Bangladesh, appropriate steps need to be taken to mitigate the harmful effects of global warming and climate change. Industries that give priority to the environment should be financed through green finance or banking. Because development can be done by damaging the environment, but it will be temporary, sustainable development should be done by protecting the environment. However, Bangladesh's financial industry lags considerably behind other countries. Given this situation, Bangladesh Bank has developed formal and official policy guidelines on green finance for banks to prevent the deterioration of the environment (Rahman et al., 2013). According to Bangladesh Bank guidelines, all banks must take appropriate measures to finance eco-friendly industries in the country. The banking industry of today thinks that every 'green' action performed now will help create a safe future, which will progressively contribute to the sustainable development of the nation. Additionally, the banks would work to enhance Bangladesh's ecology and the environment worldwide through green financing programmes. The study observed that PCBs and FCBs in Bangladesh have given a significant amount of money to eco-friendly industries through green financing, but the amount of green financing provided by SCBs and SDBs is not sufficient. This is why it can be said that the overall scenario of green finance in the banking sector is not at all satisfactory. There are many opportunities for banks to adopt green financing initiatives and strategies to save the earth's environment and build the banking sector's image in society by ensuring sustainable development in the country (Reepu, 2020).

REFERENCES

Akhter, I., Yasmin, S., & Faria, N. (2021). Green banking practices and its implication on financial performance of the commercial banks in Bangladesh. *Journal of Business Administration*, *42*(1), 1–23.

Azad, M. A. K., & Islam, M. A. (2022). Promoting green finance for sustainable development in Bangladesh. In H. Şimşek, A. Kan, M. Taş, & S. Atalay Şimşek (Eds.), *International Academician Studies Congress 2022: Change and adaptation* (pp. 395–412). Holistence Publications.

Bangladesh Bank. (2022, October–December). *Quarterly review report on sustainable finance of banks and financial institutions* (pp. 1–16). Sustainable Finance Department, Bangladesh Bank.

Bhardwaj, B. R., & Malhotra, A. (2013). Green banking strategies: Sustainability through corporate entrepreneurship. *Greener Journal of Business and Management Studies*, *3*(4), 180–193.

Bihari, S. C. (2010). Green banking towards socially responsible banking in India. *International Journal of Business Insights & Transformation*, *4*, 82–87.

Brundtland, G. H. (1987). *World commission on environment and development. Our common future*. UN.

Hoque, N., Mowla, M., Uddin, M. S., Mamun, A., & Uddin, M. R. (2019). Green banking practices in Bangladesh: A critical investigation. *International Journal of Economics and Finance*, *11*(3), 58–68.

Hoshen, M. S., Hasan, M. N., Hossain, S., Al Mamun, M. A., Mannan, A., & Al Mamun, A. (2017). Green financing: An emerging form of sustainable development in Bangladesh. *IOSR Journal of Business and Management*, *19*(12), 24–30.

Hossain, M. M., Irin, D., Islam, M. S., & Saha, S. (2013). Electronic banking services: A study on selected commercial banks in Bangladesh. *Asian Business Review*, *3*(1), 53–62.

Islam, M. S. (2014). Green banking in Bangladesh: How much implemented by the practitioners? *Abasyn University Journal of Social Sciences*, *7*(2), 189–210.

Islam, M. S., & Das, P. C. (2013). Green banking practices in Bangladesh. *IOSR Journal of Business and Management*, *8*(3), 39–44.

Masukujjaman, M. D., & Akhtar, S. (2013). Green banking in Bangladesh: A commitment towards the global initiatives. *Journal of Business and Technology (Dhaka)*, *8* (1–2), 17–40.

Meena, R. (2013). Green banking: As initiative for sustainable development. *Global Journal of Management and Business Studies*, *3*(10), 1181–1186.

Puška, A., Hodžić, I., Štilić, A., & Murtič, S. (2024). Evaluating European Union countries on climate change management: A fuzzy MABAC approach to the climate change performance index. *Journal of Green Economy and Low-Carbon Development*, *3*(1), 15–25.

Rahman, M. M., Ahsan, M. A., Hossain, M. M., & Hoq, M. (2013). Green banking prospects in Bangladesh. *Asian Business Review*, *2*(2), 59–63.

Rashid, M. H. U., & Uddin, M. M. (2018). Green financing for sustainability: Analysing the trends with challenges and prospects in the context of Bangladesh. *International Journal of Green Economics*, *12*(3–4), 192–208.

Reepu. (2020). Green investing. *Studies in Indian Place Names*, *40*(1), 15–26. ISSN: 2394-3114.

Sachs, J. D., Woo, W. T., Yoshino, N., & Taghizadeh-Hesary, F. (2019). Importance of green finance for achieving sustainable development goals and energy security. In J. D. Sachs, W. T. Woo, N. Yoshino, F. Taghizadeh-Hesary (Eds.), *Handbook of green finance* (pp. 3–12). Springer..

Sahoo, P., & Nayak, B. P. (2007). Green banking in India. *The Indian Economic Journal*, *55*(3), 82–98.

Shakil, M. H., Azam, M. K. G., & Raju, M. S. H. (2014). An evaluation of green banking practices in Bangladesh. *European Journal of Business and Management*, *6*(31), 8–16.

Ullah, M. M. (2013). Green banking in Bangladesh: A comparative analysis. *World Review of Business Research*, *3*(4), 74–83.

Ullah, M. A. (2020). Green banking in the way of sustainable development: An overview of practice and progress in Bangladesh. *Canadian Journal of Business and Information Studies*, *2*(5), 105–119.

Volz, U. (2016). *Fostering green finance for sustainable development in Asia* [ADBI Working Paper 814, Asian Development Bank Institute].

Yerpude, S., Sood, K., & Grima, S. (2022). Blockchain-Augmented digital supply chain management: A way to sustainable business. *Journal of Risk and Financial Management*, *16*(1), 7.

Zheng, G. W., Siddik, A. B., Masukujjaman, M., & Fatema, N. (2021). Factors affecting the sustainability performance of financial institutions in Bangladesh: The role of green finance. *Sustainability*, *13*(18), 1–27.

CHAPTER 15

PIXELS TO PLANET: A GLOBAL PERSPECTIVE ON SUSTAINABILITY ACROSS DIFFERENT INDUSTRIES

Prachi Gupta[a] and Shivangi Shukla Bhavsar[b]

[a]*Chitkara Business School, Chitkara University, Punjab, India*
[b]*Narayana Business School, Gujarat, India*

ABSTRACT

Purpose: *This study explores the growing significance of environmentalism and sustainability in the contemporary business landscape. Focussing on aligning industries with evolving consumer expectations, the research seeks to understand the awareness surrounding environmental conservation, sustainable development, and the adoption of an environmentally conscious lifestyle.*

Need for the study: *With environmental consciousness on the rise, understanding the initiatives taken by organisations and the utilisation of digital platforms for environmental advocacy becomes crucial. The study addresses the need to unwind the cultural shift towards sustainability and assess the effectiveness of green marketing practices in the digital age.*

Methodology: *A triangulation approach is employed, integrating secondary data from literature research with information from company reports and databases. The literature survey provides extensive insights into green marketing practices, forming the basis for an in-depth analysis. The comparative analysis and integration of findings from both sources aim to draw a comprehensive picture, identifying areas of agreement and disagreement.*

Sustainability Development through Green Economics
Contemporary Studies in Economic and Financial Analysis, Volume 114, 243–268

Published under exclusive licence by Emerald Publishing Limited
ISSN: 1569-3759/doi:10.1108/S1569-375920240000114015

Findings: *The study provides robust evidence supporting the effectiveness of green marketing practices in the digital age. Convergence between academic literature and real-world corporate practices underscores the consistency in approaches adopted by companies in leveraging digital technology to advance environmental sustainability.*

Practical implications: *The findings suggest that theory and practice converge on various aspects of green marketing, indicating its profound impact on culture, behaviours, and strategies. This research informs businesses and policymakers about the tangible benefits and shared responsibility of incorporating green practices in corporate strategies, fostering a sustainable future.*

Keywords: Environmental sustainability; green consumption; digital initiatives; green practices; marketing; triangulation method

JEL Codes: Q56; O3; M31; C12

INTRODUCTION

Over the last few years, the importance of environmental protection and sustainable development has become prominent. Consumers are now motivated to contribute to environmental protection by shifting their everyday consumption behaviour towards green consumption. This shift is crucial because excessive consumption has led to an increase in solid waste production.

Green or environmentally sustainable purchasing decisions offer an opportunity to reduce the negative environmental impact by adopting eco-friendly products. The terms 'green', eco-friendly', and 'environmentally friendly or sustainable' are often used interchangeably to describe these products.

In household consumption, groceries account for a significant share and up to one-third of the environmental impact is mainly due to packaging materials. This trend is catching on in India, where waste generation is occurring at an alarming rate, surpassing the natural degradation process and resource replacement rate. Indian consumers are more conscious of their environmental impact than consumers in Brazil, China, Australia, Russia, Canada, the USA, and Germany. EY's 2022 Sustainability Barometer found that 70% of Indian consumers consider sustainability when making purchases, compared to a much lower percentage in other countries (India EY, 2022). A study published in ScienceDirect.com also found that Indian millennials are relatively more aware of the environmental impacts of their consumption behaviour. However, despite this awareness, plastic usage remains high in India due to the need for government action to ban its production and distribution (Kanodia, 2022).

With 100% FDI allowed by Indian government through the automatic route, in the tourism and hospitality sector (IBEF, 2018), there has been significant rise in the number of international hotel brands in the country. All this has resulted in increased activities of construction, transportation, and waste generation, definitely throwing negative impact on the biodiversity. On tourism-related emissions front, just after United States, China, and Germany, India ranks fourth (Ghosh,

2018). Thereby, it becomes imperative for the hotel industry to take responsible steps towards environmental policy and implementation of sustainability practices (Sakshi et al., 2020).

The rapid digitalisation, along with advancements in technology and innovation capabilities of companies, has led to the frequent launch of new products and devices in the market. This fast-paced cycle entices customers to buy the latest models and dispose of their older ones, contributing to the growing issue of electronic waste (e-waste). The generation of e-waste is not limited to a single point but occurs throughout the value chain of manufacturing, which has detrimental effects on the environment (Shalender et al., 2023).

The concept of green theory emphasises the importance of corporate social responsibility (CSR) with a focus on sustainability and environmental practices (Suganthi, 2019). Organisations that prioritise CSR activities are more likely to adopt green practices within their operations. CSR activities enable firms to incorporate eco-friendly practices, fulfilling the social needs of stakeholders and integrating green innovation into business operations. Employees play an integral role in reducing firms' ecological footprint and there is increasing evidence that employees associate their psychological wellbeing with their activities, leading to environmental protection.

Overall, the shift towards green consumption and environmentally friendly practices is essential for mitigating the negative environmental impact of product consumption and disposal and, thus, promoting sustainable development.

PURPOSE OF RESEARCH

The accelerated pace of deterioration of the environment and the high competitiveness of market conditions have driven researchers and practitioners to focus on how green practices can be implemented to improve organisational performance. It is widely recognised that organisations contribute significantly to environmental degradation, especially with the excessive production of disposable products and the wastage of materials and energy. To address these issues, organisations can intervene and implement innovative business practices through their CSR initiatives to make the supply chain more sustainable.

By implementing various sustainable business practices, organisations can contribute to environmental preservation and benefit from cost-savings, increased employee commitment, and improved brand reputation. Businesses must integrate sustainability into their core operations and make it a way of life rather than just a conscious effort. Adopting green practices and implementing sustainable initiatives can help organisations mitigate their environmental impact and contribute to a more sustainable future.

Mele et al. (2020), in their study, suggest that the pandemic has created new challenges for businesses, such as the necessity of providing essential services, the requirement for bricolage service innovation, responsible shopping practices, and market shaping amid a crisis. The authors also suggest that the pandemic has brought to light the significance of responsible research, which refers to research pertinent to society and businesses' requirements. The authors contend that responsible research can assist organisations and society in responding to the challenges posed by the pandemic.

Objectives

1. To explore sustainable initiatives that organisations across the globe are implementing to encourage an environmentally conscious workplace.
2. To identify the digital initiatives and technologies companies use to promote environmental sustainability and how they vary across industries.
3. To understand the shift towards sustainable and eco-friendly workplace attire and its impact on organisational culture and employee behaviour.

Research Methodology

Data Collection Method

This study's data is collected via a systematic and exhaustive literature review. The literature review entails an exhaustive search for relevant research papers, academic journals, industry reports, and other credible sources about green marketing practices followed by businesses. The following steps are taken during the process of data collection:

(a) *Identification of databases*: Key academic databases are searched for peer-reviewed research papers and articles on green marketing and sustainability practices followed by organisations in various industries across the globe.
(b) *Search terms*: Relevant keywords and search terms are utilised to retrieve relevant literature. Various permutations and combinations of the terms 'green marketing', 'environmental advocacy', 'sustainable development', 'corporate sustainability', and 'eco-friendly materials' are used.
(c) *Inclusion and exclusion criteria*: Inclusion and exclusion criteria are applied to maintain the relevance and integrity of the data. Research papers and sources concentrating directly on companies' green marketing practices across industries are included. Articles that are not peer-reviewed, duplicates, and sources with insufficient data are excluded.
(d) *Screening and selection*: The identified sources are meticulously screened and relevant research papers are chosen based on their compatibility with the research objectives.

Sampling Methodology

Since this study is based on an extensive literature review, non-probability purposive sampling is used. This methodology permits the judicious selection of research papers and industry reports best suited for addressing the research hypotheses.

The examination of corporate initiatives in the context of green marketing practices involved using a purposive sampling strategy, in which a sample of close to 20 corporations was meticulously selected to ensure representation from various industries. This selection was intended to provide a comprehensive perspective of green marketing practices in various industries, such as technology, fashion, manufacturing, retail, hospitality, fast-moving consumer goods

(FMCG), and others. By focussing on a diverse sample, the research sought to uncover a vast array of environmental conservation initiatives and sustainability initiatives adopted by businesses across industries.

Data Analysis

Triangulation was employed during the data analysis process to increase the reliability of the findings. Triangulation entailed the cross-validation of data from multiple sources, including peer-reviewed research papers, industry reports, and case studies, to ensure a comprehensive and well-rounded examination of the selected corporations' and industries' green marketing practices. By way of Triangulation, the study intended to strengthen the credibility of the findings and reduce any potential biases or inaccuracies.

The combination of purposive sampling and Triangulation allowed for a robust and exhaustive analysis of corporations' green marketing initiatives, yielding valuable insights into adopting environmentally conscious practices across various industries. The findings will contribute to a greater comprehension of the current state of green marketing practices and pave the way for more effective and sustainable corporate strategies.

The literature review data collected in the study is subjected to a thematic analysis as outlined in Fig. 15.1. Specific codes and patterns under each theme are derived from the in-depth analysis of green marketing practices as extracted from the identified research papers and other secondary data on corporates' sustainability initiatives. Data from both qualitative sources are considered to develop a comprehensive topic analysis.

The themes and different codes under each theme as shown in Figs. 15.2 and 15. 3 illustrate the convergence of evidence from various perspectives and highlight the consistent trends across these areas. This enhances the validity and reliability of the overall conclusions and provides a comprehensive understanding of how these factors influence adopting eco-friendly practices in various domains.

Using this research methodology, the study aims to provide a comprehensive analysis of green marketing practices followed by companies, identifying points of parity and points of difference across industries and adding to the existing body of knowledge in the field of sustainability and corporate environmental responsibility.

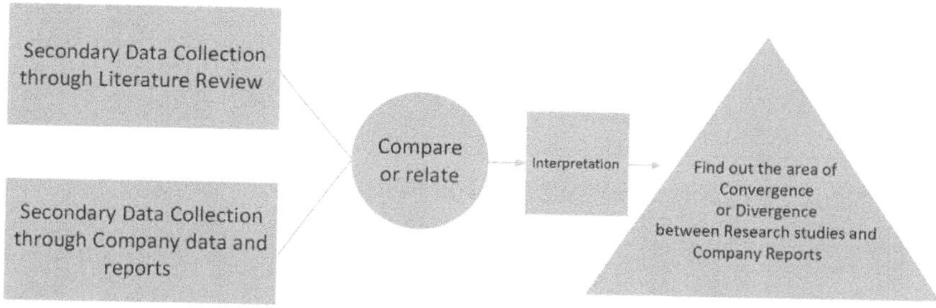

Fig. 15.1. Triangulation. *Source*: Created by authors.

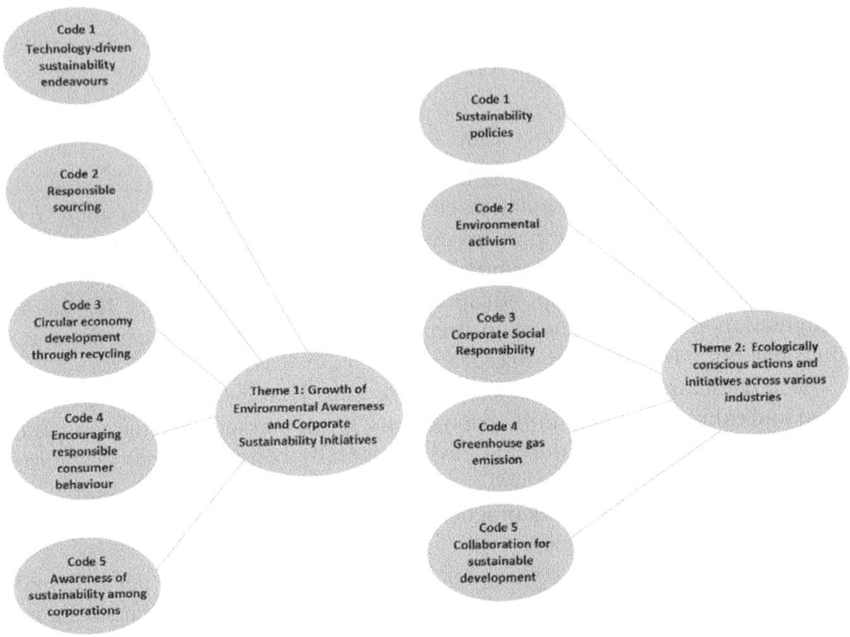

Fig. 15.2. Charting the Green Path: Environmental Awareness and Eco-conscious Actions. *Source*: Created by authors.

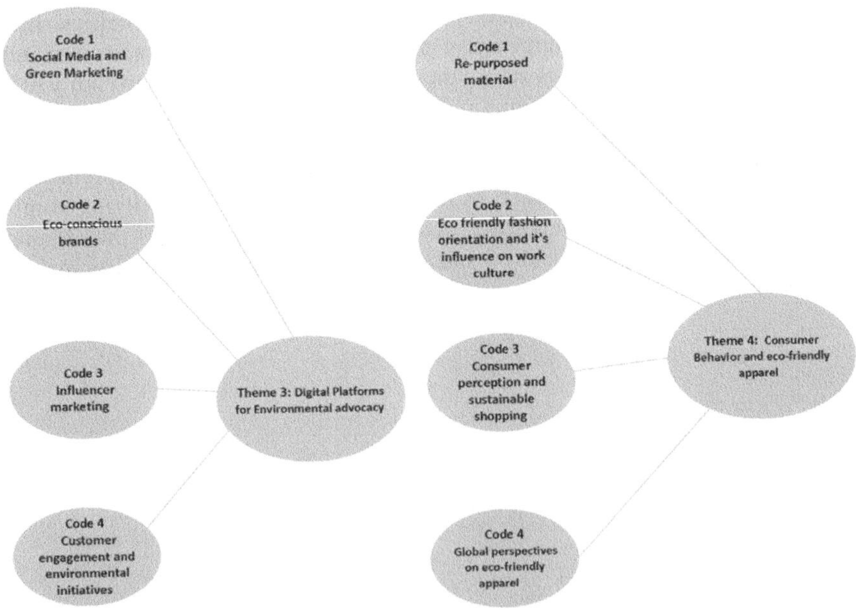

Fig. 15.3. Eco-engagement on Digital Platforms: Analysing Consumer Behaviour in Eco-friendly Apparel. *Source*: Created by authors.

HYPOTHESIS DEVELOPMENT

H1. Awareness of the importance of environment conservation and sustainable development is growing among consumers and corporations.

H2. Environmental conservation initiatives implemented or planned by organisations vary across industries.

H3. Companies, in the current age, are increasingly using digital platforms for extensive environmental advocacy and sustainability promotion.

H4. Clothing preferences in the workplace are shifting towards sustainable and eco-friendly materials, indicating the adoption of an environmentally conscious lifestyle.

ANALYSIS

H1: Awareness of the Importance of Environment Conservation and Sustainable Development is Growing Among Consumers and Corporations.

Today's customers are increasingly concerned about the environment and expect companies to be socially responsible. As a result, companies are adopting sustainable business practices, creating eco-friendly products, communicating environmental benefits, incorporating sustainability into company culture, and educating employees and customers (Verma et al., 2023).

Nestlé, a multinational food and beverage company, extensively disseminates its sustainability objectives and programmes with the help of digital technology. Its website discusses responsible sourcing, waste reduction, and community engagement. Additionally, Nestlé maintains active social media accounts on Facebook, Instagram, and Twitter to engage with consumers, educate them about sustainable practices, and promote environment-friendly products.

Nestle contributes to developing a circular economy through its endeavours to create enhanced packaging, more effective systems, and less packaging. This includes reducing the amount of freshly manufactured (or virgin) plastic they use, experimenting with reuse and refill systems, increasing the usage of paper packaging, and contributing towards adding efficiency in the collection, sorting, and recycling systems in every country where they conduct business.

In addition to this, by the year 2025, they aim to cut their consumption of virgin plastic by one-third (Sustainability at Nestle, 2023). In order to ensure that more food makes its way from the field to the table, they are working to educate customers, expand their operations, and collaborate with others in the industry.

IKEA (UK I, 2023), a multinational furniture retailer, utilises its digital platforms to communicate its sustainability efforts and encourage its customers to engage in environmentally friendly behaviours. On its website, IKEA details its environmentally responsible manufacturing practices, recycling programmes, and energy-efficient goods for customers to peruse. Because of its strong social media presence, the company can engage in conversation with customers, guide leading a more environmentally responsible lifestyle, and demonstrate a range of environment-friendly product options.

Unilever (Unilever PLC, 2023), a company that produces consumer goods, communicates its sustainability initiatives using personalised and targeted advertising. By collecting consumer data and analysing consumer preferences, Unilever tailors its marketing campaigns to specific demographics. The company emphasises sustainability-related messages that are meaningful to each population segment. Using a more individualised strategy, Unilever can better connect with consumers and raise their awareness of environmentally friendly products and practices.

Roberts and Bacon (1997) researched the complex relationships between environmental concerns and environmentally responsible consumer behaviour. This study indicates that people with higher levels of concern for the environment are more likely to engage in environmentally conscious behaviours. When this finding is applied to organisations, we find that those with a higher level of concern for the environment are more likely to implement or plan initiatives to conserve the environment.

Publication by Sheth et al. (2010) focusses on consumption with awareness, or mindful shopping, as a customer-focussed approach to environmental sustainability. This article proposes a customer-centric approach to sustainability and the importance of environmental concern in influencing consumer behaviour is emphasised to address both issues. It suggests that businesses should adjust their strategies so that they are in line with the priorities and values of consumers who are concerned about the environment.

H2: Environmental Conservation Initiatives Implemented or Planned by Organisations Vary Across Industries

Hotel Industry

Bohdanowicz (2006), in her paper, introduces the environmental impact of the hotel industry's high energy, water, and non-durable product consumption. The researcher acknowledges the need for adequate environmental protection and the growing awareness among travellers about environmental degradation. The study emphasises the need for environmentally responsible management and hotel staff to improve the situation. The paper outlines the two main paths to environmental sustainability in the hotel industry. The first involves responsible technical and behavioural practices in the sector. The second emphasises customers' need to demand 'green' practices.

The paper adds to the literature on hotel eco-initiatives and assesses how national sustainability policies and environmental awareness may affect individual establishments. The review discusses the hotel industry's energy-efficient lighting, water conservation, waste reduction, and renewable energy initiatives. The author used an email survey to examine how a country's geopolitical, economic, and sociocultural context affects hotel industry environmental attitudes and pro-ecological initiatives. The study concluded that hotel operators generally recognise environmental protection and are involved in several activities. The economy and government environmental initiatives affected hoteliers' attitudes and actions. The study suggested:

- Assessing hotel environmental initiatives.
- Examining how government policies and regulations affect hotel environmental sustainability.
- Exploring hotel-community-environmental organisation collaboration to promote sustainable tourism.
- Comparing hotel industry environmental initiatives across regions and countries.
- Exploring eco-labels and other certification schemes for hotel sustainability.

Göğüş et al. (2013) concentrate on using indicators to track innovation and sustainability in the hotel industry. This paper proposes an analytic hierarchy process (AHP)-based hierarchical decision-making model for measuring sustainable growth and innovation in the hotel industry. The model was created to obtain composite sustainable development criteria and assess individual indicators' influence on a company's sustainability. When contemplating innovation and sustainability in hotel management, the overall service quality of the hotel is the most crucial criterion. Hotel managers know the brand-building benefits of establishing a reputation for being environmentally focussed. Sustainability-driven management approaches of hotels claim to obtain a competitive advantage through sustainability, indicating that sustainability may alter the management practices of all successful businesses in the future.

Worldwide, it is being observed that hotel companies are now good environmental stewards committed to the wellbeing of their associates, communities, and guests. The hotel brands are supported by their investors, employees, and guests in their responsible environmental practices.

Many sizeable public hotel companies have committed to reducing greenhouse gas (GHG) emissions to meet the Paris Climate Agreement targets.

Retail Industry

IKEA, the multinational furniture retailer, has made significant strides in the direction of incorporating sustainability into its operations as well as its products. In the research that Gwo-Hshiung et al. (2011) conducted, IKEA is used as a case study to investigate the intention-behaviour discrepancy in green purchasing. The study highlights IKEA's commitment to environmental concern by highlighting its wide selection of sustainable and energy-efficient products, its recycling and waste reduction promotion, and its investment in renewable energy sources. IKEA is demonstrating through its actions both its commitment to environmental sustainability and its understanding of the significance of customer demand for environmentally friendly options.

(Patagonia Inc. USA (2023) retailers that sell clothing for outdoor recreation give high priority to environmental, social, and corporate governance as well as environmental activism. It has been a supporter of 1% for the Planet ever since it was founded in 1985. In 2022, it announced that all the company's profits would be donated to a charitable organisation to help finance efforts to combat climate change and other environmental issues.

E-commerce and Online Marketplaces

E-commerce has completely revolutionised the retail industry by allowing customers to shop online from the convenience of their homes. This has led to the proliferation of online marketplaces. Businesses can now promote and sell environmentally friendly products directly to end users by avoiding brick-and-mortar establishments' more traditional retail channels and instead utilising digital platforms (Saurabhadmin, 2023). This allows for a more streamlined and efficient process. Consumers get a good time to make decisions beneficial to the environment due to the proliferation of online marketplaces and platforms devoted to green initiatives, making it easier for shoppers to find and buy products that are kind to the environment.

Amazon, one of the largest e-commerce platforms in the world, offers a wide variety of environmentally friendly products in a section of its website that is specifically devoted to the topic and is called 'Amazon Sustainable Living' (Saurabhadmin, 2023). This marketplace highlights sustainable and environmentally friendly products from various brands, making it simpler for customers to locate and acquire such goods.

Etsy, an online marketplace specialising in handcrafted and vintage goods, provides a section labelled 'Eco-friendly', where vendors can list products that are kind to the environment (Brown-West, 2021). This platform allows customers to support independent retailers directly, prioritising sustainability and providing better environmental alternatives (Gebel, 2020).

Grove Collaborative Inc. (2023) is an online retailer that provides customers with environmentally friendly options for their personal care and household needs.

In addition to the eco-friendly home and beauty products that Grove Collaborative makes and sells on its own, the company also carries and sells products made by other companies in the industry. They encourage customers to make long-term sustainable choices by providing a model based on subscriptions and a curated selection of sustainable and non-toxic products. Customers can easily shop for environmentally friendly products using their online platform and have their purchases brought right to their door front.

EarthHero is another online marketplace that focusses on selling only those products that are sustainably and ethically sourced (Mancera, 2023). Its name indicates its business focus. They conduct in-depth research on the companies whose brands and products they sell to ensure they are environmentally responsible. EarthHero's mission is to make sustainable shopping more practical and approachable by operating as a one-stop shop offering various options that are kind to the environment.

Packaging waste has increased along with the growth of the e-commerce industry, adding to global warming and pollution. The Ellen MacArthur Foundation found that just 14% of all plastic packaging gets formally collected for recycling; the actual number is likely far lower (Saurabhadmin, 2023). This trash takes up valuable landfill space and emits toxic chemicals.

There is much room for improvement in the effort to decrease the amount of packaging waste caused by e-commerce. However, some companies are making strides towards adopting more sustainable packaging practices. This enhancement may involve making packing materials more recyclable, reusable, and recoverable. The growth of China's e-commerce sector and its possible effects on solid waste pollution is the focus of a study by Liang et al. (2022). Key factors to the adverse environmental effects of e-commerce are highlighted as excessive packaging, overproduction, and delivery of products. It is emphasised that considerable environmental costs are associated with the rapid growth of the express sector, pushed by the rise of China's online shopping industry. In response to this increase, environmental groups have recognised the importance of addressing plastic binding and lowering solid waste emissions. The logistics industry has identified packaging materials as a significant contributor to e-commerce trash. Vehicles, air freight, packaging, fuel manufacturing, and book manufacturing are only some e-commerce facets contributing to generating hazardous waste. The review also discusses the environmental effects of e-commerce, such as the amount of packaging needed for various shipping methods, especially for delicate or frozen products and the number of times those products are returned.

Compared to traditional brick-and-mortar stores, online shopping generates more packaging and transportation costs due to consumers' propensity to buy different things from numerous websites. The article (Kim et al., 2022) also highlights the relevance of sustainable practices by discussing the value of green technology and its part in the harmonious growth of the environment and economy. The research examines the connection between e-commerce and solid refuse emissions in China from a regional viewpoint. This research provides an essential context for understanding the evolution of eco-friendly e-commerce. It lays the framework for creating green legislation at the regional level to curb the industry's contribution to solid waste emissions.

Zhang (2023) examines the function of e-commerce in the digital marketplace and its positive effects on numerous industries. It also emphasises the impact of the COVID-19 pandemic on the expansion of e-commerce and the potential negative environmental impact. The paper proposes a comprehensive framework to comprehend the complex settings of the e-commerce environment. It seeks to fill a gap in the research on how e-commerce can achieve sustainability. Current research on sustainable e-commerce is found to be unevenly dispersed across multiple dimensions and there is an urgent need to employ government authority and raise public awareness. Delivery and logistics are the most researched topics in sustainable e-commerce, followed by policy, business, and consumers. The paper identifies a need for more support for a government perspective on effectively collaborating across sectors to achieve long-term sustainability objectives. This paper provides managerial implications for companies to pay greater attention to recurrent themes in sustainability transitions (ST) to meet shifting customer demands, ultimately impacting their capability and competitive advantage.

Tourism Industry

Seabra and Bhatt (2022) look at the research that has already been done on COVID-19 and the tourism industry's ability to survive and bounce back from future crises. It looks at possible problems and their solutions for the tourism industry to grow in a way that is sustainable after a pandemic.

The author helps bring attention to both the positive and negative impacts of COVID-19 on the travel industry. The paper gives tourism managers and destination planners a way to think about the pandemic as an opportunity and find sustainable ways to deal with the problems that will arise after the pandemic. The author says that to deal with the problems caused by the pandemic, the tourism industry must rethink, reset, and redefine itself more sustainably.

The author also talks about the steps the tourism industry needs to take towards adopting sustainable methods to ensure its survival for a long time, which can enable it to handle future crises, giving due consideration to the major stakeholders. The author also focusses on how important it is for stakeholders in the tourism industry to work together to reach sustainable development goals. The paper lays out a conceptual framework that will help tourism managers and destination planners see the pandemic as an opportunity and find sustainable ways to deal with the problems that will arise after the pandemic. The gap area of this research is that there needs to be more focus on both the supply and demand sides to find ways to get out of the crisis and make tourism businesses and destinations more resilient and long-lasting.

The development of the tourism industry and its adverse effects on the natural and social environments are discussed in the beginning. Prud'homme and Raymond (2013) emphasise sustainable development (SD) practices in the hospitality industry to mitigate these adverse effects and maximise the benefits to host populations. This paper explores the influence of sustainable development practices on consumer satisfaction and intent in the hospitality industry. Additionally, the paper discusses the difficulties hotel managers face when integrating SD practices into their business strategies and communicating their SD orientation to consumers. It emphasises the significance of consumer responsibility in daily life and how it influences hotel selection criteria, including those associated with sustainable development. Multiple factors, including government regulations, consumer demand, and competitive pressures, influence the adoption of sustainable development practices in the hospitality industry. As per the findings of the study, the consumers' selection criteria for hotels included 'charm', 'cosiness', 'SD-oriented hotel', and 'convenience'. Food, reduce-reuse-recycle (3R) practices, front desk and room, ecological concern, and access were identified as factors contributing to customer satisfaction.

Automobile Industry

Tesla, a manufacturer of electric vehicles, is widely recognised for its commitment to sustainable practices and environmental concerns. Weber and Hemmelskamp (2018) examine Tesla's business model related to the automotive industry and find that it represents a disruptive innovation. The research highlights Tesla's commitment to the environment by highlighting the company's electric vehicle production, which contributes to lower carbon emissions. Tesla's mission, accelerating the transition to sustainable transportation worldwide, reflects the company's commitment to preserving the environment.

Actions for sustainability by Tesla (Tesla report, 2022):

2021 was the year that Tesla first began measuring Scope 1 and Scope 2 greenhouse gas emissions in consideration of the GHG Protocol's guiding principles and recommendations.

In 2021, a thorough materiality analysis was conducted to determine which environmental, social, and governance (ESG) aspects were the most important for the company's varied stakeholders.

Since 2019, Tesla vehicles have been awarded a perfect score of five stars for safety from rating agencies in the USA, Europe, and Australia.

FMCG

Unilever is a global company specialising in consumer goods and has demonstrated a significant commitment to environmental sustainability. In the article that was written by Hammond and Prahalad (2009). Unilever's initiatives to implement sustainable and environmentally friendly practices are brought to the reader's attention. The authors discuss the company's commitment to reducing its environmental impact through sustainable sourcing, water and energy conservation, and waste reduction initiatives. Also discussed is the company's commitment to reducing the amount of waste it produces. Unilever Annual Report and Account (2022) is concerned about the environment because it has adopted a sustainable business model and incorporated environmental sustainability into its corporate strategy and day-to-day business operations as outlined in Fig. 15.4.

H3 Companies in the Current Age Are Increasingly Using Digital Platforms for Extensive Environmental Advocacy and Sustainability Promotion

The proliferation of digital technologies has been a significant factor in developing green marketing strategies, making it possible for businesses to interact with customers in novel and environmentally conscientious ways. The following are some high-quality content that illustrates the impact of digital technologies on environmentally conscious marketing:

Digital technologies enhancing communication channels, including social media platforms, websites, and mobile applications, have entirely transformed how businesses communicate with customers (Alkhatib et al., 2023). These channels offer an immediate and direct means of disseminating information regarding environmentally friendly products, sustainability initiatives, and CSR initiatives. By utilising these platforms, businesses could inform, inspire, and engage customers in conversations about green practices, thereby developing a customer base that is more knowledgeable and environmentally conscientious.

Patagonia, a well-known outdoor clothing and gear company, uses its website, social media platforms (such as Facebook, Instagram, and Twitter), and mobile applications to disseminate information concerning the environmental friendliness of its products, the transparency of its supply chain, and its ongoing environmental initiatives (Patagonia Activism, 2023).

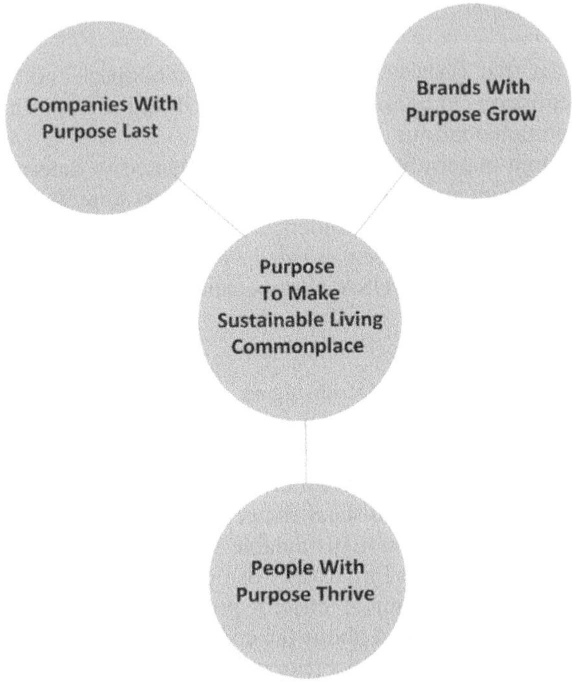

Fig. 15.4. The Unilever Compass. *Source*: Adapted from Unilever Annual Report and Accounts (2022).

Tesla, the world's leading electric vehicle manufacturer, extensively uses digital platforms to communicate its commitment to environmentally friendly initiatives and sustainable transportation solutions. Its website is a central hub for disseminating information about electric vehicles, renewable energy, and the company's mission to speed up the transition to sustainable energy worldwide (Merano, 2023). In addition, Tesla keeps active accounts on the social media platforms Facebook, Instagram, and Twitter to engage with its audience and provide updates on the company's sustainable innovations (Puška et al., 2024; Yerpude et al., 2022).

The Body Shop, a global cosmetics and skin care product brand, communicates its commitment to cruelty-free and environmentally friendly business practices using its website and social media channels (The body shop sustainability-commitments, 2023). The Body Shop provides extensive details on its website concerning its commitment to ethical sourcing, environmentally friendly packaging, and community-based economic development initiatives. Through its presence on social media platforms, the business maintains an ongoing conversation with its clientele, promoting environmentally friendly goods.

User-generated Content and Influencer Marketing

The rise of social media platforms has led to influencer marketing, where influential individuals with devoted followers promote sustainable products or lifestyles. Companies can reach a larger audience and leverage the credibility of eco-conscious influencers to endorse green initiatives when they collaborate with these individuals. In addition, user-generated content, such as reviews and testimonials, contributes to developing trust and social proof about environment-friendly products or practices, further enhancing their marketing impact.

The Body Shop, which is well known for its dedication to conducting business in an ethical and environmentally responsible manner, encourages its users to discuss their experiences with and thoughts on the company's wares (The body shop sustainability-commitments, 2023). Campaigns to boost user-generated content are run frequently by The Body Shop. These campaigns may include asking customers to submit photos of themselves using their favourite products or sharing their stories about how they incorporate sustainable practices into their everyday lives. This approach helps build a sense of community and trust, reinforcing their marketing efforts to be environmentally responsible.

Lush Retail Ltd., a British cosmetics company, significantly emphasises ethical and environmentally responsible business practices (Lusher World, 2023). They engage their customers in conversation on social media and encourage them to talk about their experiences with lush products, which are shared on the company's website and social media platforms, thus creating a sense of authenticity and trust around the brand. All this encourages others also to make decisions that are better for the environment.

Personalisation and targeted advertising are made possible by the proliferation of digital technologies, which allow businesses to collect vast amounts of information regarding customers' preferences, behaviours, and interests. Because of the information available, businesses can now segment their audiences and target specific groups with environmentally conscious marketing messages, just like the Coca-Cola Company does (The Coca-Cola Company, 2022). The ability of businesses to effectively communicate the environmental benefits of their products or services, which in turn increases the likelihood of consumer engagement and adoption of sustainable practices, is made possible by personalising their communication.

Amazon, a multinational e-commerce company, promotes environmentally friendly products by utilising its vast customer data and personalised recommendation algorithms (Pregi Sustainability, 2020). Amazon caters its product recommendations and advertising to specific target groups interested in environmentally friendly alternatives by analysing the behaviour and preferences of its customers. Using a more individualised approach, consumers are more likely to engage with environmentally friendly products and make purchases.

Coca-Cola, the world's largest beverage company, highlights the environmental benefits of its packaging and recycling efforts by customising its marketing messages to different consumer groups, using data analysis and segmentation (Coca-Cola Company, 2023). Coca-Cola aims to increase consumer engagement and encourage sustainable behaviours by providing customised messages about the company's environmental commitment. Indian millennials exhibit a preference for the environmental dimension over societal and economic considerations (Francis & Sarangi, 2022).

To promote its social and environmental mission, TOMS, a company that sells shoes and eyewear, targets customer subgroups with highly tailored emails, website content, and social media marketing campaigns to convey its commitment to environmental responsibility and demonstrate the eco-friendliness of its product offerings (TOMS, 2022). TOMS aims to increase consumer engagement and promote sustainable consumption by tailoring its messaging to align with individual interests to promote sustainable consumption.

Digital technologies provide the opportunity for experiences that are both interactive and immersive, which engage customers in a meaningful manner. It is possible to use interactive web content, virtual reality (VR), augmented reality (AR), and other similar technologies to demonstrate environmentally responsible production processes, benefits to the environment, or the impact of environmentally conscious choices as IKEA does (IKEA Global, 2017). Companies could foster a deeper connection between their customers and their environmentally conscious initiatives by providing engaging and educational experiences for their customers.

The global furniture retailer IKEA has become an early adopter of AR technology to provide customers with an improved shopping experience (IKEA Global, 2017). Customers can virtually arrange IKEA furniture in their homes using the IKEA Place mobile app, which utilises AR. This interactive experience lets customers visualise how IKEA products look and work in their space, empowering them to make more environmentally conscious decisions regarding their homes' furniture and interior design.

Patagonia, whose marketing efforts were discussed earlier, has also used interactive and immersive experiences in its campaigns. They have developed VR experiences that allow users to explore and get a first-hand feel for the natural environments they are working so hard to preserve (Patagonia Activism, 2023). Patagonia's goal in creating these all-encompassing experiences is to bring customers face-to-face with the wonder and importance of the natural world to motivate them to support causes that protect the environment.

Providing helpful direction for future research endeavours (Parida et al., 2019), introduce a complete framework that links digitisation, business model innovation, and sustainability in industrial contexts. Specifically, it highlights the role of digital technologies in encouraging business model innovation in B2B contexts and opening new revenue and value creation opportunities. The most important takeaway from this study is that digitalisation is causing a change in industrial value chains, necessitating new approaches to business to reap the benefits of different technologies fully. It highlights knowledge gaps in value creation, delivery, capture within business model innovation and their alignment to support initiatives for a sustainable industry.

In their study, Reilly and Hynan (2014) investigate 16 multinational corporations across four consumer product sectors to examine the relationship between corporate communication, sustainability, and social media. Based on external evaluations, these businesses are classified as 'Green' or 'Not Green'. The study further argues that effective corporate communication can illuminate an organisation's culture and principles. According to the findings, green businesses are more likely to include sustainability-related information in their formal corporate communication. The social media engagement of green companies far outstrips that of Not Green enterprises across all platforms evaluated. This information lends credence to the study's central thesis and shows that green businesses are the most active on social media.

H4 Workplace Clothing Preferences are Shifting towards Sustainable and Eco-Friendly Materials, Indicating the Adoption of an Environmentally Conscious Lifestyle

Sustainable fashion and accessories brand Lifestyle Over Luxury (L/L Supply) has adopted a 'circular economy' ethos that rests on the philosophy, 'the most sustainable product is one that already exists'. To accomplish this, they use upcycled resources in their manufacturing process. These materials include scraps from factories, fabrics from the end of the roll, and even plastic water bottles. Not only do they seal their boxes using biodegradable tape, but they also use biodegradable packaging whenever possible. In contrast to luxury brands that focus on producing luxury products, sustainable luxury affects whole supply chains. It incorporates the exploitation of natural resources, social and environmental issues, and the wellbeing of future generations (Sage Hill Bottle Depot, 2021). L/L Supply's approach to sustainability and the circular economy is a step in the right direction towards sustainable luxury (Kunz et al., 2020).

The sustainable shoe brand Allbirds is notable for its dedication to eco-friendly manufacturing and packaging practices. The fact that they sell out of the same box they ship in sets them apart. This deluxe packaging features 90% post-consumer recycled content and is constructed from FSC-certified paper that was ethically acquired from managed forests. Allbirds is committed to sustainability and uses various sustainable materials in its products, including sugarcane, sweet foam, tree fibre, recycled bottles, and castor bean oil. Allbirds (2021) has set a goal to source 75% of its materials sustainably by December 2025 and reduce its raw materials' carbon footprint by 25%.

GLOBAL PERSPECTIVE BY FOCUSSING ON DIFFERENT REGIONS

USA

Jin Gam (2011) says people's views on fashion and shopping affect the intention to buy eco-friendly clothing. Fashion adoption theory, which focusses on fashion ability and how it meets social and psychological needs, can be used to determine why people choose to buy eco-friendly clothes. The study found that young women in the Midwest of the USA who were interested in fashion and shopping and caring about the environment were more likely to buy clothing that was good for the environment. The clothing industry can get more young people to buy eco-friendly clothes by making shopping fun. The study gives information on how to build marketing plans that will induce more people to buy eco-friendly products and gain important information about those people. Overall, the paper shows a link between fashion, shopping, and caring about the environment in how people choose to live their lives. The results can help marketers and clothing companies develop successful, sustainable clothing that would drive people's preferences towards its purchase. More in-depth research is required to determine how fashion, shopping, and caring about the environment affect people's decisions to buy eco-friendly clothes in different places and segments.

Europe

Vita et al. (2019) in their study on 'The Environmental Impact of Green Consumption and Sufficiency Lifestyles Scenarios in Europe: Connecting Local Sustainability Visions to Global Consequences' present a new way to use backcasting to figure out how sustainable lifestyle choices affect the environment. This paper's objective is to evaluate various scenarios that reflect the lifestyles different stakeholders want. It describes sufficiency and green consumption alternatives based on the assumption that sustainable lifestyles are widely adopted, and it talks about how different scenarios affect environmental footprints and quality of life. Even though the paper does not talk about changes in culture that can be seen in how people choose to dress or what brands they buy at work, it does talk about the possible environmental effects of lifestyle changes in different areas of consumption, such as clothing and appliances. The authors say that sharing clothes and devices and making them last longer could reduce our carbon footprint by about 3%. Overall, the paper gives a clear and complete picture of the range of sustainable lifestyles and the essential options. However, more research is needed to make the scenarios closer to reality and to test them at more minor geographic scales by making them better fit the local context.

Mid-western USA

Jin Gam (2011) in the study, 'Are fashion-conscious consumers more likely to buy eco-friendly clothing?', looks at the factors that make young female consumers between the ages of 18 and 25 in the Mid-Western USA buy environment-friendly clothing (EFC). The study helps clothing companies understand the many factors that affect EFC purchases and enable them to market eco-friendly products successfully.

Sproles and Burns (1994) stated in their study that the main reasons people follow trends are related to their social and psychological needs, such as adapting to a changing society, avoiding boredom, and meeting the demands of their social groups. Literature suggests that people who like fashion and shopping are likely to look for new information about clothing goods, which can influence their desire to buy eco-apparel. Literature also shows that caring about the environment and acting in ways that are good for the environment are essential factors in the decision to buy EFC.

The paper highlights four fashion orientation factors that may affect a consumer's decision to buy EFC: fashion leadership, fashion interest, the importance of being well-dressed, and an anti-fashion attitude. The author also discusses shopping enjoyment and cost awareness as two shopping orientation factors that may affect consumers' decision to buy EFC. The clothing industry should focus on making stores fun for young, EFC customers to shop there. The results of this study mainly apply to young women in the mid-west of the USA.

Mukherjee (2015), in the study 'Environmental and Social Impact of Fashion: Towards an Eco-friendly, Ethical Fashion', highlighted the effects of the fashion business on society and the environment. The paper talks about the harmful effects of fast fashion, which focusses on new styles at low prices, resulting in increased trash and polluting the environment. The paper also talks about sustainable or ethical fashion to fix the damage that traditional production methods do to the earth and society. The author has used the term 'Reuse and Remanufacture' to protect the environment. The paper also lists different fabrics that are good for the earth, which include organic cotton, silk, wool, jute, soy silk, milk-silk, pineapple fabrics, hemp, peat, corn fibre, bamboo, and recycled fabrics made from recycled fibre. The author also talks about packaging, which adds to waste in the clothing business. Overall, the paper gives valuable information about how the fashion industry affects the earth and society and ways to make the fashion industry more sustainable and moral.

FINDINGS AND INTERPRETATION

Findings and Interpretation for H1:

The findings emphasise the importance of environmental preservation and sustainable development to consumers and businesses. Nestlé, IKEA, and Unilever use digital technologies and platforms to communicate their sustainability goals and promote environmentally responsible practices and products.

Nestlé, in its strong commitment to Sustainable Packaging, directs its efforts towards creating a circular economy by emphasising the development of more effective packaging, efficient systems, and overall, less packaging. By intending to reduce its Consumption of virgin plastic by one-third by 2025, Nestlé demonstrates its commitment to sustainable packaging that addresses environmental and food waste concerns (Sustainability at Nestle, 2023).

IKEA uses its digital platforms effectively to disseminate its sustainability initiatives to consumers, promote environmentally responsible behaviours, engage in conversations with customers, provide advice on living a more sustainable lifestyle, and promote environmentally responsible product options (IKEA Global, 2023).

Through personalised and targeted advertising, Unilever informs the public about its sustainability initiatives. This enables the company to emphasise sustainability-related messages pertinent to each demographic, effectively increasing consumer awareness of environmentally responsible products and practices (Unilever PLC, 2023).

The findings from the data captured on different corporations indicate a growing trend of companies recognising the significance of environmental preservation and sustainable development. Nestlé, IKEA, and Unilever use digital technologies and platforms to engage consumers, educate them about sustainability, and promote eco-friendly products and practices. By employing a more individualised marketing strategy, these companies can effectively convey their sustainability initiatives and encourage consumers to make environmentally responsible decisions. Significant corporations' increased emphasis on sustainability indicates a shift in consumer demands and expectations. Environmentally responsible businesses demonstrating a commitment to sustainable practices are gaining increased brand value. Nestlé, IKEA, and Unilever contribute to a more sustainable future by aligning their business practices with evolving consumer preferences through digital initiatives (Dutta, 2022).

The findings from the research paper also bring across the relation between environmental concerns and environmentally conscious behaviour in the case of both individuals and organisations. Therefore, an environment-focus strategy to be adopted by businesses is proposed so that their existence is in line with the priorities and values of consumers who are concerned about the environment.

Findings and Interpretation for H2

The authors examine environmental conservation initiatives in various industries and their efforts towards sustainability. Due to the high consumption of energy, water, and non-durable products, the hotel industry confronts significant environmental challenges. Studies emphasise the need for ethical technical and behavioural practices within the industry and the significance of 'green' practices demanded by consumers. In addition to hotels implementing initiatives such as energy-efficient lighting, water conservation, and waste reduction, there is a demand for hotels, communities, and environmental organisations to work together to promote sustainable tourism. To develop effective eco-initiatives, it is essential to comprehend the effect of national sustainability policies and environmental consciousness on specific organisations.

IKEA and Patagonia are examples of retailers committed to sustainability in the retail sector. Patagonia, an apparel retailer for outdoor recreation, is distinguished by its environmental, social, and corporate governance focus, including its pledge to donate all profits to environmental causes. The rise of e-commerce platforms enables businesses to market and sell eco-friendly products directly to consumers, making environmentally conscious options more accessible.

Although COVID-19 has impacted the tourism industry, it also presents an opportunity to develop more sustainably. For the tourism industry's long-term viability and crisis-resilience, it is essential to emphasise sustainable practices. Cooperation among stakeholders and a concentration on both the supply and demand sides are necessary for identifying sustainable solutions and achieving development goals.

Tesla's electric vehicles are a disruptive innovation in the automotive industry, contributing to reducing carbon emissions and promoting sustainable transportation. Tesla's efforts to measure greenhouse gas emissions and execute materiality analysis demonstrate the company's commitment to sustainability. Their commitment to safety is also compatible with environmental concerns since secure transportation reduces accidents and their associated environmental impacts.

The findings demonstrate that industries across all sectors recognise the significance of environmental protection and sustainable development. Businesses such as Nestlé, IKEA, Patagonia, and Tesla are proactively instituting eco-initiatives, promoting sustainable products, and reducing environmental impacts.

The emphasis on consumer demand for 'green' practices and sustainable products emphasises the significance of consumers' influence on the environmental policies of industries.

Additionally, the tourism and e-commerce industries play vital roles in promoting sustainability. Long-term success in the tourism industry will depend on its capacity to adapt and recover from crises while embracing sustainable practices. E-commerce platforms such as Amazon, Etsy, Grove Collaborative, and EarthHero facilitate consumers' access to environmentally responsible products and encourage them to make more sustainable decisions.

Across all industries, the findings indicate a growing commitment to environmental conservation initiatives. Though in two industries, hotel and e-commerce, findings from research studies and cases on corporate initiatives are only partially aligned. Corporates highlight their commitment and showcase their comprehensive initiatives, but research studies indicate the maximum challenges in implementation faced by the hotel industry. Also, relating to the e-commerce sector, companies are contributing to sustainability in various measures. However, research brings forth the detrimental impact on the environment posed by the immense growth of the e-commerce industry.

However, continuous research, collaboration, and implementation of eco-friendly practices are required to achieve long-term sustainability and reduce environmental impacts.

Findings and Interpretation for H3

The information presented supports the claim that companies in the modern era use digital platforms extensively for environmental advocacy and sustainability promotion. Several significant conclusions can be drawn from the provided data.

The proliferation of digital technologies, such as social media platforms, websites, and mobile applications, has altered how businesses communicate with consumers. Companies can now distribute information directly regarding eco-friendly products, sustainability initiatives, and CSR initiatives (Alam & Islam, 2021). These channels enable businesses to educate, inspire, and engage consumers in environmentally conscious dialogues, resulting in a customer base that is better informed and more environmentally conscious.

'Companies Embracing Environmental Advocacy Prominent businesses' such as Patagonia, Tesla, The Body Shop, and Coca-Cola are utilising digital platforms for environmental advocacy efficiently. They discuss their commitment to sustainability, eco-friendly products, ethical purchasing, and community development initiatives. They engage consumers in ongoing dialogues through their websites and active social media presence, promoting adopting environmentally responsible products and practices.

The rise of social media has facilitated influencer marketing, where influential individuals leverage their credibility to promote sustainable products or lifestyles to a larger audience. Through campaigns and interactions, companies like The Body Shop and Lush Retail Ltd. actively promote user-generated content, thereby augmenting the veracity and credibility of their environmentally responsible practices.

Digital technologies enable businesses to accumulate vast customer data, resulting in personalised marketing messages directed at specific audience segments interested in environmentally responsible products. Amazon, Coca-Cola, and TOMS use personalisation to promote eco-friendly options and sustainable behaviour.

Businesses utilise interactive web content, VR, and AR to engage customers in immersive experiences highlighting environmentally responsible production processes, environmental benefits, and the repercussions of sustainable decisions. Such technologies have been adopted by companies such as IKEA, National Geographic, The North Face, and Patagonia to inspire consumer support for conservation and sustainability.

The findings demonstrate that companies progressively utilise digital platforms for environmental advocacy and sustainability promotion. Utilising social media, websites, mobile applications, influencer marketing, and user-generated content enables businesses to interact with their audience meaningfully, nurturing authenticity and trust. In addition, personalisation enables targeted marketing messages to be sent to specific consumer segments, which increases the likelihood of engagement and adoption of sustainable practices. In addition, adopting interactive and immersive technologies demonstrates a commitment to sustainability, enabling businesses to communicate with customers on a deeper level and motivate them to support environmental causes.

Overall, the findings support the notion that digital technologies play a crucial role in the environmental advocacy efforts of contemporary businesses, facilitating communication, education, and engagement with consumers regarding eco-friendly products and sustainable practices. As companies adopt these technologies, it is anticipated that environmental consciousness will further permeate mainstream consumer behaviour, positively impacting global sustainability efforts.

Findings and interpretation for H4

Eco-friendly and sustainable materials are becoming increasingly popular in the workplace. Utilising repurposed materials, eco-friendly fabrics, and biodegradable packaging, businesses such as Lifestyle Over Luxury (L/L Supply) are growing. This indicates a developing trend of environmentally conscious workplace culture.

The findings from the literature review shed light on the cultural transition observable in today's workplace in terms of clothing and brand preferences, indicating the adoption of an environment-conscious lifestyle. By triangulating information from different sources, it is possible to understand whether the research hypothesis is supported.

The literature review includes studies conducted in various regions, including the USA, Europe, and the Midwest of the USA, providing a global perspective on the subject.

In the USA Jin Gam's (2011) study concentrates on fashion- and eco-conscious young women in the Midwest. According to this study, individuals interested in fashion and purchasing and caring about the environment are likelier to purchase eco-friendly clothing. Findings suggest that the fashion industry can promote the adoption of eco-friendly clothing by making purchasing enjoyable for younger consumers.

In Europe, Vita et al. (2019) present a study on the environmental effects of sustainable lifestyle choices. Although the study does not specifically address changes in workplace attire preferences, it examines the potential environmental effects of lifestyle changes in various areas, including apparel consumption. The findings emphasise the significance of sharing clothing and devices and extending their lifespans to reduce environmental footprints. The evaluation of these scenarios at lower geographic scales requires additional research.

Another study by de Corrêa et al. (2022) investigate the impact of sustainable products on organisations. The study emphasises organisations' responsibility to adopt sustainable practices and satisfy the growing demand for eco-friendly products. Although the study does not explicitly address workplace attire preferences, it contributes to understanding sustainable practices in various industries.

Based on the findings, there is some support for the hypothesis (*H4*) that workplace clothing preferences are shifting towards eco-friendly and sustainable materials, signifying adopting an environmentally conscious lifestyle. The studies conducted in the USA and Europe demonstrate a correlation between fashion, purchasing, and environmental awareness in the lifestyle decisions of individuals.

However, it is essential to note that the research findings are limited to regions and demographic groups. The studies predominantly concern consumer behaviour and lifestyle preferences instead of workplace-specific attire preferences. Therefore, additional research is required to investigate workplace-specific apparel preferences and brand selections to understand better the cultural shift towards eco-friendly attire in the workplace.

CONCLUSION

The study emphasises the importance of environmental preservation and sustainable development for consumers and businesses. Big corporations across different sectors recognise the significance of environmental protection and sustainable development. They use digital technologies and platforms to communicate their sustainability goals and promote environmentally responsible practices and products. The study brings across firmly the notion that digital technologies play a crucial role in the environmental advocacy efforts of contemporary businesses. Adopting interactive and immersive technologies has enabled businesses to educate, communicate, and engage with customers on a deeper level and motivate them to support environmental causes. Major global corporations' increased emphasis on sustainability indicates a shift in consumer demands and expectations. Environmentally responsible businesses demonstrating a commitment to sustainable practices are gaining increased brand value. These businesses contribute to a more sustainable future by aligning their business practices with evolving consumer preferences through digital initiatives. As companies go for comprehensive integration of technology across different functions and strategic areas, environmental consciousness will further permeate mainstream consumer behaviour, resulting in a positive impact on sustainability efforts in a holistic way.

REFERENCES

Alam, S. M., & Islam, K. M. (2021). Examining the role of environmental corporate social responsibility in building green corporate image and green competitive advantage. *International Journal of Corporate Social Responsibility*, *6*(1), 1–16. https://doi.org/10.1186/s40991-021-00062-w

Alkhatib, S., Kecskés, P., & Keller, V. (2023). Green marketing in the digital age: A systematic literature review. *Sustainability*, *15*(16), 12369, 1–16. https://doi.org/10.3390/su151612369

Allbirds. (2021). *2020 Sustainability report*. Retrieved April 29, 2023, from https://cdn.allbirds.com/image/upload/v1625161698/marketing-pages/Allbirds_Sustainability_Report_2020.pdf

Bohdanowicz, P. (2006). Environmental awareness and initiatives in the Swedish and Polish hotel industries—Survey results. *International Journal of Hospitality Management*, *25*(4), 662–682. https://doi.org/10.1016/j.ijhm.2005.06.006

Brown-West, B. (2021, December 20). Why the e-commerce supply chain has a big environmental footprint and how companies can reduce it. *Environmental Défense Fund*. Retrieved April 24, 2023, from https://business.edf.org/insights/why-the-e-commerce-supply-chain-has-a-big-environmental-footprint-and-how-companies-can-reduce-it/

Coca-Cola Company. (2023). *Sustainability*. Retrieved May 21, 2023, from https://www.coca-colacompany.com/sustainability

de Corrêa, R., de Oliveira, U. R., Abdalla, M. M., & Fernandes, V. A. (2022). Systematic literature review on sustainable products: Impact on organizations, research opportunities and future perspectives. *Cleaner Waste Systems*, *1*(Special issue), 100003, 1–13. https://doi.org/10.1016/j.clwas.2022.100003

Dutta, A. (2022, October 7). How ITC, Hindustan Unilever, Nestle, Kellogg and Dabur are using digital tech to serve you better. *Business Today*. Retrieved February 15, 2023, from https://www.businesstoday.in/magazine/features/story/how-hindustan-unilever-nestle-kellogg-and-dabur-are-using-digital-tech-to-serve-you-better-349116-2022-10-06

Francis, A., & Sarangi, G. K. (2022). Sustainable consumer behaviour of Indian millennials: Some evidence. *Current Research in Environmental Sustainability*, *4*(Special issue), 1–10. https://doi.org/10.1016/j.crsust.2021.100109

Gebel, M. (2020, December 19). What is Etsy? Everything you need to know before buying or selling on the handmade and vintage e-commerce platform for independent creators. *Business Insider*. Retrieved March 18, 2023, from https://www.businessinsider.com/guides/tech/what-is-etsy?IR=T

Ghosh, S. (2018). *Indian travellers' carbon footprint is fourth-largest in the world: Study*. Retrieved November 23, 2023, from https://india.mongabay.com/2018/05/18/ indian-travellers-carbon-footprint-is-fourth-largest-in-the-world study/

Göğüş, G., Karakadılar, İ. S., & Apak, S. (2013). Innovation and sustainable growth measurement in hotel industry: A hierarchical decision making model. *Procedia – Social and Behavioral Sciences*, *99*(Special issue), 752–761. https://doi.org/10.1016/j.sbspro.2013.10.547

Grove Collaborative Inc. (2023). *Sustainability is the only future*. Grove Collaborative. Retrieved May 15, 2023, from https://www.grove.co/g/sustainability/

Hammond, A. L., & Prahalad, C. K. (2009, October 27). *Selling to the poor*. Foreign Policy. Retrieved January 24, 2023, from https://foreignpolicy.com/2009/10/27/selling-to-the-poor/

IBEF (2018). *Indian tourism and hospitality industry analysis*. Retrieved September 24, 2023, from https://www.ibef.org/industry/indian-tourism-and-hospitality-indus try-analysis-presentation

IKEA Global. (2017, September 12). *Launch of new IKEA Place App – IKEA Global*. Retrieved March 20, 2023, from https://www.ikea.com/global/en/newsroom/innovation/ikea-launches-ikea-place-a-new-app-that-allows-people-to-virtually-place-furniture-in-their-home-170912/

IKEA Global. (2023). *IKEA global*. IKEA. Retrieved on May 25, 2023, from https://www.ikea.com/

India EY. (2022, May 11). *77% of Indian consumers expect positive changes in the financial situation, higher than the global outlook: EY report*. EY US – Home. Retrieved March 4, 2023, from https://www.ey.com/en_in/news/2022/05/seventy-seven-percent-of-indian-consumers-expect-positive-changes-in-the-financial-situation-higher-than-the-global-outlook

Jin Gam, H. (2011). Are fashion-conscious consumers more likely to adopt eco-friendly clothing? *Journal of Fashion Marketing and Management: An International Journal*, *15*(2), 178–193. Retrieved February 20, 2023, from https://doi.org/10.1108/13612021111132627

Kanodia, H. (2022, October 24). *Why Indians with means still use plastic, even when aware of its environmental impacts* [Commentary]. Mongabay. https://india.mongabay.com/2022/10/commentary-why-indians-with-means-still-use-plastic-even-when-aware-of-its-environmental-impacts/

Kim, Y., Kang, J., & Chun, H. (2022). Is online shopping packaging waste a threat to the environment? *Economics Letters, 214*(Special issue), 1–3. https://doi.org/10.1016/j.econlet.2022.110398

Kunz, J., May, S., & Schmidt, H. J. (2020). Sustainable luxury: Current status and perspectives for future research. *Business Research, 13*(2), 541–601. https://doi.org/10.1007/s40685-020-00111-3

Liang, Z., Luo, Z., Yuan, J., Li, M., Xia, Y., Che, T., Huang, L., & Liu, J. (2022). Evaluating the environmental and economic performance of municipal solid waste disposal by all – Component resource recovery. *Sustainability, 14*(24), 1–15. https://doi.org/10.3390/su142416898

Lusher world, L. (2023, November 15). *Our impact*. We are Lush. Retrieved on January 20, 2023, from https://weare.lush.com/lush-life/our-impact-reports/?_gl=1%2A1i6ds67%2A_ga%2AMTY1MjA2NjUxLjE3MDU4NjA2MDY.%2A_ga_MVBMWFB13V%2AMTcwNTg2MDYwNi4xLjEuMTcwNTg2MDYyNi4wLjAuMA

Mancera, O. (2023, January 18). *Earthhero 2022: Impact for the year!*. EarthHero. Retrieved June 12, 2023, from https://earthhero.com/blogs/blog/earthhero-2022-impact-for-the-year

Mele, C., Russo-Spena, T., & Kaartemo, V. (2020). The impact of coronavirus on Business: Developing service research agenda for a post-coronavirus world. *Journal of Service Theory and Practice, 31*(2), 184–202. https://doi.org/10.1108/jstp-07-2020-0180

Merano, M. (2023, April 6). *Tesla teases 3 next-gen vehicles, each in different segments.* TESLARATI. Retrieved September 23, 2023, from https://www.teslarati.com/tesla-master-plan-part-3-next-bus-commercial-van/

Mukherjee, S. (2015). Environmental and social impact of fashion: Towards an eco-friendly, ethical fashion. *International Journal of Interdisciplinary and Multidisciplinary Studies (IJIMS), 2*(3), 22–35. https://doi.org/10.54121/2021

Parida, V., Sjödin, D., & Reim, W. (2019). Reviewing literature on digitalization, business model innovation, and sustainable industry: Past achievements and future promises. *Sustainability (Switzerland), 11*(2), 1–18. https://doi.org/10.3390/su11020391

Patagonia Activism. (2023). *Patagonia outdoor clothing & gear*. Retrieved April 19, 2023, from https://www.patagonia.com/home/

Patagonia Inc. USA. (2023). *Environmental activism – Patagonia*. Patagonia Outdoor Clothing & Gear. Retrieved February 20, 2023, from https://www.patagonia.com/activism/

Pregi Sustainability. (2020). *7 brands that are using sustainable packaging to boost social sharing – and social good.* Pregis. Retrieved on April 22, 2023, from https://www.pregis.com/knowledge-hub/7-brands-that-are-using-sustainable-packaging-to-boost-social-sharing–and-social-good/

Prud'homme, B., & Raymond, L. (2013). Sustainable development practices in the hospitality industry: An empirical study of their impact on customer satisfaction and intentions. *International Journal of Hospitality Management, 34*(Special issue), 116–126. https://doi.org/10.1016/j.ijhm.2013.03.003

Puška, A., Hodžić, I., Štilić, A., & Murtič, S. (2024). Evaluating European Union countries on climate change management: A fuzzy MABAC approach to the climate change performance index. *Journal of Green Economy and Low-Carbon Development, 3*(1), 15–25.

Reilly, A. H., & Hynan, K. A. (2014). Corporate communication, sustainability, and social media: It's not easy (really) being green. *Business Horizons, 57*(6), 747–758. https://doi.org/10.1016/j.bushor.2014.07.008

Roberts, J. A., & Bacon, D. R. (1997). Exploring the subtle relationships between environmental concern and ecologically conscious consumer behavior. *Journal of Business Research, 40*(1), 79–89. https://doi.org/10.1016/s0148-2963(96)00280-9

Sage Hill Bottle Depot. (2021, August 10). *5 brands with compostable packaging*. Sage Hill Bottle Depot. Retrieved March 28, 2023, from https://sagehillbottledepot.ca/5-brands-with-compostable-packaging/

Sakshi, S., Cerchione, R., & Bansal, H. (2020). Measuring the impact of sustainability policy and practices in tourism and hospitality industry. *Business Strategy and the Environment, 29*(3), 1109–1126.

Saurabhadmin, E. (2023, October 4). *The environmental impact of e-commerce*. Retrieved January 18, 2023, from https://earth5r.org/convenience-comes-at-a-cost-the-environmental-impact-of-ecommerce-packaging/

Seabra, C., & Bhatt, K. (2022). Tourism Sustainability and COVID-19 pandemic: Is there a positive side? *Sustainability*, *14*(14), 8723, 1–14. https://doi.org/10.3390/su14148723

Shalender, K., Singla, B., & Sharma, S. (2023). E-waste management transition towards circular economy. In P. Srivastava, D. Ramteke, A. Bedyal, M. Gupta, & J. Sandhu (Eds.). *Handbook of research on safe disposal methods of municipal solid wastes for a sustainable environment* (pp. 80–85). IGI Global. https://doi.org/10.4018/978-1-6684-8117-2.ch006

Sheth, J. N., Sethia, N. K., & Srinivas, S. (2010). Mindful consumption: A customer-centric approach to sustainability. *Journal of the Academy of Marketing Science*, *39*(1), 21–39. https://doi.org/10.1007/s11747-010-0216-3

Sproles, G. B., & Burns, L. D. (1994). *Changing appearances: Understanding dress in contemporary society*. Fairchild Publication.

Suganthi, L. (2019). Examining the relationship between corporate social responsibility, performance, employees' pro-environmental behavior at work with green practices as mediator. *Journal of Cleaner Production*, *232*(Special issue), 739–750. https://doi.org/10.1016/j.jclepro.2019.05.295

Sustainability at Nestle. (2023). *Sustainability at Nestlé.* Nestlé Global. Retrieved March 26, 2023, from https://www.nestle.com/sustainability

Tesla report. (2022). *Environmental impact*. Tesla. Retrieved on May 11, 2023, from https://www.tesla.com/en_eu/impact/environment

The body shop sustainability-commitments. (2023). *Our sustainable development goals: The body shop*. Our Sustainable Development Goals | The Body Shop. Retrieved on June 6, 2023, from https://www.thebodyshop.com/en-gb/about-us/brand-values/sustainability/sustainability-commitments/a/a00063

The Coca-Cola Company. (2022). *The Coca-Cola Company 2022 business & sustainability report highlights*. Retrieved on May 4, 2023, from https://www.coca-colacompany.com/content/dam/company/us/en/reports/coca-cola-business-sustainability-report-2022.pdf

TOMS. (2022). Toms 2022 sustainability report. The Momentum. Retrieved June 23, 2023, from https://www.themomentum.com/reports/toms-2022-sustainability-report

UK I. (2023). *Our sustainability strategy*. IKEA. Retrieved May 19, 2023, from https://www.ikea.com/gb/en/this-is-ikea/climate-environment/the-ikea-sustainability-strategy-pubfea4c210

Unilever Annual Report and Accounts. (2022). *Delivering sustainable business performance*. Retrieved February 22, 2023, from https://www.unilever.com/https://www.unilever.com/files/92ui5egz/production/61ebc6542e967e6fb5a8d5ee05a79238c8f6e4f7.pdf

Unilever PLC. (2023, September 7). *Green growth: Sustainability solutions led by local people* Retrieved April 30, 2023, from https://www.unilever.com/news/news-search/2021/green-growth-sustainability-solutions-led-by-local-people/

Verma, J., Gagandeep, & Gupta, M. (2023). Green environmental sustainability: Initiatives by government and corporate sectors. *Handbook of research on safe disposal methods of municipal solid wastes for a sustainable environment* (pp. 212–221). IGI Global. https://doi.org/10.4018/978-1-6684-8117-2.ch015

Vita, G., Lundström, J. R., Hertwich, E. G., Quist, J., Ivanova, D., Stadler, K., & Wood, R. (2019). The environmental impact of green consumption and sufficiency lifestyles scenarios in Europe: Connecting local sustainability visions to global consequences. *Ecological Economics*, *164*(Special issue), 1–4. https://doi.org/10.1016/j.ecolecon.2019.05.002

Weber, M., & Hemmelskamp, J. (2018). Merging research perspectives on innovation systems and environmental innovation: An introduction. *International Journal of Innovation Management*, *22*(5), 1–7. https://doi.org/10.1007/3-540-27298-4_1

Yerpude, S., Sood, K., & Grima, S. (2022). Blockchain-Augmented digital supply chain management: A way to sustainable business. *Journal of Risk and Financial Management*, *16*(1), 7.

Zhang, M. (2023). Sustainability transitions in e-commerce research—Academic achievements and impediments. *Circular Economy and Sustainability*, *3*(4), 1725–1746. https://doi.org/10.1007/s43615-023-00252-7

CHAPTER 16

THE IMPACT OF POLITICAL INSTABILITY ON STOCK MARKETS IN BRICS COUNTRIES AND TÜRKIYE

Sinem Atici Ustalar[a] and Selim Şanlisoy[b]

[a]*Atatürk University, Faculty of Economics and Administrative Sciences, Erzurum, Türkiye*
[b]*Dokuz Eylül University, Faculty of Economics and Administrative Sciences, İzmir, Türkiye*

ABSTRACT

Introduction: *Political stability is an essential source of stock market dynamics. Investors are confident about countries that have higher political stability. Political stability in an economy enables investors to develop their ability to predict the future and thus to tend towards longer-term and permanent economic and financial activities.*

Purpose: *The study aimed to investigate the impact of political instability in BRICS countries and Türkiye on their stock market volatilities.*

Methodology: *The study analysed the univariate exponential generalised autoregressive conditional heteroskedasticity (EGARCH) Model. The model employed the credit default swap (CDS) 5-year USD Bond data of the BRICS countries and Türkiye to represent political instability. The daily stock exchange index return data from 1 January 2015 to 15 January 2023 was used for model estimation.*

Sustainability Development through Green Economics
Contemporary Studies in Economic and Financial Analysis, Volume 114, 269–288

ISSN: 1569-3759/doi:10.1108/S1569-375920240000114016

Findings: The results of the EGARCH model indicate that political instability is a crucial factor in stock market volatility. The coefficients suggest that when CDS increases in BRICS countries and Türkiye, the volatility of stock returns also increases. The analysis shows that the impact of political instability on the stock market of BRICS countries and Türkiye is not uniform. However, the significant effect of political instability on volatility is higher for Türkiye than for BRICS countries. This indicates that investors perceive the political risk of Türkiye to be greater than that of BRICS countries when investing in the stock market of Türkiye.

Keywords: Political instability; credit default swap; stock market; volatility; EGARCH model; BRICS; Türkiye

JEL Codes: G14; G15; G18

INTRODUCTION

In the most general sense, political instability can be defined as the instability experienced in all variables that represent the political conditions of a country. Political instability in a country affects both the economic conjuncture and the efficiency of financial markets. Political stability in an economy enables entrepreneurs to develop their ability to predict the future and thus tend towards longer-term and permanent economic activities (Şanlısoy & Kök, 2010, p. 102).

Political instability includes many political risk factors such as political chaos, terrorism, civil war, corruption, bribery, and lack of corporate governance, bringing economic and financial instability. The stability of the country's political environment where the investment is considered is an essential factor for the investment decision for both foreign direct investment and international capital flows acting as portfolio investments. Indeed, Liu et al. (2020) found that the most critical obstacles to investment for domestic and foreign investors are the lack of a stable political system and frequent changes in government policy. The effect of political instability on financial markets also impacts the countries' stock markets. However, political instability causes changes in financial market movements by affecting variables such as investors' expectations, asset prices, profitability rates, and risk perception.

In a country with high political instability, when making investment decisions, investors calculate the political risk of that country's market as high. For this reason, sudden changes in political conditions affect sudden purchases and sales in the country's stock markets. Thus, stock market volatility is expected to be high in countries with high political instability. As such, this study aims to investigate the effects of political instability in Türkiye and the BRICS countries and their stock market volatility.

In the study, time series analysis is used to analyse the effect of political instability on the stock market in Türkiye and BRICS countries. This analysis is carried out with the EGARCH model proposed by Nelson (1991), which allows the asymmetric effect of shocks on stock market volatility. In the analysis, daily returns of XU100, BVSP, IRTS, BSESN, CSI, and JTOPI exchanges of Türkiye, Brazil, Russia, India, China, and South Africa (BRICS) are used, respectively. The EGARCH model is estimated between 1 January 2015 and 15 January 2023, using daily stock market index returns. The analysis uses CDS data of Türkiye and BRICS countries to represent political instability. Daily CDS prices are used. Since the daily CDS price instantly reacts to the political changes in the country, it is used to represent political instability, especially in developing countries (Balding, 2011, p. 121). Moreover, the existence of the CDS market is essential for financial markets. For an investor, the change in the country's CDS is perceived as a signal of the country's economic-political stability (Hui & Fong, 2015, p. 174).

According to the EGARCH model results, political instability in Türkiye and BRICS countries affects the volatility of the stock market. The increase in political instability in these countries increases the volatility of stock market index returns. However, this relationship is only statistically significant for China, South Africa, India, and Türkiye. Political risk is essential for investors trading in international markets. For this reason, it is observed that the volatility of these markets is higher in emerging financial markets with high political instability, as investors assume higher political risk. As firms' exposure level to political risk increases, stock return volatility increases (Beaulieu et al., 2005). Model results also support these findings.

In the following section of the study, the concept of political instability will be explained. Then, the literature on the relationship between political instability and the stock market will be discussed. Finally, the empirical model and its results will be discussed. The result of the study is included in the conclusion section.

DEFINITION OF POLITICAL INSTABILITY

Since the 1990s, political and institutional factors have been increasingly considered in explaining the differences in macroeconomic performance between countries, in line with the views of public choice and institutional economic schools. Developed countries are known for having a more democratic structure than developing countries. However, strong institutions are crucial for the economic development of countries and are considered synonymous with a state of democracy. Therefore, the type of political regime is considered one of the most significant factors affecting growth. As a result, the impact of democratisation and the type of political regime on economic variables, especially growth, has been studied. However, empirical studies have not yet arrived at a definitive conclusion when democratisation is considered the only variable affecting growth. This situation has led to new studies in the literature on political variables affecting economic growth (Telatar, 2003, pp. 73–74).

The inclusion of political instability in these models results from these pursuits. Therefore, in determining the differences in the level of economic development among countries, the stability of the current system has come forward as the determining factor rather than the differences in the political systems of countries

(Telatar, 2003, pp. 73–74). Political instability can occur in both democratic and autocratic governments. However, the possibility of experiencing political instability and its exacerbation in democracies is lower than in dictatorial regimes. This is because the culture of reconciliation and tolerance in democratic systems reduces the severity of the environment of conflict that may arise in society. Thus, democracy prevents conflicts from turning into political crises and, therefore, economic crises (UNDP, 2002, p. 57).

Countries have different political regimes and application processes, making it difficult to reach a consensus on the definition and sources of political instability. However, two critical phenomena are commonly associated with political instability. The first is the use of force to change the political system in a country. The second is political events within the constitutional order, such as electoral polarisation, political disintegration, coalition or minority governments, frequent changes in leadership, internal conflicts, and elections.

The Union of International Associations (UIA) provides a broader definition of political instability. According to UIA, the definition of political instability is:

> lack of political continuity in the application of government tends towards sudden violent or disruptive change and fluctuation. Political instability is a function of a lack of consensus, which may arise due to colonial influence, a failure to materialize the sense of 'nationhood' in the citizenry, dictatorship, economic instability or foreign influence. Frequent changes in governments (or attempts to do so), internal dissensions and labor disputes, and involvement in border clashes with neighboring countries may also contribute to the political instability of countries. Political instability may result in social, ethnic or national disintegration and hinder progress through repression and negative change. It may also cause foreign intervention or an increase in foreign influence.[1]

Political Risk Group (PRS Group) conducted a study on political instability from a broad perspective. The study aimed to identify the sources of political instability by creating a political risk index. The political risk index was created using 12 components: government stability, socio-economic conditions, investment profile, internal conflicts, external conflicts, corruption, military influence in politics, religious influence in politics, legal regulations, ethnic tensions, democratic transparency, and bureaucracy quality (PRS, not specified year, p. 3).

The creation of political instability, political uncertainty, and political risk has an impact on economic decisions and activities by limiting the future horizon of economic units and affecting their expectations. In this case, the existence of political stability is of great importance in terms of the effectiveness of economic decisions (Şanlısoy, 2010, p. 197). In this section, we present literature on the influence of political instability on financial markets.

LITERATURE REVIEW

The literature examining the effect of political instability on country stock markets reveals that political instability affects financial asset prices, returns, and volatility (Arouri et al., 2016; Aydin et al., 2020; Bialkowski et al., 2008; Boutchkova et al., 2012; Kök et al., 2015; Liu et al., 2022; Thampanya et al., 2020). However, political instability also affects the development and integration levels of financial markets. Asteriou and Siriopoulos (2003) demonstrated with the example of Greece that political instability affects the development of the stock market. Frijns et al. (2012) discussed the effect of political crises on the integration of stock markets and revealed that political crises hurt the integration of markets.

Researchers use various variables to represent political instability in different countries. One of these variables is elections. Therefore, some studies examine the impact of elections on financial markets. Liu et al. (2022) discovered that the UK general elections decreased the FTSE100 index and increased volatility. Oehler et al. (2017) studied the effects of the Brexit Referendum on the FTSE100 return by creating a risk factor at the global level. Their research revealed that the Brexit referendum impacted returns and that the negative abnormal return increased as the companies' internationalisation degree increased. Goodell and Vahamaa (2013) and Arouri et al. (2016) concluded that the US presidential elections increased VIX volatility.

Political instability indices, prepared by researchers and institutions like the PRS Group, are often used in research to measure political instability. Apart from elections, these indices are considered indicators of political instability. Studies exploring the connection between political instability indices and stock returns and volatilities have shown that political instability impacts the returns and volatility of the stock market.

Ali and Khan (2018) and Hira (2017) investigated the relationship between political instability and stock prices of the Karachi Stock Exchange in Pakistan. According to the results obtained from the studies and political instability increases volatility in stock prices and decreases returns. Suleman (2012) examined terrorist incidents as a source of political instability and investigated their impact on the Karachi Stock Exchange. These attacks include the 11 September terrorist attacks in the USA, the 2002 suicide bombings in Bali nightclubs, the 2004–2005 train bombings in Madrid and London, and a series of sustained explosions and suicide attacks in Pakistan. It is concluded that these events negatively affected the KSE100 returns and increased the volatility of the index. Murtaza et al. (2015) and Bilal et al. (2012) also investigated the effects of political events in Pakistan and other countries on the KSE100 and reached similar results. These studies reveal that political instability or political events caused by terrorism in one country affect the stock market of another country.

Asteriou and Saratandis (2016) investigated the relationship between political instability, banking stock returns, and general stock market returns for the 1993–2013 period for OECD countries. In the study, using 27 different political instability variables, five political instability indicators are calculated from these variables. According to the analysis findings, as the political instability increases in OECD countries, the returns of the banking sector and the general stock market index decrease. On the other hand, the volatility of these indices increases with the increase in political instability. However, the effect of the five political instability indexes on the return and volatility of the stock market is heterogeneous among OECD countries. This shows that the sources of political instability differ among countries. Thampanya et al. (2020) examined the effect of political instability on the stock market in countries that are members of the Association of Southeast Asian Nations (ASEAN-5). According to the results of the analysis, the political instability of ASEAN-5 countries affects the volatility of the stock market index. However, the Indonesian and Philippine stock market volatility seems more sensitive to political instability. The stock market index volatility increase is observed in Indonesia and where political instability is also highest.

In another study, the reactions of economic decision-makers in their financial investment preferences against political instability are examined. The sensitivity of economic agents to political risks may change over time. Mehdian et al. (2008) revealed that investors are rationally more cautious and risk-averse in the face of political instability in a stock market like Türkiye, which has a long history of significant monetary, political, currency, and economic uncertainties. Günay (2016) studied the impact of domestic political risk on Türkiye's stock market in 2001–2014. According to the results, the Turkish stock market's volatility reacted to the country's political events, but this reaction decreased over time.

Several studies have examined how political instability affects individual firms and the overall stock market index. These studies suggest that political instability can impact the institutional structures of companies operating within a country. Liu et al. (2022) found that firms primarily focussing on domestic activities are more susceptible to political instability, whereas firms with increased international operations are less affected. Iqbal (2018) discovered that smaller firms are more vulnerable to political instability than larger firms. Chen et al. (2005) also found that firms with more minor foreign corporate ownership tend to experience more significant price fluctuations than those with more extensive foreign corporate ownership.

In the literature, political instability is represented by various variables, with one of them being the CDS variable of countries. In this regard, Chan et al. (2008) conducted a study to examine the relationship between CDS premiums and stock prices in seven Asian countries. The analysis was conducted over the period from January 2001 to February 2007. The authors discovered a negative correlation between CDS premiums and stock prices in these seven countries. In other words, when political instability exists in these countries, stock prices decrease.

Similarly, Feng et al. (2021) investigated the connection between CDS premiums and exchange rate markets in both G7 and BRICS countries. The analysis covered the period from 1 January 2010 to 19 August 2020. According to the findings, political instability in the G7 and BRICS countries significantly impacts the exchange rate markets. Changes in CDS premiums cause significant movements in the exchange rate markets. In addition, Kar et al. (2016) conducted a similar analysis for Türkiye. They estimated the Markow switching VAR model for the years 2009–2015. The model findings showed that Türkiye's CDS premium impacted the EUR/TL exchange rate during the relevant years.

EMPIRICAL MODEL

The study examines the impact of political instability on the stock market volatility of Türkiye and the BRICS countries using the EGARCH (1,1) model. It is widely observed that financial assets' returns tend to be fat-tailed (leptokurtic) and have volatility clusters, leading to a change in the variances of the return series over time. As a result, models with fixed variance in high-frequency time series are unsuitable, and Generalised ARCH (GARCH) and GARCH family models, which allow for variable variance over time, are commonly used. The GARCH model, created by Bollerslev (1986), is an extension of the ARCH model. The GARCH model is a generalised derivative of the ARCH model, taking into account its past values of the conditional variance. The GARCH (p,q) model is defined as:

$$y_t = \gamma x_t + \varepsilon_t \qquad \text{(Eq. 1)}$$

$$(\varepsilon_t \mid \varepsilon_{t-1}, \varepsilon_{t-2} \ldots) \sim N(0, h_t) \qquad \text{(Eq. 2)}$$

$$h_t = w_0 + \sum_{i=1}^{p} \alpha_i \varepsilon_{t-i}^2 + \sum_{j=1}^{q} \beta_j h_{t-j} \qquad i = 1, \ldots, p \text{ ve } j = 1, \ldots, q \qquad \text{(Eq. 3)}$$

In Eq. 1, x_t represents an exogenous variable and the random error. In Eq. 3, h_t represents the conditional variance of the return in period t. α_i is the ARCH term showing the past period error squares and β_j is the GARCH term showing the conditional variance's past period values. The GARCH (p,q) model allows the conditional variance of the random distribution to be linearly dependent on the past values of the squared errors and conditional variance. This model shows that it is generated by an ARMA process (Bollerslev, 1986, p. 310). Although the optimal p and q values can be determined in many analysis methods, the GARCH (1,1) model is sufficient for analysing many financial time series (Lamoureux & Lastrapes, 1990, p. 226).

In the GARCH (p,q) process, the sum of the $\alpha_i + \beta_j$ parameters represents the persistence parameter of the shocks. If $\alpha_i + \beta_j < 1$, the persistence of shocks on volatility decreases over time, while in the case of, $\alpha_i + \beta_j > 1$ the persistence of shocks on volatility increases over time. If $\alpha_i + \beta_j = 1$, the persistence of shocks on volatility is infinite and using the GARCH model is incorrect (Chou, 1988, p. 282). Engle and Bollerslev (1986) defined GARCH models as an 'Integrated GARCH (Integrated GARCH-IGARCH)' model. Bollerslev (1986) imposed a positivity constraint on the constant term of the variance model and w_0, α_i, and β_j parameters to the GARCH (p,q) model to be valid.

Black (1976) showed that stock returns are negatively related to the volatility of returns. Namely, while volatility rises with bad news in returns (excessive returns are higher than expected returns), returns decrease with good news (excessive returns are higher than expected returns). Following the study of Black (1976), this situation is now defined as the 'leverage effect'. However, the GARCH model shown in Eq. 3 shows that h_t does not depend on the sign of shocks in return, but their magnitude. However, the empirical literature has shown that financial return series exhibit fat-tail characteristics and have asymmetric responses to volatility clusters and shocks. Therefore, the magnitude of the shock to the returns and the sign is significant. For this reason, Nelson (1991) developed the 'Exponential

GARCH (EGARCH)' model, stating that the positivity constraint on the GARCH model could not measure the asymmetry in the response of financial returns to shocks. The model is defined as:

$$\log(h_t) = \alpha_0 + \sum_{j=1}^{q} \beta_j \log(h_{t-j}) + \sum_{i=1}^{p} \alpha_i \left| \frac{\varepsilon_{t-i}}{h_{t-i}} \right| + \sum_{k=1}^{r} \gamma_k \left(\frac{\varepsilon_{t-k}}{h_{t-k}} \right) \quad \text{(Eq. 4)}$$

In Eq. 4, α_0 is the constant term and α_i and β_j are the standard ARCH and GARCH terms. The γ_k parameter is the leverage parameter showing that the conditional variance response to shocks is asymmetrical. If the γ_k parameter is significant ($\gamma_k \neq 0$), shocks' effects are asymmetrical. If γ_k is significant and $\gamma_k > 0$, a past positive shock increases volatility more than a negative shock in return. If γ_k is significant and $\gamma_k < 0$, a negative shock in the past increase's volatility more than a positive shock in return. Nelson (1991) did not impose any positivity constraints on the parameters of the EGARCH model to capture the asymmetry effect.

The 5-year USD Bonds CDS is used to analyse the political instability in Türkiye and BRICS countries. When the CDS variable is added to Eq. 4, the conditional variance equation can be expressed as:

$$\log(h_t) = \alpha_0 + \sum_{j=1}^{q} \beta_j \log(h_{t-j}) + \sum_{i=1}^{p} \alpha_i \left| \frac{\varepsilon_{t-i}}{h_{t-i}} \right| + \sum_{k=1}^{r} \gamma_k \left(\frac{\varepsilon_{t-k}}{h_{t-k}} \right) + CDS_{it} \quad \text{(Eq. 5)}$$

In Eq. 5, the CDS_{it} represents the CDS of country $i$and time t. Considering the negative effect of political instability on the stock market, the effect of CDS_{it} variables on volatility is expected to be calculated positively.

The COVID-19 virus, which originated in Wuhan, China, quickly spread and became a global epidemic by 31 December 2019. Its impact has been felt all over the world. The pandemic has significantly impacted global markets, leading to an abrupt halt in economic activities. Governments worldwide have implemented various measures to manage the pandemic, resulting in economic contraction in all countries. The stock markets have also experienced significant downturns due to the pandemic's effects. To control for the impact of the COVID-19 crisis on economic models, a dummy variable is created in the EGARCH (1,1) model. The start and end dates of the crisis differ by country and are based on the IMF's policy responses to COVID-19 web page. The creation of the dummy variable is based on the start and end dates provided by the IMF for each country. In Brazil, the dates are 26 February 2020–15 January 2021; in China, 31 December 2019–1 September 2021; in India, 30 January 2020–1 May 2021; in Russia, 31 January 2020–1 June 2021; in South Africa, 5 March 2020–30 June 2021; and in Türkiye, 11 March 2020–30 June 2021.

$$\log(h_t) = \alpha_0 + \sum_{j=1}^{q} \beta_j \log(h_{t-j}) + \sum_{i=1}^{p} \alpha_i \left| \frac{\varepsilon_{t-i}}{h_{t-i}} \right| + \sum_{k=1}^{r} \gamma_k \left(\frac{\varepsilon_{t-k}}{h_{t-k}} \right) + CDS_{it} + Covid_{it} \quad \text{(Eq. 6)}$$

In Eq. 6, $Covid_{it}$ also checks for the impact of the COVID-19 crisis on the stock market volatility in country *i* for time *t*.

The EGARCH (1,1) model was used to analyse the daily closing prices of six stock market indices from 1 January 2015 to 15 January 2023. These indices represent the stock markets of six countries: Türkiye, Brazil, Russia, India, China, and South Africa (BRICS). CDS data were used to measure the political instability of these countries. The stock index returns of Türkiye and BRICS countries were calculated using a specific formula.

$$R_{it} = \ln\left(\frac{Index_{i,t}}{Index_{i,t-1}}\right) \quad \text{(Eq. 7)}$$

In Eq. 7, R_{it} represents the stock market index return of country *i* at time *t*. Daily stock market index closing prices and Daily CDS data for Türkiye and BRICS countries are obtained from the 'investing.com' website.

Daily stock market index closing prices and Daily CDS data for Türkiye and BRICS countries are obtained from the 'investing.com' website.

Since the stock markets of six countries are used in the analysis, the problem of the 'nonsynchronous trading effect' may be encountered (Olbrys & Majewska, 2017, p. 412). Since the opening-closing times of each country are different (Eun & Shim, 1989, p. 243) and countries have different national and religious holidays and unexpected events (Baumöhl & Výrost, 2010, p. 415), stocks cannot be traded on some days in the dataset. Therefore, the returns of the country's stock market indices cannot be observed synchronously. This causes the problem of asynchronous trade effect. If this problem is not taken into account while preparing the database, serious deviations occur in the moments and common moments of stock returns (Campbell et al., 1997, p. 85). Some researchers use weekly or monthly data to solve the asynchronous trade effect. However, this solution cannot capture the information in the daily data (Baumöhl & Výrost, 2010, p. 416). Another solution is the so-called "common trading window". In this method, the days when stocks are not traded are removed from the dataset and the same dates of stock trading in all countries are collected in the dataset (Eun & Shim, 1989; Olbrys, 2013; Olbrys & Majewska, 2014). In other words, the trading dates of stocks in all countries are synchronised across countries. In the study, to solve the asynchronous trade effect, the days when stock trading is not possible for all countries are excluded from the dataset. Then, the same stock trading dates in all countries are collected in the dataset.

EMPIRICAL MODEL RESULTS

It is important to note that a price series that follows a random walk is typically not stationary at the level (Herwartz, 2004, p. 197). As a result, it is crucial to examine descriptive statistics of variables and ensure that the series is stationary. Furthermore, logarithmic price series are high-frequency series and the error terms of these series tend to vary over time. Hence, it is necessary to control for heteroscedasticity in the price series. With this in mind, descriptive statistics of the countries' stock market index returns and the CDS are presented in Tables 16.1 and 16.2, respectively.

Table 16.1 contains descriptive statistics for the return of the stock market indexes in the country. The IRTS index has the highest volatility compared to all other countries, while the BSSEN index has the lowest volatility. The Skewness value indicates that the distribution of all stock market index returns is not symmetrical, distorted to the left. This means that the return series is more sensitive to negative shocks. The kurtosis value indicates whether the series has leptokurtic properties, with a critical value of three (Kallner, 2018, p. 128). The kurtosis value is over three for all stock market returns, indicating that they have a fat tail and are leptokurtic series. None of the index return series are normally distributed, as confirmed by the Jargue-Bera values that test the normality assumption of the index return series.

Table 16.2 contains the descriptive statistics of the CDS series of different countries. Russia has the highest CDS volatility, while India has the lowest. All CDS series have right-skewed distributions, which means they are sensitive to positive shocks in their related countries. Additionally, all CDS series have fat tails, making them leptokurtic. The Jargue–Bera test statistics show that the CDS series do not have a normal distribution.

Table 16.1. Descriptive Statistics of Stock Market Index Return.

	BVSP	BSESN	CSI	IRTS	JTOPI	XU100
Mean	0.0369	0.0369	0.0076	0.0333	0.0171	0.0597
Median	0.0718	0.0596	0.1088	0.1241	0.0487	0.1304
Maximum	13.0223	8.5947	6.4101	23.2044	9.0570	5.8104
Minimum	−15.9930	−14.1017	−9.1961	−48.2921	−10.4504	−10.3068
Std. Dev.	1.6423	1.1360	1.8318	2.2529	1.2286	1.4288
Skewness	−1.1149	−1.4163	−0.9922	−5.1856	−0.4640	−1.0096
Kurtosis	18.1126	23.5538	6.9014	12.0044	11.0292	8.8320
Jarque-Bera	1,812.46	3,343.41	148.80	1,164.43	507.39	295.83
Probability	0.0000	0.0000	0.0000	0.0000	0.0000	0.0000
Observations	2021	2021	2021	2021	2021	2021

Source: Authors' calculations.

Table 16.2. Descriptive Statistics of CDS.

	Brazil	China	India	Russia	South Africa	Türkiye
Mean	0.0068	−0.0217	−0.0075	−0.0482	0.0054	0.0645
Median	−0.0701	−0.0338	0.0000	−0.0112	0.0000	−0.0122
Maximum	26.7008	24.2410	9.8834	28.3088	15.0880	39.9501
Minimum	−29.9446	−29.7076	−6.2569	−20.8295	−6.6249	−13.0324
Std. Dev.	3.3546	3.2614	0.8015	3.5736	1.1025	3.0738
Skewness	0.9293	0.8610	0.8265	0.8611	2.3706	1.8793
Kurtosis	18.6455	13.9586	23.1226	11.4665	34.5720	23.3657
Jarque-Bera	1,927.97	955.74	3,166.08	579.76	7,916.31	3,331.05
Probability	0.0000	0.0000	0.0000	0.0000	0.0000	0.0000
Observations	2021	2021	2021	2021	2021	2021

Source: Authors' calculations.

The first graph illustrates Türkiye and BRICS countries' stock index return series. Volatility clustering is observed in all stock index returns, as shown in Fig. 16.1. There are significant breaks in all markets, particularly during the COVID-19 pandemic.

The graphs related to the CDS of the countries are presented in Fig. 16.2. It can be said that the COVID-19 pandemic has an effect on the CDS of Türkiye and BRICS countries.

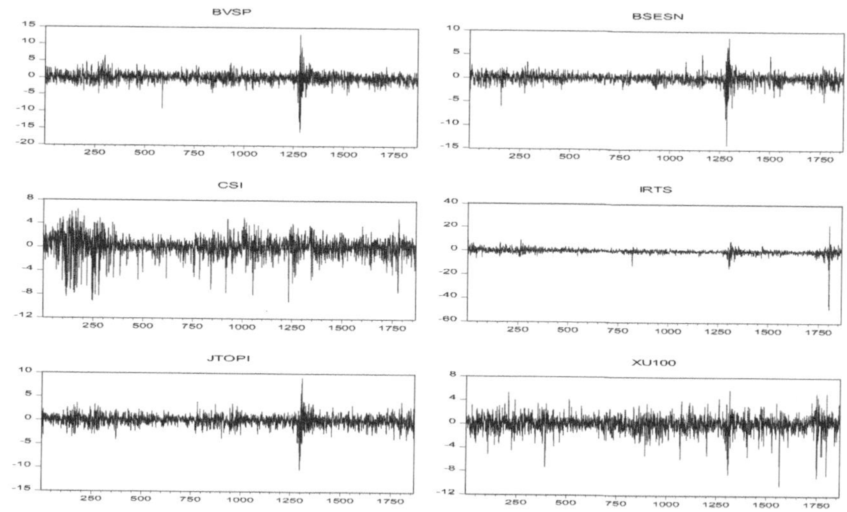

Fig. 16.1. Türkiye and BRICS Countries of the Stock Market Index Returns. *Source*: Authors' calculations.

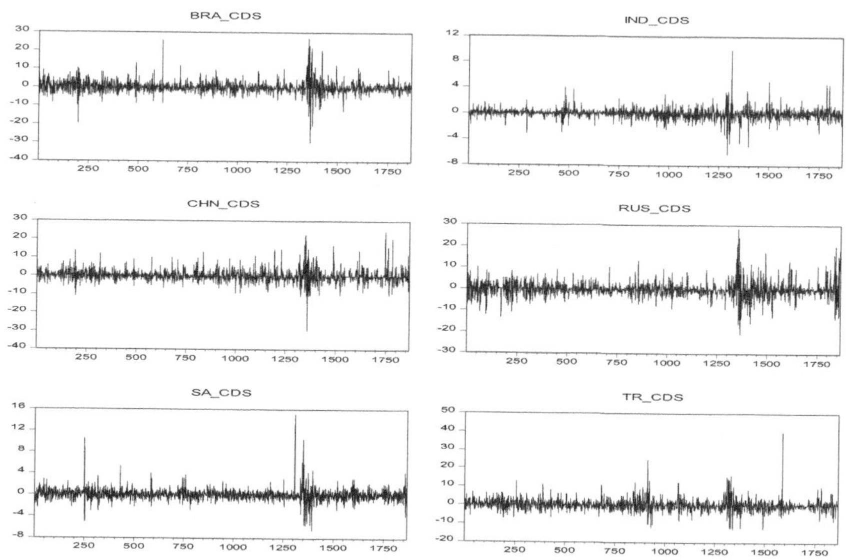

Fig. 16.2. Türkiye and BRICS Countries of the CDS. *Source*: Authors' calculations.

Unit root and stability tests of index return and CDS series are made with the Augmented-Dickey–Fuller (ADF) test, Philips–Perron (PP) test, and Kwiatkowski–Philips–Schmidt–Shin (KPSS) test. In addition, whether there is a structural break in the series is checked with the Zivot Andrews (ZA) test. The test results are shown in Tables 16.3 and 16.4.

In Table 16.3, according to the ADF and PP test results, the null hypothesis testing the existence of unit root for all return series is rejected at the 1% significance level. According to the KPSS test results, the null hypothesis testing the existence of stationarity for the return series of all countries is accepted at the 1% significance level. Thus, all index return series are stationary at I(0). In addition, since the COVID-19 period was a crisis that profoundly affected the stock markets, it is also checked whether the series had a unit root under the structural break. For this, Zivot Andrews unit root test is performed, which considers the break in the mean. According to the test results, the hypothesis that there is a unit root with a mean break for all return series is rejected at the 1% significance level. No structural break is found in all countries' average stock index returns.

The results of unit root and stationarity tests for CDS of Türkiye and BRICS countries are presented in Table 16.4. According to the results of the ADF, PP, and KPSS tests in Table 16.4, the CDS series of these countries do not contain unit roots and are stationary at the level. According to the ZA test results, there is no structural break in the average in other countries except Brazil and China. There is a structural break on average in the CDS values of Brazil and China.

Heteroscedasticity and autocorrelation test results used for stock market index returns and CDSs of Türkiye and BRICS countries are presented in Tables 16.5 and 16.6, respectively. The ARCH test is used to control the heteroscedasticity in the return series. The ARCH test is carried out by determining the optimum ARMA structure. According to the ARCH test results, the null hypothesis testing that there is no heteroscedasticity in error terms in all index returns and CDS is rejected. The error terms of all index return and CDS series have an ARCH effect. The autocorrelation test to the series is performed with the Breusch--Godfrey test. According to the test results, the null hypothesis is rejected in all series. Thus, there is autocorrelation in all index returns and CDS series.

After examining the descriptive statistics on stock market index returns and CDSs of Türkiye and BRICS countries, the EGARCH (1,1) model is applied to analyse the effect of political instability on the volatility of stock markets. Since stock market index returns and CDS series are not normally distributed and show the fat tail features, the EGARCH (1,1) model is estimated with the "GED" distribution. The results of the EGARCH (1,1) model are presented in Table 16.7.

Bollerslev (1986) showed that the w_o, α_i and β_j parameters must satisfy the positivity condition for the volatility analysis made through GARCH models to be valid. However, Nelson and Cao (1992), He & Teräsvirta (1999) showed that the positivity condition is quite restrictive and that Some estimations can have negative w alt o and alfa alt i parameters Nelson (1991) and Chen and Kuan (2002) calculated the mean of the variance equation (w_o) as negative in their EGARCH model results. In this context, when the model results in Table 16.7 are examined, the constant term of the variance equation is negative for all countries' stock return volatility.

Table 16.3. Unit Root and Stationarity Test for Stock Market Returns.

		BVSP	CSI	JTOPI	BSESN	IRTS	XU100
ADF Unit Root Test							
With Constant	*t*-Statistic	−49.5601	−39.8915	−46.683	−15.9034	−23.4031	−29.197
	Prob.	0.0001*	0.0000*	0.0001*	0.0000*	0.0000*	0.0000*
With Constant & Trend	*t*-Statistic	−49.5556	−39.8838	−46.6765	−15.9153	−23.403	−29.3948
	Prob.	0.0000*	0.0000*	0.0000*	0.0000*	0.0000*	0.0000*
Without Constant & Trend	*t*-Statistic	−49.5368	−39.9016	−46.6707	−15.8277	−23.4027	−29.0578
	Prob.	0.0001*	0.0000*	0.0001*	0.0000*	0.0000*	0.0000*
PP Unit Root Test							
With Constant	*t*-Statistic	−49.298	−40.1816	−46.6629	−45.5395	−47.4109	−44.5931
	Prob.	0.0001*	0.0000*	0.0001*	0.0001*	0.0001*	0.0001*
With Constant & Trend	*t*-Statistic	−49.2946	−40.1728	−46.6572	−45.54	−47.4477	−44.8595
	Prob.	0.0000*	0.0000*	0.0000*	0.0000*	0.0000*	0.0000*
Without Constant & Trend	*t*-Statistic	−49.2681	−40.1912	−46.6483	−45.5014	−47.4147	−44.5382
	Prob.	0.0001*	0.0000*	0.0001*	0.0001*	0.0001*	0.0001*
KPSS Stationarity Test							
With Constant	*t*-Statistic	0.0627	0.0644	0.0563	0.0841	0.0465	0.9935
	Prob.	0.0000*	0.0000*	0.0000*	0.0000*	0.0000*	0.0000*
With Constant & Trend	*t*-Statistic	0.0287	0.0675	0.0209	0.033	0.0186	0.1273
	Prob.	0.0000*	0.0000*	0.0000*	0.0000*	0.0000*	0.0000*
ZA Unit Root Test							
With Constant	*t*-Statistic	−19.4327	−40.0181	−46.8967	−18.1822	−19.7671	−29.5644
	Prob.	0.0035*	0.0054*	0.0010*	0.0000*	0.0347**	0.0071*

Source: Authors' calculations.

Notes: The critical values for the 1% significance level in the ADF and PP tests are 3.4334 with constant, −3.9626 with constant and trend and −2.5661 without constant and trend. The critical values for the 1% significance level in the KPSS test are 0.7390 with constant and 0.2160 with constant. Finally, the critical value with a constant for the ZA test is 5.3400. The values in parentheses are the probability values of the relevant *t*-statistics.

Table 16.4. Unit Root and Stationarity Test for CDS.

		Brazil	China	South Africa	India	Russia	Türkiye
ADF Unit Root Test							
With Constant	*t*-Statistic	−41.5403	−41.1315	−41.1346	−43.9974	−38.9049	−41.2784
	Prob.	0.0000*	0.0000*	0.0000*	0.0001*	0.0000*	0.0000*
With Constant & Trend	*t*-Statistic	−41.5307	−41.135	−41.1264	−44.0184	−38.997	−41.2682
	Prob.	0.0000*	0.0000*	0.0000*	0.0000*	0.0000*	0.0000*
Without Constant & Trend	*t*-Statistic	−41.5507	−41.1418	−41.1411	−44.0061	−38.91	−41.276
	Prob.	0.0000*	0.0000*	0.0000*	0.0001*	0.0000*	0.0000*
PP Unit Root Test							
With Constant	*t*-Statistic	−41.5319	−41.0318	−41.0918	−44.0002	−38.9962	−41.1834
	Prob.	0.0000*	0.0000*	0.0000*	0.0001*	0.0000*	0.0000*
With Constant & Trend	*t*-Statistic	−41.522	−41.0349	−41.0835	−44.0183	−39.0512	−41.1728
	Prob.	0.0000*	0.0000*	0.0000*	0.0000*	0.0000*	0.0000*
Without Constant & Trend	*t*-Statistic	−41.5424	−41.0427	−41.0985	−44.0092	−39.0057	−41.1845
	Prob.	0.0000*	0.0000*	0.0000*	0.0001*	0.0000*	0.0000*
KPSS Stationarity Test							
With Constant	*t*-Statistic	0.0542	0.1257	0.0478	0.2246	0.4662	0.0318
	Prob.	0.0000*	0.0000*	0.0000*	0.0000*	0.0000*	0.0000*
With Constant & Trend	*t*-Statistic	0.0467	0.0629	0.0384	0.103	0.1041	0.0326
	Prob.	0.0000*	0.0000*	0.0000*	0.0000*	0.0000*	0.0000*
ZA Unit Root Test							
With Constant	*t*-Statistic	−19.984	−23.5485	−31.9469	−19.9669	−17.4797	−41.3166
	Prob.	0.1821	0.19	0.0007*	0.0035*	0.0518**	0.0078**

Source: Authors' calculations.

Notes: The critical values for the 1% significance level in the ADF and PP tests are 3.4334 with constant, −3.9626 with constant and trend, and −2.5661 without constant and trend. The critical values for the 1% significance level in the KPSS test are 0.7390 with constant and 0.2160 with constant. Finally, the critical value with a constant for the ZA test is 5.3400. The values in parentheses are the probability values of the relevant *t*-statistics.

Table 16.5. Heteroscedasticity and Autocorrelation Test for Stock Market Returns.

	BVSP	CSI	JTOPI	BSESN	IRTS	XU100
		ARCH-LM Heterocedasticity Test				
t-Statistic	42.511	36.7634	94.6512	69.5222	9.5568	10.9675
Prob.	0.0000	0.0000	0.0000	0.0000	0.0000	0.0000
		Breusch–Godfrey Autocorrelation Test				
t-Statistic	5.5623	3.4167	3.8810	5.3588	4.1161	1.836
Prob.	0.0000	0.0001	0.0000	0.0000	0.0000	0.0379

Source: Authors' calculations.
Notes: The ARCH and Breusch–Godfrey tests are performed at 12 lags. The values in parentheses are the probability values of the relevant values.

Table 16.6. Heteroscedasticity and Autocorrelation Test for CDS.

	Brazil	China	South Africa	India	Russia	Türkiye
		ARCH-LM Heteroskedasticity Test				
t-Statistic	61.825	25.3394	4.7317	12.2789	63.415	4.9499
Prob.	0.0000	0.0000	0.0000	0.0000	0.0000	0.0000
		Breusch–Godfrey Autocorrelation Test				
t-Statistic	5.5493	2.5393	2.2032	2.5952	3.2191	4.1894
Prob.	0.0000	0.0025	0.0096	0.0002	0.0001	0.0000

Source: Authors' calculations.
Notes: The ARCH and Breusch–Godfrey tests are performed at 12 lags. The values in parentheses are the probability values of the relevant values.

For the EGARCH (1,1) model to be interpretable, the statistical significance of the parameters estimated in the model is essential. In this context, the ARCH parameter (α_i) and GARCH parameter (β_j) are positive and statistically significant in the volatility of stock market returns of all countries. The leverage parameter (γ_k), which measures the leverage or asymmetry effect, is statistically significant for the volatility of stock markets of all countries. The estimated parameters show that the political instability and the volatility of the stock market of Türkiye and BRICS countries can be analysed with the EGARCH model.

According to Table 16.7, the effect of the change in CDS on the stock market volatility of Türkiye and BRICS countries is positive. This positive effect is statistically significant for the stock markets of China, South Africa, India, and Türkiye, excluding Brazil and Russia. The 1% increase in CDS increases the volatility of China's CSI index by 8%, the volatility of South Africa's JTOPI index by about 3%, and the volatility of India's BSESN index by 5%, and finally, the volatility of Türkiye's XU100 index by about 3%. The results show that political instability in China, South Africa, India, and Türkiye increases the stock market's volatility.

The Zivot Andrews test results show no break in stock returns. However, Graph 1 indicates that the COVID-19 crisis affects the stock market. The impact of the crisis is only significant for Brazil and South Africa. These countries' stock market index volatility is increasing due to the COVID-19 crisis.

The ARCH parameter (α_i) measures how a previous shock in stock index returns affects the volatility of stock index returns. The ARCH parameter is statistically significant and positive for all countries. According to the ARCH

Table 16.7. The Effect of Political Instability on the Volatility of Stock Markets in Türkiye and BRICS Countries: EGARCH (1,1) Model Results.

Parameters	Brazil	China	South Africa	Russia	India	Türkiye
			Mean-Equation			
Constant	0.0846	0.0714	0.0072	0.0681	0.0457	0.1217
	(0.0079)*	(0.0218)**	(0.0050)*	(0.0227)**	(0.0167)**	(0.0000)*
			Variance-Equation			
CDS_{it}	0.0317	0.0869	0.0272	0.0011	0.0521	0.0266
	(0.9554)	(0.0958)***	(0.0424)**	(0.7751)	(0.0000)*	(0.0005)*
$Covid_{it}$	0.0372	−0.0023	0.0201	−0.0044	0.0069	0.0045
	(0.0358)**	(0.7781)	(0.0245)**	(0.5580)	(0.6508)	(0.8001)
w_o	−0.0821	−0.0974	−0.0864	−0.0965	−0.0866	−0.0535
	(0.0000)*	(0.0000)*	(0.0000)*	(0.0000)*	(0.0000)*	(0.0192)**
α_i	0.1478	0.1519	0.1104	0.1454	0.0846	0.1575
	(0.0000)*	(0.0000)*	(0. 0000)*	(0.0000)*	(0.0005)*	(0.0000)*
β_j	0.9445	0.9637	0.9610	0.9828	0.9576	0.8835
	(0.0000)*	(0.0000)*	(0.0000)*	(0.0000)*	(0.0000)*	(0.0000)*
γ_k	−0.1079	−0.0229	−0.1478	−0.0836	−0.1602	−0.0795
	(0.0000)*	(0.1010)***	(0.0000)*	(0.0000)*	(0.0000)*	(0.0000)*
$\alpha_i + \beta_j$	1.0923	1.1156	1.0714	1.1282	1.0422	1.0410
Half-life	7.85	6.34	10.05	4.74	16.76	17.25
GED Parameter	1.4675	1.1891	1.6214	1.3646	1.5307	1.2230
	(0.0000)*	(0.0000)*	(0.0000)*	(0.0000)*	(0.0000)*	(0.0000)*
LogLikelihood	−3,240.351	−3,424.009	−2,733.483	−3,459.742	−2,413.469	−3,120.257
AIC	3.4944	3.6917	2.9500	3.7270	2.6063	3.3633
SIC	3.5330	3.7303	2.9886	3.7626	2.6449	3.3959
HQC	3.5086	3.7059	2.9642	3.7401	2.6205	3.3753
ARCH LM	0.5710	0.5188	1.5491	0.9937	0.7036	0.7052
	(0.8668)	(0.9039)	(0.1101)	(0.4523)	(0.7492)	(0.7477)
Q(12)	8.4340	14.074	6.7747	5.8421	4.9735	12.923
	(0.3920)	(0.120)	(0.453)	(0.665)	(0.663)	(0.166)
Q²(12)	7.0175	6.6526	14.257	11.893	8.5663	8.9322
	(0.8560)	(0.880)	(0.113)	(0.454)	(0.739)	(0.709)

Source: Authors' calculations.

*, **, and *** represent 1%, 5%, and 10% statistical significance levels, respectively. The values in parentheses are the standard error values of the relevant values. They represent the AIC Akaike Information Criteria, SIC Schwartz Information Criteria, and HQC the Hannan–Quinn Criteria. The ARCH LM test is used to test the variance at 12 lags. Q and Q2 are Ljung–Box statistics used to test autocorrelation at 12 lags. The values in parentheses below the test results are the probability values of the relevant test statistics. In EGARCH models, the ARMA structure of stock market indices is also controlled in the mean equation but is not presented in the table. Accordingly, ARMA (2,2) for BVSP, ARMA (1.3) for IRTS, ARMA (2,2) for CSI, ARMA (2,3) for BSESN, ARMA (2,3) for JTOPI and XU100 ARMA (2,1) structures are used.

parameter, past shocks in BVSP, CSI, JTOPI, IRTS, BSESN, and XU100 stock index returns increase the volatility of the index returns in the current period by 0.14, 0.15, 0.11, 0.14, 0.08, and 0.15, respectively. The volatility of stock market returns is most affected by past shocks in returns in China and Türkiye.

The GARCH parameter () measures the impact of the prior period's conditional variance on the current period's conditional variance for stock market index returns. In simpler terms, it assesses the effect of a shock in the volatility of stock returns in the past period on the volatility of returns in the current period. For instance, the conditional volatility increases in the Brazilian stock market in the previous period result in a current volatility increase of 0.94. Meanwhile, the conditional volatility increase in the previous period in the stock markets of China and southern Africa leads to a current volatility increase of 0.96. The GARCH parameter is calculated to be 0.98 for Russia, 0.95 for India, and 0.88 for Türkiye. This implies that an increase in the conditional volatility of the previous period increases the current volatility of the Russian stock market index by 0.98, the Indian stock index by 0.95, and Türkiye's stock index by 0.88.

The leverage parameter (γ_k) measures whether the impact of positive and negative shocks on the return volatility of stock markets is unequal. In the case of Türkiye and BRICS countries, the leverage parameter is negative and significant, indicating the presence of a leverage effect on the volatility of their stock market returns. This implies that negative shocks cause higher volatility in these countries' stock market returns than positive shocks.

In the EGARCH (1,1) model, the parameter showing the persistence of the shocks can be calculated with the sum of $\alpha_i + \beta_j$. This is defined as the persistence parameter. This parameter shows whether the impact of the shock on the stock market index returns of Türkiye and BRICS countries will continue in the future. The parameter value showing the persistence of shocks on stock market index volatility is calculated as 1.09 for Brazil, 1.11 for China, 1.07 for South Africa, 1.12 for Russia, 1.04 for India and Türkiye. Thus, since the sum of $\alpha_i + \beta_j$ is greater than 1, shocks to BVSP, CSI, JTOPI, IRTS, BSESN, and XU100 indexes are permanent.

Within the scope of GARCH models, the half-life of the shocks can be calculated, as well as the permanence of the shocks. In this context, the half-life of the shocks is calculated with the formula $\ln(0.5)/\ln(\alpha_i + \beta_j)$ (Smallwood, 2008, p. 1170). In this context, the persistence of a shock on Brazil's stock index is approximately eight days, for China 6.34 days, for South Africa 10 days, for Russia approximately five days, for India approximately 17 days, and finally, for Türkiye 17.25 days.

According to the EGARCH (1,1) model, the diagnostic statistics are presented in Table 16.7. The ARCH-LM test reveals no heteroscedasticity issue in the conditional variance of the stock market indices of Türkiye and BRICS countries up to 12 lags. Moreover, Ljung–Box statistics demonstrate that autocorrelation disappears up to 12 lags, indicating no significant dependence on past stock returns for the stock markets of Türkiye and the BRICS countries.

CONCLUSION

One of the primary causes of financial market volatility is political instability, as stated by Balding (2011, p. 122). Investors anticipate a stable return on their financial investments. Therefore, guaranteeing the economic and political stability of the country where they invest is crucial. Although financial asset returns are not always stable, even in economically stable countries, there is evidence in the literature that political instability significantly impacts financial markets. This highlights the importance of political stability in ensuring a stable financial market.

This study focusses on how political instability in Türkiye and the BRICS countries affects the volatility of the stock market. Despite their significant contributions to the global economy, these countries have not yet achieved political stability. As a result, it is expected that the stock markets in these countries will experience increased volatility due to political instability.

The EGARCH model was used to test the impact of political instability on the stock market volatility in Türkiye and the BRICS countries. The model's findings indicate that the rising political instability in these countries has increased the volatility of their stock markets. However, the effect is only significant for China, South Africa, India, and Türkiye.

According to the model results, a higher level of political risk is involved in investing in Türkiye and BRICS countries due to the political changes in these regions. Therefore, investors willing to invest in these countries should factor in the political risk involved while making decisions. It is also observed that the stock markets of these countries are highly sensitive to political events. As a result, any political shock in these countries can lead to a sudden increase in investors' buying and selling decisions, increasing the stock market volatility.

NOTE

1. See: http://encyclopedia.uia.org/en/problem/133434.

REFERENCES

Ali, R., & Khan, R.E.A. (2018). Socioeconomic stability and variability in stock market prices: A case study of Karachi Stock Exchange. *Asian Journal of Economic Modelling*, *6*(4), 428–440.

Arouri, M., Estay, C., Rault, C., & Rouband, D. (2016). Economic policy uncertainty and stock markets: Long-run evidence from the US. *Finance Research Letters*, *18*, 136–141.

Asteriou, D., & Sarantidis, A. (2016). Political instability and stock market returns evidence from OECD countries. *Economics and Business Letters*, *5*(4), 113–124.

Asteriou, D., & Siriopoulos, C. (2003). The role of political instability in stock market development and economic growth: The case of Greece. *Economic Notes*, *29*, 355–374.

Aydin, Ü, Ekinci, R., & Tüzün, O. (2020). Effects of exchange rate shocks and political risk on the Turkish manufacturing industry: Some evidence. *Advances in Economics and Business*, *8*(4), 214–233.

Balding, C. (2011). CDS pricing and elections in emerging markets. *Journal of Emerging Market Finance*, *10*(2), 121–173.

Baumöhl, E., & Výrost, T. (2010). Stock Market integration: Granger causality testing concerning Nonsynchronous Trading effects. *Czech Journal of Economics and Finance*, *60*(4), 414–425.

Beaulieu, M. C, Cosset, J. C., & Essaddam, N. (2005). The impact of political risk on the volatility of stock returns: The case of Canada. *Journal of International Business Studies*, *36*, 701–718.

Bialkowski, J., Gottschalk, K. & Wisniewski, T. P. (2008). Stock market volatility around National elections. *Journal of Banking and Finance*, *32*, 1941–1953.

Bilal, A. R., Abu Talib, N., Haq I., Khan, M. N. A. & Islam, T. (2012). How terrorism and macroeconomic factors impact on returns: A case study of Karachi stock exchange. *World Applied Sciences Journal*, *19*(11), 1575–1584.

Black, F. (1976). Studies of stock market volatility changes. *1976 Proceedings of the American Statistical Association, Business and Economic Statistics Section* (pp. 177–181).

Bollerslev, T. (1986). Generalized autoregressive conditional Heteroscedasticity. *Journal of Econometrics*, *31*, 307–327.

Boutchkova, M., Doshi, H., Durnev, A. & Molchanov, A. (2012). Precarious politics and return volatility. *Review of Financial Studies*, *25*, 1111–1154.

Campbell, J. Y., Lo, A. W., & MacKinlay, A. C. (1997). *The econometrics of financial markets*. Princeton University Press.

Chan, K. C., Zhang, G., & Fung, H. G. (2008). On the relationship between Asian credit default swap and equity markets. *Journal of Asia Business Studies*, *4*(1), 3–12.

Chen, D. H., Bin, F. S., & Chen, C. D. (2005). The impacts of political events on foreign institutional investors and stock returns: Emerging market evidence from Taiwan. *International Journal of Business*, *10*(2), 2005.

Chen, Y. T., & Kuan, C. M. (2002). Time irreversibility and EGARCH in US stock index returns. *Journal of Applied Econometrics*, *17*, 565–578.

Chou, R. Y. (1988). Volatility persistence and stock valuations: Some empirical evidence using Garch. *Journal of Applied Econometrics*, *3*(4), 279–294.

Engle, R. F., & Bollerslev, T. (1986). Modelling the persistence of conditional variance. *Econometric Reviews*, *5*, 1–50.

Eun, C. S., & Shim, S. (1989). International transmission of stock market movements. *The Journal of Financial and Quantitative Analysis*, *24*(2), 241–256.

Feng, Q, Sun, X., Liu, C., & Li, J. (2021). Spillovers between sovereign CDS and exchange rate markets: The role of market fear. *North American Journal of Economics and Finance*, *55*, 1–22.

Frijns, B., Rad, A. T., & Indriawan, I. (2012). Political crises and the stock market integration of emerging markets. *Journal of Banking & Finance*, *36*(3), 644–653.

Goodell, J. W., & Vahamaa, S. (2013). US presidential elections and implied volatility: The role of political uncertainty. *Journal of Banking & Finance*, *37*(3), 1108–1117.

Günay, S. (2016). Is political risk still an issue for the Turkish stock market? *Borsa Istanbul Review*, *16*(1), 21–31.

He, C., & Teräsvirta, T. (1999). Properties of the autocorrelation function of squared observations for second-order GARCH processes under two sets of parameter constraints. *Journal of Time Series Analysis*, *20*, 23–30.

Herwartz, H. (2004). Conditional heteroskedasticity. *Applied time series econometrics*. Cambridge University Press.

Hira, I. (2017). Relationship among political instability, stock market returns, and stock market volatility. *Studies in Business and Economics*, *12*(2), 70–99.

Hui, C., & Fong, T. P. (2015). Price cointegration between sovereign CDS and currency option markets in the financial crises of 2007–2013. *International Review of Economics & Finance*, *40*, 174–190.

Kallner, A. (2018). Formulas. *Laboratory Statistics Methods in Chemistry and Health Sciences*, *1*, 1–140.

Kar, M., Bayat, T., & Kayhan, S. (2016). Impacts of credit default swaps on volatility of the exchange rate in Türkiye: The case of Euro. *International Journal of Financial Studies*, *4*(14), 1–18.

Kök, R., Ekinci, R., & Yalçınkaya, A. E. A. (2015). Ülke Riski Bileşenlerinin Bankacılık ve Reel Sektör Üzerine Etkileri: Türkiye Örneği, 1993–2015. *Çukurova Üniversitesi İktisadi ve İdari Bilimler Fakültesi Dergisi*, *19*(2), 151–171.

Lamoureux, C. G., & Lastrapes, W. D. (1990). Persistence in variance, structural change, and the GARCH model. *Journal of Business & Economic Statistics*, *8*(2), 225–234.

Liu, B. M., Hamdan, M., Whiteley, C., & Aminu, N. (2022). The effect of political instability on the UK stock returns: Evidence from the 2016 referendum and the major events that followed. *Theoretical Economics Letters*, *12*, 1648–1672.

Liu, R., He, L., Linag, X., & Yang, X. (2020). Is there any difference in the impact of economic policy uncertainty on the investment of traditional and renewable energy enterprises? – A comparative study based on regulatory effects. *Journal of Cleaner Production*, *255*, 1–15.

Mehdian, S., Nas, T., & Perry, M. (2008). An examination of investor reaction to unexpected political and economic events in Türkiye. *Global Finance Journal*, *18*, 337–350.

Murtaza, H., Abrar ul Haq, M., & Ali, R. (2015). *Impact of major political events on stock market returns of Pakistan* (pp. 68–83). Public Policy and Administration Research.

Nelson, D. B., & Cao, C. Q. (1992). Inequality constraints in the univariate GARCH model. *Journal of Business and Economic Statistics*, *10*, 229–235.

Nelson, D. B. (1991). Conditional heteroskedasticity in asset returns: A new approach. *Econometrica*, *59*(2), 347–370.

Oehler, A., Horn, M., & Wendt, S. (2017). Brexit: Short-term stock price effects and the impact of firm-level internationalisation. *Finance Research Letters*, *22*, 175–181.

Olbrys, J., & Majewska E. (2014). Quantitative identification of crisis periods on the major European stock markets. *La Pensée*, *76*(1), 254–260.

Olbrys, J., & Majewska E. (2017). Asymmetry effects in volatility on the major European stock markets: The EGARCH based approach. *Quantitative Finance and Economics*, *1*(4), 411–427.

Olbrys, J. (2013). Price and volatility spillovers in the case of stock markets located in different time zones. *Emerging Markets Finance and Trade*, *49*(2), 145–157.

Pastor, L., & Veronesi, P. (2012). Uncertainty about government policy and stock prices. *Journal of Finance*, *67*, 1219–1264.

Şanlısoy, S. (2010). Politik istikrarsızlık- ekonomik süreç politikaları etkileşimi, *Sosyoekonomi*, *13*(13), 192–214.

Şanlısoy, S., & Kök, R. (2010). Politik istikrarsızlık- ekonomik büyüme ilişkisi: Türkiye örneği (1987–2006). *Dokuz Eyülül Üniversitesi İktisadi ve İdari Bilimler Fakültesi Dergisi*, *25*(1), 101–125.

Smallwood, A. D. (2008). Measuring the persistence of deviations from purchasing power parity with a fractionally integrated STAR model. *Journal of International Money and Finance*, *27*, 1161–1176.

Suleman, M. T. (2012). Stock market reaction to terrorist attacks: Empirical evidence from a front line state. *Australasian Accounting Business and Finance Journal*. *6*(1), 97–110.

Telatar, F. (2003). Türkiye'de Politika Değişkenliği İle Ekonomik Büyüme Arasındaki Nedensellik İlişkileri. *İşletme ve Finans*, *211*, 71–91.

Thampanya, N., Wu, J., Nasir, M. A., & Liu, J. (2020). Fundamental and behavioural determinants of stock return volatility in ASEAN-5 countries. *Journal of International Financial Markets, Institutions and Money*, *65*, 1–51.

UNDP. (2002). *Human development report 2002: Deepening democracy in a fragmented world*. https://hdr.undp.org/content/human-development-report-2002

Vortelinos, D. I., & Saha, S. (2016). The impact of political risk on return, volatility and discontinuity: Evidence from the International Stock and Foreign Exchange Markets. *Finance Research Letters*, *17*, 222–226.

CHAPTER 17

GOING GREEN: THE EFFECTS OF MORAL OBLIGATION AND SOCIAL MEDIA ON GREEN PURCHASE INTENTION

Aamer Al Aflak and Priya Vij

University School of Business, Chandigarh University, Punjab, India

ABSTRACT

Purpose: *Green consumerism is on the rise in the 21st century, impelling businesses to prioritise environmental awareness and expand eco-products to keep up with the growing demand. This research examines how social media (SM) and moral obligations (MO) affect consumer views and their propensity to make eco-friendly choices.*

Methodology: *Data were gathered from 508 participants using an adaptive questionnaire. The proposed model was tested using 'structural equation modelling'.*

Findings: *The results show that electronic word-of-mouth (EWOM) and the intent to acquire green goods favourably impact consumer behaviour. MO positively influences attitudes and intentions to make green purchases (GPI), with attitudes acting as a mediator between MO and GPI.*

Implications: *This research is of utmost importance for marketers wanting to enhance their SM communication strategies to influence consumers' opinions*

Sustainability Development through Green Economics
Contemporary Studies in Economic and Financial Analysis, Volume 114, 289–304

Published under exclusive licence by Emerald Publishing Limited
ISSN: 1569-3759/doi:10.1108/S1569-375920240000114017

of green products and raise the possibility that they would make environmentally conscious purchases.

Keywords: Social media; moral obligation; green products; EWOM; green consumerism; consumer behaviour; green purchases intention

JEL Codes: M31; M30; Q56

1. INTRODUCTION

Environmental awareness has widely risen due to the rise in environmental concerns, leading to huge demand for sustainable products by consumers. Sustainable business practices have led companies to open multiple shop formats, products, and brands. Customers are becoming increasingly aware of the risks associated with their consumption and the threat of environmental issues. Additionally, consumer choices of goods and services negatively and indirectly impact the environment (Nekmahmud, Ramkissoon, et al., 2022). Sustainable consumption of eco-friendly products is essential for sustainable development and the usage of ecological products is one of the 'sustainable development goals' that promotes a green lifestyle by minimising the harmful environmental and health impacts (Fasoulis, 2023). Consumers are more likely to put additional effort into behaving eco-friendly and businesses are promoting green products.

Green products are made from 'non-toxic, natural, recyclable resources and eco-friendly wrapping' (Urbański & Ul Haque, 2020). To achieve longstanding corporate objectives and revenue, companies and sellers use several promotion tactics and practices to persuade customers to buy green goods (Seretny et al., 2021). Aside from that, consumer behaviour patterns, environmental concerns, and buying of green products have all been considerably affected by eco-friendly movements. Many businesses now advertise their goods through a variety of media channels to explore unexploited markets and devote more time to promoting green products (Purcărea et al., 2022). SM, which may be used for private and public purposes, is more frequently utilised to promote eco-goods (Ali et al., 2023). EWOM is one of the SM concepts that is most closely linked to it, as opposed to traditional word of mouth (WOM), which can deliver both positive and negative reviews of products and services promptly via the internet from existing, past, and future customers (Dwivedi et al., 2021). There is vast content and reviews about products and services online due to this EWOM correspondence.

The current study will focus on green products in the United Arab Emirates (UAE) in the 'fast-moving consumer goods' (FMCG) industry, specifically from Nestle, Proctor & Gamble, and Unilever. The FMCG sector is one of the largest industries, projected to expand from a global size of $11,490.9 billion in 2021 to $18,939.4 billion by 2031, with 5.1% CAGR from 2022–2031. These companies are among the top 10 companies in the world, which are also available in the UAE (Skool, 2022; Statista, 2020) that are taking initiatives to provide green products in the future. The psychological and sociological factors affecting consumers' purchase intentions for green products need to be better understood (Liang et al., 2022).

To comprehend how customers in the UAE consume green FMCG products, this research will use the 'Theory of Planned Behaviour' (TPB). TPB is a popular model for predicting the psychological factors influencing consumer behaviour. It is grounded on the notion that a person's intention depends on a structure of beliefs in the benefits and drawbacks of acting in a certain way, as well as beliefs in the social norms for doing so and control beliefs, as perceived by the person who does this (Ajzen, 1991). Despite the literature's focus on encouraging consumers to purchase eco-friendly products, SM's function in this system has received less attention. To fill a vacuum in the literature, the current research examines the impact of SM on customers' subjective norms (SNs) and attitudes and explains the motivations behind consumers' purchasing of green FMCG products using perceived behavioural control, MO, and EWOM.

2. LITERATURE REVIEW

The TPB is a socio-cognitive model used to describe specific consumer behaviours. The theory came as an extended version of the 'theory of reasoned action' (TRA) by Fishbein and Ajzen (1975), which pointed out that one's attitude towards conduct and a SN may be used to predict behavioural intentions. An attitude is a trained propensity to act consistently favourably or unfavourably towards a specific thing. As a result, attitudes result from a person's assessment of a product, service, or object (Wang et al., 2022). On the other hand, SNs are a person's propensity to adhere to societal standards and expectations. The two elements believed to be the primary indicators of behaviour intent are attitude and SNs. Despite being highly successful in explaining a wide range of acts, Ajzen enlarged the TRA model because it was later found to only account for volitional behaviours. As a result, Ajzen (1991) expanded the TRA. model to include perceived behavioural control (PBC), contributing to the TPB's development. Ajzen (1991) defined PBC as 'people's perception of how simple or difficult it is to carry out the desired behaviour'. Thus, according to the TPB model, PBC affects natural behaviour directly from PBC to the actual behaviour and indirectly by acting as a mediator to behavioural intent.

In recent years, researchers have investigated consumers' pro-environmental behaviour due to the growing concern about environmental issues from global warming, air pollution, and other ecological hazards on the earth (Berki-Kiss & Menrad, 2022; Bilro et al., 2022; Wei et al., 2021). The TPB was subsequently used to enlighten a wide range of behaviours, including soil safeguarding acts (Moshood et al., 2022), green housing (Mir Mohamad Tabar et al., 2023; Zahan et al., 2020), plastic recycling (de Oliveira et al., 2023; Liu et al., 2022), food waste behaviour (Gul et al., 2022; Sutiadiningsih et al., 2023; Zheng et al., 2023), energy saving (Fatoki, 2023; Rahmawati et al., 2023), and technology adoption (Nguyen et al., 2022). The TPB has also been successfully used to explicate consumers' intentions to use and buy environmentally friendly items (Lan et al., 2023; Nguyen et al., 2022). Consequently, the following theories are put forth:

H1. Attitude towards green products influences green purchase intentions.

H2. SNs towards green products influence green purchase intentions.

H3. Perceived behavioural control towards green products influences green purchase intentions.

Hence, the TPB has been used to describe sustainable consumption and environmental behaviour. Nevertheless, modifications were advocated, and constructs have been added. Numerous elements, including environmental awareness and concern, moral and ethical duty, beliefs, and religiosity, have been found to influence consumers' pro-environmental conduct. In order to better understand how consumers, behave towards green electronic items, the current article suggests modifying the TPB model by adding additional constructs, such as MO, SM, and green self-identity.

2.1. Moral Obligation

MO is when a person has internalised ethical principles corresponding to personal values regarding proper conduct. Existing research suggests that environmentally conscious customers favour purchasing goods that are less detrimental to the environment (Sondhi et al., 2023). However, psychological variables, such as a sense of MO or perceived morality, strongly influence people's buying of environmentally friendly products (Maior & Mantovani, 2023; Sun et al., 2022). An important factor in determining a person's ethical behaviour is their ethical obligation. Oh and Yoon (2014) claimed that MO dramatically affects one's intent to be involved in digital piracy.

Additionally, it was discovered that ethical shoppers have a strong sense of responsibility to others, which influences the things they choose to buy (Nadeau et al., 2020). Such emotions demonstrate a person's internalised moral standards and reflect their values and conceptions of good and wrong (Floriano & de Matos, 2022; Sun et al., 2022). Most studies establish that ethical responsibility directly impacts customers' propensity to buy. Other studies, including the one by Oh and Yoon (2014), showed that the ethical responsibility of individuals has an attitude-based indirect impact on purchase intentions. Hence, the following hypothesis suggested:

H4. MO has a positive impact on green purchase intentions.

H4a. MO has a positive impact on attitude.

H5. Attitude mediates the effect of MO on green purchase intention.

2.2. Social Media

SM, the Internet of Things, and the digital transformation era have significantly changed our daily social interactions. At the beginning of 2021, there were 4.33

billion SM users globally, or more than 55% of the world's population, according to a survey (Ali et al., 2023). During COVID-19, individuals became more engaged and active on SM, using Facebook and other SM platforms at higher rates (Ali et al., 2023; Gou & Perceval, 2023; Mauji & Abu-Shanab, 2023). The best source of information on all aspects of life is now social networking (Pop et al., 2020; Tazeen & Mullick, 2023). It is the easiest to obtain and the most affecting stimuli, shaping how people behave in social, organisational, and individual contexts (Guess et al., 2023; Hamadi et al., 2022; Musa et al., 2022). Many businesses have embraced it as a hub of disseminating information among all age categories due to its acceptance among users (Arli et al., 2018; Musa et al., 2022). Due to consistent and favourable SM posts on green goods, consumers are expected to believe them. The use of SM positively impacts consumers' green shopping behaviour plus their intent regarding green choices (Bedard & Tolmie, 2018; Cooley & Parks-Yancy, 2019). Social networks uphold, promote, and spread the accepted standard of environmental behaviour (Farzin et al., 2022; Nekmahmud, Naz, et al., 2022). Therefore, the resulting proposed:

H6a. SM positively influences attitude.

H6b. SM positively influences SNs.

2.3. Green Purchase Intention and Behaviour

A person's will to take on a particular action is how 'intention' is defined (Yadav & Pathak, 2016). According to the TPB, natural, passionate actions lead to success. Recently, Villavicencio and Schlesinger (2023) revealed evidence of a strong correlation between behavioural intentions and green product purchases. High-involvement consumers must make a deliberate, no-strings-attached purchase. Green purchase intents are the factors that influence a customer's green purchasing behaviour (Alambeigi et al., 2023; Villavicencio & Schlesinger, 2023). Since shopping habits are made more accessible by intention, having a green purchasing intention favours making green purchases. Therefore, it is regarded as a forecaster of buying behaviour. Earlier studies developed the following assumption (Puška et al., 2024; Yerpude et al., 2022).

H7. Green purchase intention has a positive effect on green buying behaviour.

2.4. Electronic-Word-of-Mouth

EWOM marketing consists of basic communications regarding a customer's goods or facilities, or the company itself, through compliments for the effectiveness of the product, friendliness, integrity, or efficiency, or for a particular issue that someone else has noticed and experienced (Dwivedi et al., 2021). The message conveyed may be good or harmful, depending on how the sender feels about the programmes they support (Sharma et al., 2023). The paradigm changes in message transmission has led to the loss of mainstream messaging, altering consumer behaviour. Due to the trustworthiness of personal information transfer, customers continue to favour EWOM, which significantly impacts how consumers behave. EWOM affects how consumers make decisions about what to buy (Kumar & Pandey, 2023).

H8. EWOM has a significant effect on green purchase behaviour.

3. RESEARCH METHODOLOGY

The present research was conducted in the United Arab Emirates and information was acquired from consumers in Abu Dhabi, a significant metropolitan city. The approach of purposive sampling was used to gather information. The sample size was established via 'G*Power software version 3.1.9.7' (Faul et al., 2007). This research utilised a sample of 508 respondents that complied with the allowed sample limits, but an obligatory 227 responses were required to achieve the true power of 0.95. The questionnaire was developed using a multiple-item approach and tested for reliability and validity. The characteristics were examined by a '5-point Likert scale', which ranged from 'strongly disagree (1) to agree (5) strongly'. Every component was drawn from an earlier study and changed to meet the requirements of the current study. Utilising three measuring items taken from the TPB, the three determinants of behavioural intents (ATT, SN, and PBC) were assessed (Ajzen, 1991; Jain et al., 2020; Qin & Song, 2022). Further, MO was collected from the study of (Khang et al., 2012) with a three-item scale. Finally, SM, EWOM, and green purchase behaviour were assessed using a three-item scale modified by (Kumar & Pandey, 2023) as shown in Fig. 17.1.

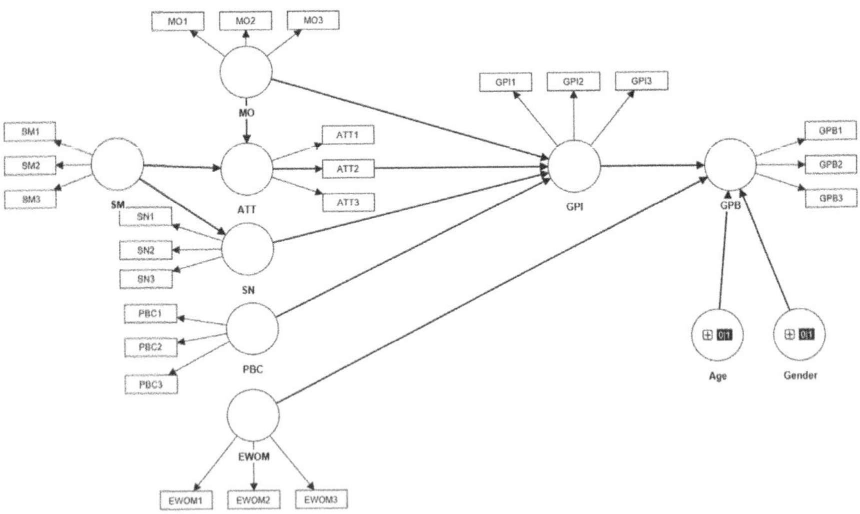

Fig. 17.1. Proposed Framework with Gender and Age as Control Variables. *Source:* Authors' own work.

4. RESULTS

4.1. Descriptive Analysis

Table 17.1 displays the outcomes of the demographic analysis. Most respondents, 59.5%, were under 32 and females comprised 40.5% of the total responses. Additionally, 250 respondents were graduates, making up 69.6% of the respondents.

4.2. Measurement Model Assessment

Table 17.2 presents an evaluation of the outcomes of the measuring model. Using 'Cronbach's Alpha (CA), Dijkstra and Henseler's rhoA (Rho_A), composite reliability (CR), and average variance extracted (AVE)', the reliability and validity of the constructs were investigated. All results for the metrics above are above the optimum cut-off point of 0.70 (Hair et al., 2017, 2020). At the same time, AVE values are above the minimum necessary value of 0.5 and vary from 0.619 to 0.787 (Shmueli et al., 2019). According to Shmueli et al. (2019), the factor loading rates are higher than the permitted threshold of 0.708.

'Heterotrait Monotrait Ratio (HTMT) is also used to test the discriminant validity'. According to Voorhees et al. (2016) and Henseler et al. (2015), all HTMT values must be smaller than 0.85. The HTMT results are displayed in Table 17.3. This demonstrates that every value is less than 0.85, representing that every construct satisfies the minimum threshold requirement. To state it explicitly,

Table 17.1. Descriptive Analysis's Results.

Age	Frequency	Percent	Educational Qualification	Frequency	Percent
Below 32	300	59.5%	Graduate	250	49.6%
32–37	150	29.8%	Post Graduate	180	35.7%
Above 37	54	10.7%	Professional	74	14.7%
	504	1		504	1
Gender			**Marital Status**		
Male	300	59.5%	Married	351	69.6%
Female	204	40.5%	Unmarried	153	30.4%
	504	100		504	100

Source: Authors' own work.

Table 17.2. Assessment of Measurements Model Results.

	Cronbach's alpha	rho_A	CR	AVE
ATT	0.834	0.842	0.900	0.751
E-WOM	0.787	0.788	0.875	0.701
GPB	0.729	0.908	0.829	0.619
GPI	0.862	0.886	0.917	0.787
MO	0.779	0.778	0.872	0.695
PBC	0.824	0.872	0.892	0.734
SM	0.826	0.833	0.897	0.743
SN	0.806	0.826	0.884	0.718

Source: Authors' own work.

Table 17.3. HTMT Ratio.

	ATT	EWOM	GPB	GPI	MO	PBC	SM	SN
ATT								
EWOM	0.675							
GPB	0.613	0.718						
GPI	0.731	0.815	0.704					
MO	0.406	0.511	0.409	0.552				
PBC	0.425	0.592	0.802	0.496	0.205			
SM	0.735	0.442	0.388	0.463	0.507	0.202		
SN	0.679	0.930	0.637	0.763	0.483	0.417	0.479	

Source: Authors' own work.

the HTMT has a max proportion of 0.85 (Henseler et al., 2015; Voorhees et al., 2016) and an allowable value of 0.9 (Gold et al., 2001). For the constructs SN and EWOM, the HTMT values were above and beyond 0.90. However, the HTMT confidence intervals were substantially within the acceptable ranges, proving that each construct met the criteria for uniqueness as indicated by Table 17.3's empirical standards.

4.3. Structural Model Assessment

Every connection between the constructs and their predictive value was examined as depicted in Fig. 17.2. A bias-corrected percentile technique was used in conjunction with the bootstrapping technique to get the appropriate p values for the assumptions provided in the research (Hair & Alamer, 2022; Sharma et al., 2022). Table 17.4 displays the findings, which showed that ATT, PBC, SN, and MO

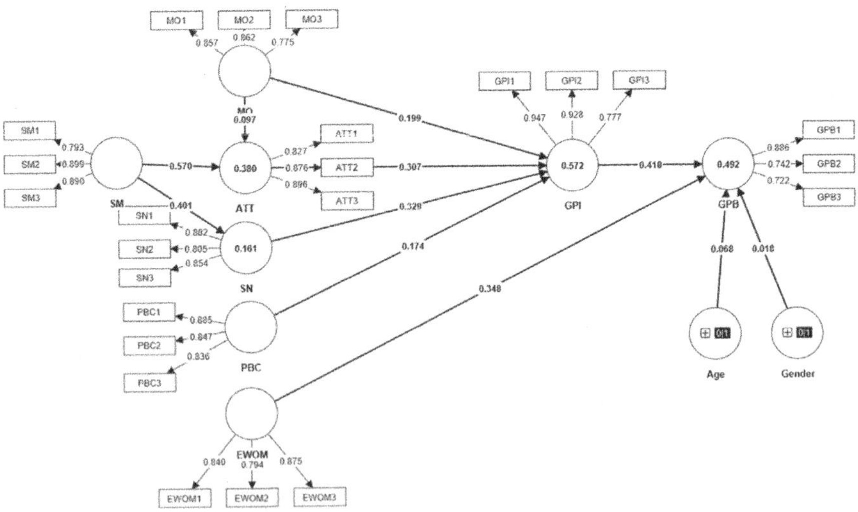

Fig. 17.2. Structural Model Assessment. *Source*: Authors' own work.

Table 17.4. Results of the Structural Model.

Hypothesis	St. beta	Sample Mean	STDEV	*T*-values	2.5%	97.5%	*P*-values	Decision Supported
ATT→GPI	0.307	0.307	0.044	6.986	0.222	0.394	0.000	Yes
EWOM→GPB	0.348	0.349	0.047	7.379	0.251	0.437	0.000	Yes
GPI→GPB	0.417	0.417	0.047	8.803	0.323	0.508	0.000	Yes
MO→ATT	0.097	0.098	0.041	2.387	0.017	0.176	0.017	Yes
MO→GPI	0.198	0.198	0.034	5.753	0.132	0.266	0.000	Yes
PBC→GPI	0.174	0.175	0.035	5.000	0.108	0.243	0.000	Yes
SM→ATT	0.571	0.571	0.045	12.599	0.477	0.656	0.000	Yes
SM→SN	0.401	0.404	0.040	10.095	0.317	0.474	0.000	Yes
SN→GPI	0.330	0.329	0.046	7.142	0.241	0.422	0.000	Yes
Age→GPB	0.068	0.067	0.066	1.024	–0.062	0.195	0.306	**No**
Gender→GPB	0.018	0.018	0.065	0.275	–0.111	0.144	0.783	**No**

Source: Authors' own work.

were significant factors in the desire to purchase green products, with St. betas of 0.037, 0.174, 0.330, and 0.198 correspondingly and $p < 0.05$. Furthermore, MO strongly impacts ATT ($p < 0.05$, $\beta = 0.098$) and SM considerably impacts ATT and SN ($p < 0.05$, $\beta = 0.571$, ($p < 0.05$, $\beta = 0.404$), respectively. Finally, EWOM positively influences GPB with ($p < 0.05$, $\beta = 0.349$) gender and age control the PLS-SEM outcomes. Age (0 for under 32 years old and 1 for over 32 years old) and gender (0 for male and female (1)) are utilised as dummy variables. SRMR, or standardised root mean square residuals, are used to assess the quality of the fit index. Less than the critical value of 0.08, the estimated model's SRMR value is 0.076 (Sharma et al., 2022).

4.4. Predictive Value of Proposed Model Outside of Sample

The study evaluates the out-of-sample predictive significance of crucial dependent variables, such as green purchase behaviour in the UAE, using the PLS prediction approach (Danks & Ray, 2018; Shmueli et al., 2019). For the PLS-SEM theoretical model, the root mean squared errors (RMSE) are computed and compared to the linear model (LM) benchmarks. Table 17.5 indicates that every Q2 predicts values greater than zero. Given their lack of predictive power over consumers' GPB, all the RMSEPLS values are higher than the RMSEM benchmarks (Shmueli et al., 2019).

4.5. Mediation Analysis

A mediation study evaluated ATT's mediating function in the link between MO and GPI. The outcomes in Table 17.6 display ($\beta = 0.30$, $t = 2.162$, $p < 0.05$) a large indirect influence of MO on GPI ($\beta = 0.307$, $t = 6.986$, $p < 0.001$). The overall impact of MO on GPI remained statistically significant. This demonstrates how attitude plays a complimentary but limited mediation function in the link between MO and GPI. So, *H5* is supported.

Table 17.5. Predictive Value Results.

	Q^2 predict	PLS-SEM_RMSE	PLS-SEM_MAE	LM_RMSE	LM_MAE
GPB1	0.426	0.745	0.612	0.622	0.46
GPB2	0.133	1	0.826	0.852	0.638
GPB3	0.139	1.039	0.843	0.818	0.592

Source: Authors' own work.

Table 17.6. Mediation Analysis.

Total Effects (MO→GPI)			Direct Effects (MO→GPI)		Indirect Effects (MO→GPI)					
Coefficient	*T*-value	*P*-value	Coefficient	Hypothesis	Coefficient	SE	*T*-value	*P*-value	CI 95%	
0.228	6.347	0.000	0.198	*H*	0.030	0.014	2.162	0.031	0.006	0.059

Source: Authors' own work.

5. CONCLUSION AND DISCUSSION

The study used the TPB model to investigate how SM, MO, and EWOM impact customers' buying intent towards green FMCG. The outcomes indicate a significant influence of the antecedents on purchase behaviour. As well as the study pointed out the positive effect of SM and EWOM on customers' intent to buy green products. Additionally, the MO of individuals plays a crucial role in their decisions to buy green goods directly and indirectly via attitude. The proposed hypotheses *H1*, *H2*, and *H3* showed a substantial connection among ATT, SN, and PBC on GPI; the results are identical to other research (Lan et al., 2023; Nekmahmud, Ramkissoon, et al., 2022). *H4*, *H4a* posits that MO has a positive impact on ATT and GPI, which indicates that MO plays a vital role in determining consumers' purchase intention; the same results are shown by (Floriano & de Matos, 2022; Kumar et al., 2023; Xuan et al., 2023). Consequently, *H5* shows that attitude mediates the relation between MO and GPI; the outcomes are in support of other research (Liao et al., 2021; Zheng et al., 2023). Furthermore, relationships among SM and ATT and SN, i.e., *H6a* and *H6b*, are significant and similar to studies (Kumar & Pandey, 2023; Nekmahmud, Naz, et al., 2022). *H7* indicated a significant relationship between GPI and GPB Relationship; the results go along with other research findings (Asl & Khoddami, 2023; Kumar et al., 2023; Qureshi et al., 2022) between EWOM and GPB and were found to be significant which meant that the *H8* supports previous studies results (Kumar & Pandey, 2023; Nekmahmud, Ramkissoon, et al., 2022).

5.1. Theoretic Implication

The research's outcomes made several hypothetical advances in our understanding of customer behaviour regarding purchase intention and the role that SM EWOM plays in encouraging consumers to purchase eco-friendly goods. Firstly, we based our research framework on Ajzen's (1991) theory of planned behaviour model. He performed his research by looking at the predicting power of ATT, SN, and PBC to forecast a person's behavioural intention. The same model was tested in this research from the perspective of purchasing green goods. To overcome the shortcomings of Ajzen's (1991) theory, we also included new constructs and variables. Previous studies pointed out the significance of extending the TPB model. They focussed on including technologies in it, but this research focussed on green FMCG and the effect of SM on one's attitude and SNs. Finally, this research enhances the existing knowledge on the effect of EWOM on purchase behaviour to buy green FMCG products.

5.2. Managerial Implication

Although there is growing consumer interest in green products, it is still being determined how consumers will positively develop their buying intentions and behaviours for these products (Fleith de Medeiros et al., 2022). However, SM has lately materially changed the nature of the connection between customers and businesses. The present research looked at the attitude and SN as precursors to purchase intent and, eventually, purchase behaviour to examine the effects of SM on buying intentions for green products. The results confirm SM's capacity to forecast attitudes and subjective standards. SM has gained popularity and is now a sought-after communication channel for businesses. Businesses now understand how valuable SM is for reaching clients and advertising their goods. SM must be fully utilised to reap the benefits for society because it has become such a vital medium for connecting with young people. The present paper examined the impact of web-based media on modifying young generations' purchase intentions towards environmentally friendly consumption through attitude and subjective standards. Resource conservation, environmental enhancement, and resource waste reduction will benefit from a shift in behaviour towards green practices. Most of the customers in the UAE are engaged in SM Thus, the research's results will aid industries in comprehending how to use these channels to improve green buying amongst UAE customers.

5.3. Limitations

The study has some limitations even though it explicitly adds to our understanding of consumer behaviour regarding green FMCG. First, the sample size is limited, hindering the generalisation of the findings. Demographic analysis and the comparison of similar environments and cultures could be included in this study in future research. Future analyses should consider the effect of variables like personal ethics and consumer personality traits and the fact that respondents' reports of their behaviour served as the basis for the consumption of green FMCG. Experiments, for instance, could be used in future studies to examine how effectively consumers choose green products.

REFERENCES

Ajzen, I. (1991). The theory of planned behavior. *Organizational Behavior and Human Decision Processes*, *50*(2), 179–211. https://doi.org/10.1016/0749-5978(91)90020-T

Alambeigi, A., Keshavarz, M., Roshanpoor, F., & Rezaei, A. (2023). Framing a model for regular and occasional consumption of green foods in developing countries. *Journal Fur Verbraucherschutz Und Lebensmittelsicherheit*, *18*(2), 147–161. https://doi.org/10.1007/S00003-023-01433-0

Ali, M., Ullah, S., Ahmad, M. S., Cheok, M. Y., & Alenezi, H. (2023). Assessing the impact of green consumption behavior and green purchase intention among millennials toward a sustainable environment. *Environmental Science and Pollution Research*, *30*(9), 23335–23347. https://doi.org/10.1007/s11356-022-23811-1

Arli, D., Tan, L. P., Tjiptono, F., & Yang, L. (2018). Exploring consumers' purchase intention towards green products in an emerging market: The role of consumers' perceived readiness. *International Journal of Consumer Studies*, *42*(4), 389–401. https://doi.org/10.1111/ijcs.12432

Asl, R. T., & Khoddami, S. (2023). A framework for investigating green purchase behavior with a focus on individually perceived and contextual factors. *Business Perspectives and Research*, *11*(1), 94–111. https://doi.org/10.1177/22785337221080505

Bedard, S. A. N., & Tolmie, C. R. (2018). Millennials' green consumption behaviour: Exploring the role of social media. *Corporate Social Responsibility and Environmental Management*, *25*(6), 1388–1396. https://doi.org/10.1002/csr.1654

Berki-Kiss, D., & Menrad, K. (2022). The role emotions play in consumer intentions to make pro-social purchases in Germany – An augmented theory of planned behavior model. *Sustainable Production and Consumption*, *29*, 79–89. https://doi.org/10.1016/j.spc.2021.09.026

Bilro, R. G., Loureiro, S. M. C., & dos Santos, J. F. (2022). Masstige strategies on social media: The influence on sentiments and attitude toward the brand. *International Journal of Consumer Studies*, *46*(4), 1113–1126. https://doi.org/10.1111/ijcs.12747

Cooley, D., & Parks-Yancy, R. (2019). The effect of social media on perceived information credibility and decision making. *Journal of Internet Commerce*, *18*(3), 249–269. https://doi.org/10.1080/15332861.2019.1595362

Danks, N. P., & Ray, S. (2018). Predictions from partial least squares models. In *Applying partial least squares in tourism and hospitality research* (pp. 35–52). Emerald Group Publishing Ltd. https://doi.org/10.1108/978-1-78756-699-620181003

de Oliveira, J. C. F., de Melo, F. J. C., Guimaraes Junior, D. S., & Miranda Sobral, E. F. (2023). Assessment of the construction industry market: A study of the barriers and drivers of sustainability practices. *International Journal of Sustainable Society*, *15*(2), 139–166. https://doi.org/10.1504/IJSSOC.2023.131692

Dwivedi, Y. K., Ismagilova, E., Hughes, D. L., Carlson, J., Filieri, R., Jacobson, J., Jain, V., Karjaluoto, H., Kefi, H., Krishen, A. S., Kumar, V., Rahman, M. M., Raman, R., Rauschnabel, P. A., Rowley, J., Salo, J., Tran, G. A., & Wang, Y. (2021). Setting the future of digital and social media marketing research: Perspectives and research propositions. *International Journal of Information Management*, 59. https://doi.org/10.1016/j.ijinfomgt.2020.102168

Farzin, M., Sadeghi, M., Fattahi, M., & Eghbal, M. R. (2022). Effect of social media marketing and eWOM on willingness to pay in the Etailing: Mediating role of brand equity and brand identity. *Business Perspectives and Research*, *10*(3), 327–343. https://doi.org/10.1177/22785337211024926

Fasoulis, I. (2023). Developments in Norway's sustainability governance in the pre-and post-2030 agenda era. *International Journal of Sustainable Society*, *15*(2), 113–138. https://doi.org/10.1504/IJSSOC.2023.131691

Fatoki, O. (2023). Antecedents of workplace energy saving behaviour: An integration of the theory of planned behaviour and norm activation model. *International Journal of Energy Economics and Policy*, *13*(4), 394–403. https://doi.org/10.32479/ijeep.13301

Faul, F., Erdfelder, E., Lang, A. G., & Buchner, A. (2007). G*Power 3: A flexible statistical power analysis program for the social, behavioral, and biomedical sciences. *Behavior Research Methods*, *39*(2), 175–191. https://doi.org/10.3758/BF03193146

Fishbein, M., & Ajzen, I. (1977). Belief, attitude, intention and behavior: An introduction to theory and research. *Contemporary Sociology*, *6*(2), 244. https://doi.org/10.2307/2065853

Fleith de Medeiros, J., Bisognin Garlet, T., Duarte Ribeiro, J. L., & Nogueira Cortimiglia, M. (2022). Success factors for environmentally sustainable product innovation: An updated review. *Journal of Cleaner Production*, *345*. https://doi.org/10.1016/j.jclepro.2022.131039

Floriano, M. D. P., & de Matos, C. A. (2022). Understanding Brazilians' intentions in consuming sustainable fashion. *Brazilian Business Review*, *19*(5), 525–545. https://doi.org/10.15728/bbr.2022.19.5.4.en

Gold, A. H., Malhotra, A., & Segars, A. H. (2001). Knowledge management: An organizational capabilities perspective. *Journal of Management Information Systems*, *18*(1), 185–214. https://doi.org/10.1080/07421222.2001.11045669

Gou, H., & Perceval, G. (2023). Does digital media use increase the risk of social-emotional delay for Chinese preschoolers? *Journal of Children and Media*, *17*(1), 1–16. https://doi.org/10.1080/17482798.2022.2118141

Guess, A. M., Malhotra, N., Pan, J., Barberá, P., Allcott, H., Brown, T., Crespo-Tenorio, A., Dimmery, D., Freelon, D., Gentzkow, M., González-Bailón, S., Kennedy, E., Kim, Y. M., Lazer, D., Moehler, D., Nyhan, B., Rivera, C. V., Settle, J., Thomas, D. R., … Tucker, J. A. (2023). Reshares on social media amplify political news but do not detectably affect beliefs or opinions. *Science*, *381*(6656), 404–408. https://doi.org/10.1126/SCIENCE.ADD8424

Gul, W., Makki, M., & Yamin, T. (2022). Water energy food security nexus: Perspectives and challenges in Balochistan, Pakistan. *International Journal of Sustainable Society*, *14*(2), 165–183. https://doi.org/10.1504/IJSSOC.2022.124863

Hair, J., & Alamer, A. (2022). Partial least squares structural equation modeling (PLS-SEM) in second language and education research: Guidelines using an applied example. *Research Methods in Applied Linguistics*, *1*(3), 100027. https://doi.org/10.1016/j.rmal.2022.100027

Hair, J., Hollingsworth, C. L., Randolph, A. B., & Chong, A. Y. L. (2017). An updated and expanded assessment of PLS-SEM in information systems research. *Industrial Management and Data Systems*, *117*(3), 442–458. https://doi.org/10.1108/IMDS-04-2016-0130

Hair, J., Howard, M. C., & Nitzl, C. (2020). Assessing measurement model quality in PLS-SEM using confirmatory composite analysis. *Journal of Business Research*, *109*, 101–110. https://doi.org/10.1016/j.jbusres.2019.11.069

Hamadi, M., El-Den, J., Azam, S., & Sriratanaviriyakul, N. (2022). Integrating social media as a cooperative learning tool in higher education classrooms: An empirical study. *Journal of King Saud University – Computer and Information Sciences*, *34*(6), 3722–3731. https://doi.org/10.1016/j.jksuci.2020.12.007

Henseler, J., Ringle, C. M., & Sarstedt, M. (2015). A new criterion for assessing discriminant validity in variance-based structural equation modeling. *Journal of the Academy of Marketing Science*, *43*(1), 115–135. https://doi.org/10.1007/s11747-014-0403-8

Jain, V. K., Gupta, A., Tyagi, V., & Verma, H. (2020). Social media and green consumption behavior of millennials. *Journal of Content, Community, and Communication*, *10*(6), 221–230. https://doi.org/10.31620/JCCC.06.20/16

Khang, H., Ki, E. J., Park, I. K., & Baek, S. G. (2012). Exploring antecedents of attitude and intention toward Internet piracy among college students in South Korea. *Asian Journal of Business Ethics*, *1*(2), 177–194. https://doi.org/10.1007/s13520-012-0017-5

Kumar, A., & Pandey, M. (2023). Social media and impact of altruistic motivation, egoistic motivation, subjective norms, and EWOM toward Green consumption behavior: An empirical investigation. *Sustainability (Switzerland)*, *15*(5). https://doi.org/10.3390/su15054222

Kumar, R., Kumar, K., Singh, R., Sá, J. C., Carvalho, S., & Santos, G. (2023). Modeling environmentally conscious purchase behavior: Examining the role of ethical obligation and green self-identity. *Sustainability (Switzerland)*, *15*(8), 1–16. https://doi.org/10.3390/su15086426

Lan, B. T. H., Phuong, T. T. L., Dat, T. T., & Truong, D. D. (2023). Factors affecting the purchase intention of products with environmentally friendly packaging of urban residents in Ho Chi Minh City, Vietnam. *Sustainability (Switzerland)*, *15*(9). https://doi.org/10.3390/su15097726

Leading FMCG companies worldwide based on sales 2020 | Statista. (n.d.). Retrieved 3, 2023, from https://www.statista.com/statistics/260963/leading-fmcg-companies-worldwide-based-on-sales/

Liang, S., Zhang, M., Chu, Y., & He, L. (2022). Should "green" be precise? The effect of information presentation on purchasing intention of green products. *Sustainability (Switzerland)*, *14*(16). https://doi.org/10.3390/su141610291

Liao, Y. K., Wu, W. Y., Pham, T. T., & Sengheang, H. (2021). Influence of environmental concerns and moral obligation on purchase intention: Evidence from Cambodia. *Asian Journal of Business Research*, *11*(2), 63–82. https://doi.org/10.14707/ajbr.210107

Liu, Q., Xu, Q., Shen, X., Chen, B., & Esfahani, S. S. (2022). The mechanism of household waste sorting behaviour—A study of Jiaxing, China. *International Journal of Environmental Research and Public Health*, *19*(4). https://doi.org/10.3390/ijerph19042447

Maior, C. S., & Mantovani, D. (2023). (Non)Monetary behaviors: How morality and status shape consumers' perceptions about sustainable actions. *Revista de Administracao Contemporanea*, *27*(3). https://doi.org/10.1590/1982-7849rac2023220068.en

Mauji, N. I., & Abu-Shanab, E. A. (2023). Are millennials in Qatar making m-commerce the future of online shopping? *International Journal of Sustainable Society*, *15*(3), 266–293. https://doi.org/10.1504/IJSSOC.2023.132890

Mir Mohamad Tabar, S. A., Rizzolo, J. B., Mazlom Khorasani, M., & Noghani, M. (2023). Social learning, neutralization, and environmental crimes: An empirical test of differential association and neutralization theories in Iran. *Society and Natural Resources*, *36*(2), 149–169. https://doi.org/10.1080/08941920.2022.2139442

Moshood, T. D., Nawanir, G., Mahmud, F., Mohamad, F., Ahmad, M. H., AbdulGhani, A., & Kumar, S. (2022). Green product innovation: A means towards achieving global sustainable product within the biodegradable plastic industry. *Journal of Cleaner Production*, *363*. https://doi.org/10.1016/j.jclepro.2022.132506

Musa, R., Nasaratnam, S., Rethinam, K., Varatharajoo, P. M., & Shanmugam, A. (2022). A study of factors influenced online shopping behavior in Malaysia: A structural approach. *WSEAS Transactions on Business and Economics*, *19*, 531–541. https://doi.org/10.37394/23207.2022.19.48

Nadeau, J., Rutter, R., & Lettice, F. (2020). Social media responses and brand personality in product and moral harm crises: Why waste a good crisis? *Journal of Marketing Management*, *36*(11–12), 1031–1054. https://doi.org/10.1080/0267257X.2020.1764080

Nekmahmud, M., Naz, F., Ramkissoon, H., & Fekete-Farkas, M. (2022). Transforming consumers' intention to purchase green products: Role of social media. *Technological Forecasting and Social Change*, *185*. https://doi.org/10.1016/j.techfore.2022.122067

Nekmahmud, M., Ramkissoon, H., & Fekete-Farkas, M. (2022). Green purchase and sustainable consumption: A comparative study between European and non-European tourists. *Tourism Management Perspectives*, *43*(November 2021), 100980. https://doi.org/10.1016/j.tmp.2022.100980

Nguyen, P. M., Vo, N. D., & Ho, N. N. Y. (2022). Exploring green purchase intention of fashion products: A transition country perspective. *Asian Journal of Business Research*, *12*(2), 87–107. https://doi.org/10.14707/ajbr.220129

Nguyen, T. M. A., Nguyen, T. H., & Le, H. H. (2022). Online shopping in relationship with perception, attitude, and subjective norm during COVID-19 outbreak: The case of Vietnam. *Sustainability (Switzerland)*, *14*(22), 1–11. https://doi.org/10.3390/su142215009

Oh, J. C., & Yoon, S. J. (2014). Theory-based approach to factors affecting ethical consumption. *International Journal of Consumer Studies*, *38*(3), 278–288. https://doi.org/10.1111/ijcs.12092

Pop, R. A., Saplacan, Z., & Alt, M. A. (2020). Social media goes the impact of social media on green cosmetics purchase motivation and intention. *Information (Switzerland)*, *11*(9). https://doi.org/10.3390/INFO11090447

Purcărea, T., Ioan-Franc, V., Ionescu, Ş.-A., Purcărea, I. M., Purcărea, V. L., Purcărea, I., Mateescu-Soare, M. C., Platon, O.-E., & Orzan, A.-O. (2022). Major shifts in sustainable consumer behavior in Romania and retailers' priorities in agilely adapting to it. *Sustainability (Switzerland)*, *14*(3). https://doi.org/10.3390/su14031627

Puška, A., Hodžić, I., Štilić, A., & Murtič, S. (2024). Evaluating European Union countries on climate change management: A fuzzy MABAC approach to the Climate Change Performance Index. *Journal of Green Economy and Low-Carbon Development*, *3*(1), 15–25.

Qin, B., & Song, G. (2022). Internal motivations, external contexts, and sustainable consumption behavior in China—Based on the TPB-ABC integration model. *Sustainability*, *14*(13), 7677. https://doi.org/10.3390/su14137677

Qureshi, M. A., Khaskheli, A., Qureshi, J. A., Raza, S. A., & Khan, K. A. (2022). Factors influencing green purchase behavior among millennials: The moderating role of religious values. *Journal of Islamic Marketing*. https://doi.org/10.1108/JIMA-06-2020-0174

Rahmawati, R., Handayani, S. R., Suprapti, A. R., Airawaty, D., & Latifah, L. (2023). Green entrepreneurship based on local characteristics and culture to support sustainable eco-tourism: A case study. *Journal of Intercultural Communication*, *23*(1), 66–75. https://doi.org/10.36923/jicc.v23i1.71

Seretny, M., Gaur, D., Sobczyk, K., & Kaabour, M. (2021). Creating a new, sustainable mindset through responsible consumption: A case study of the international chain of sustainable restaurants. *Foundations of Management*, *13*(1), 49–56. https://doi.org/10.2478/fman-2021-0004

Sharma, N., Khatri, B., & Khan, S. A. (2023). Do e-WOM persuade travelers destination visit intentions? An investigation on how travelers adopt the information from the social media channels. *Journal of Content, Community, and Communication*, *17*(9), 147–161. https://doi.org/10.31620/JCCC.06.23/11

Sharma, P. N., Liengaard, B. D. D., Hair, J. F., Sarstedt, M., & Ringle, C. M. (2022). Predictive model assessment and selection in composite-based modeling using PLS-SEM: Extensions and guidelines for CVPAT. *European Journal of Marketing*. https://doi.org/10.1108/EJM-08-2020-0636

Shmueli, G., Sarstedt, M., Hair, J. F., Cheah, J. H., Ting, H., Vaithilingam, S., & Ringle, C. M. (2019). Predictive model assessment in PLS-SEM: Guidelines for using PLSpredict. *European Journal of Marketing*, *53*(11), 2322–2347. https://doi.org/10.1108/EJM-02-2019-0189

Sondhi, S. S., Chawla, U., & Iqbal, H. (2023). Relationship between social cause, environment conservation and environmental attitude, towards promoting green purchasing behavior. *Serbian Journal of Management*, *18*(1), 27–43. https://doi.org/10.5937/sjm18-36157

Sun, Y., Li, T., & Wang, S. (2022). "I buy green products for my benefits or yours": Understanding consumers' intention to purchase green products. *Asia Pacific Journal of Marketing and Logistics*, *34*(8), 1721–1739. https://doi.org/10.1108/APJML-04-2021-0244

Sutiadiningsih, A., Purwidiani, N., Dewi, I. H. P., Hamdani, A. T., & Tho Le, H. (2023). Gastronomic experience as a motivation for tourists to choose tourist destinations in Indonesia and Vietnam. *Geojournal of Tourism and Geosites*, *47*(2), 424–431. https://doi.org/10.30892/gtg.47208-1040

Tazeen, F., & Mullick, N. H. (2023). The impact of social media platforms 'Facebook and Instagram' in influencing purchasing behaviour of green products. *Vision*. https://doi.org/10.1177/09722629221133960

Top 10 FMCG Companies in the World 2022 | M.B.A. Skool. (n.d.). Retrieved February 7, 2023, from https://www.mbaskool.com/fun-corner/top-brand-lists/17609-top-10-fmcg-companies-in-the-world.html

Urbański, M., & Ul Haque, A. (2020). Are you environmentally conscious enough to differentiate between greenwashed and sustainable items? A global consumer perspective. *Sustainability (Switzerland)*, *12*(5), 1–25. https://doi.org/10.3390/su12051786

Villavicencio, M., & Schlesinger, W. (2023). Brand attitude and frugality as a lifestyle: Evidence from coffee shop customers. *Springer Proceedings in Business and Economics*, 83–88. https://doi.org/10.1007/978-3-031-32894-7_10

Voorhees, C. M., Brady, M. K., Calantone, R., & Ramirez, E. (2016). Discriminant validity testing in marketing: An analysis, causes for concern, and proposed remedies. *Journal of the Academy of Marketing Science*, *44*(1), 119–134. https://doi.org/10.1007/s11747-015-0455-4

Wang, D., Weisstein, F. L., Duan, S., & Choi, P. (2022). Impact of ambivalent attitudes on green purchase intentions: The role of negative moods. *International Journal of Consumer Studies*, *46*(1), 182–199. https://doi.org/10.1111/ijcs.12663

Wei, J., Zhao, X., Liu, Y., & Yang, X. (2021). Measuring purchase intention towards green power certificate in a developing nation: Applying and extending the theory of planned behavior. *Resources, Conservation and Recycling*, 168. https://doi.org/10.1016/j.resconrec.2020.105363

Xuan, V. N., Loan, L. T., Hoa, N. M., & Dao, N. T. (2023). Using a unified model of TPB, N.A.M., and SOBC to investigate the energy-saving behaviour of urban residents in Vietnam: Moderation role of cultural values. *Sustainability (Switzerland)*, *15*(3). https://doi.org/10.3390/su15032225

Yadav, R., & Pathak, G. S. (2016). Young consumers' intention towards buying green products in a developing nation: Extending the theory of planned behavior. *Journal of Cleaner Production*, *135*, 732–739. https://doi.org/10.1016/j.jclepro.2016.06.120

Yerpude, S., Sood, K., & Grima, S. (2022). Blockchain-augmented digital supply chain management: A way to sustainable business. *Journal of Risk and Financial Management*, *16*(1), 7.

Zahan, I., Chuanmin, S., Fayyaz, M., & Hafeez, M. (2020). Green purchase behavior towards green housing: an investigation of Bangladeshi consumers. *Environmental Science and Pollution Research*, *27*(31), 38745–38757. https://doi.org/10.1007/s11356-020-09926-3

Zheng, F., Zhao, C., Ajina, A. S., & Poulova, P. (2023). Decoding the dilemma of consumer food over-ordering in restaurants: An augmented theory of planned behavior model investigation. *Sustainability (Switzerland)*, *15*(11). https://doi.org/10.3390/su15118735

INDEX

Printed and bound by CPI Group (UK) Ltd, Croydon, CR0 4YY

17/09/2026

14964139-0001